Word Recognition in
Beginning Literacy

Word Recognition in Beginning Literacy

Edited by

Jamie L. Metsala
University of Maryland

and

Linnea C. Ehri
CUNY Graduate Center

LEA

LAWRENCE ERLBAUM ASSOCIATES, PUBLISHERS
1998　Mahwah, New Jersey　　　　　　　　London

Lawrence Erlbaum Associates, Inc., Publishers
10 Industrial Avenue
Mahwah, NJ 07430

Cover design by Kathryn Houghtaling Lacey

Library of Congress Cataloging-in-Publication Data

Word recognition in beginning literacy / edited by Jamie L.
Metsala and Linnea C. Ehri
      p.   cm.
   Includes bibliographical references and index.
   ISBN 0-8058-2898-2 (cloth : alk. paper). —ISBN 0-
8058-2899-0 (pbk. : alk. paper)
   1. Word recognition. I. Metsala, Jamie L. II. Ehri,
Linnea C.
   LB1050.44.W67 1998   97–40338
   372.46'2—dc21   CIP

10 9 8 7 6 5 4 3 2 1

Contents

Preface

This edited volume grew out of a conference sponsored by the National Reading Research Center, funded through the Office of Educational Research and Improvement by the U.S. Department of Education. The purpose of the conference was to bring together beginning reading experts from the fields of education and the psychology of reading and reading disabilities so that they could present and discuss their research findings and theories about how children learn to read words, instructional contexts that facilitate this learning, background experiences prior to formal schooling that contribute, and sources of difficulty in disabled readers. Presenters wrote drafts of their chapters prior to the meeting; these were read by others and discussed at the meeting, and revisions were written to produce this volume.

Chapters in Part I focus on the importance of the internal cognitive processes of developing readers and on explanations of their growth and development. Authors in Part II of the book address the development of reading-related phonological skills in disabled readers and programs aimed at teaching disabled readers. Chapters in Part III present studies of word recognition in the context of the early home environment, and also examine several beginning reading programs in the classroom. Also, the principles that make early literacy instruction motivating to students are addressed, and the impact of early reading success on later reading habits are examined.

Ehri (chap. 1) begins by identifying the processes that develop as beginners learn to recognize written words. Ehri considers the different ways that words might be read and proposes a detailed developmental model, including the role of alphabetic processes and spelling knowledge in acquiring mature word recognition skills. Ehri emphasizes that although a method of instruction is not prescribed herein, it is paramount to take into consideration the cognitive and linguistic processes to be targeted in such instruction.

Goswami examines the importance of spelling patterns that correspond to rhymes in the spoken language on children's reading acquisition (chap. 2). She argues that the high level of regularity of orthographic analogies at the rhyme level, as well as children's early sensitivity to rhymes in spoken English, combine to make this a functionally important unit for beginning readers. Goswami compares the reading acquisition processes involving rhyme across a number of languages, and concludes with a section on how to incorporate the importance of rhyme units into classroom instruction.

Stahl and Murray extend the discussion of phonological awareness skills and address how these interact with basic reading skills in word recognition (chap. 3). These authors first examine the multidimensional aspects of phonological awareness skills because research has accumulated to expose earlier notions as too simplistic. A new and more detailed model of the role of these phonological awareness skills in acquiring skilled word recognition is proposed.

In Chapter 4, Metsala and Walley examine aspects of spoken language growth that may be prerequisites to phonological awareness skills. These authors argue that the phoneme emerges first as a perceptual processing unit that results from growth in vocabulary size and structure, and only later emerges as a unit that can be accessed and manipulated in awareness and reading tasks. Walley and Metsala present a model suggesting the seeds from which phonemic awareness develops.

In the following chapter, Brown argues that one can achieve a different kind of understanding of the endpoint of the reading process if one adopts the "adaptive analysis" approach that has recently received wide attention in other areas of psychological research, such as memory and perception. According to this approach, skilled adult processing is seen as an optimal processing strategy, given the statistical nature of the task at hand (chap. 5). Brown shows that this approach can be used to understand a number of core issues in the study of adult skilled reading, and he discusses the potential of such approaches for understanding the word recognition acquisition process.

Siegel begins Part II by exploring the cognitive processes that have most often been identified as major hurdles for disabled readers (chap. 6). She examines how phonological processing deficits are manifested in reading disabled children across different languages. Siegel also discusses the modularity of phonological processes and their role in word recognition development in disabled readers.

Torgesen and Burgess expand the discussion of reading-related phonological processes across the earliest years of reading acquisition (chap. 7). These authors examine whether reading-related phonological processes show sufficient stability across early reading development to qualify as a proximal cause of reading disabilities. Three reading-related phonological processes are identified, phonological awareness, short-term phonological memory, and rapid automatic naming. The relationship between these three processes and measures of reading ability over the period of early reading acquisition are reported. Torgesen and Burgess discuss the practical applications of their findings for diagnoses and intervention for reading disabled children.

In chapter 8, Wise, Olson, Ring, and Johnson present their research on computer-supported reading programs for disabled readers. Their research is driven by the questions of how these instructional programs can establish foundation skills in phonological and orthographic processing, and how they can ensure that these skills are integrated and applied to reading in context.

Part II closes with a chapter by Gaskins describing the reading program implemented at Benchmark School, a school for struggling readers in Grades 1 through 8 (chap. 9). Gaskins outlines the specific forms of word knowledge that the students at Benchmark School appear to lack and then how the literacy instruction is targeted at these specific knowledge deficits. Gaskins' theory of instruction builds strongly on targeting the cognitive processes outlined in previous chapters.

In Part III, Cunningham and Stanovich examine the effects of exposure to print as a variable that can account for individual differences in both specific mechanisms practiced in reading, and, more generally in vocabulary, reading comprehension and verbal ability (chap. 10). These authors present a longitudinal investigation relating widening achievement disparities to differences in cumulative print exposure. Cunningham and Stanovich provide evidence that early success in beginning reading acquisition affects lifetime reading habits.

Baker, Fernandez Fein, Scher, and Williams extend the context of examining reading development to include early home experiences (chap. 11). Baker and her colleagues examine home experiences such as book reading and environmental print reading, with a focus on defining effects on the child's development of print knowledge and phonological awareness. These authors also examine sociocultural differences in home experiences related to word recognition and implications from their findings are briefly discussed.

Contributors of previous chapters briefly mention the importance of spelling in the development of reading and literacy. Treiman expands on this and presents evidence that supports the incorporation of spelling instruction into beginning reading instruction (chap. 12). Treiman examines the spelling properties of the English orthographic system and children's spelling development within this orthographic context. Treiman argues that spelling instruction benefits both phonemic awareness and learning to read. A focus on approaches to spelling instruction in the early years concludes her chapter.

Calfee explores and analyzes major features of his literacy program, Word Work (chap. 13). Word Work is a decoding-spelling program that also includes policies and practices found in literature-based classrooms. This program includes teaching strategies for literature analyses, as well as explicit strategies for analyzing English spelling-sound relations. Calfee explains how Word Work differs from typical phonics programs and presents three case studies to illustrate this unique program of instruction.

Tracey and Morrow discuss the aspects of learning environments, such as physical, as well as task characteristics, that motivate children in beginning literacy. Studies show that increasing the motivation of the children to read leads to increased levels of literacy involvement and achievement. Surveying current instructional practices in both phoneme awareness and phonics instruction, these authors examined whether word recognition instruction in the classroom most often includes the motivating principles outlined in this chapter.

Pressley, Wharton-McDonald, and Mistretta examine the classrooms of nine first-grade teachers selected by administrators in their districts as exceptional teachers. Pressley and his colleagues develop a bottom-up approach to characterize literacy instruction in each classroom. Three classrooms that exhibit excellent first-grade literacy instruction on criterion variables are identified and the commonalties of these three classroom models are compared and summarized. One classroom is presented in detail to provide an example of an excellent first-grade reading program.

In summary, the chapters in this collection bring a variety of perspectives to bear on a single cluster of problems involving the acquisition of word reading ability. It is our keen hope that the insights and findings of the research reported here will influence and become incorporated into the development of practicable, classroom-based instructional programs that succeed in improving children's ability to become skilled readers. Moreover, we hope that these insights and findings will become incorporated into the working knowledge that teachers apply when they teach their students to read, and into further research on reading acquisition.

—Jamie L. Metsala and Linnea C. Ehri

I
▼▼▼▼▼▼▼

BASIC PROCESSES IN BEGINNING WORD RECOGNITION

1

▼▼▼▼▼▼▼

Grapheme–Phoneme Knowledge Is Essential for Learning to Read Words in English

Linnea C. Ehri
Graduate School of the City University of New York

Currently there is much interest in the question of how children learn to read, particularly as a result of debates about whether instruction should follow phonics or whole-language prescriptions. The purpose of my chapter is to sidestep the instructional issue, to focus on the learner rather than the teacher, and to clarify how alphabetic processes are central in learning to read words as indicated by theory and evidence. Research on this topic is too extensive to cover fully in this chapter. I have dealt with this problem by mentioning limited evidence to support my claims with the belief that this evidence is representative of and not contradicted by the larger pool of evidence. (For a more complete picture, see Adams', 1990, book, *Beginning to Read*.)

In my chapter, I argue that grapheme–phoneme knowledge, also referred to as *alphabetic knowledge*, is essential for literacy acquisition to reach a mature state. It is important to include spelling as well as reading in this picture, because learning to read and learning to spell words in English depend on processes that are tightly interconnected (Ehri, 1997). As the chapter unfolds, the nature of this connection becomes apparent.

Processes Versus Methods

In considering how children learn to read words, one can focus on methods of teaching reading, or one can focus on processes that develop as beginners learn to read. In this chapter, I focus on processes rather than methods. It is important to be clear about this. I see too many instances where processes are confused with methods and an argument erupts that is unresolvable because the parties are talking about two different things.

3

Let me give you an example. What does the term *sight word learning* mean to you? What kind of mental image does this term evoke? Teachers who say "I object to it," or "I support it," or "I do it everyday with my students" are referring to a method of instruction. They probably envision students speeding through a set of flash cards as fast as they can, practicing how to read single words.

A very different reaction to this term is to think of sight word learning as a process, as something that all beginners go through to attain skill in reading. Holding this meaning, one envisions the mind of the reader and perhaps imagines a mental dictionary lodged somewhere in the left hemisphere. The dictionary holds all the written words and spoken words that are familiar to the reader. The dictionary is linked to the reader's eyes such that when the eyes light on words that exist in the dictionary, the pronunciations and meanings of the words are immediately activated in memory.

It is important to realize that reading processes can be described separately from reading methods, and that no particular instructional method is entailed by any process. When I talk about sight word learning as a process, I am not suggesting anything about the activities that teachers should impose on students to help them learn sight words. Many different activities might do the job.

Also, it is important to realize that, by singling out word reading processes and talking about their development, I am not suggesting that the processes should be taught in isolation. Likewise, I am not arguing against teaching them in context. The point is that I am not making any declarations about how to teach the processes.

What I want to do is set aside questions about instruction, and try to achieve a clearer view of the reading processes that instruction is intended to develop in students. In doing this, I am not suggesting that instruction is unimportant; quite the opposite. Explicit, directed instruction is essential for enabling most children to acquire enough proficiency with the alphabetic system to become skilled readers and writers of English. The reason for focusing on processes separate from instruction is to clarify what the target of instruction is, where instruction should be aimed, and how instruction should be evaluated for its effectiveness. In my view, teachers need to understand the processes that their instruction is aimed at teaching and the behaviors that indicate whether students are progressing along the lines expected in learning to read. Teachers need this knowledge to evaluate and improve the effectiveness of their instructional efforts.

Basic Processes to Explain

Learning to read involves two basic processes. These processes are captured in the simple view of reading (Gough & Tunmer, 1986; Hoover & Gough, 1990). One process involves learning to decipher the print; the other involves comprehending the meaning of the print. When children attain reading skill, they learn to perform both of these processes in a way that allows their attention to focus on the meaning of the text while the mechanics of reading, including deciphering, operate unobtrusively and out of awareness for the most part. How do beginners achieve this mature state of reading? Can simple practice of reading text lead to mature forms of reading, just as practice of learning to speak leads to mature speaking abilities? Is there anything special about reading that might be hard to learn and might not be acquired through practice? To answer these questions, we need to clarify the nature of the processes involved in reading and learning to read.

It is important to note that children acquire comprehension skill in the course of learning to speak. Listening comprehension processes are very similar to reading comprehension processes, as Hoover and Gough (1990) showed. However, children do not acquire deciphering skill in the course of learning to speak. This achievement requires special experiences that do not occur in the normal course of conversations between parents and children, or even in sessions where parents read books to their children.

Liberman (1992) argued elegantly and persuasively that humans are equipped for learning to produce and comprehend spoken language easily, but they are not equipped for learning to decode written language easily despite the greater powers of the eye than the ear for processing information. Processing spoken language is not governed by "end" organs such as eyes and ears, but rather is governed by central phonological structures in the brain. Processing speech is not a matter of processing sounds, but instead is a matter of processing combinations of rapidly executed, co-articulated, motoric gestures that are controlled by central processes in the brain. Such processing far exceeds the limits of the ear. The critical phonemic segments that speakers and listeners must process do not lie in the signal itself; rather they lie in the brain and are detected and processed successfully by speakers and listeners because they both possess the same mental equipment.

These facts about speech make it apparent why learning to decipher print is not the "natural" process that learning to speak is. The brain is specialized for processing spoken language, but it has no special central equipment for processing written language. In order for reading and writing skills to develop, what needs to happen is that written language must penetrate and gain a foothold in the central equipment used to process speech. Graphemes must become attached to "deep" phonemes, not simply to "surface" sounds within words. Such penetration and attachment, however, are not straightforward steps, because speech is seamless on the surface, with no breaks signaling phonemic units. Special experiences are needed to engage the brain in deciphering print.

The basic question to be answered is how learners acquire the deciphering skills that give their eyes access to language comprehension processes that are programmed for mouths and cars rather than eyes. The answer proposed in this chapter is that access is gained through the acquisition of unobtrusively functioning deciphering skills that involve two types of structures, one nested within the other. The larger structure is lexical and consists of specific words as units with orthographic, phonological, and semantic identities. Nested within words are structures consisting of graphemes linked to phonemes.

Before taking up the matter of how deciphering skills are acquired in a way that allows print to symbolize speech at a deep level, it is important to identify what deciphering skills are and how they operate as part of the reading process.

Reading Words in Text

The interactive model of reading adapted from Rumelhart (1977) and displayed in Fig. 1.1 enables us to describe how words are processed during the act of reading. The center box represents a central processor that receives information from the eyes and interprets it. The boxes around the center depict the various information sources that are stored in readers' memory and are used to recognize and interpret text. Readers' knowledge of language enables them to recognize sentences and their meanings. Readers have factual, experiential, and schematic knowledge about the world. This enables them to understand ideas and to fill in parts of a text where meanings are assumed to be known and thus are not stated explicitly. Readers use their metacognitive knowledge to monitor the quality of their comprehension, to verify that the information makes sense and meets specific purposes, and to detect when repairs are necessary. Memory for a text is constructed as readers use these knowledge sources to comprehend the sentences and paragraphs in that text. Readers' understanding of the text is stored in memory, accessed to understand subsequent text, and revised to accommodate new information.

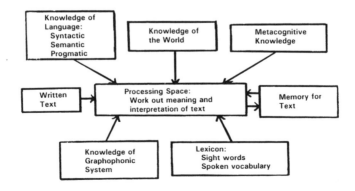

FIG. 1.1. Interactive model of text reading, depicting the sources of knowledge.

At the bottom of Fig. 1.1 are depicted two knowledge sources that enable readers to process letters and words in the text, referred to as *deciphering skills*. Readers' knowledge of the graphophonic system enables them to convert letters into sounds in order to decode unfamiliar words. *Lexical knowledge* refers to something like a dictionary of words that readers hold in memory, including the written forms of words known by sight. All of the knowledge sources in Fig. 1.1 operate together to facilitate text comprehension.

Let us take a closer look at how readers read words as they process text. We can identify at least five different ways (Ehri, 1991, 1994). Readers might read words:

1. By assembling letters into a blend of sounds, referred to as *decoding*.
2. By pronouncing and blending familiar spelling patterns, a more advanced form of decoding.
3. By retrieving sight words from memory.
4. By analogizing to words already known by sight.
5. By using context cues to predict words.

In each case, the processes differ. As readers attain skill, they learn to read words in all five ways.

One way to read words is to determine the sounds of letters and blend them into pronunciations that approximate real words. This is a strategy that enables readers to read words they have never before seen. To use this strategy, readers must know how letters typically symbolize sounds in words, not only single letters but digraphs such as *th, sh, ea, ow*. This is a slower way of reading words than sight word reading (Ehri & Wilce, 1983; Perfetti & Hogaboam, 1975). In reading English, this strategy works sometimes but not always, because many spellings have variable or irregular pronunciations.

Whereas beginning readers decode words by attacking individual letters, more advanced readers process chunks of letters when they decode words. They learn how letter chunks are pronounced from their experiences reading and writing different words that share common letter patterns. When they see new words containing these patterns, they can pronounce the patterns as units without having to subdivide them into graphophonic units. Table 1.1 contains a list of common chunks found at the ends of single-syllable words in English (Stahl, Osborn, & Lehr, 1990), as well as a list of common affixes occurring in words (Becker, Dixon, & Anderson-Inman, 1980). Studies show that words having common letter patterns are easier to decode by readers who are familiar with the patterns (Bowey & Hansen, 1994; Juel, 1983; Laxon, Coltheart, & Keating, 1988; Treiman, Goswami, & Bruck, 1990).

A very different way to read words is by sight. Consider the list of words in Table 1.2 taken from Adams and Huggins' (1985) test of sight word

TABLE 1.1
Common Spelling Patterns in Words

Common Endings (Rime Spellings) of Single-Syllable Words						
-ack	-all	-ain	-ack	-ale	-ame	-an
-ank	-ap	-ash	-at	-ate	-aw	-ay
-eat	-ell	-est				
-ice	-ick	-ide	-ight	-ill	-in	-ine
-ing	-ink	-ip	-ir			
-ock	-oke	-op	-ore	-or		
-uck	-ug	-ump	-unk			

Common Affixes						
-al	-able	-ate	-ant			
-ed	-en	-er	-ent			
-ize	-ist	-ing	-ive	-ite	-ion	-ic
-ful	-ly	-less	-ment	-ness	-ous	
com-	con-	de-	dis-	ex-	im-	in-
or-	pre-	pro-	re-	un-		

reading. You can probably read them easily. Why do we take this as evidence for sight word reading? Because these words cannot be read accurately by decoding letters into sounds. They have unusual spellings that do not conform to the conventional spelling system. Readers have to remember how to read these words in order to read them accurately. Adams and Huggins selected these words to show that sight word reading is a very different way to read words than is decoding. However, it is important to note that sight word reading is not limited to strangely spelled, difficult-to-decode words. With sufficient practice, all words acquire status as sight words.

When readers read words by sight, they access information stored in memory from previous experiences reading the words (Ehri, 1992). This process is used to read words that have been read several times before. Sight of the written word activates its spelling, pronunciation, and meaning immediately in memory, without any decoding steps required. Reitsma's (1983) evidence suggests that even first graders can retain sight words in memory, after reading the words as few as four times. You can tell when readers are reading words by sight because they read the words as whole units, with no

TABLE 1.2
Words From Adams and Huggins' (1985) Test of Sight Word Reading

none	island	busy	bouquet	rhythm
calf	depot	yacht	fiance	heights
break	react	suede	guitar	
prove	sugar	tongue	chauffeur	

pauses between sounds, and they read the words within one second of seeing them (Ehri & Wilce, 1983).

There is one property of sight word reading that distinguishes it from the other ways of reading words. This property makes sight word reading especially valuable for text reading. When sight words are known well enough, readers can recognize their pronunciations and meanings *automatically* (LaBerge & Samuels, 1974). That is, they can read these words without expending any attention or effort decoding the words. They recognize these words instantly, even when they try to ignore them.

To experience automatic word recognition, look at Fig. 1.2. Move across the rows from left to right and say the name of each picture as quickly as you can. Ignore the words printed on the pictures. Did you find it impossible to ignore the words? Most readers do. This is evidence that your mind is processing the words automatically, despite your intention to ignore the words.

In psychological research, this is known as the Stroop phenomenon. Studies using the picture–word interference task have shown that not only the pronunciations but also the meanings of words are recognized automatically (Ehri, 1977; Golinkoff & Rosinski, 1976; Rosinski, Golinkoff, & Kukish, 1975) and that readers as young as the end of first grade can read familiar words automatically (Guttentag & Haith, 1978). It turns out that automat-

FIG. 1.2. Picture-naming task to demonstrate that words are processed automatically despite the reader's intention to ignore them. From "Learning to Read and Spell Words" by L. Ehri, *Journal of Reading Behavior, 19,* 5–11. Copyright 1987 by National Reading Conference. Reprinted by permission.

icity of word reading is the secret of efficient text reading. We consider this matter shortly.

Another way to read words is by analogy (Baron, 1977; Bowey & Hansen, 1994; Cunningham, 1976; Gaskins, et al., 1988; Glushko, 1979, 1981; Goswami, 1986, 1988; Laxon et al., 1988; Marsh, Freidman, Welch, & Desberg, 1981). Readers may read a new word by recognizing how its spelling is similar to a word they already know as a sight word. They access the similar sight word in memory and then adjust the pronunciation to accommodate the new word, for example, reading *fountain* by analogy to *mountain*, or *brother* by analogy to *mother*. Goswami (1990) found that beginning readers can use their knowledge of rhyming words to read words by analogy. However, having some decoding skill appears to be required for beginners to analogize by accessing sight words in memory (Ehri & Robbins, 1992).

One final way to read words is by using context cues such as pictures and the preceding text to make predictions about upcoming words. As portrayed in the interactive model in Fig. 1.1, readers can use their knowledge about language, their knowledge of the world, and their memory for the text already read to guess the identities of some words as they read text. Some words are easier to predict than others. For example, function words such as *to* and *the* are easier than content words such as *farmer*, *truck*, and *corn*. This way of reading words is evident in the miscues that readers produce when they read text aloud. When words are misread, the words substituted often fit the sentence structure and meaning, indicating that context influenced how the words were read (Biemiller, 1970; Clay, 1968; Goodman, 1976; Weber, 1970).

Predicting words based on context cues, however, does not account for the way that readers read most words in text (Stanovich, 1980). Studies of the predictability of words in text indicate that, on average, 25% to 30% of the words can be guessed correctly. However, the most important content words that carry the most meaning are the least predictable, with only 10% guessed correctly (Gough & Walsh, 1991). Thus, for readers to guess words effectively, they must know most of the surrounding words in a text. To read these accurately, readers must use processes other than contextual guessing.

Having identified the various ways to read words, let us consider how words are processed during text reading. First, consider eye movements. How do you think readers' eyes move when they read a line of print? Do the eyes sweep across the page like a video camera, or do they move in jerks, moving and stopping, moving and stopping? If you observe someone read a page of text, you will discover that the eyes move in fairly regular jerks, stopping to fixate on words and then jumping to the next fixation point. Studies reveal that the eyes fixate on practically every word in a text, sometimes more than once (McConkie & Zola, 1981; Rayner & Pollatsek, 1989). Few words are skipped, usually only high-frequency function words such as *the*. Even words that can be predicted with 100% accuracy are not skipped. This indicates that the eyes are picking up and processing each word during text reading. According to the interactive model of reading in Fig. 1.1, multiple processes operate in parallel in readers' heads as they read text, and their minds coordinate all of these processes. The eyes light on one word after another. The mind picks them up. The reader's attention and interpretative powers are focused on determining what events, information, and ideas are being represented—what the text means.

Of the various ways to read words identified here, there is one way that enables text reading to operate the most efficiently. If readers can recognize words automatically, then word reading can be executed unconsciously. Each of the other ways of reading words requires conscious attention, however slight. If readers attempt to decode the word, or to find an analogous word in memory, or to use context to predict what the word might be, their attention is shifted at least momentarily to the word itself to solve the puzzle regarding the word's identity, regardless of how easy it is to decode the word or to guess it. This suggests that being able to read words by sight automatically is the key to skilled reading of text. This allows readers to process words in text quickly, without attention directed at the word itself.

Although sight word reading is the most efficient way to read words in text, readers may not know all of the words by sight, so the other four means of reading words must be available to identify unknown words. However, this is not their only contribution. Perfetti (1985) proposed an interactive model in which sight word reading is *supported* by the other ways of reading words. Imagine that a skilled reader is reading a text. Most of the words are known by sight. Sight word reading is a fast-acting process, faster than all the other forms of word reading, so this is how the words are identified. As each sight word is fixated, its meaning and pronunciation are triggered in memory quickly and automatically. However, the other word reading processes do not lie dormant; their contribution is not to *identify* words in the text, but rather to *confirm* the identity already determined. Confirmatory processes are thought to happen automatically as well. Knowledge of the graphophonic system confirms that the word's pronunciation fits the spelling on the page. Knowledge of syntax confirms that the word fits into the structure of the sentence. World knowledge and text memory confirm that the meaning of the word is consistent with the text's meaning up to that point. Having confirmation from multiple sources, that is, redundancy operating during text reading, is a highly important feature. It serves to maintain highly accurate reading, to make the reader sensitive to errors, and to provide a means of self-correction when errors disrupt comprehension.

Sensitivity to redundancy in text may explain miscue differences distinguishing good from poor beginning readers. Both good and poor readers have been observed to substitute the same proportion of syntactically appropriate words when they misread words in texts, indicating that both good and poor readers are influenced by context to the same extent (Biemiller, 1970). However, good readers are much more likely to self-correct their errors than are poor readers (Clay, 1969), supporting the idea that confirmatory processes operate to a greater extent in good readers than in poor readers.

Let me remind you that in order for readers to be able to read text easily and make sense of it, a large proportion of the words must be familiar and easily read. The rule of thumb is that if students can read at least 98% of the words in a text, the text is considered easy. If students can read 90% to 95% of the words, the text is at their instructional level. If students fall much below 90%, the text becomes frustrating for them (Johns, 1991). These high values underscore the importance of readers' acquiring large sight vocabularies as well as acquiring the various strategies for figuring out unfamiliar words.

Although several ways to read words in and out of context can be distinguished, the type of word reading that most directly supports text reading is sight word reading, at least in English. Moreover, I suggest that establishing sight words in memory is the way that written language gains a foothold in the central mechanisms that regulate speech. This allows readers to use their knowledge of speech to process written language.

SIGHT WORD LEARNING REQUIRES ALPHABETIC KNOWLEDGE

Sight words are words that readers have read accurately on earlier occasions. They read the words by remembering how they read them previously. The term *sight* indicates that sight of the word activates that word in memory, including information about its spelling, pronunciation, typical role in sentences, and meaning (Ehri, 1992). To explain sight word reading, we must specify how readers are able to look at printed words they have read before and recognize those specific words while bypassing thousands of other words, including those with very similiar spellings or meanings. Moreover, we must specify how readers are able to store and remember new words easily after reading them only a few times (Reitsma, 1983). The kind of process we have found to be at the heart of sight word learning is a *connection-forming* process: Connections are formed that link the written forms of words to their pronunciations and meanings. This information is stored in the reader's mental dictionary or lexicon.

What kinds of connections are formed to store sight words in memory? You are probably familiar with the traditional view, which holds that readers memorize associations between the visual shapes of words and their meanings. For example, if you outlined the borders of the following words, each would exhibit a distinctive shape:

dog   green   tent   on   ate

However, in my research I have found that this view is incorrect (Ehri, 1992).

Consider the feat that skilled readers perform when they read words by sight. They are able to recognize in an instant any one of many thousands of words. They recognize one unique word and bypass many other similarly spelled words. For example, consider all the words that must be overlooked to read the word "stick" accurately: not only *stink, slick,* and *slink,* which have similar shapes as well as letters, but also *sting, sling, string,* as well as *sick, sing,* and *sink.* Moreover, skilled readers can remember how to read new sight words with very little practice. Memorizing arbitrary associations between the shapes and meanings of words cannot explain how skilled readers do what they do. Sight word reading must involve remembering letters in the words. These are the distinctive cues that make one word different from all the others.

Findings of my research indicate that readers learn sight words by forming connections between graphemes in the spellings and phonemes underlying the pronunciations of individual words. The connections are formed out of readers' general knowledge of grapheme–phoneme correspondences that recur in many words. Graphemes are the functional letter units symbolizing phonemes. Phonemes are the smallest units of "sound" in words. Readers look at the spelling of a particular word, they pronounce the word, and they apply their graphophonic knowledge to analyze how letters symbolize individual phonemes detectable in the word's pronunciation. This secures the sight word in memory (Ehri, 1980, 1984, 1987, 1991, 1992, 1994; Ehri & Saltmarsh, 1995; Ehri & Wilce, 1979, 1980, 1983, 1986, 1987a).

Figure 1.3 reveals how beginning readers might analyze several different words to secure them as sight words in memory. In this figure, capital letters designate the spellings of words, lower-case letters between slashes indicate phonemes, and lines linking letters to phonemes indicate connections. Notice that in some spellings, more than one letter combines to form the grapheme that is linked to a phoneme (e.g., *sh, ch, th*). Notice that sounds consisting of a vocalic consonant plus schwa, /əl/ or /ər/, may be treated as one graphophonic unit (Treiman, 1993). Alternatively, beginners may be taught to separate these into two units in order to conform to the principle that all syllables must have a vowel (Gaskins, Ehri, Cress, O'Hara, & Donnelly, 1996). Notice that although the grapheme *g* is known to symbolize either /j/ or /g/ in words, in the word *giggle,* the letter *g* gets remembered as the phoneme /g/, not /j/, because the pronunciation of the word specifies /g/. In this way, the spelling is bonded to the word's pronunciation and meaning. The bonded unit is stored in memory as that word. The next time the reader sees the word, he or she can retrieve the word from memory to read it. Perfetti (1992) described a similar process for representing words in memory.

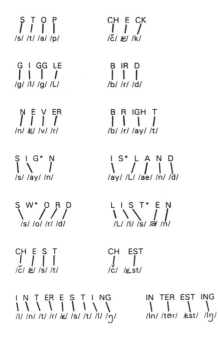

FIG. 1.3. Illustration of the connections formed in memory between graphemes and phonemes, or between consolidated graphemes and syllabic units, to remember how to read specific words.

Note what graphophonic knowledge readers must possess to secure complete representations of sight words in memory. Readers need sufficient familiarity with letter shapes. They need to know how to distinguish the functional graphemic units that typically symbolize phonemes in words. They need to know how to segment pronunciations into constituent phonemes that match up to the graphemes they see in spellings. It is in performing this graphophonic analysis for individual words that the spellings of words penetrate and become attached to readers' knowledge of spoken words in a way that links written language to the central mechanisms governing spoken language.

In analyzing words graphophonically, readers attempt to achieve an optimum match by searching pronunciations for distinguishable phonemes that graphemes suggest are present in the word. For example, we observed fourth graders segment words such as *pitch* into four phonemes corresponding to the graphemes *p-i-t-ch,* but they segmented *rich* into three phonemes matched to the graphemes *r-i-ch* (Ehri & Wilce, 1980). A phoneme corresponding to *t* can be found in articulating these words, but it is not distinguished without a spelling to suggest it.

The process of forming connections allows readers to remember how to read not only words containing conventional letter–sound correspondences such as *stop*, but also words that have less regular spellings. Connections that might be formed to remember irregular words are illustrated in Fig 1.3. Note that the same types of connections are evident. It turns out that most of the letters in irregular words conform to grapheme-phoneme conventions, for example, all but *s* in *island*, all but *w* in *sword*, all but *t* in *listen*, all but *g* in *sign*. In remembering letters that do not correspond to phonemes, readers may remember them as extra visual forms, may flag them as silent in memory, or may remember a special spelling pronunciation that includes the silent letter, for example, remembering *listen* as *lis-ten* or *chocolate* as *choc-o-late* (Drake & Ehri, 1984; Ehri, 1984; Ehri & Wilce, 1982).

Spellings of words are like maps that lay out the phonological forms of words visually. Readers need to become skilled at computing these mapping relations very quickly when they read words. Knowledge of letter–sound relations provides a powerful mnemonic system that bonds the written forms of specific words to their pronunciations in memory. Once the graphophonic spelling system is known, readers can learn to read words and build a lexicon of sight words easily.

Capabilities That Enable Sight Word Learning in Beginners

There are three graphophonic capabilities that enable beginners to secure complete representations of sight words in memory: knowledge of letter shapes, knowledge of how graphemes typically symbolize phonemes in words, and phonemic segmentation skill. Evidence for the importance of letter knowledge and phonemic segmentation skill in building a sight vocabulary can be found in many studies. For example, Share, Jorm, Maclean, and Matthews (1984) compared the value of 39 characteristics measured in kindergartners at the beginning of school as predictors of word reading skill after 1 and 2 years of instruction. They found that phonemic segmentation and letter-name knowledge were the top predictors of word reading ability, better even than vocabulary knowledge and parent–child book reading experiences, with *r*s ranging from .58 to .68. Several training studies have confirmed that teaching beginners phonemic segmentation, particularly when it is combined with letter knowledge, facilitates the development of word reading skills in beginners (Ball & Blachman, 1991; Bradley & Bryant, 1979, 1985; Lundberg, Frost, & Peterson, 1988; and several others).

It is important to recognize that these skills are strong predictors of beginning reading, not only because they enable sight word reading but also because they are not easily acquired by youngsters. Liberman, Shankweiler, Fischer, and Carter (1974) showed that segmenting words into phonemes is much harder for beginners than is segmenting words into syllables. This is because there are no breaks signaling where one phoneme ends and the next begins in the pronunciations of words. Rather, phonemes overlap and are co-articulated, yielding a seamless stream of sound. Special experiences are needed to help beginners become skilled at recognizing and manipulating phonemes in words. Studies have shown that even adults who have never learned to read an alphabetic orthography have much difficulty identifying phonemes in speech (Mann, 1986; Morais, Alegria, & Content, 1987; Read, Zhang, Nie, & Ding, 1986).

It is important to recognize that acquiring phonemic awareness requires getting in touch with "deep" phonemes in words rather than surface sounds, as explained previously. According to our theory, graphemes must become attached to these deep phonemes in order for sight words to become well secured in lexical memory. Helping students do this may be facilitated by teaching them how to monitor articulatory gestures, that is, how to use lip and tongue movements to signal phoneme boundaries. For example, the following sequence of movements are involved in saying "top": the tongue touching the roof of the mouth, the mouth opening, and then the lips coming together. Each movement corresponds to a different phoneme. Such awareness and monitoring are taught in the Auditory Conceptualization in Depth Program designed by Lindamood and Lindamood (1975) to remediate reading and spelling difficulties.

It is important to recognize that the aim of phonemic segmentation training is to help learners discover the phonemic segments that allow the spellings of words to become attached to the phonological representations of words in memory. The errors of children who are naive about the spellings of words reveal how phonemic analysis can run off course if left to operate independently of spellings. For example, observations by Henderson (1981), Read (1971, 1975), and Treiman (1993), among others, revealed that some naive learners think that the second sound in *important* is /n/ rather than /m/, that the initial sound in *dress* is the same as the initial sound in *jumper*, that the second consonant in *skate* is /g/, and that the sound between /b/ and /p/ in *bump* consists of one rather than two phonemes. Although children's insights are accurate, discovering these facts about phonetics is not helpful for matching spellings to pronunciations. It is more adaptive to conceptualize the sound structure of words so that it dovetails with graphemes in the spellings of words. It is possible for learners to tinker with the phonological representations of words, but it is not possible to alter spellings that are fixed by the conventional system. According to my theory, the connection-forming process for storing words in memory is facilitated when potential discrepancies between spellings and pronunciations can be reconciled in this way.

Not only phonemic segmentation but also letter learning is difficult for beginners; here, the burden is on memory (Ehri, 1983). Children must remember the shapes, names, and typical sounds of 52 upper- and lower-case letters. These abstract visual forms and labels lack any meaning, making it especially difficult to retain the letter information in memory. Methods of teaching the letters that incorporate meaning into the learning process, that provide mnemonic devices for enhancing memory, and that involve the child in extensive practice should speed up the course of letter learning. An example of letters that are made much easier to learn is found in the Letterland program (Wendon, 1994). For example, the letter *s* is drawn as a snake, and children learn to refer to it as "Sammy Snake." Both shapes of *h* (*H* and *h*) are drawn to depict "Hairy Hat Man." The alliteration in the labels clarifies the critical sounds to be associated with the letters. The letter shapes are retained more easily in memory because they assume the shapes of the characters. Children can look at a letter, be reminded of the character's shape, recall the character's name, and then find the critical sound at the beginning of the name. In our research, we have found such mnemonics to be effective in teaching letter–sound relations (Ehri, Deffner, & Wilce, 1984).

Children who come to school knowing most of their letters have a substantial head start in learning to read. Knowing the names of letters makes the process of learning letter–sound relations easier, because most of the letters contain relevant sounds in their names. Children who come to school knowing few letters are extremely limited in the progress they can make in learning to read until they learn most of the letters, as becomes apparent later in this discussion.

Phonemic segmentation and letter knowledge are capabilities that benefit sight word learning when children first begin learning to read. In later years, as learners encounter words that are longer and more complex, they need to acquire additional knowledge about the alphabetic system, knowledge involving syllabic and morphemic spelling patterns. This knowledge is needed to extend the development of sight word reading beyond a graphophonic level.

Phases of Development in Sight Word Learning.

In studying the course of development of sight word learning, I have found that different types of connections predominate at different points in development (Ehri, 1991, 1994, 1995). To provide an overview, sight word learning begins as a nonalphabetic process involving memory for connections between selected visual cues and words. However, once learners acquire some knowledge about the alphabetic writing system, sight word learning changes into an alphabetic process involving connections between letters in written words and sounds in their pronunciations. At first, connections are partial, linking salient letters to sounds. When readers acquire full knowledge of the alphabetic system, complete connections can be formed between graphemes in spellings and phonemes in the pronunciations of words. As sight words accumulate in memory in fully analyzed forms, letter patterns recurring in different words become consolidated into multiletter units symbolizing phonological blends. Alphabetic connections linking all of the letters in spellings to their pronunciations enable mature readers to represent thousands of words uniquely in their mental lexicons and to locate the pronunciations and meanings of these words accurately and automatically when seeing them in print (Ehri, 1980, 1984, 1987, 1992; Perfetti, 1992).

PHASES OF

SIGHT WORD LEARNING

Pre-alphabetic Phase

"look"

Partial Alphabetic Phase

/s/ /puّ/ /n/

Full Alphabetic Phase

/s/ /p/ /u̯/ /n/

Consolidated Alphabetic Phase

/sp/ /uّn/

FIG. 1.4. Example of the connections formed to remember how to
read words by sight at each phase
of development.

To capture the changes that occur in the development of sight word reading, I have distinguished four phases characterized by the involvement of the alphabetic system. This system represents the regularities that underlie the written forms of English words and that all learners must internalize in order to build a fully functioning sight vocabulary. The term *alphabetic* indicates not simply that words consist of letters, but also that the letters function as symbols for phonemes and phoneme blends in the words. The four phases are: pre-alphabetic, partial alphabetic, full alphabetic, and consolidated alphabetic. Each phase is labeled to reflect the predominant type of connection that links the written forms of sight words to their pronunciations and meanings in memory. These are illustrated in Fig. 1.4.

Pre-Alphabetic Phase

During the pre-alphabetic phase, beginners remember how to read sight words by forming connections between selected visual attributes of words and their pronunciations or meanings and storing these associations in memory. Gough and Hillinger (1980) described this as a process of paired associate learning. We called this *visual cue reading* (Ehri & Wilce, 1985). Gough, Juel, and Griffith (1992) showed that pre-alphabetic readers select single salient visual cues to remember words. In one case, a thumbprint appearing next to a word was found to be the salient cue. When it accompanied the word, children could read the word. When it did not, the word was not recognized. Other examples of salient visual cues that readers might use to form connections are the two round eyes in *look* (see Fig. 1.4), the tail dangling at the end of *dog*, and two humps in the middle of *camel* (Gough, Juel, & Roper/Schneider, 1983).

This phase is called pre-alphabetic because, in contrast to subsequent phases, letter–sound relations are not involved in the connections. When pre-alphabetic readers are observed to read print in their environment, such as stop signs and fast-food restaurant signs, they do this by remembering visual cues accompanying the print rather than the written words themselves; for example, the golden arches behind the McDonalds' sign rather than initial *M* in the name. Masonheimer, Drum, and Ehri (1984) selected children who could read environmental print and presented the print with one letter altered; for example, *Pepsi* changed to *Xepsi*. Children failed to notice the change. This occurred not because children ignored letters in the signs (McGee, Lomax, & Head, 1988), but because they did not store the letters in memory as part of the connections that prompted their reading of the signs.

One interesting consequence of the fact that pre-alphabetic connections do not involve ties between letters and sounds is that readers are not held to specific pronunciations of printed words. In studies by Goodman and Altwerger (1981) and Harste, Woodward, and Burke (1982), children were observed to connect print to ideas and to produce variable rather than exact wordings; for example, reading *Crest* as "brush teeth" or "toothpaste," and reading *Dynamints* as "fresh-a-mints." This lack of correspondence at the phonemic level but equivalence at the semantic level indicates that the connections formed in lexical memory at this phase are between salient visual cues and meanings of words. This contrasts with later phases, in which the involvement of letter–sound connections restricts the word accessed in memory to a single pronunciation linked to the word's spelling (Ehri & Wilce, 1987b).

The pre-alphabetic phase is really a phase that occurs by default, as Byrne (1992) pointed out. Young children have a desire to remember how to read words, but they cannot take advantage of systematic relations between letters and sounds. By default, they resort to noticing and remembering visually salient cues. However, in most cases these cues are unreliable, because they recur in several words. Also, they are hard to remember because most are arbitrary; for example, the thumbprint, or the tall posts in *yellow* (Mason, 1980).

Partial Alphabetic Phase

During the next phase, beginners remember how to read sight words by forming partial alphabetic connections between only some of the letters in written words and sounds detected in their pronunciations. Because first and final letters are especially salient, these are often selected as the cues to be remembered. We called this *phonetic cue reading*. To remember sight words in this way, partial alphabetic readers need to know the relevant letter–sound correspondences and they need to be able to segment initial and final sounds in words. For example, to remember how to read *spoon*, beginners might detect initial /s/ and final /n/ segments in their pronunciation of the word, and recognize that the letters they see, *s* and *n*, symbolize these sounds, as shown in Fig. 1.4. Recognizing these connections is facilitated by the fact that the names of these letters contain the relevant sounds (i.e., "ess" and "en"; Templeton & Bear, 1992; Treiman, 1993). These connections are retained in memory and enable learners to remember how to read *spoon* the next time they see it. The reason why the connections formed are partial rather than complete is that readers lack full knowledge of the spelling system, particularly vowels; also, they do not know how to segment speech into phonemic units that match up with the array of graphemic units.

Ehri and Wilce (1985) showed how readers at these two phases differed in their sight word learning. They found that beginners in the pre-alphabetic phase had an easier time remembering how to read words that had unique visual forms but bore no relationship to sounds (e.g., *WcB* for *elephant*), whereas beginners in the partial alphabetic phase had an easier time remembering how to read words containing salient cues linking letters to sounds (e.g., *LFT* for *elephant*). Cardoso-Martins (1996) recently replicated this study in Brazil with Portuguese-speaking children.

Rack, Hulme, Snowling, and Wightman (1994) confirmed the phenomenon of phonetic cue reading in children. They showed that beginners remembered how to read words better when the spellings provided connections that were phonetically close rather than distant. For example, beginners were taught to read two different spellings of *garden,* either *kdn* or *bdn*. Both /k/ and /b/ differ from /g/, but /k/ is closer phonetically to /g/ because /k/ and /g/ are articulated at the same place in the mouth, in the back. (Say these sounds to yourself to detect similarities and differences.) Results showed that students learned to read *kdn* more easily than *bdn*. Thus, even though both spellings contained incorrect letters, the letter that enabled the formation of a plausible graphophonic connction was the one that facilitated sight word learning.

Byrne and Fielding-Barnsley (1989, 1990) studied what type of training was required to move readers from the pre-alphabetic phase to the partial alphabetic phase. They found that students had to be taught to perceive shared sounds in words, to segment initial sounds in the pronunciations of words, and to recognize how letters symbolized initial sounds in words. These three skills had to be acquired in combination to enable beginners to deduce and transfer alphabetic information from training words to transfer words.

There is an advantage to forming connections out of partial phonetic cues rather than visual cues. Ehri and Wilce (1985) and also Mason (1980) found that phonetic cue readers remembered how to read words much better than did visual cue readers. This is because phonetic cue readers had a system available to support memory. Knowing the alphabetic system greatly facilitates the task of forming and remembering relevant connections between written words and their pronunciations. In contrast, visually based connections are idiosyncratic rather than systematic and are often arbitrary, making them much harder to remember.

Full Alphabetic Phase

During the full alphabetic phase, beginners remember how to read sight words by forming complete connections between letters seen in the written forms of words and phonemes detected in their pronunciations. This is possible because readers understand how most graphemes symbolize phonemes in the conventional spelling system (Venezky, 1970). In applying this knowledge to form connections for sight words, spellings become amalgamated or bonded to pronunciations of words in memory (Ehri, 1992; Perfetti, 1992). For example, in learning to read *spoon,* full phase readers recognize how the five letters correspond to four phonemes in the word, including how *oo* symbolizes /u/ (see Fig. 1.4). I have already described this form of sight word learning previously.

One advantage of representing sight words more completely in memory is that word reading becomes much more accurate. Whereas phonetic cue readers' limited memory for letters may cause them to misread *soon* or *spin* as *spoon*, full alphabetic readers' representations eliminate confusion because their representations are sufficiently complete to distinguish easily among similarly spelled words. This difference in the tendency to confuse similarly spelled words was apparent in a study comparing readers in the partial phase with readers in the full alphabetic phase (Ehri & Wilce, 1987b).

Another characteristic distinguishing full-phase from partial-phase readers is the ability to decode words never read before, by blending letters into a pronunciation. This knowledge enables full-phase readers to form fully connected sight words in memory. In a study by Ehri and Wilce (1987a), beginners who were partial-phase readers were assigned to one or another of two treatments. The experimental group was taught to read words by converting all of the letters to sounds, thus enabling them to process words like readers in the full phase. The control group was given practice associating individual letters to sounds, a treatment that was not expected to advance them beyond the partial phase in their reading. Following training, subjects received a sight word learning task. They were given several trials to practice reading a list of 15 similarly spelled words with corrective feedback on each trial. The full-phase readers mastered the list within three trials, whereas the partial-phase readers read only 40% of the words after seven learning trials.

The difficulty exhibited by partial-phase readers was confusing words having similar letters, for example, *bend* and *blond, drip* and *dump, lap* and *lamp, stab* and *stamp*. These results reveal the great advantage to word reading that occurs at the full alphabetic phase.

Although full-phase readers are able to decode words, this graphophonic assembly strategy for reading words is supplanted by sight word reading for words that are practiced sufficiently often. The advantage of sight word reading over decoding is that sight word reading operates much faster. In a study by Ehri and Wilce (1983), students in first, second, and fourth grades read familiar sight words much faster than simply spelled nonsense words. In fact, good readers were able to read the sight words as rapidly as they could name single digits, indicating that the words were read as single unified wholes rather than as letters identified sequentially. Unitization is taken to indicate that spellings of sight words are fully bonded to their pronunciations in memory.

It is not until beginners are capable of establishing fully connected sight words in memory that they can read new words by analogy to known sight words. In a study by Ehri and Robbins (1992), we found that beginners in the full alphabetic phase were able to read new words by analogy to known words, whereas beginners in the partial alphabetic phase were not. Rather than analogize, partial-phase readers tended to mistake the new words for the known words because of shared letter cues; for example, misreading the new word *save* as the word they had learned to read *cave*. Our explanation is that partial-phase readers do not store their sight words in memory in sufficient letter detail to recognize how they are similar to yet different from similarly spelled new words. In contrast, readers in the full phase possess full representations of sight words plus decoding skill, both of which support an analogy strategy.

Consolidated Alphabetic Phase

The ability of readers in the full alphabetic phase to retain complete infor-mation about the spellings of sight words in memory makes it possible for their print lexicons to grow rapidly as they encounter many different words in their reading. As fully connected spellings of more and more words are retained in memory, letter patterns that recur across different words become consolidated. Repeated experience reading a letter sequence that symbolizes the same phoneme blend across different words yields a consolidated unit. Consolidation allows readers to operate with multiletter units that may be morphemes, syllables, or subsyllabic units such as onsets and rimes. These letter patterns become part of a reader's generalized knowledge of the spelling system.

Larger letter units are valuable for sight word reading because they reduce the memory load involved in storing sight words in memory. For example, -*est* might emerge as a consolidated unit in a reader's memory from its occurrence in several sight words known by the reader—*nest, pest, rest, test, vest, west,* and *crest.* Knowing -*est* as a consolidated unit means that the graphemes and phonemes have been analyzed and bonded. Knowing this should ease the task of forming connections to learn the new word, *chest* as a sight word. Whereas full-phase readers would need to form four separate connections linking *ch, e, s,* and *t* to the phonemes /č/, /e/, /s/, /t/, respectively, a consolidated phase reader would need to form only two separate connections, *ch,* and *est,* linked to /č/ and /est/, respectively. Another example of connections formed from consolidated units is shown in Fig. 1.4.

If a reader knew units such as *est, tion, in,* and *ing* as consolidated units, the task of learning longer sight words such as *question* and *interesting* would be easier. Another contribution of consolidated units to sight word reading is that they speed up the process of accessing words by facilitating letter identification (Juel, 1983; Venezky & Massaro, 1979).

A number of studies have shown that older readers are more sensitive to letter co-occurrence patterns than beginning readers. For example, Leslie and Thimke (1986) gave first and second graders a word-search task and found that students reading at a second-grade level were sensitive to the difference between legally sequenced and illegally sequenced letters in non-words, whereas first graders were sensitive only to the difference between familiar and unfamiliar real words. This suggests that second grade is when children's sight vocabularies grow large enough to support the consolidation of frequently occurring letter patterns into units.

Also, there is evidence that words containing more familiar letter patterns are read more accurately by students than are words containing unfamiliar patterns even when the words are constructed out of the same grapheme–phoneme correspondences (Treiman, Goswami, & Bruck, 1990). Such effects are more apparent in advanced beginning readers than in novice beginners, indicating the contribution of a larger sight vocabulary to knowledge of common spelling patterns (Bowey & Hansen, 1994).

A study by Juel (1983) showed that knowledge of letter patterns enables more mature readers to read familiar words faster. She found that fifth graders who were shown words that shared letter patterns with many other words were able to read those words faster than words having less common letters. However, this factor made little difference to second graders who were influenced primarily by the decodability of the words. Thus, word reading speed may be facilitated by knowledge of letter patterns sometime after second grade.

To summarize, I have suggested that the development of sight word learning occurs in several phases differing from each other in the involvement of alphabetic knowledge. The pre-alphabetic phase occurs by default because beginners lack much knowledge or ability to use letters in their sight word reading, so this phase makes little contribution to subsequent phases of development. In contrast, the three alphabetic phases—partial, full, and consolidated—are closely related and extend development from immature to mature forms of sight word learning.

SIGHT WORD LEARNING REQUIRES SPELLING KNOWLEDGE

Most people take it as a given that reading and spelling are different things. However, this can be questioned. The term *spelling* is actually ambiguous. It can function as a verb to refer to the act of spelling a word by writing it; however, it can also function as a noun to refer to the product that is written, the word's spelling, consisting of a sequence of letters. Spellings of words are the targets not only of spelling behavior but also of reading behavior. Talking about spellings of words for reading blurs the separation between reading and spelling.

Another factor muddying the waters is uncertainty about which behaviors count as spelling and which count as reading. One can spell words by writing them. One can also recognize whether spellings are correct or incorrect as the words are being *read*; for example, *rane* versus *rain*. When one writes out words, one usually *reads* the words to verify their correctness. To the extent that spellers do this when they spell, reading as well as spelling contribute to the final spelling product.

Although the ambiguity and overlap might appear hopeless, some basic distinctions can be salvaged. Words have spellings, that is, prescribed sequences of letters. Spellings of words are the targets of three literacy acts:

1. Writing spellings.
2. Reading spellings to determine their pronunciations and meanings.
3. Noticing when spellings are incorrect as they are read.

It turns out that these three literacy acts are very closely related (Ehri, 1997).

There is evidence that when readers read text, they automatically notice when words are misspelled. McConkie and Zola (1981) planted misspellings in text, and they recorded readers' eye movements as they read the text. They found that normal eye movement patterns were disrupted when readers saw words as subtly misspelled as *fracture* and *garden* written *fraoture* and *garben*, even when these words appeared in highly predictable contexts. This is evidence that reading and spelling processes are intertwined during the act of reading.

Correlational findings reveal that the three literacy acts are closely related. I have extracted correlations from various studies in which students were asked to read a list of words, or to write words to dictation, or to distinguish correct from incorrect spellings of words. From Table 1.3 one can see that reading and spelling performances were highly related in these studies. The high values are not explained by more general factors, such as intelligence. For example, in the Greenberg, Ehri, and Perin (1997) study, the partial correlation remained the same when Peabody Picture Vocabulary scores were removed. Note that most of the correlations are above $r = .70$, bringing them close to reliability values that are expected between tests that measure one capability. Such high correlations indicate that similar if not identical processes are measured by these tasks.

Let us consider knowledge sources and processes that are involved in these three acts involving spellings to see what makes them much more similar than different. We can distinguish two types of knowledge that people use to read and spell words (Ehri, 1986). They possess knowledge about the spellings of specific words held in memory as a result of their experiences reading those particular words. Earlier, I portrayed this knowledge as involving graphophonic connections linking spellings to pronunciations. People also possess knowledge about the general alphabetic system. This includes phonemic segmentation and blending, grapheme–phoneme and phoneme–grapheme relations, and spelling patterns that recur in different words. It

TABLE 1.3

Correlations Among Reading Words, Producing Correct Spellings
of Words, and Recognizing Misspellings of Words at Various
Grade Levels Across Different Studies (from Ehri, 1997)

Studies Grade Levels	Read: Spell	Read: Rec. Missp.	Spell: Rec. Missp.
Juel, Griffith, and Gough (1986) Different words were read, spelled, and recognized.			
First graders	.84	.74	.76
Second graders	.77	.69	.68
Griffith (1987) Same words were read and spelled.			
First graders	.83		
Third graders	.84		
Greenberg, Ehri, and Perin (1997) Different words were read and spelled.			
Third through fifth graders	.86		
Jorm (1981) Same words were read and spelled.			
Fourth through sixth graders	.85		
Griffith (1991) Different words were spelled and recognized.			
Third graders			.80
Ehri and Wilce (1982) Different words were spelled and recognized.			
Seventh graders			.77
College students			.78

does not include memorized rules that people can state verbatim but have little idea how to apply (Beck, 1981). By alphabetic knowledge, I mean *working* knowledge that people actually apply to read and spell.

Typically, beginners are taught grapheme–phoneme correspondences when they begin school. These associations are easier to learn if students already know the names of letters, because most letter names include relevant sounds, for example /t/ in *tee,* and /k/ in *kay.* Read (1971), Treiman (1993), and others showed that beginners make use of letter-name knowledge in their attempts to invent spelling of words. We have shown that beginners use this knowledge also in remembering how to read words (Ehri & Wilce, 1985).

Although letter names take care of 25 associations, there are several more to be learned that are not found in names. Whereas grapheme–phoneme relations are used for reading, phoneme–grapheme relations are used for spelling. It turns out that correspondences for reading are not completely isomorphic with correspondences for spelling. There are about 40 distinctive phonemes in English, but 70 letters or letter combinations to symbolize phonemes. This makes pronouncing spellings easier than writing correct spellings (Cronnell, 1978).

Whereas beginners utilize graphemes and phonemes to read and spell, once students gain more experience with words, they consolidate graphemes and phonemes that recur across different words into multiletter units that are used to read and spell. The earliest units to become consolidated are probably the common affixes and common spelling patterns that were shown in Table 1.1.

This view of systematic alphabetic knowledge is broader than that offered by Venezky (1970) and by Hanna, Hanna, Hodges, and Rudorf (1966). It includes regularities that others regard as irregularities; for example, sounds that are spelled in more than one way, and letter sequences that include silent letters. The feature that makes a letter or letter sequence systematic is its recurrence in several different words. Of course, I am talking about *potential* systematic knowledge here. These sources of regularity are all available for learners to incorporate into their working knowledge of the system. Whether they actually do is another matter.

The other type of knowledge used for reading and spelling consists of information about the spellings of individual words. As I have explained, word-specific knowledge is constructed out of students' knowledge of the general alphabetic system. Knowledge of the system functions as a mnemonic tool, enabling students to retain letter-specific information about individual words in memory.

In English, specific word learning is necessary because variable spellings are possible. For example, *telephone* might be spelled conventionally in several ways, as *teliphone, tellafoan,* or *telufown.* To the extent that learners see one spelling and process its grapheme–phoneme connections, they remember this spelling and not the alternatives, as has been shown in various studies (Ehri, 1980; Ehri & Wilce, 1986; Reitsma, 1983). Of course, any of these alternatives is much easier to remember than spellings that lie outside the system; for example, spelling *telephone* as *komikeh*. This illustrates how knowledge of the system is central for remembering the written forms of specific words for use in both reading and spelling acts.

It is important to note that my view differs from other views that regard word-specific memory as comprising visual configurations of words or serial lists of letters but not rules and regularities (Kreiner & Gough, 1990). My view is that knowledge of the system is the primary stuff used to build word-specific memory.

Although reading words and spelling words involve very similar processes, it is obvious that we can read words better than we can spell words. The reason is that more bits of information must be remembered for correct spelling than for correct reading. When a student remembers how to read a familiar word, he or she accesses essentially one bit of information from memory, an amalgam consisting of the word's spelling, pronunciation, and meaning. However, when the student remembers how to spell a familiar word, he or she must access *several* bits of information from memory consisting of individual letters in the proper order.

What is the nature of the representations that enable students to write out all the letters in words correctly? Results of our research indicate that the spelling-pronunciation-meaning amalgams formed in memory to read words are also useful for spelling words. In several studies, we have taught beginners to read specific words and then have asked them to spell the words. In most cases, transfer from reading to spelling was evident (Ehri, 1997). However, reading did not enable most subjects to spell the words *perfectly*. Typically, students could spell a greater proportion of the letters correctly than they could spell entire words correctly: 70% to 80% of the letters versus 30% to 40% of the words. This suggests that perfect spelling requires more than the amalgams formed from reading practice.

What kinds of letters make spellings especially hard to remember? According to our theory, letters that do not conform to the alphabetic system should be harder to remember. Letter sequences that recur in few other words and are not built out of conventional grapheme–phoneme correspondences should cause problems. When there are many graphemes that might symbolize a phoneme, as in the case of *schwa* vowels, remembering the particular grapheme is harder. Graphemes having no correlates in sound should elude memory; for example, doubled letters and silent letters.

Let us examine some words that have parts known to be difficult to spell. I have listed in Table 1.4 some spelling demons identified by Fry, Polk, and Fountoukidis (1984). What makes these words difficult to spell? According

TABLE 1.4
Spelling Demons With Difficult Parts Underlined
(Taken From Fry et al., 1984)

lieutenant	sergeant	receipt	aisle
unnecessary	accommodate	muscle	yacht
conscientious	noticeable	pneumonia	vacuum

to our theory, students remember best those letters that conform to their knowledge of the alphabetic system, especially letters that can be connected unambiguously to phonemes within words. They have the hardest time remembering letters that lie outside the alphabetic system as they know it. Inspection of these demons reveals that all contain problem letters, including nonconventional graphemes, doubled letters, silent letters, *schwa* vowels (i.e., the nondistinctive vowel pronounced "uh" in unstressed syllables), and uncommon spelling patterns that I have underlined. Notice how variable the spellings of *schwa* vowels can be, as evidenced in these words—*a, e, ou, ea, o, i*—hence, the difficulty of remembering which letter is correct. Kreiner and Gough (1990) showed that spellers make more errors on *schwa* vowels than on unambiguously pronounced vowels.

Waters, Bruck, and Malus-Abramowitz (1988) compared students' ability to spell words that exhibited different kinds of spelling regularities. The children were in third through sixth grades. The hardest words to spell were those having letters that fell outside the system, words such as *aisle* and *yacht*. Less difficult were words whose regularity depended on knowing the spellings of root words and affixes; for example, *sign* related to *signal* and *shortage*. Easier than these were words that might be spelled in alternative, equally legitimate ways, for example, *detail* versus *detale*. The easiest words to spell were completely regular words with few alternative legal spellings. These findings are consistent with our theory.

To summarize, the point of this discussion is to suggest that learning to read words and learning to spell words are very closely related, because growth in both cases requires knowledge of the alphabetic system. Becoming a skilled reader as well as a skilled writer necessitates learning the alphabetic system. This involves at the outset learning graphophonemic relations that provide the foundation for learning a wide variety of spelling patterns.

Spelling Helps Reading and Reading Helps Spelling During Development

Results of several studies indicate that learning to read and learning to spell are reciprocally related, particularly when children first learn to read and write words. To review, according to our theory, students retain word-specific information in memory when they learn to read words, and this information is available to support spelling performance. Likewise, learning how to produce more complete spellings of words contributes to sight word reading.

We observed transfer from reading to spelling in a study with second graders (Ehri, 1980). Students practiced reading the spellings of eight made-up words until they could read them perfectly. Half of the students read one plausible letter sequence, and half read an alternative sequence. Examples of the pairs of spellings are:

wheople versus *weepel*	*wh* versus *we*
bischun versus *bistion*	*ch* versus no *ch*
ghirp versus *gurp*	*i* versus no *i*

Both forms were pronounced identically. After a 4-minute delay, students wrote from memory the spellings that they had read. They recalled 69% of the words perfectly, indicating that substantial transfer from word reading to word spelling occurred despite alternative ways to spell the words. Even when students misspelled the words, they restricted their letter choices to those they had seen in the words rather than phonemically equivalent alternatives. Adjacent to the word pairs printed here are letters distinguishing the two spellings. We found that students included these letters in their misspellings only if they saw the letters in the words they studied, not if they didn't see the letters. This indicates that word specific knowledge retained from reading experiences influenced second graders' spellings.

Results of another study (Ehri & Wilce, 1986) also revealed the impact of reading words on students' memory for their spellings. In this study, we used words containing medial flaps that are pronounced more like /d/ in American English, but might be spelled with either *d* or *t*. Examples of the words we used are:

huddle, modify, pedigree versus *meteor, glitter, attic.*

Second graders were exposed orally or in writing to 12 words containing these medial flaps. Half of the subjects practiced reading the words; the other half heard and repeated the words but never saw spellings. Subjects practiced the words on one day and then wrote spellings on the next day. Half of the words contained flaps spelled *d* and half contained flaps spelled *t*.

We expected that students who read the words would connect graphemes to phonemes and would remember the flap in each word as /d/ or /t/ according to its spelling, whereas students who only listened to the words would spell the flap phonetically as /d/ in most of the words. This was what we found. Subjects who read the words spelled 84% of the flaps accurately, whereas controls spelled only 64%. By chance we would expect 50% accuracy.

Whereas students in the made-up word (Ehri, 1980) study, spelled words shortly after they read them, students in the flap study spelled words on a different day. Despite the delay, students' spellings still reflected memory for word-specific information, indicating that memory was long term.

In the second flap study, we found that students' memory for complete spellings of the words was weak, only 31%, probably because the words contained problem letters such as doubled consonants. The fact that word-specific effects were nevertheless evident in spellings shows that if students have partial letter information about specific words in memory, they do not ignore this knowledge and invent a spelling. Rather, they access the letters they remember and invent the part they do not remember.

The focus of transfer effects from reading to spelling in these studies involved specific words. In another laboratory study, we manipulated students' knowledge of the alphabetic system by training kindergartners to decode words. We found that this reading treatment boosted their spelling performance (Ehri & Wilce, 1987a). Foorman, Francis, Novy, and Liberman (1991) reported similar findings in a classroom-based study.

To summarize, results of these studies confirm that reading impacts spelling in beginners. When beginners read words, they retain word-specific information in memory and they access this to spell the words. When readers receive reading instruction that improves their general knowledge of the alphabetic system, this benefits their spelling ability as well.

It is clear that reading influences spelling in beginners. Also, there is evidence that spelling influences reading. Morris and Perney (1984) had first graders invent spellings of words before the students had received any formal reading instruction. Most children knew all the letters of the alphabet but they were able to spell few words correctly, only 9%. Students' productions were scored to reflect whether all the sounds were spelled with plausible letters and whether letter choices were conventional. Results revealed a surprisingly high correlation, .68, between spellings invented at the beginning of the school year, and reading achievement scores at the end of the year. The correlation rose to .82 between mid-year spelling scores and year-end reading scores. The likely explanation is that invented spellings reflect children's knowledge of the spelling system that determines how quickly they get off the ground and make progress in learning to read.

We performed a short-term experiment with beginners to examine the effects of spelling training on word reading (Ehri & Wilce, 1987b). In this study, we manipulated learners' knowledge of the general alphabetic system. The students were kindergartners selected because they had limited ability to read words and could not decode. Experimental students were taught to spell words phonetically by segmenting them into phonemes and symbolizing the phonemes with graphemes. Control students practiced isolated phoneme–grapheme associations. Then students were given several trials to learn to read a set of 12 similarly spelled words. Comparison of performances revealed that spelling-trained students learned to read significantly more words than did control students. Our explanation is that spelling instruction improved students' working knowledge of the alphabetic system. With this knowledge they were able to form more complete grapheme–phoneme connections to remember how to read the words than control students.

In our study, spelling instruction improved students' ability to learn to read a set of words with practice, but it did not improve their ability to decode unfamiliar words, presumably because it did not include lessons in how to assemble and blend graphemes into phonemes. However, Uhry and Shepherd (1993) conducted a spelling training experiment and found that training did improve students' decoding ability. Their findings suggest that spelling instruction can improve decoding ability if it is structured to include blending.

In sum, it is likely that the reason why instruction in spelling contributes to word reading ability is that spelling instruction helps beginners acquire knowledge of the alphabetic system, which benefits processes used in reading.

Reading and Spelling in Normal and Disabled Readers

We have shown that reading and spelling processes are highly related in normally developing readers. What about disabled readers? In two studies examining the relationship between word reading and word spelling abilities in disabled readers separately from normal readers, results verified that reading and spelling performances were strongly correlated in both groups. However, the correlations were not quite as high for disabled readers as they were for normal readers, indicating that the underlying processes may be less interconnected and interdependent in disabled readers.

Guthrie (1973) examined 19 normal second-grade readers and 19 older disabled readers matched to normals in reading age. He gave them word reading and spelling recognition tasks involving both words and pseudowords. Correlations between the reading and spelling tasks were all positive and strong, but those among normal readers were substantially higher than those among disabled readers:

	Spell/Read Words	Spell/Read Pseudowords
Normal readers	$r = .84$	$r = .91$
Disabled readers	$r = .68$	$r = .60$

In another study, Greenberg, Ehri, and Perin (1997) compared 72 normal readers in third, fourth and fifth grades with 72 adults matched to the normals in reading age. The adults were severely disabled readers enrolled in adult literacy programs. Greenberg et al. gave tasks to measure spelling production, word reading, and pseudoword reading:

	Spell/Read Words	Spell/Read Pseudowords
Normal readers	r = .86	r = .62
Disabled readers	r = .57	r = .41

As in Guthrie's study, all the correlations were postive and significantly greater than zero, but normal readers' values were substantially higher than those of disabled readers. The difference was not attributable to differences in the size of the standard deviations between the two groups.

Our interpretation is that the lower correlations among disabled readers signal the reason for their difficulty learning to read and spell. Their progress is impaired because their word reading and word spelling processes have not become sufficiently integrated. Poorer integration may arise from inadequate detection of "deep" phonemes in words, or deficient knowledge of the alphabetic system. Both of these deficiencies would be expected to impair the process of establishing sight words in memory, by limiting the strength of the bonds formed between spellings and pronunciations and limiting the attachment of spellings to deep phonemes within the central speech processing system.

This explanation received some support in the Greenberg et al. (1997) study. They found that even though the adult disabled readers and child normal readers were matched in their word reading skill, the adults performed much worse on phonemic awareness and nonword decoding tasks, indicating that their knowledge of the alphabetic system and knowledge of deep phonemes were poorer.

Ehri and Saltmarsh (1995) compared normal first-grade readers to older disabled readers in a sight word learning task. They found that the disabled readers took significantly longer to learn to read the words than did normal readers when learning scores were adjusted for reading age. Moreover, reaction times to read the words indicated that the sight words were not as well secured in memory among disabled readers as among normal readers. These findings add support to the view that the connection-forming processes involved in sight word learning are impaired among disabled readers. Whereas normal readers reach the consolidated phase in their sight word learning, disabled readers may remain at the partial alphabetic phase in their development.

CONCLUSION

Theory and evidence presented in this chapter reveal that learning to read is fundamentally an alphabetic process. There is no way that beginners can attain mature levels of reading and writing without acquiring knowledge of the alphabetic system and utilizing this to build a vocabulary of sight words. Moreover, getting off the ground in learning to read is not easy. Beginners must accomplish some very difficult tasks. They must retain in memory 52 upper- and lower-case letter shapes and learn how these letters operate singly or in combination to symbolize phonemes in words. They must learn how to find the invisible seams in the flow of speech in order to segment words into phonemes. Their knowledge of graphemes and phonemes must be put to use to penetrate the phonological structure of words buried deep in the speech centers of their brains and to attach spellings of words to these representations.

Phonemic awareness and letter knowledge are important determiners of reading acquisition during the first couple of years. However, further growth requires acquisition of alphabetic knowledge that involves multiletter units, or spelling patterns. Learning to read and learning to spell become closely intertwined during development because each draws on the same knowledge sources in memory. Although the same processes operate in poor readers as in good readers, reading and spelling are not as closely intertwined. Word memory remains difficult when the letters or connections that must be remembered lie outside learners' knowledge of the alphabetic system. This may explain the greater difficulty that disabled readers have in learning to read.

My focus has involved describing how alphabetic processes are central in learning to read. I have said little about instruction. However, my reason for going into detail about reading acquisition processes in learners was to lay out a map that teachers might use to guide their efforts. My claim is that teachers need to understand these processes so that they hold a target in mind when they teach students to read, they can tell whether these processes are being acquired by their students, they can identify how particular aspects of their instruction develop these processes, they can tell whether instruction is working as it should, and they can figure out how to modify instruction to improve its effectiveness. What I propose may appear to be a tall order indeed, but this is what effective, intelligent teaching is all about. Effective teachers are not robots who follow teacher manuals blindly and religiously and who turn the burden of effective instruction over to curriculum materials. Rather, effective teachers are intelligent, reasoning, informed problem solvers who undstand what they are doing.

In giving teachers direction in how to think about the processes they need to teach, I would offer the following as fundamental:

1. At the outset of instruction, beginners need to learn all their letters and learn how to use their letter knowledge to penetrate speech processes. Letter learning includes recognizing the shapes of letters as well as recalling and writing letter shapes from memory. It includes learning the names of

letters as well as the most frequent sounds they symbolize. It includes learning how to group letters to form graphemes that symbolize sounds. Facility with letters is essential for learners to operate alphabetically with words. Learners cannot be expected to make adequate progress without acquiring facility with letters.

2. At the same time, beginners need to break the sound barrier and become aware that words contain phonemes with acoustic and articulatory properties. As this awareness is cultivated, it needs to dovetail with knowledge about sounds in letter names and sounds depicted in the spellings of words. Mastery is evidenced when children can generate phonetically complete and graphemically plausible spellings of words they have never seen written.

3. Teachers need to monitor beginners' progress in acquiring letter knowledge and phonemic awareness to make sure that it is occurring for each student. In kindergarten and first-grade classrooms there is tremendous variability among students in this respect. Teachers will need to exert extra effort with students who enter school lacking this knowledge or who find it more difficult to acquire.

4. First-grade teachers need to adopt as a primary goal that of helping students reach the full alphabetic phase in their sight word reading. For students, this means learning the major grapheme–phoneme correspondences, vowel correspondences being most important. This means being able to segment pronunciations of words into phonemes, being able to segment spellings of words into graphemes, recognizing how the two match up, and retaining these connections in memory.

5. To support sight word learning, students need to acquire strategies for reading unfamiliar words by both decoding and analogizing. These strategies should be easier to teach to students once they reach the full alphabetic phase in their sight word reading.

6. Students need to acquire word spelling as well as word reading competencies. At the outset, spelling instruction should focus on helping students invent phonetically complete spellings of words as well as inventing spellings that are graphemically plausible in terms of the conventional system. Learning the spellings of specific words by memorizing word lists should not begin until students understand how the conventional system works graphophonically. Once this point is reached, remembering the spellings of specific words will be much easier, so spelling instruction can shift to this learning activity.

7. In addition to learning the spellings of specific words, another goal of spelling instruction should be to cultivate students' knowledge of the alphabetic system. This should include not only graphophonic correspondences but also knowledge of consolidated units including root words, affixes, and families of related words. The more that students understand about the alphabetic system, the easier time they should have retaining information about individual words in memory for reading as well as for spelling words.

The guidance I offer is directed at teachers who provide literacy instruction during the primary grades. In my view, it is during this period that teachers make their greatest contribution to students' ultimate reading success, by making sure that the alphabetic foundation for learning to read is well established. This view receives support from studies showing that correlations between reading in first grade and reading in later grades is very high (Juel, 1988). Early on, the ground to cover includes teaching phonemic awareness, letter knowledge, decoding, sight word reading, and spelling as well as teaching how these skills are incorporated into text reading and writing. Students will have a better chance of achieving subsequent milestones with the proper foundation in place. Later milestones include achieving speed and automaticity in reading sight words during text reading, and advancing to the consolidated phase in acquiring knowledge and use of the alphabetic system for reading and writing. Teaching beginners to read effectively is not easy, particularly if children are at risk for reading disability. It requires a professionally trained teacher who understands the processes I have discussed here, who knows how to cultivate them through instruction, and who can tell through observation and assessment whether each student is making satisfactory progress.

AUTHOR NOTES

Portions of this paper were drawn from the following papers:

Ehri, L. (1995). Phases of development in learning to read words by sight. *Journal of Research in Reading, 18*, 116–125. Reprinted by permission of L. Ehri and Blackwell Publishers.

Ehri, L. (1997). Learning to read and learning to spell are one and the same, almost. In C. Perfetti, L. Rieben, & Fayol, M. (Eds.), *Learning to spell* (pp. 237–269). Hillsdale, NJ: Lawrence Erlbaum Associates.

Ehri, L. (1997). Sight word reading in normal readers and dyslexics. In B. Blachman (Ed.), *Cognitive and linguistic foundations of reading acquisition and intervention* (pp. 163–189). Hillsdale, NJ: Lawrence Erlbaum Associates.

Ehri, L. (1998). Word reading by sight and by analogy in beginning readers. In C. Hulme & M. Joshi (Eds.), *Reading and spelling: Development and disorders* (pp. 87–111). Hillsdale, NJ: Lawrence Erlbaum Associates.

Ehri, L. (in preparation). The unobtrusive role of words in reading text. In A. Watson, A. Badenhop, & L. Giorcelli (Eds.), *Accepting the literacy challenge* (pp.). Australia: Ashton Scholastic.

REFERENCES

Adams, M. (1990) *Beginning to read: Thinking and learning about print.* Cambridge, MA: MIT Press.

Adams, M., & Huggins, A. (1985). The growth of children's sight vocabulary: A quick test with educational and theoretical implications. *Reading Research Quarterly, 20*, 262–281.

Ball, W., & Blachman, B. (1991). Does phoneme segmentation training in kindergarten make a difference in early word recognition and developmental spelling? *Reading Research Quarterly*, *26*, 49–66.

Baron, J. (1977). Mechanisms for pronouncing printed words: Use and acquisition. In D. LaBerge & S. Samuels (Eds.), *Basic processes in reading: Perception and comprehension* (pp. 175–216). Hillsdale, NJ: Lawrence Erlbaum Associates.

Beck, I. (1981). Reading problems and instructional practices. In L. Resnick & P. Weaver (Eds.), *Reading Research: Advances in Theory and Practice* (Vol. 2, pp. 53–95). New York: Academic.

Becker, W., Dixon, R., & Anderson-Inman, L. (1980). *Morphographic and root word analysis of 26,000 high frequency words*. Eugene: University of Oregon College of Education.

Biemiller, A. (1970). The development of the use of graphic and contextual information as children learn to read. *Reading Research Quarterly*, *6*, 75–96.

Bowey, J., & Hansen, J. (1994). The development of orthographic rimes as units of word recognition. *Journal of Experimental Child Psychology*, *58*, 465–488.

Bradley, L., & Bryant, P. (1979). The independence of reading and spelling in backward and normal readers. *Developmental Medicine and Child Neurology*, *21*, 504–514.

Bradley, L., & Bryant, P. (1985). *Rhyme and reason in reading and spelling*. Ann Arbor: University of Michigan Press.

Byrne, B. (1992). Studies in the acquisition procedure for reading: Rationale, hypotheses and data. In P. Gough, L. Ehri, & R. Treiman (Eds.), *Reading acquisition* (pp. 1–34). Hillsdale, NJ: Lawrence Erlbaum Associates.

Byrne, B., & Fielding-Barnsley, R. (1989). Phonemic awareness and letter knowledge in the child's acquisition of the alphabetic principle. *Journal of Educational Psychology*, *81*, 313–321.

Byrne, B., & Fielding-Barnsley, R. (1990). Acquiring the alphabetic principle: A case for teaching recognition of phoneme identity. *Journal of Educational Psychology*, *82*, 805–812.

Cardoso-Martins, C. (1996, August). *Alphabetic access route in beginning reading acquisition in Portuguese: The role of letter-name knowledge*. Paper presented at the Biennial ISSBD Conference, Quebec City, Canada.

Clay, M. (1968). A syntactic analysis of reading errors. *Journal of Verbal Learning and Verbal Behavior*, *7*, 434–438.

Clay, M. (1969). Reading errors and self-correction behavior. *British Journal of Educational Psychology*, *39*, 47–56.

Cronnell, B. (1978). Phonics for reading vs. phonics for spelling. *Reading Teacher*, *32*, 337–340.

Cunningham, P. (1976). Investigating a synthesized theory of mediated word identification. *Reading Research Quarterly*, *11*, 127–143.

Drake, D., & Ehri, L. (1984). Spelling acquisition: Effects of pronouncing words on memory for their spellings. *Cognition and Instruction*, *1*, 297–320.

Ehri, L. (1977). Do adjectives and functors interfere as much as nouns in naming pictures? *Child Development*, *48*, 697–701.

Ehri, L. (1980). The development of orthographic images. In U. Frith (Ed.), *Cognitive processes in spelling* (pp. 311–338). London: Academic.

Ehri, L. C. (1983). Summaries and a critique of five studies related to letter-name knowledge and learning to read. In L. Gentile, M. Kamil, & J. Blanchard (Eds.), *Reading research revisited* (pp. 131–153). Columbus, Ohio: C. E. Merrill.

Ehri, L. (1984). How orthography alters spoken language competencies in children learning to read and spell. In J. Downing & R. Valtin (Eds.), *Language awareness and learning to read* (pp. 119–147). New York: Springer-Verlag.

Ehri, L. (1986). Sources of difficulty in learning to spell and read. In M. Wolraich & D. Routh (Eds.), *Advances in developmental and behavioral pediatrics* (pp. 121–195). Greenwich, CT: JAI Press.

Ehri, L. (1987). Learning to read and spell words. *Journal of Reading Behavior*, *19*, 5–31.

Ehri, L. (1991). Development of the ability to read words. In R. Barr, M. Kamil, P. Mosenthal, & P. Pearson (Eds.), *Handbook of reading research* (Vol. II, pp. 383–417). New York: Longman.

Ehri, L. (1992). Reconceptualizing the development of sight word reading and its relationship to recoding. In P. Gough, L. Ehri, & R. Treiman (Eds.), *Reading acquisition* (pp. 107–143). Hillsdale, NJ: Lawrence Erlbaum Associates.

Ehri, L. (1994). Development of the ability to read words: Update. In R. Ruddell, M. Ruddell, & H. Singer (Eds.), *Theoretical models and processes of reading* (4th ed., pp. 323–358). Newark, DE: International Reading Association.

Ehri, L. (1995). Phases of development in learning to read words by sight. *Journal of Research in Reading, 18,* 116–125.

Ehri, L. (1997). Learning to read and learning to spell are one and the same, almost. In C. Perfetti, L. Rieben, & M. Fayol (Eds.), *Learning to spell* (pp. 237–269). Hillsdale, NJ: Lawrence Erlbaum Associates.

Ehri, L., Deffner, N., & Wilce, L. (1984). Pictorial mnemonics for phonics. *Journal of Educational Psychology, 76,* 880–893.

Ehri, L., & Robbins, C. (1992). Beginners need some decoding skill to read words by analogy. *Reading Research Quarterly, 27,* 12–26.

Ehri, L., & Saltmarsh, J. (1995). Beginning readers outperform older disabled readers in learning to read words by sight. *Reading and Writing: An Interdisciplinary Journal, 7,* 295–326.

Ehri, L., & Wilce, L. (1979). The mnemonic value of orthography among beginning readers. *Journal of Educational Psychology, 71,* 26–40.

Ehri, L., & Wilce, L. (1980). The influence of orthography on readers' conceptualization of the phonemic structure of words. *Applied Psycholinguistics, 1,* 371–385.

Ehri, L., & Wilce, L. (1982). Recognition of spellings printed in lower and mixed case: Evidence for orthographic images. *Journal of Reading Behavior, 14,* 219–230.

Ehri, L. C., & Wilce, L. S. (1983). Development of word identification speed in skilled and less skilled beginning readers. *Journal of Educational Psychology, 75,* 3–18.

Ehri, L., & Wilce, L. (1985). Movement into reading: Is the first stage of printed word learning visual or phonetic? *Reading Research Quarterly, 20,* 163–179.

Ehri, L., & Wilce, L. (1986). The influence of spellings on speech: Are alveolar flaps /d/ or /t/? In D. Yaden & S. Templeton (Eds.) *Metalinguistic awareness and beginning literacy* (pp. 101–114). Portsmouth, NH: Heinemann.

Ehri, L., & Wilce, L. (1987a). Cipher versus cue reading: An experiment in decoding acquisition. *Journal of Educational Psychology, 79,* 3–13.

Ehri, L., & Wilce, L. (1987b). Does learning to spell help beginners learn to read words? *Reading Research Quarterly, 22,* 47–65.

Foorman, B., Francis, D., Novy, D., & Liberman, D. (1991). How letter–sound instruction mediates progress in first-grade reading and spelling. *Journal of Educational Psychology, 83,* 456–469.

Fry, E., Polk, J., & Fountoukidis, D. (1984). *The reading teacher's book of lists.* Englewood Cliffs, NJ: Upper Saddle River: Prentice-Hall.

Gaskins, I., Downer, M., Anderson, R., Cunningham, P., Gaskins, R., Schommer, M., & The Teachers of Benchmark School. (1988). A metacognitive approach to phonics: Using what you know to decode what you don't know. *Remedial and Special Education, 9,* 36–41.

Gaskins, I., Ehri, L., Cress, C., O'Hara, C., & Donnelly, K. (1996). Procedures for word learning: Making discoveries about words. *The Reading Teacher, 50,* 312–327.

Glushko, R. J. (1979). The organization and activation of orthographic knowledge in reading aloud. *Journal of Experimental Psychology: Human Perception and Performance, 5,* 674–691.

Glushko, R. J. (1981). Principles for pronouncing print: The psychology of phonography. In A. M. Lesgold & C. A. Perfetti (Eds.), *Interactive processes in reading* (pp. 61–84). Hillsdale, NJ: Lawrence Erlbaum Associates.

Golinkoff, R., & Rosinski, R. (1976). Decoding, semantic processing and reading comprehension skill. *Child Development, 47*, 252–258.

Goodman, K. (1976). Reading: A psycholinguistic guessing game. In H. Singer & R. Ruddell (Eds.), *Theoretical models and processes of reading* (2nd ed., pp. 497–508). Newark, DE: International Reading Association.

Goodman, Y., & Altwerger, B. (1981). *Print awareness in preschool children—a working paper: A study of the development of literacy in preschool children* (Occasional Paper No. 4). Tucson: University of Arizona, Program in Language and Literacy.

Goswami, U. (1986). Children's use of analogy in learning to read: A developmental study. *Journal of Experimental Child Psychology, 42*, 73–83.

Goswami, U. (1988). Orthographic analogies and reading development. *Quarterly Journal of Experimental Psychology, 40*, 239–268.

Goswami, U. (1990). A special link between rhyming skill and the use of orthographic analogies by beginning readers. *Journal of Child Psychology and Psychiatry, 31*, 301–311.

Gough, P., & Hillinger, M. (1980). Learning to read: An unnatural act. *Bulletin of the Orton Society, 30*, 180–196.

Gough, P., Juel, C., & Griffith, P. (1992). Reading, spelling and the orthographic cipher. In In P. Gough, L. Ehri, & R. Treiman (Eds.), *Reading acquisition* (pp. 35–48). Hillsdale, NJ: Lawrence Erlbaum Associates.

Gough, P., Juel, C., & Roper/Schneider, D. (1983). Code and cipher: A two-stage conception of initial reading acquisition. In J. A. Niles & L. A. Harris (Eds.), *Searches for meaning in reading/language processing and instruction* (32nd Yearbook of the National Reading Conference, pp. 207–211). Rochester, NY: National Reading Conference.

Gough, P., & Tunmer, W. (1986). Decoding, reading, and reading disability. *Remedial and Special Education, 7*, 6–10.

Gough, P., & Walsh, S. (1991). Chinese, Phoenicians, and the orthographic cipher of English. In S. Brady & D. Shankweiler (Eds.), *Phonological processes in literacy: A tribute to Isabelle Y. Liberman* (pp. 199–209). Hillsdale, NJ: Lawrence Erlbaum Associates.

Greenberg, D., Ehri, L., & Perin, D. (1997). Are word-reading processes the same or different in adult literacy students and third–fifth graders matched for reading level? *Journal of Educational Psychology, 89*, 262–275.

Griffith, P. (1987). *The role of phonological and lexical information in word recognition and spelling.* Unpublished doctoral dissertation, University of Texas, Austin.

Griffith, P. (1991). Phonemic awareness helps first graders invent spellings and third graders remember correct spellings. *Journal of Reading Behavior, 23*, 215–233.

Guthrie, J. (1973). Models of reading and reading disability. *Journal of Educational Psychology, 65*, 9–18.

Guttentag, R., & Haith, M. (1978). Automatic processing as a function of age and reading ability. *Child Develoment, 49*, 707–716.

Hanna, P., Hanna, J., Hodges, R., & Rudorf, E. (1966). *Phoneme–grapheme correspondences as cues to spelling improvement.* Washington, DC: U.S. Government Printing Office.

Harste, J., Woodward, V., & Burke, C. (1984). *Language stories and literacy lessons.* Portsmouth, NH: Heinemann.

Henderson, E. (1981). *Learning to read and spell: The child's knowledge of words.* DeKalb: Northern Illinois University Press.

Hoover, W., & Gough, P. (1990). The simple view of reading. *Reading and Writing: An Interdisciplinary Journal, 2*, 127–160.

Johns, J. (1991). *Basic reading inventory* (5th ed.). Dubuque, IO: Kendall/Hunt.

Jorm, A. (1981). Children with reading and spelling retardation: Functioning of whole-word and correspondence-rule mechanisms. *Journal of Child Psychology and Psychiatry, 22*, 171–178.

Juel, C. (1983). The development and use of mediated word identification. *Reading Research Quarterly, 18*, 306–327.

Juel, C. (1988). Learning to read and write: A longitudinal study of fifty-four children from first through fourth grade. *Journal of Educational Psychology, 80*, 437–447.

Juel, C., Griffith, P., & Gough, P. (1986). Acquisition of literacy: A longitudinal study of children in first and second grade. *Journal of Educational Psychology, 78*, 243–255.

Kreiner, D., & Gough, P. (1990). Two ideas about spelling: Rules and word-specific memory. *Journal of Memory and Language, 29*, 103–118.

LaBerge, D., & Samuels, J. (1974). Toward a theory of automatic information processing in reading. *Cognitive Psychology, 6*, 293–323.

Laxon, V., Coltheart, V., & Keating, C. (1988). Children find friendly words friendly too: Words with many orthographic neighbours are easier to read and spell. *British Journal of Educational Psychology, 58*, 103–119.

Leslie, L., & Thimke, B. (1986). The use of orthographic knowledge in beginning reading. *Journal of Reading Behavior, 18*, 229–241.

Liberman, A. (1992). The relation of speech to reading and writing. In R. Frost & L. Katz (Eds.), *Orthography, phonology, morphology, and meaning* (pp. 167–177). New York: Elsevier/North-Holland.

Liberman, I., Shankweiler, D., Fischer, F., & Carter, B. (1974). Reading and the awareness of linguistic segments. *Journal of Experimental Child Psychology, 18*, 201–212.

Lindamood, C., & Lindamood, P. (1975). *Auditory discrimination in depth.* Boston: Teaching Resources Corporation.

Lundberg, I., Frost, J., & Peterson, O. (1988). Effects of an extensive program for stimulating phonological awareness in preschool children. *Reading Research Quarterly, 23*, 263–284.

Mann, V. (1986). Phonological awareness: The role of reading experience. *Cognition, 24*, 65–92.

Marsh, G., Freidman, M., Welch, V., & Desberg, P. (1981). A cognitive-developmental theory of reading acquisition. In G. Mackinnon & T. G. Waller (Eds.), *Reading research: Advances in theory and practice* (Vol. 3, pp. 199–221). New York: Academic.

Mason, J. (1980). When do children begin to read: An exploration of four-year-old children's letter and word reading competencies. *Reading Research Quarterly, 15*, 203–227.

Masonheimer, P., Drum, P., & Ehri, L. (1984). Does environmental print identification lead children into word reading? *Journal of Reading Behavior, 16*, 257–272.

McConkie, G., & Zola, D. (1981). Language constraints and the functional stimulus in reading. In A. Lesgold & C. Perfetti (Eds.), *Interactive processes in reading* (pp. 155–175). Hillsdale, NJ: Lawrence Erlbaum Associates.

McGee, L., Lomax, R., & Head, M. (1988). Young children's written language knowledge: What environmental and functional print reading reveals. *Journal of Reading Behavior, 20*, 99–118.

Morais, J., Alegria, J., & Content, A. (1987). The relationships between segmental analysis and alphabetic literacy: An interactive view. *Cahiers de Psychologie Cognitive, 7*, 415–438.

Morris, D., & Perney, J. (1984). Developmental spelling as a predictor of first grade reading achievement. *Elementary School Journal, 84*, 441–457.

Perfetti, C. (1985). *Reading ability.* New York: Oxford University Press.

Perfetti, C. (1992). The representation problem in reading acquisition. In P. Gough, L. Ehri, & R. Treiman (Eds.), *Reading acquisition* (pp. 107–143). Hillsdale, NJ: Lawrence Erlbaum Associates.

Perfetti, C., & Hogaboam, T. (1975). The relationship between single word decoding and reading comprehension skill. *Journal of Educational Psychology, 67*, 461–469.

Rack, J., Hulme, C., Snowling, M., & Wightman, J. (1994). The role of phonology in young children learning to read words: The direct-mapping hypothesis. *Journal of Experimental Child Psychology, 57*, 42–71.

Rayner, K., & Pollatsek, A. (1989). *The psychology of reading*. Upper Saddle River, NJ: Prentice-Hall.

Read, C. (1971). Pre-school children's knowledge of English phonology. *Harvard Educational Review, 41*, 1–34.

Read, C. (1975). *Children's categorization of speech sounds in English* (Research Report No. 17). Urbana, IL: National Council of Teachers of English.

Read, C., Zhang, Y., Nie, H., & Ding, B. (1986). The ability to manipulate speech sounds depends on knowing alphabetic writing. *Cognition, 24*, 31–44.

Reitsma, P. (1983). Printed word learning in beginning readers. *Journal of Experimental Child Psychology, 75*, 321–339.

Rosinski, R., Golinkoff, R., & Kukish, K. (1975). Automatic semantic processing in a picture–word interference task. *Child Development, 46*, 243–253.

Rumelhart, D. (1977). Toward an interactive model of reading. In S. Dornic (Ed.), *Attention and performance* (Vol. 6, pp. 573–603). New York: Academic Press.

Share, D., Jorm, A., Maclean, R., & Matthews, R. (1984). Sources of individual diferences in reading achievement. *Journal of Educational Psychology, 76*, 1309–1324.

Stahl, S., Osborn, J., & Lehr, F. (1990). *Beginning to read: Thinking and learning about print by Marilyn Jager Adams: A summary*. Urbana–Champaign, IL: Center for the Study of Reading.

Stanovich, K. (1980). Toward an interactive-compensatory model of individual differences in the development of reading fluency. *Reading Research Quarterly, 16*, 32–71.

Templeton, S., & Bear, D. (Eds.). (1992). *Development of orthographic knowledge and the foundations of literacy: A memorial festschrift for Edmund H. Henderson*. Hillsdale, NJ: Lawrence Erlbaum Associates.

Treiman, R. (1993). *Beginning to spell*. New York: Oxford University Press.

Treiman, R., Goswami, U., & Bruck, M. (1990). Not all nonwords are alike: Implications for reading development and theory. *Memory & Cognition, 18*, 559–567.

Uhry, J., & Shepherd, J. (1993). Segmentation/spelling instruction as a part of a first-grade reading program: Effects on several measures of reading. *Reading Research Quarterly, 28*, 218–233.

Venezky, R. (1970). *The structure of English orthography*. The Hague, Netherlands: Mouton.

Venezky, R. L., & Massaro, D. W. (1979). The role of orthographic regularity in word recognition. In L. Resnick & P. Weaver (Eds.), *Theory and practice of early reading* (pp. 85–107). Hillsdale, NJ: Lawrence Erlbaum Associates.

Waters, G., Bruck, M., & Malus-Abramowitz, M. (1988). The role of linguistic and visual information in spelling: A developmental study. *Journal of Experimental Child Psychology, 45*, 400–421.

Weber, R. (1970). A linguistic analysis of first grade reading errors. *Reading Research Quarterly, 5*, 427–451.

Wendon, L. (1994). *Letterland*. Cambridge, England: Letterland Ltd.

2

▼▼▼▼▼▼▼

The Role of Analogies
in the Development of Word Recognition

Usha Goswami
Behavioural Sciences Unit
Institute of Child Health
University College, London

Word recognition in beginning literacy poses a particular set of problems. The most important of these is how written words represent spoken words. Writing systems were invented to communicate the spoken language, and most writing systems do this systematically, by using an alphabet, a syllabary, or a set of logographs (characters, like $ or %) that convey meaning. Because English is an alphabetic language, children who are learning to read English must learn the systematic correspondences between alphabetic letters (or groups of letters) and sounds. This means that learning written language requires some understanding of spoken language. This is not surprising when one considers that writing systems are designed to convey speech.

In this chapter, we consider how the ability to reflect on spoken language might help a child to learn to read English. We investigate the most consistent level at which the English writing system (or orthography) represents sound (phonology), and examine whether English-speaking children use this level in reading acquisition. This entails the use of orthographic analogies in reading. We then contrast the strategies used by children learning to read English with those used by children learning to read other languages. Finally, we discuss the implications of the analogy research for classroom teaching.

ACQUIRING SPOKEN VERSUS WRITTEN LANGUAGE

Consider briefly the immense task that faces an infant who is beginning to acquire spoken language. The infant is faced with the problem of distin-

41

guishing units of meaning within an apparently seamless stream of speech. Although adults help to segment the speech stream by occasionally uttering words in isolation, exaggerating the pronunciation of key words, and so on, research has now established that infants are able to discriminate stimuli differing by a single phonetic segment within the first few months of life. For example, a 1-month-old infant can recognise when a *p* sound changes to a *b* sound (Eimas, Siqueland, Jusczyk, & Vigorito, 1971). In principle, this gives the infant the capacity to distinguish words from each other, because a phoneme is the smallest unit of sound that changes the meaning of a word. A word like *bat* is distinguishably different from *pat*, and *tab* is different from *tap*, because *b* differs from *p*. However, the ability to distinguish between these words is probably an emergent property of the development of speech perception (see Metsala & Walley, Chap. 4, this volume).

The task facing a young child who is learning to read seems somewhat easier. Although the child has to work out how units of meaning are represented by strings of letters, words in print are already segmented, because there are gaps between separate words on the page. Second, the target words are usually familiar—by the age of 5, children have acquired fairly extensive spoken vocabularies, and most early reading books take account of their reader's language level. Third, at least at first glance, the phonemic units are already picked out for the child by the letters in each word, because alphabetic letters correspond to phonemes. Thus, it would seem that all that the child has to do to solve the problem of word recognition is to learn the correspondences between letters and phonemes. After all, if infants can recognize phonemic contrasts, surely it cannot be that difficult for children to segment spoken words into phonemes, to learn how the 26 alphabet letters represent these phonemes, and to blend the phonemes represented by these different letters into words?

The puzzle for psychologists has been that children, at least some children, do experience genuine difficulties with the task of learning to read. We now know that one source of these difficulties is a lack of *phonological awareness*. Although the ability to differentiate phonemes such as *p* and *b* is innate, the ability to become aware, or to consciously realise, that the *p* sound is different from the *b* sound is not innate. Whereas almost all children learn to comprehend and produce spoken language (even children who have severe educational difficulties), not all children find it easy to learn to read, even children who are doing very well at school in other respects. Individual differences in phonological awareness distinguish children who will become good readers from children who will become poor readers (e.g., Stanovich, Nathan, & Zolman, 1988). Poor phonological skills discriminate poor readers, whether the children with reading problems have general educational difficulties or not.

THE SPELLING SYSTEM OF ENGLISH

An additional problem, of course, is that the alphabet does *not* consistently represent the phonemes of spoken English. The spelling system of English was developed to keep the spelling of root meanings (morphemes) constant. For example, the root morpheme *heal* is used in the word *health*, leading to different pronunciations for the same spelling. There are also identical pronunciations for different spellings (e.g., *heal–feel, light–site*; see Katz & Feldman, 1981, 1983). This is very different from the spelling system used for a language like Serbo-Croatian. In Serbo-Croatian, the alphabet follows the principle "Spell a word like it sounds, and speak it the way it is spelled" (see Frost & Katz, 1992). If these principles were applied to written English, *health* would be pronounced "heelth," and *light* would be spelled *lite*. The difference between English and Serbo-Croatian can be described as a difference in *orthographic transparency*. In Serbo-Croatian, each letter represents only one phoneme, and each phoneme is represented by only one letter, and thus the relationship between spelling and sound is transparent. English is orthographically nontransparent, because letters can represent more than one phoneme, and phonemes can be represented by more than one letter.

Many other Indo-European languages, such as German, Spanish, and Greek, are also orthographically transparent for reading (although not necessarily for spelling). These languages all have writing systems that demonstrate a high level of *consistency* in the correspondence between letters and phonemes. It is interesting to note that these countries do not have a debate about the best method of teaching initial reading. In fact, in Austria and Greece, the sequence in which the letters and their sounds are taught in school is decided by the government, and all schools follow the same teaching sequence. In Greece, they even use the same reading book. This lack of debate is probably a consequence of the high orthographic transparency of German and Greek. Because there is a 1:1 mapping between graphemes and phonemes, a phonics system of teaching initial reading is highly successful.

Although English does not have a 1:1 mapping between graphemes and phonemes, we can still calculate how many times a letter like *a* or *b* has the same pronunciation across different words. In a recent analysis of the statistical properties of the English orthography, Treiman, Mullennix, Bijeljac-Babic, and Richmond-Welty (1995) carried out such calculations for all of the consonant-vowel-consonant (CVC) words of English (vowels in this analysis included vowel digraphs like *ai* or *ea*, in which two letters represent one sound). Treiman et al. found that the pronunciation of the initial and final consonants was reasonably predictable. The first consonant (C_1) was pronounced the same in 96% of CVC words, and the final consonant (C_2) was pronounced the same in 91% of CVC words. However, the pronunciation

of vowels turned out to be very variable. Individual vowels were only pronounced the same in 51% of CVC words, and when Treiman et al. considered
the initial consonant and the vowel as a unit (C_1V), then only 52% of CVC
words sharing a C_1V spelling had a consistent pronunciation, even though
initial consonants alone were so predictable. The greatest consistency of
vowel pronunciation occurred when the vowel and final consonant were
considered as a unit (VC_2). Treiman et al. found that 77% of CVC words
sharing a VC_2 spelling had a consistent pronunciation. This analysis shows
that the spelling system of English becomes more consistent when rhyming
families of words are considered (*heal–deal–meal/health–wealth–stealth*).

In fact, the number of different VC_2 units in written English can be
calculated as well. Stanback (1992) analyzed the different VC_2 patterns in
the 43,041 syllables making up the 17,602 words in the Carroll, Davis, and
Richman (1971) word frequency norms for children. She found that the entire
corpus was described by 824 VC_2 units, 616 of which occurred in rhyme
families. Wylie and Durrell (1970) pointed out that nearly 500 primary grade
words were derived from a set of just 37 rimes (see Fig. 2.1). These analyses
of the spelling system of English suggest that there are significant advantages
in learning about VC_2 units (i.e., spelling units that represent rhymes) during
reading acquisition.

LEVELS OF PHONOLOGICAL AWARENESS

If the spelling patterns that correspond to rhymes are important for reading
acquisition in English, then a sensitivity to rhyme may represent an important
level of phonological awareness for children who are learning to read English.
Although phonological awareness was initially measured at the level of the

-ack	-ail	-ain	-ake	-ale
-ame	-an	-ank	-ap	-ash
-at	-ate	-aw	-ay	-eat
-ell	-est	-ice	-ick	-ide
-ight	-ill	-in	-ine	-ing
-ink	-ip	-ir	-ock	-oke
-op	-ore	-or	-uck	-ug
-ump	-unk			

FIG. 2.1.   The 37 rimes in the Wylie and Durrell (1970) analysis of primary
grade texts.

phoneme, we now know that phonological awareness can be measured at more than one level (see Fig. 2.2). Two other levels of phonological awareness have also been distinguished: *syllabic* awareness and *onset-rime* awareness.

Phonemic awareness refers to the awareness that a word like *cup* consists of three phonemes, corresponding to the letters *c*, *u*, *p*. However, phonemic awareness appears to develop relatively late, and also develops partly as a *consequence* of learning to read and to spell (see Goswami & Bryant, 1990). Syllabic awareness and onset-rime awareness both appear to be present *before* a child begins to learn to read. *Syllabic awareness* is the ability to detect constituent syllables in words. For example, a word like *popsicle* has three syllables, whereas a word like *dinner* has two. Syllabic awareness appears to be present by at least age 4 (e.g., Liberman, Shankweiler, Fisher, & Carter, 1974). *Onset-rime awareness* is the ability to detect that a single syllable can have two units: the onset, which corresponds to any initial consonants in the syllable; and the rime, which corresponds to the vowel and to any following consonants (i.e., to VC_2 units; see Treiman & Chafetz, 1987). For example, the onsets in *health*, *stealth*, and *wealth* are the sounds made by the letters *h*, *st*, and *w*, respectively. The rime is *ealth*. Whereas onsets are optional in English syllables, rimes are mandatory (words like *eat* and *up* have no onsets). Onset-rime awareness is also present by at least age 4 (Bradley & Bryant, 1983), and may even emerge as young as 2 or 3, via experience of nursery rhymes and such (Maclean, Bryant, & Bradley, 1987).

Onset-rime awareness and phonemic awareness are not completely distinct, however. Many English words have single-phoneme onsets; that is,

1. Syllables	'din'	+	'ner'
	'zig'	+	'zag'
	'cup'	+	'cake'
2. Onsets/Rimes	'd' + 'in'	+	'n' + 'er'
	'z' + 'ig'	+	'z' + 'ag'
	'c' + 'up'	+	'c' + 'ake'
3. Phonemes	'd' + 'i' + 'n'		'n' + 'e' + 'r'
	'z' + 'i' + 'g'		'z' + 'a' + 'g'
	'c' + 'u' + 'p'		'c' + 'A' + 'k'

FIG. 2.2. Levels of phonological awareness.

they begin with a single consonant. As we have seen, the pronunciation of this initial consonant is highly predictable, being similar in 96% of English words. Similarly, some English words have single-phoneme rimes. A word like *zoo* or *tree* has a rime that consists of a single phoneme, albeit a vowel digraph. Thus, an awareness of onset-rime units within words *necessarily* entails a developing awareness of phonemes. Although studies have shown that onset-rime awareness precedes phonemic awareness in most English-speaking children (Kirtley, Bryant, Maclean, & Bradley, 1989; Treiman & Zukowski, 1991), this general conclusion refers to *awareness of every constituent phoneme in words*, rather than to awareness of particular phonemes such as the initial phoneme.

PHONOLOGICAL AWARENESS
AND LEARNING TO READ

A large number of studies have shown that phonological awareness measured at all three of these levels is important for reading development (e.g., Cunningham, 1990; Fox & Routh, 1975; Juel, 1988; Perfetti, Beck, Bell, & Hughes, 1987; Snowling, 1980; Stanovich, Cunningham, & Cramer, 1984; Stanovich, Cunningham, & Feeman, 1984; Tunmer & Nesdale, 1985; Vellutino & Scanlon, 1987; Wagner, 1988, Yopp, 1988; see also Stahl & Murray, chap. 3, this volume; Torgeson & Burgess, chap. 7, this volume). Some studies, however, have suggested a particularly strong connection between rhyme awareness and early reading (e.g., Bradley & Bryant, 1978, 1983; Ellis & Large, 1987; Holligan & Johnston, 1988). As we have seen, such a connection may be important because of the spelling system of English, which is highly consistent at the VC_2 unit level. Words that share VC_2 units usually rhyme (e.g., *heal, meal, deal*).

LEVELS OF PHONOLOGICAL AWARENESS AND
LEARNING TO READ PARTICULAR ORTHOGRAPHIES

Phonological awareness has also been shown to be an important predictor of reading development in other orthographies, including highly transparent orthographies and orthographies like Chinese and Japanese (e.g., Caravolas & Bruck, 1993; Cossu, Shankweiler, Liberman, Tola, & Katz, 1988; Gombert, 1992; Huang & Hanley, 1995; Lundberg, Olofsson, & Wall, 1980; Mann, 1986; Naslund & Schneider, 1991; Porpodas, 1993; Schneider & Naslund, in press; Wimmer, Landerl, Linortner, & Hummer, 1991; Wimmer, Landerl, & Schneider, 1994). However, when studies of other languages have included a measure of rhyme awareness, they generally have failed to find a strong connection between rhyming and reading (although see Lundberg et al., 1980). For example, a study in German by Wimmer et al. (1994) found that rhyme awareness in German children was not connected to early reading development at all. Instead, rhyme only became an important predictor of reading later in development, when German children were acquiring automaticity. This pattern is the opposite of that found in studies in English, where the predictive strength of rhyme measures appears early, and may drop out by the age of 6 years (e.g., Stanovich, Cunningham, & Cramer, 1984). Thus, a particularly strong connection between rhyming and early reading does not appear to hold for orthographies other than English.

This raises the interesting possibility that the level of phonological awareness that is most predictive of reading development may vary with the orthography that is being learned. Different levels of phonological awareness may interact with the statistical properties of the orthography (its transparency), so that the spelling units that offer the most consistent mappings to phonology in a particular orthography become particularly salient to the phonologically aware learner. For children who are learning to read English, this means that rhyme awareness should be an important predictor of learning to read, and that the spelling sequences that reflect rimes—VC_2 units— should have a special functional salience. For children who are learning to read more transparent orthographies, phonemic awareness may be a more important predictor of learning to read, and individual grapheme–phoneme correspondences may have a special salience.

ORTHOGRAPHIC ANALOGIES
AND RIME UNITS IN ENGLISH

In fact, there is quite a lot of evidence that rimes are functionally important units for young readers of English. Most of this evidence comes from research into children's use of orthographic *analogies* in reading. An orthographic analogy involves using a shared spelling sequence to make a prediction about a shared pronunciation. For example, a child who knows how to read a word like *beak* could use this word as a basis for reading other words with shared spelling segments, such as *peak*, *weak*, and *speak*, or *bean*, *bead*, and *beat*. Notice that in order to use a word like *beak* as a basis for reading a new word like *peak*, the child is making a prediction about the pronunciation of the new word that is based on the shared rime. In order to use *beak* as a basis for reading *bean*, however, the child is making a prediction about the pronunciation of a spelling unit that crosses the onset-rime boundary. The shared spelling sequence *bea-* in *beak* and *bean* corresponds to the onset and part of the rime (C_1V).

When children's ability to use a word like *beak* as a basis for reading analogous words like *peak* and *bean* is assessed experimentally, it turns out that rime analogies are easier than analogies based on the onset and part of the rime. Rime analogies also emerge first developmentally, appearing in children's spontaneous reading behavior before onset analogies or analogies based on the onset and part of the rime. For example, in some of my first analogy experiments, I asked 5-, 6-, and 7-year-old children to play a clue game about working out words (Goswami, 1986, 1988; see Fig. 2.3). In this game, the children learned to read clue words such as *beak*, and were then asked to read new words like *peak* and *bean*, using their clue to help them. The children were pretested on the latter words prior to learning the clue words, to make sure that they really were new to the children, and the clue words remained visible during the testing phase, to make sure that the children did not forget them. The results showed that words like *peak* were easier to read by analogy to the clue word than were words like *bean*. This finding was particularly marked for the younger children.

In subsequent work, I have shown that analogies based on rimes are typically the *only* analogies made by very young readers (Goswami, 1993). Once a child has been reading for a period of around 6 to 8 months, then other analogies are also observed, such as analogies between the onset and part of the rime (*beak–bean*), analogies between shared vowel digraphs (*beak–heap*), and analogies between onsets (*trip–trim*). Analogies between onsets have only been studied using consonant clusters (Goswami, 1991). In a clue word study in which children learned clue words like *trip* as a basis for decoding new words like *trim* (shares initial consonant cluster), and clue words like *desk* as a basis for decoding new words like *risk* (shares final consonant cluster), I found that analogies were restricted to the shared consonant clusters that corresponded to onsets. The children made a signifi-

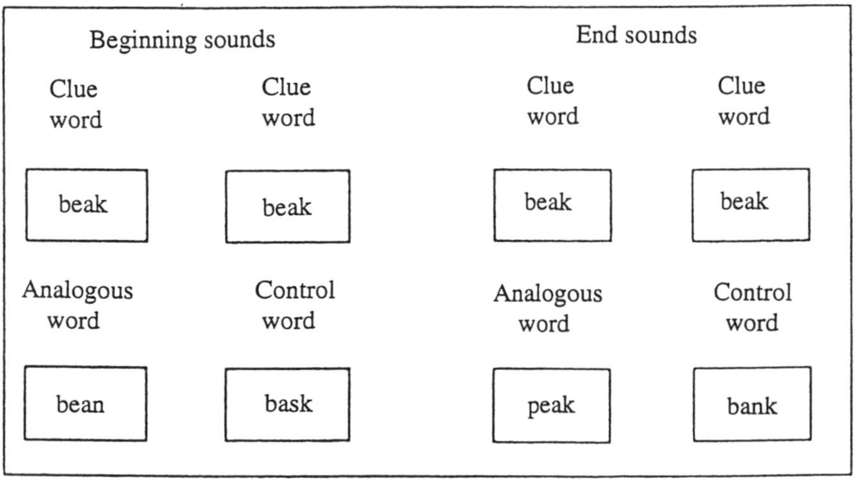

Beginning sounds		End sounds	
Clue word	Clue word	Clue word	Clue word
beak	beak	beak	beak
Analogous word	Control word	Analogous word	Control word
bean	bask	peak	bank

FIG. 2.3.   The clue word task.

cant number of analogies between clue words like *trim* and test words like *trot*. They did not use analogies between clue words like *desk* and test words like *risk*, even though these words also shared consonant clusters with the clue words. Thus, for consonant clusters, the phonological (onset-rime) status of the shared spelling sequence appears to have a clear effect on children's analogies.

Such analogies are not simply an artifact of the clue word technique of showing children words in isolation, because they are also observed when children are reading stories rather than playing the clue game (Goswami, 1988, 1990a). If a clue word is embedded in the title of a story, and analogous words appear in the story text, then children who learn the clue word as part of the title read more of the analogous words in the story correctly than do children who do not learn the clue word as part of the title. This analogy effect operates *in addition* to the effects of story context. The context of the story helps the children in both experimental groups to read the analogous words in the text correctly, but the children who learn the clue word via the story title have a significant extra advantage. Finally, orthographic analogies really do depend on shared spelling patterns, and are not the result of a simple form of rhyme priming. If children are taught to read a clue word like *head*, which is analogous in spelling to a rhyming word like *bread* but not analogous in spelling to a rhyming word like *said*, then most analogies are restricted to the rhyming words with shared spelling patterns (Goswami, 1990a).

The orthographic analogy evidence that rimes are functionally important units for young readers of English has now received support from a number of studies using converging methods (e.g., Bowey & Hanson, 1994; Bruck & Treiman, 1992; Ehri & Robbins, 1992; Goswami, 1986, 1988, 1991; Muter, Snowling, & Taylor, 1994; Treiman, Goswami, & Bruck, 1990; Wise, Olson, & Treiman, 1990). However, there is one important link that remains to be discussed, and that is the link between analogies and phonological skills. From the research discussed so far, we know (a) that rhyme awareness is an important predictor of reading development in English, (b) that young children use rimes in their reading, and (c) that the rime is the level at which the English orthography has the greatest consistency (VC_2 units). A connection between these three facts remains to be established experimentally. For example, (a) and (b) may be related because children with better rhyming skills use more rime analogies. Similarly, (b) and (c) may be related because rimes are useful units for learning to read English. Finally, (a), (b), and (c) may all be related. Phonological skills predict reading development in all orthographies, but the special connection between rhyming and reading in English may be a direct result of the statistical properties of the English orthography, which makes rime units particularly useful for word recognition in English.

EVIDENCE FOR A CONNECTION BETWEEN
(a) AND (b): RHYME AWARENESS
AND RIME ANALOGIES IN ENGLISH

As noted previously, (a) and (b) may be related because children with better rhyming skills use more rime analogies. There is some evidence that this is the case, at least when rhyming and analogy use are measured in children of the same age (Goswami, 1990b; Goswami & Mead, 1992). In our studies, we examined whether children's performance in the clue word analogy task was more strongly related to their performance in some phonological awareness tasks than others. For example, in Goswami (1990b), I gave 6- and 7-year-old children the Bradley and Bryant oddity task, which measures onset-rime awareness, and a phoneme deletion task developed by Content, Morais, Alegria, and Bertelson (1982). In the first task, children have to detect the odd word out in sets of words like *fan, cat, hat, mat*; and in the second children are asked to delete either the first (*beak–eak*) or the last (*beak—bea*) phoneme in spoken words.

The results showed that there was a specific connection between onset-rime knowledge and rime analogies. Onset-rime skills were related to analogizing even after controlling for vocabulary skills and phoneme skills, whereas phoneme deletion did not retain a significant relationship with analogising after controlling for vocabulary skills and onset-rime knowledge. In a related study by Goswami and Mead (1992), we included more phonological measures, such as syllable and phoneme segmentation, and we included a test of nonsense word reading (*vep, hig*) as well. We then looked at the relationship between the different phonological variables and analogy use after controlling either for reading age alone, or for both reading age and nonsense word reading. Each set of equations produced a consistent set of results. If reading age was controlled, then the onset-rime measures retained a significant relationship with rime analogies (these measures were the rhyme oddity task and onset deletion), but the phonemic measures did not (these measures were final consonant deletion and phoneme segmentation). In contrast, both the phonemic and the onset-rime measures retained significant relationships with onset-and-part-of-the-rime (*beak–bean*) analogies. When reading age and nonsense word reading were controlled, then the only variables to retain a significant relationship with rime analogies were the oddity rhyme measures. The only variables to retain a significant relationship with onset-and-part-of-the-rime analogies were the consonant deletion measures. Because onset-and-part-of-the-rime analogies require segmentation of the rime, this is not really surprising. Knowledge about rhyme seems to have a strong and specific connection to children's use of rime analogies, whereas analogies between spelling sequences corresponding to the onset-and-part-of-the-rime are related to more fine-grained phonological knowledge about phonemes.

EVIDENCE FOR A CONNECTION BETWEEN
(b) AND (c): ANALOGIES IN OTHER ORTHOGRAPHIES

As noted earlier, young English-speaking children may use rime analogies in their reading because the rime is the level at which the English orthography has the greatest consistency. One way to examine this connection, which is the connection between facts (b) and (c) discussed earlier, is to study children's use of analogies in orthographies other than English. It is important to note that analogy is not necessarily a strategy that young children apply consciously, although we can certainly teach children to use analogies (see later discussion). Rather, in my research analogy is conceived of as an automatic process, driven by the level of a child's phonological knowledge and by the nature of the orthographic–phonological relations that operate in a particular orthography (see also Goswami, in press; Goswami, Gombert, & Fraca de Barrera, in press). From this perspective, analogies should operate in every writing system. However, analogies in a very transparent orthography would reflect grapheme–phoneme relations, and analogies in English would reflect rime-based coding.

One way of comparing the salience of rime units in languages other than English is to study nonsense word reading. Matched nonsense words can be derived that either have rimes that are familiar from real words, as in the English example *dake* (*cake, make*), or unfamiliar (*daik*). The rime spelling pattern *-aik* does not occur in any real words in English. This means that although children can read a nonsense word like *dake* by using a rime analogy or by assembling its constituent grapheme–phoneme correspondences, they can only read a matched nonsense word like *daik* by assembling its constituent grapheme–phoneme correspondences.[1]

Similar sets of nonsense words can be derived for other languages. The importance of rime units in reading these different orthographies can then be assessed by the magnitude of the difference in reading accuracy and reading speed between nonsense words with familiar rimes (e.g., *dake*) compared to nonsense words with unfamiliar rimes (e.g., *daik*) in each orthography. This difference for English, French, and Greek[2] is shown in Fig. 2.4 (see Goswami, Gombert, & Fraca de Barrera, in press; Goswami, Porpodas, & Wheelwright, 1997, for more detailed information about these experiments). Greek is highly transparent, French is less transparent than Greek

---

[1]These two word types were matched for lower-level orthographic frequency using positional bigram frequencies.

[2]This description somewhat simplifies the comparisons that were possible, as we could not derive monosyllables with unfamiliar rimes in Greek. The Greek data are taken from longer nonsense words with familiar versus unfamiliar spelling patterns for the *rhyming* portions of the words. The English and French data are from monosyllables, as described in the text.

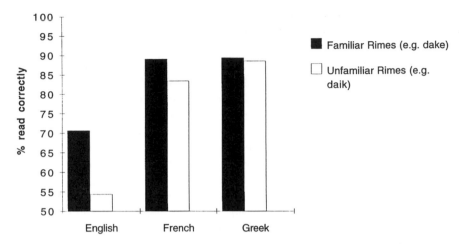

FIG. 2.4. The rime/rhyme familiarity effect in English, French, and Greek.

but more transparent than English, and English is the least transparent of the three languages. As the figure shows, the rime familiarity effect varies with orthographic transparency. The largest effect was found in English, a smaller effect was found in French, and there was no effect of orthographic familiarity at the level of the rhyme at all for the Greek children.

In fact, these cross-linguistic studies also showed that spelling patterns for *rhymes* in bisyllabic and trisyllabic words were very salient to children who were learning to read English. If a nonsense word shared a rhyme spelling pattern with a real word (e.g., *bomic–comic*, *taffodil–daffodil*), then it was easier to read than a nonsense word that did not (e.g., *bommick*, *tafoddyl*). Again, this difference was not found for the other languages studied. This raises the intriguing possibility that the importance of rhyme awareness for predicting reading development in English is picking up a level of analysis that goes *beyond* monosyllabic words. Rhymes and rimes are not necessarily the same units when words of more than one syllable are considered. For example, *behind* and *unwind* share the rime of the second syllable and also rhyme, whereas *wagon* and *melon* share the rime of the second syllable but do not rhyme (examples from Brady, Fowler, & Gipstein, in preparation). In some phonological awareness tasks using multi-syllabic words, Brady et al. found that rhyme awareness precedes rime awareness in 4- and 5-year-old children. Thus, the spelling sequences that reflect rhymes in words of more than one syllable (e.g., *agon* in *wagon*) may be more important than individual rimes. It should be noted that future research may prove the rime perspective to be a limited one, with *rhyme* rather than rime being a more important variable in explaining reading development in English.

THEORETICAL REASONS FOR PROPOSING
A CONNECTION BETWEEN (a), (b), AND (c):
INTERACTIVE THEORIES OF READING
DEVELOPMENT

I turn finally to the possibility that all of the evidence for facts (a), (b), and (c) discussed previously is related, namely to the possibility that the special connection between rhyming and reading in English is a direct result of the statistical properties of the English orthography, which make rime units particularly useful for word recognition in English, and thus lead to rimes being functional units in beginning reading. Although there is little direct evidence for this possibility at the moment, it is consistent with a number of recent *theories* of reading development that have proposed that children's phonological knowledge plays a role in the development of their orthographic representations (e.g., Ehri, 1992; Goswami, 1993; Hatcher, Hulme, & Ellis, 1994; Perfetti, 1992; Stuart & Coltheart, 1988). Although only some of these theories focus on rimes, the general spirit of interactive theories is consistent with the special connection between rhyming and reading discussed previously. Traditional stage models of reading, such as those proposed by Frith (1985), and by Marsh, Friedman, Welch, and Desberg (1980), are not consistent with this special connection.

In traditional stage models of learning to read (Frith, 1985; Marsh et al., 1981), children are thought to begin to learn to read by using holistic strategies (the logographic stage), to progress to using letter–sound correspondences (the alphabetic stage), and to finally become able to use orthographic strategies that involve larger spelling units. This stage sequence has been taken to be invariant across orthographies, a view that may prove misguided (e.g., Porpodas, 1995; Wimmer, 1993). According to stage models, the approach that children take to the task of learning to read is qualitatively different at different stages of the reading process, although earlier strategies remain available as the later stages are attained.

In contrast, the newer interactive models of learning to read conceptualize reading as an interactive developmental process from the very earliest phases. These new theories propose that children's orthographic knowledge is founded in their phonological skills. In other words, the phonological knowledge that children *bring with them* to reading plays an important role in establishing orthographic recognition units from the earliest phases of development. During the developmental process, phonological and orthographic knowledge continuously interact in increasingly refined ways. A child's phonological knowledge will partly determine that child's learning about the orthography, and that orthographic learning will in turn change the level of the child's phonological knowledge. Because phonological knowledge can be measured at more than one level, it is possible that different levels of phonological awareness will interact with the statistical properties of the orthography that is being learned. Variations in the statistical properties of different orthographies mean that children who are learning to read in different orthographies may at first develop *different* orthographic representations (Goswami, Gombert, & Fraca de Barrera, in press; Goswami, Porpodas, & Wheelwright, 1997). The spelling units that offer the most *consistent* mappings to phonology in a particular orthography will be most salient to the phonologically aware learner.

For children learning to read English, these should be spelling units that correspond to rimes (Goswami, 1993). These are the VC_2 units that Treiman et al. (1995) showed will provide the most consistent mappings from orthography to phonology as far as vowel pronunciations are concerned. We know that most children have good rhyming skills when they enter school, and thus this knowledge about rhyme should lead them to identify spelling units for rimes (see Goswami & Bryant, 1990). The development of orthographic recognition units that code rimes will in turn offer significant advantages in terms of pronunciation consistency over orthographic recognition units that code separate vowels and the C_1V. Thus, children who are learning to read English may develop orthographic representations that accord a special status to rime units, whereas children who are learning to read more transparent orthographies may not. Notice that initial and final consonants (C_1 and C_2) may also benefit from this interactive process, because according to Treiman et al.'s statistical analysis these English spelling units also have highly consistent links to sound (see Ehri, chap. 1, this volume). Eventually, the interactive nature of the relationship between orthographic and phonological knowledge will help children to learn about all the constituent phonemes in words. Learning to spell will also significantly enhance this process (see Treiman, chap. 12, this volume).

ORTHOGRAPHIC ANALOGIES AND CLASSROOM PRACTICE

Let us summarize the position that we have reached so far. I discussed evidence that the most consistent links between the English spelling system and the sounds of spoken language occur at the level of the rime, that onset-rime awareness develops early in children, that there is a special link between rhyme (onset-rime) awareness and early reading in English, that children use rime analogies when they are reading, that children with better onset-rime skills make more rime analogies, that rime units have a special status for children who are learning to read in English, and that the special status of rime units does not hold for more transparent orthographies. I then proposed that one way of integrating all of these findings was to think of reading development as a process of increasing interaction between phonological and orthographic knowledge. Although the level of phonological knowledge that is important for initial reading may vary with the orthography that is being learned, it was proposed that, for children who are learning to read English, links between phonology and orthography at the level of the rime may be particularly important.

If this is true, then we can predict that *teaching* children about rime analogies during initial reading instruction should be highly beneficial to their reading progress. There is some evidence that this is the case, although findings have been mixed (Bruck & Treiman, 1992; Ehri & Robbins, 1992; Peterson & Haines, 1992; Walton, 1995; White & Cunningham, 1990; Wise, Olson, & Treiman, 1990). So far, however, the interpretation of most of these studies has been limited by the use of fairly short training sessions, rather few analogy examples, and the occasional lack of adequate control groups. Nevertheless, I discuss two of the longer training studies in some depth, to illustrate the potential importance of including some instruction about rime analogies in a program of initial reading instruction.

In a study conducted in Canada, Peterson and Haines (1992) provided instruction in reading by rime analogy to a kindergarten group of 5- to 6-year-olds. A second group of children from the same classes acted as unseen controls. The experimental group was taught using a rime training method based on word families. Ten rime families were used during a training period of one month. Each child was given individual training with each family, in sessions lasting approximately 15 minutes each. In a given session, one word from the family being studied would be introduced (e.g., *ball*), and segmented into its onset and rime (*b-all*). A new word from the family was then added, also segmented into its onset and rime (e.g., *f-all*). The rime similarity was pointed out to the child and emphasized, and four more analogous words were gradually added in the same fashion (e.g., *mall, wall, hall, gall*). This word family approach, which entails the inclusion of more than one example of a rime-analogous word, may be important for learning. Research in problem solving by analogy has found that the provision of multiple example analogies significantly benefits learning (e.g., Brown & Kane, 1988; Goswami, 1992).

Peterson and Haines (1992) then assessed the effects of their rime analogy training by giving the children a posttest that involved reading new words by analogy to new clue words. This analogy test was also given to the control children from the same classrooms. The two groups of children had shown equivalent performance in this test prior to training, but at posttest the rime-trained group significantly outperformed the control group. The importance of an interactive relationship between phonology and orthography was also shown in this study. Peterson and Haines found that the children with better phonological segmentation skills benefited most from the analogy training, and that rime analogy training in turn benefited the development of segmentation skills. Similar findings have been reported by Ehri and Robbins (1992), who found that children who were good segmenters benefited more from rime analogy training than did children who were poor segmenters. However, the latter study used an artificial orthography.

Another positive result for rime analogy training was reported by White and Cunningham (1990), who also used a word family approach to analogy training. However, in contrast to Peterson and Haines, they included phonological training in their study as well. The children who took part were 290 6- and 7-year-olds in a particular school district in Hawaii. A group of teachers were trained to use an analogy reading program based on onsets and rimes, and the progress of the children in their classrooms was compared to that of a group of control children from comparable schools in the same district whose teachers had not received this analogy training.

The training period lasted for an entire year. The first 4 months were spent in phonological training, and the next 8 months were spent in linking phonology and orthography via analogy. The rime analogy training was based on learning 200 clue words and their rime families. The 200 key words were chosen to reflect major spelling patterns, in order to enable analogies to many other words (e.g., *look–book, took, cook*; *nine–pine, mine, fine*). As each key word was learned, it was written up on a "word wall" in the classroom (see Gaskins, chap. 9, this volume). For example, the children might learn about the *nine* family by being presented with a new word from one family, such as *spine*. They would have to decide to which family this new word belonged, and how to pronounce it. Similar instruction was then given in spelling.

At the end of the school year, the children in the analogy classrooms were significantly ahead of the children in the control classrooms in standardized measures of *both* decoding and reading comprehension. White and Cunningham reported similar results in a follow-up study conducted a year later, which involved an equally large group of children. As well as supporting the importance of including instruction about rime analogies in any program of reading instruction, the successful outcome of this study also provides support for the interactive models of reading development outlined previously. White and Cunningham's program placed explicit emphasis on linking orthographic and phonological information at the level of the rime, and this interactive approach may have been an important component of its success. Similar results concerning the linkage of orthographic and phonological information (using plastic letters) have been reported by Bradley and Bryant (1983), and by Hatcher, Hulme, and Ellis (1994).

INTEGRATING ORTHOGRAPHIC ANALOGIES INTO YOUR CLASSROOM

The research discussed here has shown that there are three important points to bear in mind when introducing rime analogies into your own classroom. These are: provide phonological instruction about rhymes, provide orthographic instruction about rimes, and make the links between the two very explicit.

Providing Phonological Instruction About Rhymes

Phonological instruction about rhyme can be introduced in multiple ways. One of the most obvious ways is to use nursery rhymes. The goal of this instruction is to increase children's *awareness* of the rhyming words. For example, this can be done by: (a) changing some of the rhyming words and asking the children to correct you ("Humpty Dumpty had a great fright!"); (b) making up variations on nursery rhymes ("Humpty Dumpty sat on a chair! Humpty Dumpty went to the fair!"); or (c) getting the children to be rhyme detectives, and to check whether matching words in nursery rhymes really do rhyme. A surprising number do not: For example *Jack and Jill* rhymes *water* with *after*, and *Baa Baa Black Sheep* rhymes *dame* with *lane*. Helping the children to sort out the real rhymes will provide valuable experience in learning about rhyme.

Providing Orthographic Instruction About Rimes

The best way to introduce orthographic instruction about rimes is to use rhyming families of words. The easiest way to teach children to use rime analogies is to make up a clue game of your own, based on these different rhyming families. To do this, you simply choose the spelling pattern or clue word that you want to teach, and then use it as a basis for analogies. For example, you could use a clue word from a favorite class story.[3]

- Begin by drawing the children's attention to the rhyme family that you are using. For example, read them the story that uses the clue word, asking them to spot all the rhymes for the clue word as you read. You could then reread the story, pausing at the rhymes, so that the children have to supply them.

---

[3]More detailed descriptions of how to use rime analogies in the classroom can be found in *Phonics That Work!* by Janiel Wagstaff (1994), and *Phonics They Use*, by Patricia Cunningham (1992). A special set of stories for teaching clue words and their associated rime spelling patterns has been devised by Rod Hunt for the *Oxford Reading Tree Rhyme and Analogy Programme*, edited by Usha Goswami (1996).

- Next, spell the clue word for the children, using a concrete material such as plastic letters or fuzzy felt letters stuck onto a board (you need letters that you can move around). Make a gap between the onset and the rime.
- Now make another word from the same family, also with plastic letters. Put it on the board underneath the clue word, and align the onset and rime in both words.
- Ask the children to read the new word for you, using the rime from their clue word, and working out the onset from their letter knowledge or from an alphabet frieze.
- Alternatively, you can ask the children to nominate rhyming words to spell, and help them to use the clue word to spell them.

Linking Phonological and Orthographic Instruction

The best way to link the phonological instruction with the orthographic instruction is to model the process of making the analogy for the children, using guided response questions. The kind of guided response questions that you use might be as follows (using the example clue word *cap*):

> How can we use our clue to read this word? What is our clue word? Yes, it's *cap*. What are the letters in *cap*? Yes, *c, a, p*. And what are the letters in this new word? Yes, *t, a, p*. So which bit of the new word can our clue help us with? Which part of the words are the same? That's right, the *a, p* part. What sound do the letters *a, p* make in *cap*? Yes, *ap*. So what sound do they make here? Yes, it must be *ap*. So now we just need the sound for the beginning letter, which is—yes, *t*. What is the sound for *t*? We can check on the alphabet frieze. Yes, *t* makes a "t" sound, like in *teddy*. So our word is?—yes, *t-ap*, *tap*. So we can use *cap* to figure out *tap*, because they rhyme.

To use analogies in spelling, you simply reverse this procedure ("So if *tap* rhymes with *cap*, how do we know what letters to use to write the end part?" etc.). To use analogies for multisyllabic words, you divide each syllable into onsets and rimes, and so on. The goal of the clue game is to teach children to use analogies spontaneously in their own reading and spelling. As they practice making rime analogies, the children can learn that the English spelling system is not as capricious as it may seem.

SUMMARY

At the beginning of this chapter, I set out to examine the problem of how written words represent spoken words. We have seen that although English is an alphabetic language that uses individual letters to represent individual phonemes, the nontransparent nature of the English orthography means that the most *consistent* links between spelling and sound occur at the level of the rime (VC$_2$ units). Rimes are usually groups of phonemes, corresponding to vowels and final consonants, and the final consonant helps to determine the pronunciation of the vowel.

We have also seen that there is a special relationship between rhyme awareness and reading development in English, a relationship that may not hold for more transparent orthographies. This suggests that phonological awareness at the level of the rhyme may be particularly important for learning to read English, because of the consistency of spelling units for rimes (VC$_2$ units). Theoretically, this relationship can be modeled in terms of the *interactions* between phonological and orthographic knowledge that are important for reading development. Phonological knowledge at the level of the rhyme helps children to become aware of rime units in word spellings, and this orthographic insight in turn helps to develop phonemic knowledge of all the constituent phonemes in a word.

Finally, we have seen that the way to implement the spirit of interactive models of reading development in the classroom is to teach children explicitly about the *relationships* between spelling patterns and sound patterns. One way to achieve this is to teach children to use rime analogies. This instruction will encompass phonology (rhymes), orthography (rimes), and the connection between the two (analogies). Of course, it is important to note that there is more to learning to read than the use of rime analogies. As the other chapters in this book make clear, literacy processes in the home, instruction at other phonological levels, print exposure, and many other factors also play an important role in beginning literacy. However, rime analogies are an important part of achieving word recognition in English, and some instruction about rime analogies is easy to incorporate into any classroom program for the teaching of reading.

REFERENCES

Bowey, J. A., & Hansen, J. (1994). The development of orthographic rimes as units of word recognition. *Journal of Experimental Child Psychology, 58*, 465–488.

Bradley, L. & Bryant, P. E. (1978). Difficulties in auditory organisation as a possible cause of reading backwardness. *Nature, 271*, 746–747.

Bradley, L. & Bryant, P. E. (1983). Categorising sounds and learning to read: A causal connection. *Nature, 310*, 419–421.

Brady, S., Fowler, A., & Gipstein, M. (in preparation). *Questioning the role of syllables and rimes in early phonological awareness.* Manuscript submitted for publication.

Brown, A. L., & Kane, M. J. (1988). Preschool children can learn to transfer: Learning to learn and learning by example. *Cognitive Psychology, 20*, 493–523.

Bruck, M., & Treiman, R. (1992). Learning to pronounce words: the limitations of analogies. *Reading Research Quarterly, 27*(4), 374–389.

Caravolas, M., & Bruck, M. (1993). The effect of oral and written language input on children's phonological awareness: A cross-linguistic study. *Journal of Experimental Child Psychology, 55*, 1–30.

Carroll, J. B., Davies, P. & Richman, B. (1971). *Word frequency book.* New York: American Heritage Publishing Company.

Content, A., Morais, J., Alegria, J., & Bertelson, P. (1982). Accelerating the development of phonetic segmentation skills in kindergarteners. *Cahiers de Psychologie Cognitive, 2,* 259–269.

Cossu, G., Shankweiler, D., Liberman, I. Y., Katz, L., & Tola, G. (1988). Awareness of phonological segments and reading ability in Italian children. *Applied Psycholinguistics, 9,* 1–16.

Cunningham, A. E. (1990). Implicit vs. explicit instruction in phonemic awareness. *Journal of Experimental Child Psychology, 50,* 429–444.

Cunningham, P. M. (1992). *Phonics they use: Words for reading and writing* (2nd ed.). New York: HarperCollins.

Ehri, L. C. (1992). Reconceptualizing sight word reading. In P. B. Gough, L. C. Ehri, & R. Treiman (Eds.), *Reading acquisition* (pp. 107–143). Hillsdale, NJ: Lawrence Erlbaum Associates.

Ehri, L. C., & Robbins, C. (1992). Beginners need some decoding skill to read words by analogy. *Reading Research Quarterly, 27*(1), 12–28.

Eimas, P. D., Siqueland, E. R., Jusczyk, P., & Vigorito, J. (1971). Speech perception in infants. *Science, 171,* 303–306.

Ellis, N. C., & Large, B. (1987). The development of reading: As you seek, so shall ye find. *British Journal of Psychology, 78,* 1–28.

Fox, B., & Routh, D. K. (1975). Analysing spoken language into words, syllables and phonemes: A developmental study. *Journal of Psycholinguistic Research, 4,* 331–342.

Frith, U. (1985). Beneath the surface of developmental dyslexia. In K. Patterson, M. Coltheart, & J. Marshall (Eds.) *Surface dyslexia* (pp. 301–330). Cambridge, UK: Academic.

Gombert, J. E. (1992). *Metalinguistic development.* Hemel Hempstead, England: Harvester-Wheatsheaf.

Goswami, U. (1986). Children's use of analogy in learning to read: A developmental study. *Journal of Experimental Child Psychology, 42,* 73–83.

Goswami, U. (1988). Orthographic analogies and reading development. *Quarterly Journal of Experimental Psychology, 40A,* 239–268.

Goswami, U. (1990a). Phonological priming and orthographic analogies in reading. *Journal of Experimental Child Psychology, 49,* 323–340.

Goswami, U. (1990b). A special link between rhyming skills and the use of orthographic analogies by beginning readers. *Journal of Child Psychology and Psychiatry, 31,* 301–311.

Goswami, U. (1991). Learning about spelling sequences: The role of onsets and rimes in analogies in reading. *Child Development, 62,* 1110–1123.

Goswami, U. (1992). *Analogical reasoning in children.* Hillsdale, NJ: Lawrence Erlbaum Associates.

Goswami, U. (1993). Toward an interactive analogy model of reading development: Decoding vowel graphemes in beginning reading. *Journal of Experimental Child Psychology, 56,* 443–475.

Goswami, U. (Ed.). (1996). *The Oxford reading tree rhyme and analogy programme.* Oxford, England: Oxford University Press.

Goswami, U. (in press). Integrating orthographic and phonological knowledge as reading develops: Onsets, rimes and analogies in children's reading. In R. Klein & P. McMullen (Eds.), *Converging methods for understanding reading and dyslexia* (pp.).

Goswami, U., & Bryant, P. E. (1990). *Phonological skills and learning to read.* Hillsdale, NJ: Lawrence Erlbaum Associates.

Goswami, U., Gombert, J., & De Barrera, F. (in press). Children's orthographic representations and linguistic transparency: Nonsense word reading in English, French and Spanish. *Applied Psycholinguistics.*

Goswami, U., & Mead, F. (1992). Onset and rime awareness and analogies in reading. *Reading Research Quarterly, 27*(2), 152–162.

Goswami, U., Porpodas, C., & Wheelwright, S. (1997). Children's orthographic representations in English and Greek. *European Journal of Psychology of Education, 12*(3), 273–292.

Hatcher, P. J., Hulme, C., & Ellis, A. W. (1994). Ameliorating early reading failure by integrating the teaching of reading and phonological skills: The phonological linkage hypothesis. *Child Development, 65*, 41–57.

Holligan, C., & Johnston, R. S. (1988). The use of phonological information by good and poor readers in memory and reading tasks. *Memory and Cognition, 16*, 522–532.

Huang, H. S., & Hanley, R. J. (1995). Phonological awareness and visual skills in learning to read Chinese and English. *Cognition, 54*, 73–98.

Juel, C. (1988). Learning to read and write: A longitudinal study of 54 children from first through fourth grades. *Journal of Educational Psychology, 80*, 437–447.

Katz, L., & Feldman, L. B. (1981). Linguistic coding in word recognition: Comparisons between a deep and a shallow orthography. In A. M. Lesgold & C. A. Perfetti (Eds.), *Interactive processes in reading* (pp. 157–166). Hillsdale, NJ: Lawrence Erlbaum Associates.

Katz, L., & Feldman, L. B. (1983). Relation between pronunciation and recognition of printed words in deep and shallow orthographies. *Journal of Experimental Psychology: Learning, Memory, and Cognition, 9*, 157–166.

Katz, L., & Frost, R. (1982). *Orthography, phonology, morphology and meaning.* Holland: Elsevier Science.

Kirtley, C., Bryant, P., Maclean, M., & Bradley, L. (1989). Rhyme, rime and the onset of reading. *Journal of Experimental Child Psychology, 48*, 224–245.

Liberman, I. Y., Shankweiler, D., Fischer, F. W., & Carter, B. (1974). Explicit syllable and phoneme segmentation in the young child. *Journal of Experimental Child Psychology, 18*, 201–212.

Lundberg, I., Olofsson, A., & Wall, S. (1980). Reading and spelling skills in the first school years predicted from phonemic awareness skills in kindergarten. *Scandanavian Journal of Psychology, 21*, 159–173.

Maclean, M., Bryant, P. E., & Bradley, L. (1987). Rhymes, nursery rhymes and reading in early childhood. *Merrill-Palmer Quarterly, 33*, 255–282.

Mann, V. A. (1986). Phonological awareness: The role of early reading experience. *Cognition, 24*, 65–92.

Marsh, G., Friedman, M. P., Welch, V., & Desberg, P. (1980). The development of strategies in spelling. In U. Frith (Ed.), *Cognitive processes in spelling* (pp. 339–353). London: Academic.

Muter, V., Snowling, M., & Taylor, S. (1994). Orthographic analogies and phonological awareness: Their role and significance in early reading development. *Journal of Child Psychology & Psychiatry, 35*, 293–310.

Naslund, J. C., & Schneider, W. (1991). Longitudinal effects of verbal ability, memory capacity and phonological awareness on reading performance. *European Journal of Psychology of Education, 6*(4), 375–392.

Perfetti, C. (1992). The representation problem in reading acquisition. In P. B. Gough, L. C. Ehri, & R. Treiman (Eds.), *Reading acquisition*, (pp. 145–174). Hillsdale, NJ: Lawrence Erlbaum Associates.

Perfetti, C., Beck, I., Bell, L., & Hughes, C. (1987). Phonemic knowledge and learning to read are reciprocal: A longitudinal study of first grade children. *Merrill-Palmer Quarterly, 33*, 283–319.

Peterson, M. E., & Haines, L. P. (1992). Orthographic analogy training with kindergarten children: Effects on analogy use, phonemic segmentation, and letter-sound knowledge. *Journal of Reading Behaviour, 24,* 109–127.

Porpodas, C. (1993). The relation between phonemic awareness and reading and spelling of Greek words in the first school years. In M. Carretero, M. Pope, R. J. Simons, & J. I. Pozo (Eds.), *Learning and instruction,* (Vol. 3, pp. 203–217). Oxford, UK: Pergamon.

Porpodas, C. (1995, December). *How Greek first grade children learn to read and spell: Similarities with and differences from established views.* Paper presented at the COST-A8 workshop on early interventions promoting reading acquisition in school, Athens, Greece.

Schneider, W., & Naslund, J. C. (in press). The impact of early phonological processing skills on reading and spelling in school: Evidence from the Munich longitudinal study. In F. E. Weinert & W. Schneider (Eds.), *Individual development from 3 to 12: Findings from the Munich longitudinal study.* Cambridge, UK: Cambridge University Press.

Snowling, M. J. (1980). The development of grapheme–phoneme correspondence in normal and dyslexic readers. *Journal of Experimental Child Psychology, 29,* 294–305.

Stanback, M. L. (1992). Syllable and rime patterns for teaching reading: Analysis of a frequency-based vocabulary of 17,602 words. *Annals of Dyslexia, 42,* 196–221.

Stanovich, K. E., Cunningham, A. E., & Cramer, B. R. (1984). Assessing phonological awareness in kindergarten: Issues of task comparability. *Journal of Experimental Child Psychology, 38,* 175–190.

Stanovich, K. E., Cunningham, A. E., & Feeman, D. J. (1984). Intelligence, cognitive skills and early reading progress. *Reading Research Quarterly, 19,* 278–303.

Stanovich, K. E., Nathan, R. G., & Zolman, J. E. (1988). The developmental lag hypothesis in reading: Longitudinal and matched reading-level comparisons. *Child Development, 59,* 71–86.

Stuart, M., & Coltheart, M. (1988). Does reading develop in a sequence of stages? *Cognition, 30,* 139–181.

Thorstad, G. (1991). The effect of orthography in the acquisition of literacy skills. *British Journal of Psychology, 82,* 527–537.

Treiman, R., & Chafetz, J. (1987). Are there onset- and rime-like units in printed words? In M. Coltheart (Ed.), *Attention & performance XII* (pp. 281–298). Hillsdale, NJ: Lawrence Erlbaum Associates.

Treiman, R., Goswami, U., & Bruck, M. (1990). Not all nonwords are alike: Implications for reading development and theory. *Memory & Cognition, 18,* 559–567.

Treiman, R., Mullennix, J., Bijeljac-Babic, R., & Richmond-Welty, E. D. (1995). The special role of rimes in the description, use and acquisition of English orthography. *Journal of Experimental Psychology, General, 124,* 107–136.

Treiman, R., & Zukowski, A. (1991). Levels of phonological awareness. In S. Brady & D. Shankweiler (Eds.), *Phonological processes in literacy* (pp. 67–83). Hillsdale, NJ: Lawrence Erlbaum Associates.

Tunmer, W. E., & Nesdale, A. R. (1985). Phonemic segmentation skill and beginning reading. *Journal of Educational Psychology, 77,* 417–527

Vellutino, F. R., & Scanlon, D. M. (1987). Phonological coding, phonological awareness and reading ability: Evidence from a longitudinal and experimental study. *Merrill-Palmer Quarterly, 33,* 321–363.

Wagner, R. K. (1988). Causal relations between the development of phonological processing abilities and the acquisition of reading skills: A meta-analysis. *Merrill-Palmer Quarterly, 34,* 261–279.

Wagstaff, J. M. (1994). *Phonics that work! New strategies for the Reading/Writing Classroom.* New York: Scholastic.

Walton, P. D. (1995). Rhyming ability, phoneme identity, letter-sound knowledge and the use of orthographic analogy by prereaders. *Journal of Educational Psychology, 87,* 587–597.

White, T. G., & Cunningham, P. M. (1990, April). *Teaching disadvantaged students to decode by analogy.* Paper presented at the annual meeting of the American Educational Research Association, Boston.

Wimmer, H. (1993). Characteristics of developmental dyslexia in a regular writing system. *Applied Psycholinguistics, 14,* 1–33.

Wimmer, H., Landerl, K., Linortner, R., & Hummer, P. (1991). The relationship of phonemic awareness to reading acquisition: More consequence than precondition but still important. *Cognition, 40,* 219–249.

Wimmer, H., Landerl, K., & Schneider, W. (1994). The role of rhyme awareness in learning to read a regular orthography. *British Journal of Developmental Psychology, 12,* 469–484.

Wise, B. W., Olson, D. K., & Treiman, R. (1990). Subsyllabic units as aids in beginning readers' word learning: Onset-rime versus post-vowel segmentation. *Journal of Experimental Child Psychology, 49,* 1–19.

Wylie, R. E., & Durrell, D. D. (1970). *Elementary English, 47,* 787–791.

Yopp, H. K. (1988). The validity and reliability of phonemic awareness tests. *Reading Research Quarterly, 23,* 159–177.

3

▼▼▼▼▼▼▼

Issues Involved in Defining Phonological Awareness and Its Relation to Early Reading

Steven A. Stahl
The University of Georgia

Bruce Murray
Auburn University

The first exposure to the concept of phonological awareness for many educators and psychologists came from the publication of *Language by Ear and by Eye*, edited by James Kavanaugh and Ignatius Mattingly in 1972. In this volume, Mattingly, Harris Savin, and Donald Shankweiler and Isabelle Liberman discussed the relation between an awareness of phonological segments (then called *linguistic awareness*) and learning to read. Shankweiler and Liberman's research drew from the work in speech perception done at the Haskins Laboratories (e.g., Liberman, Cooper, Shankweiler, & Studdert-Kennedy, 1967), which found that spoken words could not be acoustically analyzed into discrete phonological segments because the phonemes, which could be thought of abstractly as separate elements, were "folded" together into units. "Before he can map the visual message to the word in his vocabulary, [the child] has to be consciously aware that the word *cat* that he knows—an apparently unity syllable—has three separate segments" (Shankweiler & Liberman, 1972, p. 309). Shankweiler and Liberman suggested that difficulties in phonological awareness were at the root of many reading problems.

The basic premise that "phonological awareness is related to reading" has been conclusively established by research in the years since Kavanaugh and Mattingly's landmark volume. However, we have yet to specify what we mean by the terms of the equation. What kind of "phonological awareness" is related to reading? About what kind of relation are we talking? And how are we defining *reading*. The purpose of this chapter is to review some of the relevant work related to defining these terms, and to propose a model

65

of how phonological awareness might be related to reading at different stages of the development of both phonological awareness and reading.

DEFINING PHONOLOGICAL AWARENESS

Over the years, phonological awareness has been defined in a number of ways. At first it was defined as a single concept. Researchers created tasks that required what they thought was phonological awareness, assuming that different tasks all reflected general metalinguistic ability. Thus, Liberman (1973) used a tapping task, in which students needed to tap a wooden dowel for every phoneme in a word (see also Liberman, Shankweiler, Fischer, & Carter, 1974); Rosner (1974) had children mentally remove phonemes from a word; and Fox and Routh (1975) had children tell the first sound of a word. All of these tasks require some degree of phonological awareness. With these different tasks, it was little wonder that children appeared to acquire phonological awareness at different ages in different studies!

In retrospect, the tasks varied considerably, involving different processes and different levels of linguistic and metalinguistic knowledge (Stahl & Murray, 1994). In subsequent research, the different tasks were compared empirically, to see which best represents phonological awareness, or whether there were different types of phonological awareness (e.g., Beach, 1992; Yopp, 1988). More recently, phonological awareness has been defined in terms of the content and the processes acting on that content, adding new constructs such as "linguistic complexity" (Treiman, 1985) and "phoneme identity" (Byrne & Fielding-Barnsley, 1989, 1990). Commonly used tasks include:

- Rhyming, either by recognizing rhymes or rhyme production.
- Word-to-word matching tasks, which involve having a child determine whether a series of words begins or ends with the same sound, or which word in a set is the "odd one out."
- Sound-to-word matching tasks, which ask whether a particular sound, uttered explicitly by the examiner, can be found in a word.
- Full segmentation, requiring a child to articulate separately each phonemic segment in a spoken word or to report the number of segments in a word.
- Partial segmentation (also called *phoneme isolation*), in which the child is asked to segment one sound. Sometimes this involves separating an onset from a rime (e.g., /k/ /at/) or breaking up a rime (/ka/ /t/).
- Blending—the "flip side" of segmentation—which involves having a child combine sounds that are spoken separately into a word (e.g., recognizing that /k/ /a/ /t/ is cat).

- Deletion and manipulation—in deletion tasks, such as Rosner's Auditory Analysis Test (1975), a child is told to mentally remove a portion of a word to make another word (e.g., "Say coat. Now say it again without the /k/.")

In more complex manipulation tasks, children may be asked to remove a phonemic segment and put it elsewhere in the word to make a new word, or to perform other complex manipulations, such as in pig Latin (Savin, 1972). Making sense of the experimental literature about phonological awareness has been muddled by comparisons of these different tasks.

LEVELS OF DIFFICULTY

In a synthesis of the literature on reading acquisition, Adams (1990) theorized that the various tasks used to measure phonological awareness fall into five levels of difficulty. The most primitive level, according to Adams, consists of having an ear for the sounds of words, as revealed by the ability to remember familiar rhymes (e.g., Maclean, Bryant, & Bradley, 1987). A second level consists of the ability to recognize and sort patterns of rhyme and alliteration in words, which requires a more focused attention to sound components; this ability is revealed in oddity tasks (e.g., Bradley & Bryant, 1983). A third level requires familiarity both with the division of syllables into phonemes and with the sounds of isolated phonemes; this level is indicated by blending tasks and syllable-splitting tasks (e.g., isolating initial phonemes). A fourth level of difficulty covers tasks that require full segmentation of component phonemes (e.g., a tapping test; Liberman, 1973). At the fifth and most difficult level are tasks requiring children to add, delete, or otherwise move phonemes and to regenerate the resultant word or pseudoword (e.g., Rosner, 1974).

Simple and Complex Phonological Awareness

Yopp (1988) attempted to resolve empirically the problem of defining phonological awareness. She gave 10 different measures of phonological awareness to a group of kindergartners in order to determine the reliability and relative difficulty of each measure and to assess task validity through correlation with a pseudoword decoding task. Yopp also carried out a factor analysis, which identified two skills influencing test performance: a simple phonemic awareness factor (seen in segmentation, blending, sound isolation, and phoneme counting tests), and a compound phonemic awareness factor (seen in tasks that require holding a sound in memory while performing additional operations). There are some problems with Yopp's (1988) factor analysis. The first relates to the analysis itself. The first factor found had an eigenvalue of 5.87, accounting for 58.7% of the variance. The second factor had an eigenvalue of 0.94, accounting for an additional 9.5% of the variance, and eigenvalues for other factors drop off slowly, accounting for less and less of the variance. Because the eigenvalue for Yopp's second factor is beneath the conventional cutoff of 1.0, and because the first factor accounts by itself for the majority of variance, a one-factor solution rather than Yopp's two-factor solution might be more appropriate. Using somewhat different measures, we found that a single factor, rather than two factors, seemed to best describe our data (Stahl & Murray, 1994). Our basic data looked much like Yopp's, but, given the eigenvalue of 1.0 criterion, we discounted the second factor. When performances on different tasks (blending, full segmentation, partial segmentation, and deletion) were used for analysis, a single factor accounted for 72.6% of the common variance (eigenvalue = 2.91). When we forced a two-factor solution and attempted various rotations, the first factor was still significantly more pronounced.

Linguistic Complexity

Although Yopp (1988) posited two clearly different levels of phonological awareness, she also noted disparities across the tasks commonly used to assess the construct. Items varied greatly both between and within measures derived from the same type of task. For example, some blending tasks used nonsense words whereas some used real words; some had more short consonant-vowel-consonant (CVC) words, whereas others contained more words with consonant blends.

One important source of variability not controlled in Yopp's tasks was linguistic level. According to Treiman (1992), syllables seem to break most readily between the onset (any beginning consonants) and the rime (the vowel and any final consonants). The rime is further divided into the vowel nucleus and the coda, or any final consonants. For instance, most people find it easier to divide *stamp* into /st/ and /amp/ than into other dichotomous parts. This tendency is illustrated by the unintended slips of the tongue (spoonerisms) people construct when they are torn between synonyms by blending the onset of one word with the rime of another (e.g., *tons of soil* for *sons of toil*). Treiman (1992) simulated this by asking adults to combine *frail* and *slat* into one new word. The majority (62%) responded with *frat,* which moved the onset of the first word onto the rime of the second; very few responded with *frait,* which would have required a division within a rime. Because of the significance of onsets and rimes within words, it is more difficult, for example, to delete the initial phoneme in *trick* than in *tick*. To delete /t/ from *trick* involves breaking up the blended phonemes within an onset, but in *tick* deleting /t/ only requires separating the onset from the rime. Based on Treiman's notions, it should be easier to break a syllable between an onset and a rime than to separate the coda from the rest of the word, and more difficult still to split cluster onsets such as /sl/ or cluster codas such as /st/ or /mp/.

Yopp used or adapted extant tasks of phonological awareness. Items on the tasks varied considerably in terms of the levels of linguistic analysis required to perform each task. Thus, one cannot be sure whether the performance differences found between tasks resulted from differences in the inherent degrees of task difficulty or from differences in linguistic complexity.

We reexamined the items on Yopp's (1988) measures. We assigned a weight for each level of linguistic complexity tapped (Stahl & Murray, 1994). Recognition of a rhyme was assigned a value of 1, manipulating onset and a rime a value of 2, manipulating vowel and coda a value of 3, manipulating phonemes within a cluster onset a value of 4, and manipulating phonemes within a cluster coda a value of 5. We rated each item on linguistic complexity and averaged these ratings for each task. When we correlated task ratings with the mean score obtained by Yopp's subjects on each task, we found a .95 correlation between our post hoc measure of task difficulty and the levels of difficulty obtained by Yopp. This suggested that linguistic complexity may be an important factor in phonological awareness. It also suggested that Yopp's measures may have confounded linguistic complexity and task.

In our study, we prepared four tasks (blending, full segmentation, partial segmentation, and deletion), each with an equal number of items at different levels of linguistic complexity (Stahl & Murray, 1994). Our design was such that it allowed us to examine the differential effects of both task and linguistic complexity. When we analyzed our measures by linguistic complexity across the different tasks, we found support for our hypothesis that onset-rime separation was easier than breaking up a rime by segmenting vowel and coda, which in turn was easier than breaking a cluster onset or rime into constituent phonemes.

As mentioned earlier, when we used tasks to define phonological awareness, a single factor accounted for 72.6% of the common variance. We also conducted a factor analysis with levels of linguistic analysis used to define phonological awareness. The scores at the various levels, summed across tasks, were used in the analysis. In this analysis, one factor accounted for substantially more of the common variance, 81.7% (eigenvalue = 3.32). We concluded that defining phonological awareness by levels of linguistic complexity better accounted for our data than defining phonological awareness by task, because when the subtests were analyzed by that grouping, the factor analysis accounted for 9% more of the total variance, even though both approaches accounted for high amounts of the total variance and both would be considered to be adequate.

Phoneme Identity

Both the task approach and the linguistic levels approach tend to view phonological awareness mechanistically. That is, according to these views, the task of phonological awareness involves performing some mental manipulation to a spoken word. In contrast, a third approach to defining phonological awareness, phonemic identity (Byrne & Fielding-Barnsley, 1989), views the task as concept formation.

The germ of the concept of phoneme identity was suggested by Lewkowicz (1980), who tried to explain how children could segment syllables into phonemes despite the linguistic problem of the acoustic unity of a syllable. Lewkowicz speculated that children must look for familiar elements in the stretched pronunciations of syllables. What becomes familiar are the vocal gestures and their accompanying sounds that children come to recognize as recycled across words. These vocal gestures come to have identities (from the Latin *idem*, meaning "same") when they are recognized as the same vocal gestures used across different words.

The identity view of phonological awareness has important implications for teaching. In identity-based teaching, one teaches the identities of a small number of phonemes in a variety of words. In segmentation training, one teaches isolating the sounds as a skill that one can perform with any word, rather than with only words whose phonemes were mastered. Byrne and Fielding-Barnsley (1989, 1993) used identity teaching and segmentation teaching with samples of preschoolers. The identity group was taught to recognize only the phonemes /s/ and /m/ in words by isolating and stretching these phonemes. This group received guided practice in reliably selecting words beginning or ending with these phonemes (i.e., sound-to-word matching). The segmentation group received practice in isolating the beginning and ending sounds of the same words, using a larger set of phonemes. Both groups learned letter–phoneme correspondences for the letters *s*, *m*, *b*, and *f*, which appeared in a reading analog task during posttesting. For example, children given the word *mow* were asked, "Is this *sow* or *mow*?" This task involves phonetic cue reading (Ehri, 1991), because participants need only focus on the first letter sound as a cue to correctly respond. They were also asked to respond to words beginning with *f* and *b*, for which phoneme identities had not been explicitly taught. Although the groups were not directly compared, possibly because the small sample size lacked power to distinguish performance differences, the identity group appeared to fare somewhat better in leading children to master the phonetic cue reading task. Furthermore, sound-to-word matching scores (an identity measure) were a better predictor of phonetic cue reading ability for identity participants ($r = .49$) than segmentation scores were for segmentation-trained participants ($r = .20$) on the phonetic cue reading measure. Byrne and Fielding-Barnsley also observed informally that children seemed to enjoy the identity work more and that it required little corrective feedback.

Five children from each teaching program mastered phonetic cue reading with the untrained letters *f* and *b*, suggesting that these children had acquired a larger sense of phoneme awareness that permitted them to use simple correspondence information to quickly get a handle on the identities of these phonemes and succeed in phonetic cue reading.

Murray (1995) replicated the Byrne and Fielding-Barnsley (1989) study using a larger sample size. Murray found that kindergarten children trained to segment spoken words made greater gains than an identity group on measures of phoneme manipulation, such as blending and partial and full segmentation, but that the children with identity training were better able to transfer their knowledge to a measure of phonetic cue reading. The Byrne and Fielding-Barnsley (1989) and Murray (1995) studies suggest strongly that it is important to include phoneme identity in any definition of phonological awareness.

RELATIONSHIPS AMONG PHONOLOGICAL AWARENESS SKILLS

In our earlier study (Stahl & Murray, 1994), we found a clear hierarchy among three tasks—blending, deletion, and partial segmentation. Partial segmentation (which we termed *phoneme isolation*) seems to be the first task mastered. A series of scattergrams suggested that partial segmentation, at least of an onset and rime, seems to reliably precede the ability to blend and delete phonemes. That partial segmentation was nearly always present in children who could blend and delete phonemes suggests that it is a necessary condition for these manipulations. The sequence of partial segmentation to blending and deletion is complicated by a number of other factors. First, reading ability seems to mediate blending and deletion. The scattergram analysis indicated that some degree of reading ability, as measured by reading words on a preprimer list, also seems to be precede blending and deletion ability. This minimum level was surprisingly high—into the first reader range for both tasks—suggesting that a fairly high level of word recognition is necessary for children to blend and delete phonemes in spoken words. This confirms the findings of Perfetti, Beck, Bell, and Hughes (1987) with similar tasks. Second, we believe that the construct of phoneme identity seems to underlie the ability to perform all of these tasks.

We did not include phoneme identity tasks in our 1994 study, but a later study (Murray, 1995) included a phoneme identity measure.[1] He found that

---

[1]The instrument we used was a modification of Torgesen and Bryant's (1994) Test of Phonological Awareness (TOPA). The TOPA is designed to be a word-to-word matching test with illustrations of the words to be matched. Children are directed, for example, to notice pictures of *leg, lamp, hand,* and *fish,* and to "mark the one that begins with the same sound as *leg.*" To make the test more

children performed similarly on this measure of phoneme identity as they did on a measure of partial segmentation. From this pattern of results, it is possible that partial segmentation measures may be strongly influenced by children's ongoing development of phoneme identities.

The importance of linguistic complexity suggests a sequence of learning the identity of phonemes in simpler contexts before locating them in more difficult linguistic contexts. For example, recognizing the phoneme /s/ when it serves as an onset, as in *sun,* is easier than finding it when it is part of a time, as in *gas,* which would be easier, in turn, then recognizing it as part of a complex onset, such as in *star,* or as part of a complex rime coda as in *wrist.*

WHAT DO WE MEAN BY *IS RELATED TO?*

There are two relationships we can posit that phonological awareness can have to reading: correlational, and necessary but not sufficient. ("Necessary and sufficient" and "sufficient but not necessary" are logically implausible.) These relationships can be demonstrated using scattergrams. At this point, we do not tell you which variables are illustrated but instead do so later, because here we want to concentrate on the relationships rather than what they mean. The scattergram shown in Fig. 3.1 is a classical correlation pattern. The r here is about .79, which is a strong correlation. Notice that both variables rise together. This could suggest that these two measures are measuring the same thing. Because correlation does not imply causality, it could also mean that a third variable, to which both are related, could be causing the relationship.

In contrast, the scattergram in Fig. 3.2 shows what could be a necessary but not sufficient relationship. In this relationship, there were children who could not do either task very well and students who did both tasks well. There were also students who did the first task well but not the second, but few children who did the second well but not the first. Let's divide this into quadrants. In a correlation, the coefficient would assess the number of children in quadrant B and quadrant C. In this case, as in many cases reported in the literature, this correlation would be high because most of the children in the study fell into one of those two quadrants. However, the real information is in the other quadrants. One can analyze this statistically (we used McNemar's Test, a nonparametric statistic), but the picture is informative by itself.

In our work with phonological awareness, this type of pattern was the most common for a number of reasons. First, most variables tended to have

---

explicit, the examiner pronounced the target phoneme in isolation, telling children that "lamp begins with /l/," and asking them to "mark the one that begins with /l/, as in *leg.*" By this modification, the TOPA became a sound-to-word matching test, operationalizing the identity view of phoneme awareness as knowledge of particular phoneme identities across words.

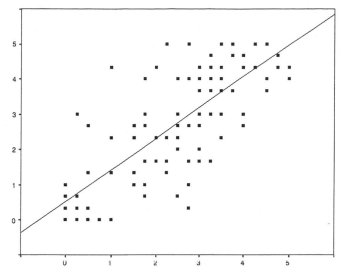

FIG. 3.1. Scattergram illustrating a correlational relationship.

ceiling effects. There are only 26 letters of the alphabet, children generally either can or cannot segment a word, and so on. Although most research in this area analyzes these variables as if they have a full range and are normally distributed, these are not variables with a full range and their distribution tends to be skewed. Second, these relationships make theoretical sense. From Liberman's (1973) work onward, it has been assumed that phonological

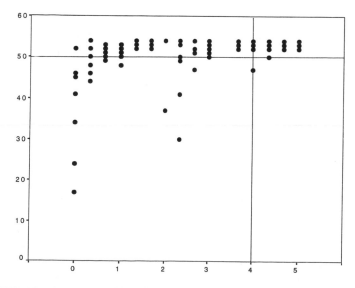

FIG. 3.2. Scattergram illustrating a necessary but not sufficient relationship.

awareness entered into a causal relationship with reading. There is evidence from training studies, from Bradley and Bryant's (1983) study to their successors, that phonological awareness or lack thereof does seem to be causally related to success or failure in reading. The scattergram analysis shows this most closely. If two variables enter into a causal relationship, especially if one or both variables would tend to have a skewed distribution, then one would expect to see a "necessary but not sufficient" pattern, as in Fig. 3.2.[2]

The variables in Fig. 3.1 are the measure of phoneme identity and a partial segmentation measure, discussed earlier. Because these covary, one might assume (within the caveat of correlation not implying causality) that these measures are assessing the same or similar skills. Thus, a partial segmentation measure might be measuring phoneme identity knowledge. The variables in Fig. 3.2 are alphabet knowledge and blending. This suggests, as noted previously, that alphabet knowledge (the y-axis) is necessary but not sufficient for the ability to partially segment words (the x-axis), because there are many subjects who know nearly all letters and can segment, some who know few letters and cannot segment, some who know letters but cannot segment, and one who can blend but do not know at least 50 letters of the alphabet.

In this research, regression and correlation have been used extensively to examine these relationships. However, they may be misleading, because variables do not fit together in ways appropriate for correlational analysis.

HOW DO WE DEFINE *READING*?

There are a number of ways to define *reading*, hence the confusion about the goals of reading programs (see Stahl, 1997a). Proponents of different instructional models tend to view the concept of reading in different ways. For example, some people tend to view reading purely in terms of decoding, whereas whole language theorists tend to view reading in terms of responding to and appreciating literature. These differing views have led to the acrimonious debates that have typified our field. When we talk about reading, in whatever context, it is important to state exactly what aspect of reading we are talking about.

In relation to phonological awareness, reading has been defined strictly in terms of word recognition. This is appropriate, because phonological awareness has been posited to underlie a person's learning of sound–symbol relations or of orthography, which in turn underlies the larger purposes of reading.

---

[2]If two variables are both skewed, as is typical in this type of research, then the presence of a third variable could cause this pattern. Thus, as in other basically correlational research, one cannot impute causality. However, this pattern is consistent with a "necessary but sufficient" pattern.

We assume that readers go through a series of stages as they learn to recognize words. Although we rely on Ehri (1991) for the names of these stages, similar stages have been proposed by Chall (1996), Frith (1985), Gough, Juel, and Griffith (1992), and McCormick and Mason (1986). In all of these models, the development of word recognition goes through roughly three stages, what Ehri (1991) called *visual cue reading, phonetic cue reading,* and *phonological recoding.*

Visual Cue Reading

In visual cue reading, children recognize words by purely visual means. Studies of visual cue reading further indicate that readers do not use visual patterns of whole words as retrieval cues, but rather select specific features of a visual array for this purpose (Gough, Juel, & Griffith, 1992). The reader might select a letter shape, a memorized spelling (e.g., for a name), a distinctive logo, a picture, or the bent corner of a card, and ignore the sequence of remaining letters. For example, Gough et al. (1992) asked 4- and 5-year-old children to learn to read four words presented on flash cards. One card in each child's collection of words to be learned was soiled with a distinct thumbprint in one corner. The children were trained by standard paired-associate learning methods to a criterion of two successive perfect trials. The card with the thumbprint was always learned first. However, when the same word was presented on a clean card, fewer than half of the children could then recognize it. Moreover, when the children were shown a blank card with a thumbprint, nearly all reported the word they had seen on the original thumbprinted card. The same results occurred when they were shown a different word with a thumbprinted corner.

One explanation for these results is that young children with no means of remembering words other than visual cue reading tend to associate words and their meanings with whatever salient visual cue is available—in this case, the thumbprint. It was the thumbprint, rather than the sequence of letters of the word, that elicited their association during the test trials. In a similar demonstration, preschoolers learned to read four dissimilar four-letter words by the same anticipation and correction method, and then were asked to identify the words from half of the spelling. For example, they were asked to recall *pony* from the letters *po,* or from *ny.* Children who could not identify the word from half the spelling were twice as likely to recognize it when shown the other half. This suggests that visual cue readers select a visual feature from part of the word to make their associations, rather than using the entire visual configuration.

Visual cue reading may be used by children to recognize logos. Whole language advocates suggest that children may learn about print initially through examination of logos, such as the arches for McDonald's. However, the research of Masonheimer, Drum, and Ehri (1984) and Stahl and Murray (1993) suggests that prereaders process logos as pictures and do not analyze print. Masonheimer et al. found that children were insensitive to alterations of the print within a logo, such as placing *xepsi* within a Pepsi logo. Stahl and Murray found that kindergarten children's knowledge of the alphabet predicted their recognition of words taken from logos written in block print significantly better than their recognition of the logos themselves.

Although word representations acquired by visual cue reading tend not to be memorable, reliable, or easily learned, paired association of visual cues with word meanings is the standard default strategy used by untaught beginners in their attempts to recognize words (Byrne, 1992). Ehri and Wilce (1985) found that preschoolers and kindergartners who read no words found it easier to read spellings that were visually distinctive (e.g., **yMp** for *turtle*) than spellings that used the sounds values of letters (e.g., **GRF** for *giraffe*). Children who could read some words found the less visually distinctive sound spellings easier, and learned them more accurately in fewer trials.

Use of a phonological recoding strategy is possible only with syllabic and alphabetic writing systems, in which spellings map the sequential pronunciations of sounds in spoken words. To profit from the advantage offered by alphabetic orthographies, the beginner must gain insight into the alphabetic principle, namely that spellings in written words map onto phonemes in spoken words. Understanding this principle does not come easily to children (Gough & Hillinger, 1980). Byrne (1992) taught preschoolers to recognize pairs of words that differed only in their initial consonants (e.g., *fat* and *bat*; *fin* and *bin*). Although most of the children learned to identify these words, they did not learn that the initial letter represented a sound found in other words; when asked to distinguish *fun* and *bun* or *fell* and *bell*, their responses were at chance levels. In contrast, these preschoolers were able to generalize symbols linked to meanings. For example, after learning to identify *little boy* and *big boy* and *little truck* and *big truck*, they were above chance in differentiating *little fish* and *big fish*. This suggests that young children can generalize symbols that refer to meaning, but they are quite unlikely to generalize symbols that encode phonemes.

Phonetic Cue Reading

Children move slowly from visual cue reading to a full analysis of a word's spelling. The first step is usually a transitional phase that Ehri (1991) called *phonetic cue reading*. In phonetic cue reading, the beginner uses some letters in words (typically the initial or boundary letters) to generate one or more sounds in the spoken equivalent of the word, thereby narrowing the ranges of choices for contextual guessing. This reduces the memory burden occasioned by the rote associations of visual cue reading, because it replaces the arbitrary link of selected visual cues with a systematic link through letter–sound associations. For instance, instead of remembering that *yellow* has "two sticks" in the middle, the beginner can access the phoneme /y/ and guess a color name beginning with that sound, presuming he or she has determined from context that the unfamiliar word names a color.

Phonetic cue reading affects children's reading and writing in a number of different ways. Phonetic cue readers can readily fingerpoint words in memorized text (Ehri & Sweet, 1991), enabling children to pair spoken and printed words.Their misreadings of words tend to preserve initial or boundary sounds (Biemiller, 1970). Also, phonetic cue readers rarely make semantically related misreadings that are not phonetically related (e.g., "sneaker" for *Nike*), because they use letter-sound information to monitor their reading (Stahl & Murray, 1993). Instead, phonetic cue readers who cannot recognize a word tend to provide no response instead of producing a semantically acceptable guess (Biemiller, 1970). Finally, children's early invented spellings tend to preserve these letters or their equivalents (Ehri & Wilce, 1987; Gillet & Temple, 1990).

Disadvantages of Phonetic Cue Reading. Although phonetic cue reading offers a decided advantage over the arbitrary associations of visual cue reading, it is not without its drawbacks. In contrast with more skilled readers who can phonologically recode using the entire spelling, children who read via phonetic cues show inconsistency in reading the same word across trials. In one study these beginners could read only about 35% of the words they had read correctly on the previous trial, less than half the number correctly reread by children who could recode most of the spelling sequence (Ehri & Wilce, 1987). Words with similar spellings (e.g., **pots, post, spot, stop**) require more learning trials for phonetic cue readers than those with dissimilar spellings (McCutchen & McDowell, 1969). Given these limitations, readers who have taken the qualitative leap from visual to phonetic cue reading must still take the quantitative steps toward fuller analysis and use of complete spelling sequences in phonological recoding.

Phonological Recoding

Another means of accessing the meanings of printed words is phonological recoding; that is, generating an approximate pronunciation of a word from spelling cues to retrieve meaning. (This is also called "cipher" reading; Gough et al., 1992). Phonological recoding serves as a self-teaching mechanism for word recognition as well as a backup mechanism for skilled readers to access less familiar words (Jorm & Share, 1983; Share, 1995). Expert phonological recoding involves generating pronunciations from entire spellings of words. Whatever teaching method is used to lead children into independent word recognition, it is increasingly clear that would-be readers of alphabetic languages must learn to reproduce spoken words by using complete spellings as maps to pronunciation (Adams, 1990; Ehri, 1991; Jorm & Share, 1983).

Children use a number of means to identify words. Sometimes children use a "sounding-out"strategy, involving sequential translation of letters to sounds. The ability to sound words out develops from a slow, attention-demanding, and laborious process to one that is rapid, at least partially automatic, and relatively effortless. More skillful phonological recoding probably develops as children learn to recognize syllabic or intrasyllabic word parts as units (e.g., when they learn that the -*tion* suffix reliably encodes the syllable /shun/). Such sophisticated spelling knowledge is characteristic of the orthographic stage of reading development (Frith, 1985) and probably represents an instance of chunking smaller units into larger ones (Rozin & Gleitman, 1977). Just as children discard their training wheels as they learn to maintain balance on a moving bicycle, novice readers put aside laborious sounding and blending routines as they begin to perceive larger orthographic units.

Other times children use an analogy strategy, as described by Goswami (chap. 2, this volume). In such a strategy, the child uses a known word to decode an unknown word. We suggest that the successful use of an analogy strategy is dependent on a child's full encoding of the known word (Gaskins, Ehri, Cress, O'Hara, & Donnelly, 1996). Without such full encoding, the child is likely to confuse that word with others with similar rime patterns, and make errors that would be classified as phonetic cue errors. It is only at the orthographic stage that a child is able to choose effectively and consistently among analogues.

Development of Recoding Skill.   Monaghan (cited in Ehri, 1991), in a longitudinal study of recoding acquisition, described phases she observed in the development of the skill of pronouncing pseudowords. At first, the children articulated the sounds represented by letters but could not blend. Next, they learned to sound out and blend, but their efforts were slow and effortful. In a transitional stage, they learned to recode in a quiet voice or by silently moving their lips before saying the word. Finally, they could read the pseudowords rapidly without moving their lips. Monaghan's observations suggest that the skill of phonological recoding develops from a slow overt process to a fast silent one. Moreover, skilled recoding depends on moving from sounding and blending based on single letters to mentally dividing a word into pronounceable multiletter units (e.g., consonant and vowel digraphs) and recognizing the signaling influence of nearby letters (e.g., a final *e*). More sophisticated knowledge of orthographic constraints is characteristic of later stages of word recognition development (Frith, 1985).

DEFINING READING IN THE PHONOLOGICAL AWARENESS LITERATURE

We reviewed a selected set of studies to examine how reading has been assessed in phonological awareness studies, including both training studies and correlational studies. In the 24 training studies we looked at, 14 used a measure of decoding, including pseudoword decoding. Eight used a measure of word recognition. Only one used a measure of phonetic cue reading. Measures of connected text reading were used in four studies.

Word recognition involves a series of increasingly more sophisticated knowledge of letters and sounds and how they map unto the speech stream. However, word recognition in isolation is not the same as word recognition in context. Adams and Huggins (1985) found that children can read words somewhat more accurately in context than they can in isolation. This effect has been found by a number of other researchers, although different researchers have found different magnitudes of the effects (cf. Goodman, 1983; Nicholson, 1991). In context, word recognition processes interact with comprehension-driven processes. This interaction is suggested to be more pronounced with younger or less competent readers (Stanovich, 1980), such as those who are the participants in phonological awareness studies.

Reading words in isolation is a more focused test of the effects of phonological awareness on reading than contextual measures. We assume that phonological awareness most directly affects the learning of sound–symbol relationships and their use in decoding and word recognition. Reading connected text does involve decoding, but also involves some use of contextual information (e.g., Adams & Huggins, 1985). This may be especially true for beginning readers. If phonological awareness training has strong effects on measures of decoding but lesser effects on measures of oral reading of connected text, this would support the view that phonological awareness specifically affects sound–symbol knowledge. Using broader measures of reading would also enable richer models of reading acquisition, including the use of contextual information and how it interacts with phonological and orthographic information.

ALPHABET KNOWLEDGE AND PHONOLOGICAL AWARENESS

In the research on phonological awareness, there is an unstated assumption that some level of phonological awareness combined with alphabet knowledge is necessary for children to learn to decode. There is an assumption, in Adams (1990) among others, that alphabet knowledge is separate from phonological knowledge. In our research and others, however, we found that alphabet knowledge seems to precede the simplest level of phonological awareness that we tested. We discovered evidence of this in a number of studies. Lomax and McGee (1987) tested a multicomponent model of emergent reading. They examined 81 3-, 4-, 5-, and 6-year-olds on a variety of measures, using LISREL analysis to examine relationships among variables. They found that the children's "graphic awareness" factors (consisting of measures of letter orientation, letter discrimination, and word discrimination) accounted for 99% of the variance in their phonemic awareness factor (consisting of two word-to-word matching tasks, one with beginning sounds and one with final sounds, and an auditory discrimination task). These tasks seem rather different than those that we would use. In their meta-analysis of the effects of phonological awareness training, Wagner and Rashotte (1993) found that only those programs that combined phonological awareness training with alphabet recognition (and, consequently, spelling) had a significant effect on reading achievement (e.g., Bradley & Bryant, 1983). (An exception is the study by Lundberg, Frost, & Petersen, 1988, which found significant effects on a reading measure from a program that did not include letter training.)

Other studies more directly tested the effects of alphabet knowledge on phonological awareness. Wagner, Torgesen, and Rashotte (1994), in a longitudinal study of the relations between early reading and reading-related abilities, found that letter-name knowledge appeared to have a causal relationship with phonological processing. Stahl and Murray (1994), using scattergram analysis, found that alphabet knowledge seems necessary for phonological awareness. They found only one child who could successfully recognize and manipulate onsets and rimes but who was unable to recognize at least 45 of 54 letter forms. This finding suggests that knowledge of letter identities may be necessary for phonological awareness, although, of course, not sufficient.

Why might this be? One explanation might be that having a concrete referent, such as a letter, may make it easier to understand an abstract entity such as a phoneme (e.g., Hohn & Ehri, 1993). This could be tested by using another concrete mediator, such as the symbols developed by Calfee, Chapman, and Venezky (1972). Another explanation might be that phonological awareness and alphabet knowledge may both be mediated through exposure to alphabet books. Such books typically include both letter-name information and phonological information about initial sounds (*b* is for *bear*). It may be that children who are read alphabet books, and thus understand how *b* is for *bear*, will learn both letter names and be able to isolate phonemes.

We pursued this second possibility through an experimental study. We gave three treatments to different groups of prekindergarteners, a total of 42 students in three classes. In the first group, the teacher read conventional alphabet books. In the second, the teacher read books chosen to contain the letter names only, without reference to the sound values, such as Martin and Archambault's (1989) *Chicka-Chicka-Boom-Boom*. The third group, a control, read only storybooks. All groups gained in print concepts and letter knowledge over the course of the study. The conventional alphabet group made significantly greater gains in phoneme awareness than did the group that read the letter-name books without sound values, suggesting that conventional alphabet books may be one route to the development of phonological awareness. However, these gains were relatively small in an absolute sense. In addition, the storybook reading class, for reasons we believe were irrelevant to the treatment, also made significant gains in phonological awareness.

This study provides tentative support for the notion that alphabet books can mediate phonological awareness. The notion that *b* is for *bear* or *m* is for *mouse* may require children to construct the concept of phoneme identity, which in turn enables the children to partially segment sounds from spoken words. We suggest, along with Yaden, Smolkin, and MacGillivray (1993), that in order for children to understand *how b* could stand for *bear* they must begin to look at words phonologically. Yaden et al., in an ethnographic study of children's alphabet book reading, found evidence that they went through a period of disequilibrium when listening to alphabet books. This disequilibrium was resolved when they were able to focus on the phonological, rather than semantic, aspects of words.

HOW DOES PHONOLOGICAL AWARENESS RELATE TO READING?

Table 3.1 shows the possible definitions of *phonological awareness, is related to,* and *reading* discussed so far. It is not enough to posit that phonological awareness is related to reading; we must posit which aspect of phonological awareness is related to which aspect of reading in which way.

Our tentative model is shown in Fig. 3.3. Working from data from several of our studies, confirmed by findings of others in the field, we can find some

TABLE 3.1
Possible Relationships Among Terms

Phonological Awareness	Is Related To	Reading
Rhyming	Correlation	Visual cue reading
Partial segmentation	Necessary but not sufficient	Alphabet knowledge
Identity		Phonetic cue reading
Blending		Phonological recoding
Deletion		
Full segmentation		

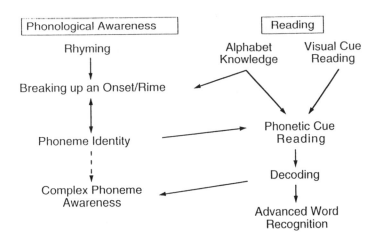

FIG. 3.3. Possible relations among phonological awareness and reading.

probably causal links using the logic of our scattergrams. As noted earlier, alphabet knowledge seems to be related to phoneme identity, possibly through alphabet book reading (Murray, Stahl, & Ivey, 1996). Alphabet knowledge may mediate phoneme identity learning through either the process of confronting *why b* might be for *bear*. Children also may use alphabet letters as concrete mediators for phonemes. Hohn and Ehri (1993) directly compared phonological awareness training with and without simultaneously training subjects on letter names. They found that the letter-name training produced somewhat superior performance on measures of phonological awareness. As noted earlier, Wagner and Rashotte (1993), in a meta-analysis of phonological awareness training studies, found that only those training programs that included some letter or spelling training had a significant effect on children's acquisition of written words. In contrast, Read, Yun-Fei, Hong-Kin, and Bao-Qing (1986) found that literate adult readers of a non-alphabetic language had difficulties with complex phonological awareness tasks. In addition, Morais, Cary, Alegria, and Bertelson (1979) found that illiterate adults could not similarly perform complex phonological awareness tasks. Both sets of researchers suggested that their research emphasizes the key role of an alphabetic language for developing phonological awareness. We suggest that it is the alphabet itself that is responsible for that relation.

The alphabet may also mediate the development of phonological awareness through children's invented spelling. As children move from prephonetic spelling, in which the letters used bear no relation to the sounds in the words (*xgrs* for *giraffe*), to early phonemic spellings, where the children use the initial and sometimes the final consonant sounds to represent the whole word (*b* or *br* for *bear*), they are beginning to analyze the spoken word. Having a letter to represent that sound seems to be the beginning of the establishment of phonemic identity. The relationship between phonological awareness and invented spelling may be reciprocal. Tangel and Blachman (1992) found that a phonological awareness training program improved children's invented spelling as well.

The concept of phoneme identity is closely related to the ability to segment a part of a spoken word, as evidenced by scattergrams in the Murray (1995) study, shown in Fig. 3.1 above. We see the relation between phoneme identity and partial segmentation as more correlational. Conceptually, it makes sense to see these two abilities as covarying; that is, as children learn the identities of more phonemes, they are better able to isolate their sounds in spoken words.

Partial segmentation (as well as alphabet knowledge and other print concepts) seems to underlie the ability to read words. We speculate that partial segmentation is needed for phonetic cue reading, because noticing initial letters in words and connecting those to sounds seems highly similar to segmenting initial sounds in spoken words. In addition, Byrne and Fielding-Barnsley (1989) and Murray (1995) found that phoneme identity seemed to be necessary for phonetic cue reading.

Phoneme awareness also seems to influence fingerpoint reading, another important precursor to the development of word recognition. Ehri and Sweet (1991) found that phoneme awareness, as measured by success on a training task, accounted for a significant amount of variance in fingerpointing to words in a memorized book. When this variable was in the equation, other variables commonly used in early reading studies, such as alphabet knowledge and word recognition, failed to contribute significant amounts of variance.

Phonetic cue reading, in turn, would lead to more advanced knowledge of words, such as the cipher reading discussed by Ehri (1991) and Gough, Juel, and Griffith (1992). This advanced knowledge, in its own turn, would enable children to perform more complex phonological awareness tasks, such as blending, deletion, and full segmentation. A number of researchers—including Beach (1992), Perfetti, Beck, Bell, and Hughes (1987), and Stahl and Murray (1993)—found that the relationship between phoneme awareness and reading is a reciprocal one, with success with simple phoneme awareness tasks, such as segmentation of initial consonants, preceding simple word recognition, but that some recognition of words typically precedes more advanced phonological awareness abilities, such as deletion.

What we have tried to do is to simplify a greatly complex body of literature. To us, the notion of phoneme identity is a crucial one, because it seems to be a bridge between alphabet knowledge and phonological awareness and phonological awareness and early decoding. However, phoneme identity is a relatively new concept. Whether its central role holds up is yet to be determined.

OTHER SPECULATIONS

When we talk to a class of inservice or preservice teachers, we always try to clearly distinguish phonological awareness from phonics. We have not always been successful. Students in our classes, despite our best efforts, still confuse the two constructs. Up until recently, the two seemed to be clearly distinct—phonological awareness had to do with spoken words, phonics with written words. However, the concept of phoneme identity seems to be midway between the notions of phonics and the more mechanical notions of phonological awareness. The evidence for this view is that alphabet knowledge seems to be implicated in the development of phoneme identity. Thus, what we have been calling "phonological awareness" may indeed be something akin to the processes of learning letter–sound relations and using them to decode words. At the least, the distinctions between phonological awareness and phonics may be finer than many think.

Second, if one looks at the factors that we have identified as crucial for the development of phonological awareness (and, through phonological awareness, word recognition), it seems that all of them are ordinarily fostered in a home environment with a literacy press. As Adams (1990) described such a home, it contains not only alphabet books, but magnetic letters on the refrigerator, alphabet blocks, *Sesame Street*, and other media for learning about the alphabet. The children are read to from a variety of storybooks for a significant amount of time each day. Through the modeling of reading and alphabet play, children develop not only alphabet knowledge and phoneme identity knowledge, but also a broader knowledge of the functions and forms of reading and literacy. The presence of so many activities that foster literacy in the stereotypical home with a strong literacy press may suggest why all of these early reading skills are so strongly correlated, and why factor analyses tend to produce single factor solutions.

Stressing the key role of the home, however, begs the question of why some children fail to read in supportive environments. It also begs the question of how to teach children who are significantly behind their peers because of the early lack of phonological awareness (Stahl, 1997b).

The model shown in Fig. 3.3 suggests that all of these basic literacy skills grow together—that they are entwined rather than separate skills that should be taught through targeted programs. Instead, the most desirable way of developing these early literacy skills is through a supportive literacy environment in a home with a strong literacy press (McClain, 1995). Many homes do not provide such a press. Adams (1990) contrasted her reading to her son with parents and children studied by Teale (cited in Adams, 1990). She observed that, by reading to her son for 30 to 45 minutes per day, her child will come to first grade with over a 1,000 hours of literacy experience that children who have not been read to at home will lack. Making up these

1,000 hours becomes a difficult if not insurmountable job for the school. Understanding how key early literacy skills fit together can make early instruction more efficient and help us bridge this yawning gap.

REFERENCES

Adams, M. J. (1990). *Beginning to read: Thinking and learning about print.* Cambridge, MA: MIT. Press.

Adams, M. J., & Huggins, A. W. (1985). The growth of children's sight vocabulary: A quick test with education and theoretical implications. *Reading Research Quarterly, 20*, 262–281.

Beach, S. A. (1992). *Toward a model of the development of reader resources in the emergence and acquisition of literacy skill.* Unpublished doctoral dissertation, University of California at Riverside.

Biemiller, A. (1970). The development of the use of graphic and contextual information as children learn to read. *Reading Research Quarterly, 6*, 75–96.

Bradley, L., & Bryant, P. E. (1983). Categorizing sounds and learning to read—a causal connection. *Nature, 301*, 419–421.

Byrne, B. (1992). Studies in the acquisition procedure for reading: Rationale, hypotheses, and data. In P. B. Gough, L. C. Ehri, & R. Treiman (Eds.), *Reading acquisition.* Hillsdale, NJ: Lawrence Erlbaum Associates.

Byrne, B., & Fielding-Barnsley, R. (1989). Phonemic awareness and letter knowledge in the child's acquisition of the alphabetic principle. *Journal of Educational Psychology, 81*, 313–321.

Byrne, B., & Fielding-Barnsley, R. (1990). Acquiring the alphabetic principle: A case for teaching recognition of phoneme identity. *Journal of Educational Psychology, 82*, 805–812.

Byrne, B., & Fielding-Barnsley, R. (1993). Evaluation of a program to teach phonemic awareness to young children: A 1-year follow-up. *Journal of Educational Psychology, 85*, 104–111.

Calfee, R., Chapman, R., & Venezky, R. (1972). How a child needs to think to learn to read. In L. W. Gregg (Ed.), *Cognition in learning and memory* (pp. 139–182). New York: Wiley.

Chall, J. S. (1996). *Stages of reading development* (2nd ed.). New York: Harcourt Brace.

Ehri, L. C. (1991). Development of the ability to read words. In R. Barr, M. L. Kamil, P. B. Mosenthal, & P. D. Pearson (Eds.), *Handbook of reading research* (Vol. II, pp. 383–417). White Plains, NY: Longman.

Ehri, L. C., & Sweet, J. (1991). Fingerpoint-reading of memorized text: What enables beginners to process the print. *Reading Research Quarterly, 26*, 442–462.

Ehri, L. C., & Wilce, L. S. (1985). Movement into reading: Is the first stage of printed word learning visual or phonetic? *Reading Research Quarterly, 20*, 163–179.

Ehri, L. C., & Wilce, L. S. (1987). Cipher versus cue reading: An experiment in decoding acquisition. *Journal of Educational Psychology, 79*, 3–13.

Fox, B., & Routh, D. K. (1975). Analyzing spoken language into words, syllables, and phonemes: A developmental study. *Journal of Psycholinguistic Research, 4*, 331–342.

Frith, U. (1985). Beneath the surface of developmental dyslexia. In K. E. Patterson, J. C. Marshall, & M. Colheart (Eds.), *Surface dyslexia: Neuropsychological and cognitive studies of phonological reading* (pp. 301–330). Hillsdale, NJ: Lawrence Erlbaum Associates.

Gaskins, I. W., Ehri, L. C., Cress, C., O'Hara, C., & Donnelly, K. (1996). Procedures for word learning: Making discoveries about words. *The Reading Teacher, 50*, 312–328.

Gillet, J. W., & Temple, C. (1990). *Understanding reading problems* (3rd ed.). Glenview, IL: Scott-Foresman.

Goodman, K. S. (1983). A linguistic study of cues and miscues in reading. In L. M. Gentile, M. L. Kamil, & J. S. Blanchard (Eds.), *Reading research revisited* (pp. 187–192). Columbus, OH: Merrill.

Gough, P. B., & Hillinger, M. L. (1980). Learning to read: An unnatural act. *Bulletin of the Orton Society, 30*, 179–196.

Gough, P. B., Juel, C., & Griffith, P. L. (1992). Reading, spelling, and the orthographic cipher. In P. B. Gough, L. C. Ehri, & R. Treiman (Eds.), *Reading acquisition* (pp. 35–48). Hillsdale, NJ: Lawrence Erlbaum Associates.

Hohn, W. E., & Ehri, L. C. (1983). Do alphabet letters help prereaders acquire phonemic segmentation skill? *Journal of Educational Psychology, 75*, 752–762.

Jorm, A. F., & Share, D. L. (1983). Phonological recoding and reading acquisition. *Applied Psycholinguistics, 4*, 103–147.

Kavanaugh, J. F., & Mattingly, I. C. N. (1972). *Language by ear and by eye.* Cambridge, MA: MIT Press.

Lewkowicz, N. K. (1980). Phonemic awareness training: What to teach and how to teach it. *Journal of Educational Psychology, 72*, 686–700.

Liberman, A. M., Cooper, F. S., Shankweiler, D. P., & Studdert-Kennedy, M. (1967). Perception of the speech code. *Psychological Review, 74*, 431–461.

Liberman, I. Y. (1973). Segmentation of the spoken word and reading acquisition. *Bulletin of the Orton Society, 23*, 65–77.

Liberman, I. Y., Shankweiler, D., Fischer, F. W., & Carter, B. (1974). Reading and the awareness of linguistic segments. *Journal of Experimental Child Psychology, 18*, 201–212.

Lomax, R. G., & McGee, L. M. (1987). Young children's concepts about print and reading: Toward a model of reading acquisition. *Reading Research Quarterly, 22*, 237–256.

Lundberg, I., Frost, J., & Peterson, O.-P. (1988). Effects of an extensive program for stimulating phonological awareness in preschool children. *Reading Research Quarterly, 23*, 263–284.

Maclean, M., Bryant, P., & Bradley, L. (1987). Rhymes, nursery rhymes, and reading in early childhood. *Merrill-Palmer Quarterly, 33*, 255–281.

Martin, B., Jr., & Archambault, J. (1989). *Chicka-chicka-boom-boom.* New York: Simon & Schuster.

Masonheimer, P. E., Drum, P. A., & Ehri, L. C. (1984). Does environmental print identification lead children into word reading? *Journal of Reading Behavior, 16*, 257–271.

McClain, V. P. (1997). *Literacy press: How families promote literacy.* Unpublished doctoral dissertation, The University of Georgia, Athens.

McCormick, C. E., & Mason, J. M. (1986). Intervention procedures for increasing preschool children's interest in and knowledge about reading. In W. H. Teale & E. Sulzby (Eds.), *Emergent literacy: Writing and reading* (pp. 90–115). Greenwich, CT: Ablex.

McCutcheon, B. A., & McDowell, E. E. (1969). Intralist similarity and acquisition and generalization of word recognition. *The Reading Teacher, 23*, 103–107.

Morais, J., Cary, L., Alegria, J., & Bertelson, P. (1979). Does awareness of speech as a sequence of phones arise spontaneously? *Cognition, 7*, 323–331.

Murray, B. A. (1995). *Which better defines phoneme awareness: Segmentation skill or identity knowledge?* Unpublished doctoral dissertation, University of Georgia, Athens.

Murray, B. A., Stahl, S. A., & Ivey, M. G. (1996). Developing phoneme awareness through alphabet books. *Reading and Writing: An Interdisciplinary Journal, 8*, 307–322.

Nicholson, T. (1991). Do children read words better in context or in lists: A classic study revisited. *Journal of Educational Psychology, 83*(4), 444–450.

Perfetti, C. A., Beck, I. L., Bell, L., & Hughes, C. (1987). Phonemic knowledge and learning to read are reciprocal: A longitudinal study of first grade children. *Merrill-Palmer Quarterly, 33*, 283–319.

Read, C., Yun-Fei, Z., Hong-Kin, N., & Bao-Qing, D. (1986). The ability to manipulate speech sounds depends on knowing alphabetic writing. *Cognition, 24*, 31–44.

Rosner, J. (1974). Auditory analysis training with prereaders. *The Reading Teacher, 27*, 379–384.

Rosner, J. (1975). *Helping children overcome learning difficulties.* New York: Walker.

Rozin, P., & Gleitman, L. (1977). The structure and acquisition of reading. In A. S. Reber & D. L. Scarborough (Eds.), *Toward a psychology of reading* (pp. 1–76). Hillsdale, NJ: Lawrence Erlbaum Associates.

Savin, H. B. (1972). What the child knows about speech when he starts to learn to read. In J. F. Kavanaugh & I. C. Mattingly (Eds.), *Language by ear and by eye* (pp. 319–326). Cambridge, MA: MIT Press.

Shankweiler, D., & Liberman, I. Y. (1972). Misreading: A search for causes. In J. F. Kavanaugh & I. G. Mattingly (Eds.), *Language by eye and by ear* (pp. 293–317). Cambridge, MA: MIT Press.

Share, D. L. (1995). Phonological recoding and self-teaching: *Sine qua non* of reading acquisition. *Cognition, 55*, 151–218.

Stahl, S. A. (1997a). Models of reading instruction: An introduction. In S. A. Stahl & D. A. Hayes (Eds.), *Instructional models in reading* (pp. 1–29). Hillsdale, NJ: Lawrence Erlbaum Associates.

Stahl, S. A. (1997b). Teaching children with reading problems to recognize words. In L. Putnam (Ed.), *Readings on language and literacy: Essays in honor of Jeanne S. Chall* (pp. 131–154). Cambridge, MA: Brookline Books.

Stahl, S. A., & Murray, B. A. (1993). Environmental print, phonemic awareness, letter recognition, and word recognition. In D. J. Leu & C. K. Kinzer (Eds.), *Examining central issues in literacy research, theory, and practice: Forty-second yearbook of the National Reading Conference* (pp. 227–233). Chicago: National Reading Conference.

Stahl, S. A., & Murray, B. A. (1994). Defining phonological awareness and its relationship to early reading. *Journal of Educational Psychology, 86*, 221–234.

Stanovich, K. E. (1980). Toward an interactive-compensatory model of individual differences in the development of reading fluency. *Reading Research Quarterly, 16*, 32–71.

Tangel, D. M., & Blachman, B. A. (1992). Effect of phoneme awareness instruction on kindergarten children's invented spellings. *Journal of Reading Behavior, 24*, 233–262.

Torgesen, J. K., & Bryant, B. R. (1994). *Test of phonological awareness.* Austin, TX: Pro-Ed.

Treiman, R. (1992). The role of intersyllabic units in learning to read and spell. In P. B. Gough, L. C. Ehri, & R. Treiman (Eds.), *Reading acquisition* (pp. 85–106). Hillsdale, NJ: Lawrence Erlbaum Associates.

Treiman, R. (1985). Onsets and rimes as units of spoken syllables: Evidence from children. *Journal of Experimental Child Psychology, 39*, 161–181.

Wagner, R. K., & Rashotte, C. A. (1993, April). *Does phonological awareness training really work? A meta-analysis.* Paper presented at annual meeting, American Educational Research Association, Atlanta, GA.

Wagner, R. K., Torgesen, J. K., & Rashotte, C. A. (1994). Development of reading-related phonological processing abilities: New evidence of bidirectional causality from a latent variable longitudinal study. *Developmental Psychology, 30*, 73–87.

Yaden, D. B., Smolkin, L. B., & MacGillivray, L. (1993). A psychogenetic perspective on children's understanding about letter associations during alphabet book readers. *Journal of Reading Behavior, 25*, 43–68.

Yopp, H. K. (1988). The validity and reliability of phonemic awareness tests. *Reading Research Quarterly, 23*, 159–177.

4

▼▼▼▼▼▼▼

Spoken Vocabulary Growth and the Segmental Restructuring of Lexical Representations: Precursors to Phonemic Awareness and Early Reading Ability

Jamie L. Metsala
University of Maryland, College Park

Amanda C. Walley
University of Alabama at Birmingham

In this chapter, we present a model of the development of spoken word recognition, the processes involved in matching speech input to lexical patterns stored in memory. Our lexical restructuring model was formulated to account for developmental changes in the structure of spoken word representations and the growth of phonological awareness (see also Metsala, 1997a, 1997b; Walley, 1993b). According to this model, the representations supporting spoken word recognition become increasingly segmental with spoken vocabulary growth, and this change makes possible explicit access to phonemic units. We propose that lexical restructuring is a protracted process that extends into early and even middle childhood. This restructuring is influenced by the words that are known at a given point in time and that must be distinguished from one another for successful recognition. Variations across children in lexical growth and in the restructuring process contribute to individual differences in phonemic awareness, and thus success in learning to read an alphabetic orthography (for a similar position, see Fowler, 1991).

We first outline two theoretical positions on the developmental origins of the phonemic segment, each of which is grounded in research on adult spoken word recognition and infant speech perception. Two models of adult recognition are described, and then we survey studies of infant perception contrasting the earliest inferences drawn from this work concerning the initial status of the phoneme with more recent interpretations. Second, we examine work pointing to the emerging segmental structure of speech representations in late infancy, which has been widely attributed to vocabulary growth; this attribution serves as a primary impetus for our model. Third, we describe the main claims of the model, which is unique in its focus on spoken word recognition in early and middle childhood, and then review empirical findings that support its predictions regarding the protracted emergence of segmental representations. Fourth, we discuss evidence for the proposed link between the emergence of the segment as an implicit, perceptual unit of spoken word representation and processing, and as a more explicit and accessible cognitive unit that can be harnessed for the reading task. Specifically, we consider basic spoken language development and its relation to phonemic awareness, as well as the speech perception difficulties of reading-disabled children. Our overriding goal is to bring together what have often been viewed as separate developmental domains—namely, basic speech processing, phonemic awareness, and early reading. The links across these three domains require further scrutiny, and our model is only a starting point in this endeavor.

THE DEVELOPMENTAL ORIGINS OF THE SEGMENT

A Preformed or Emergent Unit? The Accessibility and Emergent Positions

The empirical relations between phonemic awareness and reading success are now well established. Both children and adults with greater phoneme segmentation and manipulation ability demonstrate superior word reading skill for alphabetic orthographies, which rely on phoneme–letter correspondences. Prereaders and poor readers do not perform very well in phoneme segmentation and manipulation tasks (for a description and analysis of such tasks, and discussion of their relation to early reading, see Stahl & Murray, chap. 3, this volume). Importantly, there are two main theoretical positions regarding the developmental origins of the segment, each of which tends to be associated with a particular stance on the causal relation between phonemic awareness and early reading ability (for elaboration, see Fowler, 1991; Walley, 1993b).

According to the traditional accessibility position, phonemic segments are highly modularized and largely available only for that purpose for which they evolved, namely basic speech processing. Although these units may be present and functional even in infancy, they are not accessible at an explicit, conscious level before reading experience with an alphabetic orthography or with metacognitive development more generally (e.g., Gleitman & Rozin, 1977; Liberman, Shankweiler, & Liberman, 1989; Morais, Cary, Alegria, &

Bertelson, 1979; Rozin, 1976).[1] This position is largely adevelopmental in that the perceptual units that support speech processing are viewed as essentially preformed. Neither phonemic segments nor the lexical structures they comprise undergo any change in their fundamental nature.

Although many reading researchers agree that experience with an alphabetic system enhances phonemic awareness (see, e.g., Ehri, 1984; cf. Morais et al., 1979; Morais, Bertelson, Cary, & Alegria, 1986), some degree or level of phonological awareness is an important precursor to early reading success (e.g., Share & Stanovich, 1995). There has, however, been little attention paid to the development of the phoneme prior to its emergence as a consciously accessible unit that can be deployed for reading purposes. Studies pointing to the stability of reading-related phonological processes from a young age (see Torgesen & Burgess, chap. 7, this volume) make understanding the origins and growth of the segment in the prereading period a priority. Our focus is on developmental research that speaks to this crucial issue, but that has been largely overlooked by those interested in the acquisition of reading-related abilities.

Research on spoken word recognition and speech perception in childhood supports a more recently influential account of the development of the segment, which we refer to as the "emergent" position. According to this position, the phoneme is not an integral, hard-wired aspect of speech representation and processing. Rather, the phoneme emerges with spoken language experience as a result of interactions between vocabulary growth and performance constraints (e.g., Ferguson, 1986; Jusczyk, 1986, 1993; Lindblom, 1992; Lindblom, MacNeilage, & Studdert-Kennedy, 1983; Nittrouer & Studdert-Kennedy, 1987; for additional references, see Walley, 1993b). In an elaboration of this position, we have stressed the gradual, twofold nature of this change. Over the course of early and middle childhood, the phoneme emerges first as an implicit perceptual unit that is used in basic speech processing, and only later as an explicit unit that can be deployed for reading-related activities (Metsala, 1997a; Walley, 1993b; see also Fowler, 1991).

According to this emergent position, phonemic awareness is not "simply" a problem of accessing underlying units of speech representation, but also is limited by the very nature of these representations, which undergo substantial developmental change. Our Lexical Restructuring Model (LRM): emphasizes the impact of continued vocabulary growth on spoken word

---

[1]More specifically, the prereader's difficulty in explicitly attending to phonemes has been attributed to the contextually dependent manner in which these units (more so than syllables, e.g.) are encoded in the speech waveform (e.g., Gleitman & Rozin, 1977; Liberman, Shankweiler, Liberman, Fowler, & Fischer, 1977). However, this same factor may also underlie more fundamental developmental differences in both speech perception and production (e.g., Nittrouer & Studdert-Kennedy, 1987; Nittrouer et al., 1989).

recognition in childhood, and what such growth encompasses; and delineates specific relations that might be expected among basic speech processing, phonemic awareness, and early reading ability. To explicate the emergent position and our model, we turn now to models of adult spoken word recognition and then to studies of infant speech perception.

Models of Adult Spoken Word Recognition

Spoken word recognition is widely regarded as a process by which a given word is perceived in the context of other words in memory, or is discriminated from various lexical alternatives (see Luce, 1986). This theoretical assumption is also central to our model. For now, let us consider how it is realized in two models of adult recognition: the cohort model and the Neighborhood Activation Model (for detailed evaluations of these and other models, see Cutler, 1995; Nygaard & Pisoni, 1995). Both models are concerned specifi-cally with spoken word recognition, which has developmental priority over visual word recognition.

In the cohort model (e.g., Marslen-Wilson, 1987, 1989), the emphasis is on the temporal course of spoken word recognition. There are two core components of recognition: the multiple activation or access of all word candidates that are consistent with word-initial speech input (about the first 100 ms to 150 ms of a word, or one to two phonetic segments), and the selection of a particular candidate through the elimination of competitors that are inconsistent with subsequent input. The model therefore accounts for the fact that adult listeners can recognize words on the basis of partial speech input, before they have heard the entire word (e.g., Grosjean, 1980; cf. Bard, Shillock, & Altmann, 1988).

A more elaborate treatment of the structural organization of the lexicon is provided by the Neighborhood Activation Model (NAM; e.g., Goldinger, Luce, & Pisoni, 1989; Luce, 1986). According to NAM, the speed or accuracy with which a target word is recognized depends on its similarity neighborhood structure, which encompasses the number and degree of confusability of words that overlap, on a segmental basis, with the target, and the frequency of the word and the combined frequency of the word's neighbors.

In both models, recognition involves discrimination among segmentally structured lexical representations that are activated in parallel on the basis of speech input.[2] In the selection component of the cohort model, activated word candidates are also monitored in parallel, such that no cost is incurred for the processing of large versus smaller cohorts. In contrast, in NAM the ease of recognizing a word depends on the number and nature of activated,

---

[2]Although there is considerable evidence that adult's lexical representations are segmentally structured (see Pisoni & Luce, 1987), this view is not uncontroversial (see Walley, 1993b).

and thus competing, words. In support, adult recognition is better for high-frequency words with few neighbors than for low-frequency words with many neighbors (e.g., Goldinger et al., 1989).

These assumptions are useful for conceptualizing how recognition might differ in young versus older listeners and how development might proceed. In particular, children's lexical representations may not, at the outset, have the segmental structure needed to support recognition from partial speech input. However, their lexicons grow rapidly, which might precipitate the implementation of more detailed, segmental units of representation. Yet this restructuring may be gradual, because vocabulary growth continues to be substantial throughout much of childhood. Thus, recognition by children and older listeners should differ for some time. We next examine the extent to which these expectations are supported by infant speech perception studies.

Infant Speech Perception

Much of what we know about the development of speech perception comes from studies of infants (for review, see Aslin, Pisoni, & Jusczyk, 1983; Jusczyk, 1995; Werker, 1991). This focus on infancy can be traced to the seminal study of Eimas, Siqueland, Jusczyk, and Vigorito (1971), who found that 1- to 4-month-old infants discriminated synthetic consonant–vowel stimuli varying in voice-onset time (a speech cue that signals, e.g., the difference between *bat* and *pat*) in a categorical and thus adultlike manner. That is, infants discriminated stimuli from different phonemic categories (/b/ vs. /p/), but not stimuli from within the same category. Because categorical perception was widely considered to uniquely characterize human perception of speech, these data were interpreted as indicating that phonemic segments and/or their associated features are specified innately, or constitute part of our biological makeup for speech processing.

The finding that young infants discriminate stimuli differing by a single phonemic segment was subsequently extended to a variety of other contrasts (see Aslin et al., 1983; Jusczyk, 1995; Werker, 1991). However, two other results quickly called into question the view that this early capacity is species- and speech-specific. First, similarities were observed in the perception of speech by humans and nonhumans (e.g., Burdick & Miller, 1975; Kuhl & Padden, 1982). Second, similarities in the perception of nonspeech patterns by adults and infants were found (e.g., Jusczyk, Pisoni, Walley, & Murray, 1980; Pisoni, Carrell, & Gans, 1983). These results suggested that basic speech processing is mediated by general auditory, as opposed to speech-specific mechanisms. However, as Miller and Eimas (1994) noted, there are problems in choosing between these theoretical alternatives: Cross-species parallels in perception do not necessarily imply the same underlying mechanism, and a modularized speech processor might be "fooled" by sufficiently complex nonspeech stimuli (cf. Fowler, 1995).

Still, other observations cannot be readily accommodated within the "speech is special" framework. Although young infants can discriminate a wide variety of speech contrasts, older infants do not always perform so impressively even for their native language, and perception may not approach adultlike levels until middle childhood or beyond (e.g., Flege, & Eefting, 1986; Nittrouer & Studdert-Kennedy, 1987; Walley, Flege, & Randazza, 1998). This discrepancy has been attributed in part to the different tasks used to assess perception across age levels (e.g., Jusczyk, 1992; Studdert-Kennedy, 1986). Those paradigms used to assess infant perception have, for the most part, yielded only discrimination data, which are not sufficient to support the claim that speech is perceived at a linguistic as opposed to a more general auditory level. Most important, discrimination could be mediated by holistic processes, and not by the detection of localized, segmental differences.

In fact, there is little positive evidence that infants' speech representations are, at the outset, structured in terms of segments. In a series of experiments addressing this issue, Jusczyk and colleagues (see Jusczyk, 1992, 1993) showed that young infants are sensitive to the presence of a common syllable, but not a common phoneme in sets of stimuli. In addition, the results of several studies (see Cooper & Aslin, 1989; Jusczyk, 1995) suggest that pro- sodic information, which is distributed globally throughout the speech wave- form, is more likely to capture infants' attention than segmental information. For example, soon after birth, infants prefer to listen to child-directed speech or "Motherese," in which prosodic features (such as intonation contour, stress, and pauses) are typically exaggerated, rather than to adult-directed speech (e.g., Cooper & Aslin, 1990; Pegg, Werker, & McLeod, 1992). New- borns also distinguish between passages spoken in their native language versus a foreign one, even when the passages are low-pass filtered, and their segmental content thus largely removed (Bertoncini, Bijeljac-Babic, Jusczyk, Kennedy, & Mehner, 1988). Such early sensitivity to prosodic information may provide infants with a starting point for parsing the stream of speech around them into increasingly smaller and linguistically relevant units, such as clauses, phrases and words (e.g., Hirsh-Pasek et al., 1987; Jusczyk & Aslin, 1995; Jusczyk et al., 1992). The word may, in turn, serve as a crucial point of entry to the segmental level of the native language. When and how, more precisely, do infants gain such entry?

Cross-linguistic studies of infant perception help to provide an answer. These studies suggest that infants from a given language community can initially discriminate a wide range of both native and nonnative contrasts. However, sensitivity to the latter generally wanes over the second 6 months of life—at around the same time that infants are becoming more sensitive to native language sound properties. For example, Werker and Tees (1984) tested infants from Canadian-English speaking homes aged 6 to 8 months, 8 to 10 months, and 10 to 12 months. Although the youngest infants discriminated English, Hindi, and Nthlakampx consonantal contrasts, only some of the infants from the middle age group discriminated the foreign contrasts, and those from the oldest group discriminated the English contrast only. In addition, 9-month-old American and Dutch infants prefer to listen to lists of words from their native language, whereas 6-month-olds do not; however, when the words are low-pass filtered, leaving only prosodic information that is similar for English and Dutch, older infants exhibit no preference, suggesting that they are beginning to focus on the individual sound segments comprising the utterances (Jusczyk, Friederici, Wessels, Svenkerund, & Jusczyk, 1993). More recently, Jusczyk, Luce, and Charles-Luce (1994) showed that, by 9 months of age, infants are sensitive to language-specific phonotactic sequences, including their frequency distribution.

Such enhanced sensitivity to native language contrasts has been attributed by many to the onset of early word learning, when sounds first become interfaced with meaning (but see, e.g., Kuhl, Williams, Lacerda, Stevens, & Lindblom, 1992). This interfacing is, for example, central to Jusczyk's (1992, 1993) model of word recognition and phonetic structure acquisition (WRAPSA). According to WRAPSA, general auditory analyzers first yield a detailed but transient description of an incoming acoustic signal, and it is this analysis that mediates infants', adults', and nonhumans' basic perception (e.g., discrimination) of various speech and nonspeech patterns. However, crucial to the attainment of word recognition ability is the development of an interpretive scheme, which debuts around 9 to 12 months of age. This interpretive scheme provides a more selective and enduring representation of the speech signal (in the form of syllables, for much of childhood) by weighting information from the preliminary auditory analyzers, such that features critical for signaling meaningful distinctions are given prominence, and those that are irrelevant are rendered less discriminable. Thus, the infant begins to learn that *bat* means something different than *pat*, but that physically different renditions of *bat* are equivalent. Not only does this model account for infants' and adults' perception of native and nonnative speech patterns, it also speaks to other requisite (e.g., memory-related) abilities for word recognition (cf. Kuhl, 1993). More generally, this model attempts to explain how infants' perceptual abilities are relevant to later language learning. As yet there is, however, little empirical evidence directly linking attentional shifts in speech perception to vocabulary development. In particular, such shifts have not, within a given infant or group of infants, been tied to "recognitory comprehension," or the ability to make a correct behavioral response to a spoken word without extralinguistic, contextual support (e.g., Thomas, Campos, Shucard, Ramsay, & Shucard, 1981). For example, would 9- to 12-month-olds be more likely to respond correctly when told to "Look at the dog!" by various native, as opposed to nonnative, English speakers?

In summary, some researchers have begun to reevaluate the status of the segment as an early perceptual unit, and there has been a growing consensus that phonetic/phonemic segments are emergent units of speech perception (see Studdert-Kennedy, 1993; Walley, 1993a). Yet, the related issues of what constitute the primary structural units of infant perception, the extent to which these are speech-specific, and whether their development proceeds in an active or passive manner have not been resolved. Fortunately, there is additional evidence from studies of toddlers' first word representations, as well as from another, until recently neglected area—namely, phonetic perception and spoken word recognition in childhood—that supports the emergent position, and the claims of our LRM more specifically.

EARLY WORD REPRESENTATIONS

The first lexical representations of the older infant/toddler (about 9–12 months to 18 months of age) may be holistic or undifferentiated in that there is little intraword differentiation and interword organization. Because the child's vocabulary is still very small, there would be little need to represent words in any systematic and detailed manner (e.g., as sequentially arrayed phonemic segments). Instead, words might be represented and recognized on the basis of individual salient characteristics or their overall acoustic shape or prosodic structure (e.g., Jusczyk, 1986; Menyuk & Menn, 1979). Representations might also be holistic because the child is in the process of establishing a lexical base. This is a multifaceted task that includes segmenting words from continuous speech, noting correspondences between recurring speech patterns and non-linguistic events, discovering the relevant nonphonological (e.g., semantic and syntactic) features of words, translating sound sequences into articulatory sequences that can be used in production, and so on (e.g., Menyuk & Menn, 1979). All this must be accomplished in addition to any momentary recognition task—matching an input speech pattern to representations already in memory. Systematic and detailed segmental matching may therefore exceed the child's attentional and/or memory capacity, such that words are instead stored and retrieved as unanalyzed wholes.

These expectations are consistent with the emergent view of the development of the phoneme in that segmental information is not, at the outset, used at the level of perceptual representations that are accessible in real time and relevant to word recognition (see Aslin & Smith, 1988). However, the empirical evidence for the holistic nature of early word recognition is not extensive or direct; rather, it derives from a limited number of perceptual studies in late infancy and toddlerhood, and from studies of early word productions.

Perception

Only a few studies have assessed speech perception in late infancy and toddlerhood—as the child gains entry to the native language proper and begins to show signs of comprehending words. Although the lower limit on this ability is often placed at 9 months, based largely on observational work (e.g., Benedict, 1979; Huttenlocher, 1984), experimental studies of recognitory comprehension yield a more conservative estimate (for discussion, see Walley, 1993b); for example, Thomas et al. (1981) found that 13-month-olds, but not 11-month-olds, looked longer at the referents of words that were familiar, according to maternal report, than they did at the referents of unfamiliar words. In studies concerned with phonetic perception, objects, such as blocks with faces on them, are assigned nonsense names, pairs of which differ only in their initial consonant (e.g., "bak" vs. "mak") and children are asked to point to one of the objects. Under these conditions, they have difficulty perceiving single phoneme differences. For example, Shvachkin (1973) reported that 18-month-old Russian children could correctly distinguish a "bak" from a "zub" or a "mak" from a "zub," but not a "bak" from a "mak." Similar results have been reported for 17- to 22-month-old American children (Garnica, 1973) and even for 3-year-olds (Edwards, 1974). More recently, Werker and Baldwin (see Werker & Pegg, 1992) found that 19-month-olds, but not younger children, look longer at a pictured object when presented with a matching a test word (e.g., *dog*), as opposed to a minimal pair nonword, a phonetically dissimilar nonword, or a phonetically dissimilar real word (e.g., *bog*, *luf*, or *car*).[3] Thus, older infants and toddlers show the beginnings of access to segmental information for highly familiar words, but this ability is certainly not fully developed.

Production

The speech perception data suggest that phonemes, as linguistic units that distinguish sound patterns in terms of their meaning, are less salient for older infants and toddlers than they are for adults. This difference is mirrored in early speech productions, which have proved more tractable for study (albeit primarily through observational, rather than experimental methods; but see, e.g., Gerken, 1994). In the production literature, there is a more long-standing consensus that segments do not serve as early units of speech representation, and that children's first lexical representations are holistic in nature (see Ferguson, 1986; Studdert-Kennedy, 1986; Suomi, 1993; Walley, 1993b; for models relating the development of production and perception, see Menn & Matthei, 1992; Suomi, 1993; Vihman, 1993).

On the one hand, the first 50-word stage of production (beginning anywhere from 9 to 18 months of age) is characterized by little phonetic vari-

---

[3]This study employed a single picture presentation format, rather than the four-alternative format used by Thomas et al. (1981); however, the phonetic similarity of targets and foils was not systematically varied in the earlier study—a difference that could account for the discrepancy in the age estimates obtained.

ability or "mobility," such that some words seem "fixed" (Bloch, 1913, cited in Ingram, 1979). Some pronunciations are quite accurate, and more advanced than later ones; others persist in falling short of the rest of the child's productions (sometimes referred to in the literature as progressive and regressive "phonological idioms," respectively). On the other hand, some early words are highly variable in form. A classic example is that of K, who offered 10 different renditions of *pen* within one half-hour (Ferguson & Farwell, 1975); another is Jennika, who produced three phonological variants of *blanket* on the same day (Ingram, 1979). Thus, there is considerable interword and intraword variability in the child's early speech, and phonemes do not seem to exist initially as functional, commutable, and "crystallized" elements in his or her phonological repertoire (e.g., Studdert-Kennedy, 1986). Rather, "There is some word-by-word learning to pronounce . . . in which the whole word is an indivisible target" (Menyuk & Menn, 1979, p. 63).

According to many researchers then, it is the word, not the phoneme, that serves as the basic unit of early phonological contrast—a position perhaps most evident in Ferguson's work (e.g., Ferguson, 1986). The word is primary because it is the simplest nonprosodic unit with which the child can accomplish communicative intent; it represents the first major interface between sound and meaning in development (Studdert-Kennedy, 1986), as well as in online spoken language processing (e.g., Marslen-Wilson, 1987). Some place greater emphasis on the initial importance of larger units, such as intonational phrases (e.g., Moskowitz, 1973; Peters, 1983), whereas others stress the role of the syllable (e.g., Jusczyk, 1993; Menyuk & Menn, 1979); indeed, there may be individual as well as cross-language differences in reliance on different processing units (Cutler, Mehler, Norris, & Segui, 1989; Menyuk & Menn, 1979). Nevertheless, there is general agreement that development entails the increasing differentiation of speech representations, such that "Smaller units (syllables, clusters, segments) become more definitely located within [larger ones, such as the] word" (Ferguson, 1986, p. 50). Ferguson emphasized that this discovery or construction of a phonological system by the child does not center around the phoneme, but proceeds gradually via "lexical diffusion," or in a word-dependent manner (cf. Jakobson, 1968).

The Vocabulary Growth Spurt
and the Beginnings of Segments

Although early phonological development has been characterized as a period in which lexical representations of a holistic nature predominate, one major event that may prompt a change in the nature of these representations is the vocabulary growth spurt, or naming explosion. Whereas the child's first 50 words or so are acquired slowly and one at a time, after this point (i.e., from about 18 months to 3 years of age), many children show a large and sudden increase in the number of words they can produce and comprehend (see Reznick & Goldfield, 1992). As a growing number of words overlap in their acoustic properties, there should be considerable pressure to implement more fine-grained (e.g., segmental) representations. Such representations would facilitate fast and accurate discrimination of a growing base of lexical alternatives (e.g., Charles-Luce & Luce, 1990; Jusczyk, 1986; Walley, 1993b), and support more efficient articulation (e.g., Lindblom, 1992; Menn, 1983; Studdert-Kennedy, 1986).

With respect to how lexical restructuring proceeds, Jusczyk (1986, 1993) proposed that a word recognition network might first be organized around the spectral onset characteristics of syllables, such that words with similar onsets are located close to one another. This organization, which mirrors the temporal structure of input patterns and capitalizes on the saliency and robustness of word-initial information, would narrow the set of items to be searched and enhance the speed and accuracy of recognition. According to Jusczyk, the development of segmental representations might go forward in a similar manner, but perhaps only later when learning to read, especially as unfamiliar words are encountered (see also Ferguson, 1986; Peters, 1983; Vihman, 1981). Yet greater detail about similar syllables might have to be represented earlier.

Locke (1988) suggested that beginning with the vocabulary growth spurt, children are increasingly likely to encounter minimal pairs of words (e.g., *cat* and *hat*) and thus to realize that some words differ in only one part. In support, there is a high degree of synchrony in the number of different initial consonants and the number of words produced by 2-year-olds (Stoel-Gammon, 1991). There is also the early-occurring phenomenon of homonymy, or the use of a single sound pattern to produce two or more phonologically similar words (e.g., [aš] for *cheese, sausage, sock,* and *slipper*; Vihman, 1981). According to Ingram (1985), however, homonymy eventually declines because of increases in phonetic inventory size, which, in turn, are the result of vocabulary increases.[4] As Schwartz (1988; see also Studdert-Kennedy, 1987) proposed:

> [Such] word associations may enable the child to recognize similarities and ultimately differences between the phonetic forms for different words both in perception and in production. This may allow the child to form categories of word structures and perhaps facilitate the extraction of segments or features that are shared by certain words and differentiate others. . . . [That is, eventually] the child must progress to a point of extracting smaller units. [Homonymy] may be one of the ways in which this progression occurs. (p. 216)

---

[4]The emergence of segments would also promote further vocabulary growth, in that a limited pool of highly productive elements with recombinatorial power would support more efficient storage of lexical items in memory (e.g., Lindblom, 1992).

We concur with the increasingly influential notion that vocabulary growth serves as an important mechanism for prompting the differentiation of lexical representations and enhancing the discriminative power of the recognition process. More generally, there is a trend from wholes to parts that can be found across many areas of perceptual-cognitive development (see Aslin & Smith, 1988). However, our LRM focuses on spoken word recognition beyond late infancy and toddlerhood. In addition, it is concerned with how the increasingly segmental nature of representations provides the foundations for explicit segmentation ability and thus early reading success (see also Fowler, 1991).

LATER WORD REPRESENTATIONS

The Lexical Restructuring Model

The first claim of our LRM is that young children recognize words in a more holistic manner than do older children and adults, due to both the continued segmental restructuring of lexical representations and processing limitations that arise from the demands of a rapidly growing vocabulary. Therefore, despite similarities in basic phonetic perception by infants and adults, these should be differences in young children's and adults' performance for tasks that more closely resemble word recognition.

Although the emergence of segments may have sudden beginnings or be precipitated by the vocabulary growth spurt, the segmental restructuring of lexical representations may be quite gradual, extending into early and middle childhood (Fowler, 1991; Walley, 1993b). The central reason for such protracted restructuring, according to our model, is that there is still substantial spoken vocabulary growth after age 3 (the upper limit on the growth spurt) and prior to extensive reading and writing experience. That is, there are changes in the absolute size of children's lexicons, and the rate of vocabulary increase is still quite dramatic over the preschool and early elementary school years. Anglin (1989), for example, estimated that 4-year-old preschoolers know 2,500–3,000 words, first graders know 7,000–10,000 words, and fifth graders know 39,000–46,000 words. In addition, there are increases in the familiarity status of individual words and changes in the organizational structure among words based on their sound-similarity relations or segmental overlap.

The advantages of more segmental, adultlike representations, such as the ability to recognize words from partial speech input, may not be immediately apparent after lexical restructuring. Early decisions based on segmental processing of speech input may tax children's attention and memory resources and cause recognition errors when new words are presented. Thus, children may continue to rely on holistic processing, or pay greater attention to information distributed throughout the speech input, until vocabulary knowledge becomes more stable.

The second claim of our model is that lexical restructuring does not occur in an all-or-none manner, or on a systemwide basis, but rather is gradual and word-specific, depending on such factors as overall vocabulary size or rate of expansion, as well as the familiarity status and sound-similarity relations among individual words in the child's lexicon.

A growing vocabulary necessitates recognition among words of increasing similarity in their phonological structure. In the adult word recognition literature, "neighborhood density" has typically been defined in terms of the number of words in the lexicon that differ from a given target word by a one-phoneme substitution, deletion, or addition (Logan, 1992; Luce, 1986). Words with many similar-sounding neighbors reside in "dense" neighborhoods. Thus, recognizing the word *big* will require a more fine-grained representation for a child who also knows the words *bag, bug, bib, bit, dig*, and *wig,* than for a child who does not. Some words do not have many similar-sounding neighbors, even in the adult lexicon (e.g., *girl*); these words reside in "sparse" neighborhoods. According to our model, words residing in dense neighborhoods will need to be segmentally represented earlier in development than will words from sparse neighborhoods. As new words enter the lexicon, they must be analyzed for their phonological structure and cross-referenced with existing representations to facilitate efficient storage and online recognition. Thus, children's performance on word recognition tasks should be better (i.e., most adultlike) for words in dense neighborhoods, and developmental differences greatest for words in sparse neighborhoods.

Another important factor in our model is the familiarity status of individual words. Word familiarity depends on at least two factors: experienced frequency and age of acquisition (AOA). Experienced frequency and AOA are correlated, but not identical. For example, *cartoon,* is acquired early by most children, but is not necessarily heard often relative to many other words; *cartilage,* on the other hand, is learned later by most people, but could be heard frequently by some (e.g., medical students). In the adult literature, it has been suggested that early-acquired words have more robust or detailed representations than later-acquired ones (e.g., Brown & Watson, 1987), and recent research indicates that AOA, when unconfounded with word frequency, may have a greater influence on recognition performance (e.g., Morrison & Ellis, 1995; but see Garlock, Walley, Randazza, & Metsala, 1998). To date, however, there has been little developmental research examining the relative impact of these two dimensions of word familiarity on recognition. Therefore, in our model, words that are acquired at a young age, as well as words that are heard frequently, are assumed to undergo more extensive segmental restructuring and to be recognized better by childrcn (in a more adultlike manner) than are later-acquired or infrequently encountered words.

The third claim of our model is that the gradual segmental restructuring of lexical representations plays a primary role in the development of explicit segmentation ability (i.e., phonemic awareness). That is, the phoneme emerges first at an implicit level for the perceptual representation and processing of spoken words, and thus only later as a cognitive unit that can be consciously accessed and manipulated. According to this claim then, implicit and explicit segmentation ability should follow similar developmental trends, with the latter delayed relative to the former. Furthermore, because word characteristics, such as familiarity and neighborhood density, are the causal mechanisms underlying restructuring of lexical representations, we might expect to observe a relation in performance across implicit and explicit tasks for specific items (e.g., better performance in both recognition and awareness tasks for high-frequency words with many neighbors than for low-frequency word with few neighbors).

The fourth claim of our model is that deficits in lexical restructuring play a causal role in reading-disabled children's difficulties with phonological processing, phonemic awareness, and reading ability. If lexical representations do not become segmentalized in a developmentally appropriate manner or time frame, children should be unable to access phonemes and to learn the relation between phonemes and graphemes (i.e., decipher the alphabetic code). Therefore, our model offers a developmental framework for understanding the pervasive phonological processing deficits observed in individuals with reading disabilities. Reading-disabled children should show particular deficits for unfamiliar words or words with few similar sounding neighbors, and their performance on spoken word recognition tasks should resemble that of younger children with similar vocabulary knowledge and lexical representations. To what extent are these claims of our model supported by the existing empirical data?

Empirical Evidence for Gradual Lexical Restructuring

Phonetic Perception in Childhood

Studies of phonetic perception by children support the first claim of our model that speech/lexical representations are initially holistic and only gradually become segmentally structured during early and middle childhood. Despite the impressive discrimination capacities of infants, a number of studies have indicated that phonetic perception remains incomplete or nonadultlike for several years (for review, see Barton, 1980). For example, children aged 2 years, 11 months to 3 years, 5 months were asked to discriminate the pairs *rake/lake*, *wake/rake*, and *wake/bake* using either recorded, synthetically produced, or live stimuli (Strange & Broen, 1981). All of the children performed above chance on all three contrasts in at least one of the stimulus conditions. Nevertheless, even in this highly constrained testing situation, there was a high degree of variability among subjects. Along similar lines, Zlatin and Koenigsknecht (1976) examined discrimination of voiced and voiceless stop consonants. Two-year-olds required a greater difference for successful discrimination than did 6-year-olds or adults. Even 6-year-olds required a greater difference than did adults when the voiced/voiceless discrimination involved a velar pair (e.g., *goat/coat*).

More recently, Nittrouer and Studdert-Kennedy (1987) showed that 3- to 5-year-olds were less sensitive than were 7-year-olds and adults to frequency information in fricative noise when identifying stimuli along an /s–š/ continuum. Identification functions were also shallower for children when compared to adults, indicating that their phoneme categories are less well defined (see also Burnham, Earnshaw, & Clark, 1991; Walley et al., 1998). A follow-up study revealed that 5-year-olds' productions were more affected than were 7-year-olds' and adults' by vocalic context, or coarticulated information distributed across the speech waveform (Nittrouer, Studdert-Kennedy, & McGowan, 1989). Moreover, studies with disyllabic stimuli indicate that children under the age of 7 years may attempt to extract syllables rather than phonetic segments from the speech stream (Nittrouer, 1992). In some cases, phonetic development may not be complete until young adulthood. Flege and Eefting (1986) showed that the /da/-/ta/ boundary occurred at a longer mean voice-onset time (VOT) value in both English-and Spanish-speaking adults when compared to their 9-year-old counterparts. These boundary differences were still observed when English-speaking adults were compared with 11-, 13-, and 17-year-olds.

Spoken Word Recognition in Childhood

Studies of the development of spoken word recognition support the first and second claims of LRM—namely, that recognition shifts gradually through middle childhood from being based on holistic to segmental processes, and that this shift is a result of changes in the characteristics of individual words, such as familiarity and neighborhood density. Next we highlight supporting results from three tasks that have been used to study speech representation and spoken word recognition in children.

Similarity Judgments. Similarity judgments are obtained from classification tasks in which subjects are typically given triads of speech stimuli and asked to select the pair that best goes together, and provide some indication of what speech information is most salient to listeners. Treiman and Baron (1981) employed this sort of task with kindergartners, first graders, and adults and presented triads such as /bI/, /ve/, and /bo/. Adults made more common phoneme classifications (e.g., judged /bI/ and /bo/ as most similar), whereas children made more global similarity classifications (e.g., judged /bI/ and /ve/ as similar), even when they were specifically reinforced for making common phoneme classifications. These findings were extended by Treiman and Breaux (1982) to three-phoneme syllables (e.g., /bIs/, /diz/, /bun/) in both training and memory procedures. In the first experiment, similarity training was more effective for preschoolers when compared to phoneme training. Phoneme training was more effective for adults. In a second experiment, subjects were taught the three syllables as the names of three animals. When tested immediately after the training phase, children were more likely to confuse syllables that were globally similar. Adults were more likely to confuse syllables that shared a phoneme (see also Walley, Smith, & Jusczyk, 1986).

More recently, Byrne and Fielding-Barnsley (1993) showed that similarity effects may underlie children's apparent recognition of phoneme relations. For example, when children are asked whether *bowl* or *shed* begins with the same sound as *beak*, children sometimes give the adultlike answer *bowl*. However, *beak* and *bowl* not only share a common initial phoneme, they are also more globally similar than are *beak* and *shed*. To address the confounding of these variables, two versions of this phoneme identity task were developed. In the first version, common phoneme relations and overall similarity relations were purposely confounded such that the words which shared a common phoneme were also more similar on global ratings (e.g., *beak, bowl, shed*). In the second version, one of the test words again shared a common phoneme with the target, but the foil was more globally similar (e.g., *beak, bowl, dig*). Kindergartners performed better when phoneme identity was confounded with global similarity, suggesting that children do base their judgments on overall acoustic characteristics. Byrne and Fielding-Barnsley also showed that performance on the unconfounded version of this task was more strongly related to pseudoword reading and spelling ability than was performance on the confounded version. Thus, phonemes are not very salient to young children, but children's growing sensitivity to this unit is important to later reading ability.

Mispronunciation Detection.   Mispronunciation detection tasks involve presenting listeners with intact and mispronouced words in stories, sentences, or in isolation and asking them to detect which words are mispronounced. Adults detect mispronunciations in word-initial position more accurately but more slowly than noninitial mispronunciations (e.g., Cole & Perfetti, 1980; Walley & Metsala, 1990). This pattern of performance has been interpreted as indicating that adults pay particular attention to the first one or two phonemic segments in a word during recognition and lexical access; less attention is paid to the middles and ends of words, because the identity of segments in these positions is highly constrained by word-initial information (for additional references, see Marslen-Wilson, 1989; Walley, 1993b).

According to our model, however, lexical representation and processing are more holistic in nature for young children versus older children and adults. This is primarily because overall vocabulary growth in early through middle childhood is still substantial, and the familiarity and neighborhood similarity relations among individual words in the young child's lexicon are very dynamic. Therefore, word beginnings are not very predictive and young children must pay more attention to information throughout a word in order to identify it.

In support, children's mispronunciation identifications are less influenced by the position in a word of an error than adult's performance, especially when words are presented in isolation (e.g., Cole & Perfetti, 1980; Walley, 1987; Walley & Metsala, 1990). Walley (1987), for example, assessed mispronunciation detection for isolated words presented either with or without a picture referent. When pictures were present, 5-year-olds showed greater sensitivity to word-initial than word-final mispronunciations, and greater sensitivity to word-initial mispronunciations than did 4-year-olds. No position effect was observed for 5-year-olds in the no-picture condition or for 4-year-olds in either condition (i.e., when lexical constraints were weaker). In a perceptual judgment task, Walley (1988) presented 5-year-olds and adults with isolated words in which white noise either replaced or was added to phonemes in the initial, medial, or final syllables. Adults rated words with either noise replacing or added to initial phonemes more poorly than words with noninitial disruptions, whereas children's ratings were not influenced by the positional manipulation and were higher than adults' for words with initial disruptions.

More recently, we examined children's and adults' detection of errors in words varying in age-of-acquisition or AOA (Walley & Metsala, 1990; see also Walley & Metsala, 1992). We used adults' subjective estimates of AOA to select our stimuli, because previous research indicated that these estimates are reliable and valid. For example, when adults estimate that a word is learned at age 3, then 3-year-olds can correctly select a corresponding picture. We divided our stimuli into three AOA categories—"early," "current," and "late" vis-à-vis the age of our youngest, 5-year-old subjects (e.g., *policeman, propeller,* and *pavilion*). All words were of low frequency according to adult objective counts and were matched across AOA categories in terms of various structural characteristics (e.g., initial consonant); a similar mispronunciation was then constructed for items across AOA categories (e.g., /t/ for /p/ in the words mentioned previously).

Our subjects heard both mispronounced and intact versions of each word and indicated whether a given stimulus was said "right" or "wrong" by pointing to either a happy or a sad face. We found that 5- and 8-year-olds were as sensitive (as indexed by d') to errors in early words as were adults. Eight-year-olds were as sensitive as adults to errors in current words, whereas 5-year-olds were less able to discriminate the mispronounced and intact versions of current and late words. Each of the age comparisons was significant for the late words. These findings indicate that recognition for young children varies as a function of word familiarity, with performance being most adultlike for early-acquired words.

Gating Paradigm. In the gating paradigm, listeners are presented with increasing amounts of speech input from word onset and asked to identify the target word after each "gated" trial. For example, the listener may hear the initial 100 msec of the word on the first trial, then the initial 150 msec, 200 msec, and so on for subsequent trials, until all of the word has been presented. Adults can identify many words on the basis of partial input, and recognize high-frequency words and words in context on the basis of less input than low-frequency words or words without context (Grosjean, 1980). In fact, high-frequency, one-syllable words in sentences can be recognized from as little as 150 msec of input, or less than half the speech signal corresponding to the entire word.

Several developmental studies employing this paradigm have shown that children aged 5 to 7 years need more speech input than do adult listeners to correctly recognize words (e.g., Elliott, Hammer, & Evan, 1987; Walley, 1988; Walley, Michela, & Wood, 1995). This age effect is found even for one-syllable words that are highly familiar to young children (Elliott et al., 1987). However, these are systematic improvements in recognition performance during childhood, presumably as a result of increases in vocabulary knowledge; thus, although first graders need more input than adults to recognize gated words, they need less input than kindergarteners (Walley et al., 1995).

More recently, Metsala (1997a) examined word recognition by 7-, 9-, 11-year-olds, and adults using the gating task as a function of word frequency and neighborhood density. Overall, the amount of speech input needed to recognize the test words decreased systematically with age. Of more interest however, age interacted with lexical characteristics. Specifically, the two youngest age groups needed more speech input to recognize low-frequency words and words from sparse neighborhoods than did the oldest group of children and adults. For high-frequency words from sparse neighborhoods, 7-year-olds needed more speech input than did 11-year-olds, and all three child groups needed more input than did the adults. There were no developmental differences in the recognition of high-frequency words from dense neighborhoods.

These findings support the first two claims of our model. First, changes in spoken word recognition continue into early childhood and are related to an individual word's frequency and neighborhood structure. Even the youngest group of children recognized high-frequency words in dense neighborhoods on the basis of as little speech input as adults. Second, the observed frequency by neighborhood density interaction across age groups suggests that word frequency and neighborhood structure underlie or prompt segmental restructuring and processing of a lexical item. Specifically, high-frequency words are segmentally represented/processed and therefore recognized on the basis of minimal speech input, except when there are many online competitors (i.e., in dense neighborhoods). On the other hand, low-frequency words can be recognized on the basis of little input only if they reside in a dense neighborhood. Presumably these words have experienced pressure to undergo segmental restructuring to a greater extent or earlier than low-frequency words with few neighbors.

Previous adult studies have been inconsistent with respect to the effect of neighborhood density. In naming latency tasks, Luce (1986) found an advantage for all words in sparse versus dense neighborhoods (see also Goldinger, Luce, & Pisoni, 1989). According to his Neighborhood Activation Model, words from sparse neighborhoods have the least online competition and should therefore be easiest to recognize. This main effect of neighborhood density is inconsistent with Metsala's (1997a) observed frequency by neighborhood density interaction. This interaction has, however, also been observed in adults' lexical decision performance (Luce, 1986) and in studies of visual word naming (e.g., Andrews, 1992; Seidenberg & McClelland, 1989). The effects of these two factors on children's spoken word recognition needs further examination (see Garlock et al., 1998).

Taken together, the developmental research suggests that even though children begin to be sensitive to segmental information with the onset of the vocabulary growth spurt, segmental restructuring continues into middle childhood and processing of spoken words remains relatively holistic into the early school years. This more holistic processing occurs despite the fact that the point at which a given word can be structurally differentiated from others on a left-to-right, segmental basis occurs earlier in the smaller lexicons of young children. In a study by Charles-Luce and Luce (1990), 5- and 7-year-olds' production lexicons were found to consist predominantly of short, high-frequency words, the recognition of which might well be accomplished by global, as opposed to more segmental and thus capacity-demanding processing (cf. Dollaghan, 1994; Logan, 1992). However, the perceptual evidence we have reviewed indicates that by about 4 or 5 years of age, children are not completely unable to use partial speech input and do not need to hear all of a word in order to recognize it (consistent with an emerging ability to use segments or "chunks" of segments). In support of vocabulary expansion as the basis for a shift from global to more segmentally based processing, Charles-Luce and Luce found that as the size of the lexicon increases, so too does the number of similar neighbors that a given word has. There is, in turn, a trend toward denser similarity neighborhoods that goes hand in hand with developmental increases in the ability to organize and attend to the segmental and temporal properties of words.

THE LINKS BETWEEN LEXICAL RESTRUCTURING, PHONEMIC AWARENESS, AND READING ABILITY

The third claim of our LRM is that explicit segmentation ability depends on the emerging segmental structure of lexical representations. That is, phonemic awareness is limited by the very nature of the phonological representations being accessed and manipulated; if representations are not adequately segmented, it should not be possible for children to perform cognitive operations on individual phonemes. We therefore predict a close relationship between changing lexical representations and phonemic awareness, with the latter delayed relative to the former. As well, beginning phonemic awareness should depend on language development specifically, rather than on general metacognitive ability or reading experience.

The fourth claim of our model is that the phonological deficits in reading disabilities are due, in part, to atypical development in lexical restructuring. Next, we discuss the empirical support for these two claims of the model and thus attempt to integrate findings across largely disparate bodies of literature. In particular, we relate the model to empirical findings in the following areas: the relationship between language development and phonological awareness, and the link between implicit speech processing difficulties in reading-disabled children and lexical restructuring.

Language Development and Phonological Awareness

What does research reveal about the relationship between the development of basic speech and emerging phonological awareness skills? Only a few studies have examined this relationship empirically. One area of investigation has attempted to ascertain whether language and metalinguistic skills interact or develop autonomously (e.g., Smith & Tager-Flusberg, 1982; Webster & Plante, 1995). The logic is that if basic language ability and metalinguistic abilities are intertwined, then there should be strong interrelationships between measures of each—the interaction hypothesis. Alternatively, metalinguistic awareness might develop as a function of metacognitive abilities that arise in middle childhood and be independent of basic language ability—the autonomy hypothesis. These two hypotheses parallel the emergent versus accessibility positions outlined earlier, although the interaction–autonomy issue has been applied more broadly (e.g., to the domain of syntactic development).

Webster and Plante (1995) assessed the relationship between productive phonology and phonological awareness in a longitudinal study of 45 children over a 2- to 3-year period. Beginning at age 3½, children's productive phonology was measured every 6 months using the Khan-Lewis Phonological Analysis test, which provides a measure of the intelligibility of a child's speech. Importantly, children were selected to represent a wide range of articulatory abilities at study onset, yet performed in the normal range on tests of nonverbal intelligence, receptive language, and speech and hearing discrimination. Two metaphonological tasks, also administered every 6 months, consisted of rhyme and alliteration detection. The three main findings were: (a) children with underdeveloped productive phonologies were much less likely to perform at criterion on the two measures of phonological awareness; (b) increases over time on the production measure predicted significant increases in the likelihood of reaching criterion on the two metaphonological tasks—specifically, as production improved, there was an exponential growth in phonological awareness; and (c) change in rank on the phonological measure, rather than age, predicted increasing phonological awareness. These investigators concluded that "The development of primary phonology is a causal factor in the development of phonological awareness, but not the reverse" (p. 54).

Similar studies with young prereaders support the interaction hypothesis, namely that metaphonological skills develop as a function of basic phonological development. For example, Chaney (1994) examined the relationship among social class, language development, metalinguistic awareness, and emergent literacy in 4-year-old preschoolers (see also Chaney, 1992). She found that a standardized test of basic language development (the Preschool Language Scale—Revised) was most highly associated with performance on a composite test of phonological awareness (consisting of phoneme synthesis, rhyme detection, mispronunciation detection, and initial sound detection identification). Measures of social and family literacy accounted for unique variance beyond age and language ability in measures of overall print awareness, alphabetic concepts, and concepts about books. However, these latter variables did not predict additional variance in the phonological awareness composite, once age and language had been taken into account.

Chaney's (1992, 1994) findings support a general link between basic language ability and phonological awareness. She concluded that "The young child's success in solving metalinguistic problems is not so dependent on an ability to step back from meaning as on the state of linguistic knowledge of a particular linguistic structure . . ." (Chaney, 1992, p. 512). Webster and Plante's (1995) findings concerning the relationship between productive phonology and phonological awareness support the more specific hypothesis of our LRM—namely, that there is a strong causal relationship between basic phonological development and the emergence of phonological awareness tasks within individual children. Further, Chaney (1992) found that 4-year-olds' spoken vocabulary scores were significantly related to a composite phonological awareness score, which is also consistent with our model.

Metsala and Stanovich (1995) examined the relationship between overall vocabulary development, lexical representation (word–nonword status), and phonemic awareness. Sixty preschoolers (4- and 5-year-olds) performed better on two measures of phonemic awareness (isolating initial phonemes and onset-rime blending) for words than for nonwords. Furthermore, there were (age-partialed) correlations between a receptive vocabulary measure, as in Chaney's (1992) sample of 4-year-olds, and in Bowey and Patel's (1988) sample of 5- and 6-year-olds. These findings support the prediction of our model that rudimentary phonemic awareness develops prior to the onset of reading and provide preliminary evidence for a specific link between vocabulary knowledge and phonemic awareness. Vocabulary size and familiarity of individual lexical items both play the role in our model of propelling the segmental restructuring of lexical representations, and it is primarily this restructuring that mediates beginning phonemic awareness. These claims are supported by the finding that children with larger vocabularies performed better on phonemic awareness tasks and that performance on these tasks was better for familiar than unfamiliar items (cf. Bowey & Francis, 1991).

Metsala and Stanovich (1995) also examined the relationship among nonword repetition, vocabulary growth, and phonemic awareness. Previously, nonword repetition, especially for "unwordlike" nonwords, has been thought of as a measure of phonological short-term memory capacity (e.g., Gathercole, 1995; Gathercole & Baddeley, 1993; cf. Snowling, Chiat, & Hulme, 1991). Gathercole, in particular, proposed that phonological short-term memory influences vocabulary growth in young children. In contrast, Metsala and Stanovich suggested that it is the degree of segmental structure of lexical items that influences nonword repetition ability. The reasoning is that segmental representations are necessary for a nonword to be adequately represented in the first place. They maintained that correlations between nonword repetition accuracy and vocabulary size reflect this mediating influence of segmental representations. In support, they found that a measure of explicit segmental structure (i.e., phonemic awareness) had a unique relationship with vocabulary size, even after age and nonword repetition scores were partialed. However, nonword repetition did not predict unique variance in vocabulary, after age and a phonemic awareness measure were partialed. These findings are consistent with our proposal that extent of lexical restructuring, or segmental representation, influences implicit phonological tasks (such as nonword repetition) and is related to the development of a child's vocabulary.

Bowey and Patel (1988) assessed two hypotheses that are relevant to these issues. By the first, independent metalinguistic hypothesis, metalinguistic ability presupposes cognitive control that does not develop until middle childhood. By the second, general language development hypothesis, metalinguistic skills are highly correlated with basic spoken language development, more so than with any general cognitive factor. Both phonological and syntactic awareness tests were employed as metalinguistic measures, word reading and reading comprehension tests as reading measures. Bowey and Patel found that metalinguistic awareness did not account for additional unique variance in word reading or reading comprehension after basic language development was entered into the regression analysis. Similarly, basic language development did not account for variance in beginning word reading or comprehension after variance due to metalinguistic awareness was controlled. It was therefore concluded that although metalinguistic awareness does contribute to reading development, such awareness is dependent on basic language development.

In summary, children as young as 3 to 4 years of age can perform many tasks that are traditionally used to measure phonological awareness. This is a powerful argument against the view that metalinguistic skills develop solely as a function of the ability to reflect upon the structure of language, independent of its meaning, only after approximately 5 or 6 years of age. Instead, there is evidence for a strong relation between early vocabulary development and the emergence of phonological awareness ability. These findings are consistent with our LRM, but certainly additional research is needed to strengthen its viability. To this end, we are, for example, currently examining performance over the preliteracy and early literacy periods on both implicit spoken word recognition tasks and explicit phonemic awareness tasks for words that vary in age of acquisition, frequency of occurrence, and neighborhood structure (Garlock et al., 1998). Such studies will help us better understand the emergence of phonemic awareness and early reading success (see also McBride-Chang, 1995).

The Lexical Restructuring Model and Reading Disabilities

Reading-disabled children display phonological processing deficits for diverse tasks that do not require explicit access to or manipulation of phonemes (for review see Siegel, chap. 6, this volume). We believe that examining such findings from a developmental perspective may help to explain the implicit or phonological core deficits in reading disabilities.

Phonological deficits in reading-disabled children have variously been attributed to less robust, underspecified, or degraded phonological representations. We propose that segmental restructuring of lexical items does not progress in a developmentally appropriate manner for such reading-disabled children. Many of the deficits of reading-disabled children do, in fact, parallel spoken word recognition in younger children, for whom more holistic processing of speech input appears to be the norm. First, reading-disabled children rely on lexical context to recognize ambiguous word onsets to a greater degree than do nondisabled readers (Reed, 1989; Snowling, Goulandris, Bowlby, & Howell, 1986). Similarly, 3- to 5-year-olds' production and perception of syllables and individual phonemes are more influenced by contextual factors than are those of 7-year-olds and adults (see Nittrouer, 1992). Second, younger children require more speech input than do older children and adults to recognize spoken words (e.g., Elliott et al., 1987; Walley et al., 1995), as do reading-disabled children (Metsala, 1997b). Third, young children's recognition performance differs most from older children's and adults' for words that are least familiar (e.g., Metsala, 1997a; Walley & Metsala, 1990, 1992). Similarly, reading-disabled subjects perform most poorly when stimuli are unfamiliar, multisyllabic, or degraded (e.g., Brady, Shankweiler, & Mann, 1983). Finally, reading-disabled children (e.g., De Weirdt, 1988; Godfrey, Syrdal-Lasky, Millay, & Knox, 1981) and young children (e.g., Walley et al., 1998) both display shallower slopes in their identification functions for phonetic categories, indicating that these categories or segments are more broadly tuned than they are for normal readers and older listeners.

In order to adduce more definitive support for the fourth claim of our LRM, Metsala (1997b) tested whether spoken word recognition differed between reading-disabled and normally achieving children as a function of word frequency and neighborhood density. On a speech gating task, reading-disabled children in Grades 1 through 6 needed more input from word-onset to recognize words with few similar sounding neighbors than did same-age peers. For the youngest children in the sample, the amount of speech input needed predicted individual differences in word and pseudoword reading beyond the variance accounted for by overall vocabulary size and phonemic awareness measures. Young reading-disabled children displayed this variation in lexical processing even when matched for vocabulary size with nondisabled peers.

Metsala's (1997b) observation that individual differences on the gating task were predictive of young children's reading, but not older children's, supports two conclusions. First, there appears to be a direct link between spoken word recognition and reading performance. This conclusion is supported by recent connectionist models of the reading process, which demonstrate that inadequately specified phonological representations impair generalization of the alphabetic code (i.e., the statistical regularities between phonemes and graphemes) to novel word or pseudoword input—precisely the same problem experienced by disabled readers (e.g., Brown, 1997; Metsala & Brown, 1998). Second, the speech–reading relationship may be developmentally limited (see Stanovich, 1986). That is, segmental representations and processing of speech input may affect developmentally early attempts to decipher the alphabetic code for reading. Later word decoding in reading may reflect this early experience, more than continuing deficits in underlying cognitive/perceptual abilities. Certainly, more research is needed to substantiate the causal relationship between segmental representations in speech and reading disabilities (see also, Elbro, 1996; Elbro, Nielsen, & Peterson, 1994; Snowling et al., 1991).

CONCLUSIONS

We have outlined two very different positions regarding the developmental origins of the phonemic segment. By the accessibility position, the phoneme is functional in early infancy as a unit of speech perception, but is inaccessible for conscious manipulation until before substantial reading experience/exposure. By the emergent position, phonemes are not preformed perceptual units and only develop gradually over childhood. As we have shown, there is a growing body of evidence to support this position and our LRM more specifically. According to this model, lexical representations become more segmental in early through middle childhood primarily as a result of spoken vocabulary growth (i.e., changes in absolute vocabulary size, familiarity of individual lexical items, and neighborhood structures). Thus, the development of phonemic awareness abilities is limited by the very nature of those speech representations being accessed and manipulated. At the same time, then, our model provides a framework for understanding the phonological processing deficits in reading disabilities, although clearly further empirical support is needed in this area and other respects.

We also view our model as having important implications for future applied research on phonemic awareness, beginning reading, and reading disabilities. The programs described in this volume that impact phonemic awareness and beginning reading and spelling may be the very programs that impact lexical restructuring. One important implication of our model, then, is that early attention to vocabulary growth may be a key component in the early detection of children at risk for reading difficulties. The stability of phonological processing through the preschool years and onward (see Torgesen & Burgess, chap. 7, this volume) should serve as a strong impetus for finding earlier interventions for promoting successful reading acquisition by more children. With a better understanding of lexical restructuring in childhood, earlier identification and intervention strategies may be found.

ACKNOWLEDGMENTS

The authors wish to thank Rebecca Treiman for her comments on an earlier version of this manuscript, and Vicki Garlock for her input into our formulation of these research issues. Support for the preparation of this chapter was provided by a grant from the National Reading Research Center to the first author, and by grant HD30398 from the National Institute for Child Health and Human Development to the second author. Inquiries can be sent to either author at the following addresses: Amanda C. Walley, Department of Psychology, University of Alabama at Birmingham, UAB Station, Birmingham, AL 35294-1170 (e-mail: SBSF080@UABDPO.DPO.UAB.EDU); Jamie L. Metsala, Department of Human Development, University of Maryland, College Park, MD 20742 (e-mail: jm251@umail.umd.edu).

REFERENCES

Andrews, S. (1992). Frequency and neighborhood effects on lexical access: Lexical similarity of orthographic redundancy? *Journal of Experimental Psychology: Learning, Memory, and Cognition, V18*(2), 234–254.

Anglin, J. M. (1989). Vocabulary growth and the knowing–learning distinction. *Reading Canada, 7,* 142–146.

Aslin, R. N., Pisoni, D. B., & Jusczyk, P. W. (1983). Auditory development and speech perception in infancy. In M. M. Haith & J. J. Campos (Eds.), *Carmichael's manual of child psychology: Vol. II. Infancy and the biology of development* (pp. 573–687). New York: Wiley.

Aslin, R. N., & Smith, L. B. (1988). Perceptual development. *Annual Review of Psychology, 39,* 435–473.

Bard, E. G., Shillock, R. C., & Altmann, G. T. M. (1988). The recognition of words after their acoustic offsets in spontaneous speech: Effects of subsequent context. *Perception & Psychophysics, 44,* 395–408.

Barton, D. (1980). Phonemic perception in children. In G. H. Yeni-Komshian, J. F. Kavanagh, & C. A. Ferguson (Eds.), *Child phonology: Vol. 2, perception* (pp. 97–116). New York: Academic.

Benedict, H. (1979). Early lexical development: Comprehension and production. *Journal of Child Language, 6,* 183–200.

Bertoncini, J., Bijeljac-Babic, R., Jusczyk, P. W., Kennedy, L. J., & Meher, J. (1988). An investigation of young infants' perceptual representations of speech sounds. *Journal of Experimental Psychology: General, 117,* 21–33.

Bowey, J. A., & Francis, J. (1991). Phonological analysis as a function of age and exposure to reading instruction. *Applied Psycholinguistics, 12,* 91–121.

Bowey, J. A., & Patel, R. (1988). Metalinguistic ability and early reading achievement. *Applied Psycholinguistics, 9,* 367–383.

Brady, S., Shankweiler, D., & Mann, V. (1983). Speech perception and memory coding in relation to reading ability. *Journal of Experimental Child Psychology, 35,* 345–367.

Brown, G. D. A. (1997). Developmental and acquired dyslexia: A connectionist comparison. *Brain and Language, 59,* 207–235.

Brown, G. D. A., & Watson, F. L. (1987). First in, first out: Word learning age and spoken word frequency as predictors of word familarity and word naming latency. *Memory & Cognition, 15,* 208–216.

Burdick, C. K., & Miller, J. D. (1975). Speech perception by the chinchilla: Discrimination of sustained /a/ and /i/. *Journal of the Acoustical Society of America, 58,* 415–427.

Burnham, D. K., Earnshaw, L. J., & Clark, J. E. (1991). Development of categorical identification of native and non-native bilabial stops: Infants, children and adults. *Journal of Child Language, 18,* 231–260.

Byrne, B., & Fielding-Barnsley, R. (1993). Recognition of phoneme invariance by beginning readers: Confounding effects of global similarity. *Reading and Writing, 6*, 315–324.

Chaney, C. (1992). Language development, metalinguistic skills, and print awareness in three-year-old children. *Applied Psycholinguistics, 13*, 485–514.

Chaney, C. (1994). Language development, metalinguistic awareness, and emergent literacy skills of 3-year-old children in relation to social class. *Applied Psycholinguistics, 15*(3), 371–394.

Charles-Luce, J., & Luce, P. A. (1990). Similarity neighborhoods of words in young children's lexicon. *Journal of Child Language, 17*, 205–215.

Cole, R. A., & Perfetti, C. A. (1980). Listening for mispronunciations in a children's story: The use of context by children and adults. *Journal of Verbal Learning and Verbal Behavior, 19*, 297–315.

Cooper, R. P., & Aslin, R. N. (1989). The language environment of the young infant: Implications for early perceptual development. *Canadian Journal of Psychology, 43*, 247–265.

Cooper, R. P., & Aslin, R. N. (1990). Preference for infant-directed speech in the first month after birth. *Child Development, 61*, 1584–1595.

Cutler, A. (1995). Spoken word recognition and production. In J. L. Miller & P. D. Eimas (Eds.), *Speech, language, and communication* (pp. 97–136). San Diego, CA: Academic.

Cutler, A., Mehler, J., Norris, D., & Segui, J. (1989). Limits of bilingualism. *Nature, 340*, 229–230.

De Weirdt, W. (1988). Speech perception and frequency discrimination for good and poor readers. *Applied Psycholinguistics, 9*, 163–183.

Dollaghan, C. A. (1994). Children's phonological neighborhoods: Half empty or half full? *Journal of Child Language, 21*, 257–271.

Edwards, M. L. (1974). Perception and production in child phonology: The testing of four hypotheses. *Journal of Child Language, 1*, 205–219.

Ehri, L. C. (1984). How orthography alters spoken language competencies in children learning to read and spell. In J. Downing & R. Valtin (Eds.), *Language awareness and learning to read* (pp. 119–147). New York: Springer-Verlag.

Eimas, P. D., Siqueland, E. R., Jusczyk, P. W., & Vigorito, J. (1971). Speech perception in early infancy. *Science, 171*, 304–306.

Elbro, C. (1996). Early linguistic abilities and reading development: A review and a hypothesis. *Reading and Writing: An Interdisciplinary Journal, 8*, 453–485.

Elbro, C., Nielsen, I., & Peterson, D. K. (1994). Dyslexia in adults: Evidence for deficits in non-word reading and in the phonological representation of lexical items. *Annals of Dyslexia, 44*, 205–226.

Elliott, L. L., Hammer, M. A., & Evan, K. E. (1987). Perception of gated, highly familiar spoken monosyllabic nouns by children, teenagers, and older adults. *Perception & Psychophysics, 42*, 150–157.

Ferguson, C. A. (1986). Discovering sound units and constructing sound systems: It's child's play. In J. S. Perkell, & D. H. Klatt (Eds.), *Invariance and variability in speech processes* (pp. 36–51). Hillsdale, NJ: Lawrence Erlbaum Associates.

Ferguson, C. A., & Farwell, C. B. (1975). Words and sounds in early language acquisition. *Language, 51*, 419–439.

Flege, J. E., & Eefting, W. (1986). Linguistic and developmental effects on the production and perception of stop consonants. *Phonetica, 43*, 155–171.

Fowler, A. E. (1991). How early phonological development might set the stage for phonological awareness. In S. Brady & D. Shankweiler (Eds.), *Phonological processes in literacy: A tribute to Isabelle Y. Liberman* (pp. 97–117). Hillsdale, NJ: Lawrence Erlbaum Associates.

Fowler, C. A. (1995). Speech production. In J. L. Miller & P. D. Eimas (Eds.), *Speech, language, and communication* (pp. 29–61). San Diego, CA: Academic.

Garlock, V. M., Walley, A. C., Randazza, L. A., & Metsala, J. L. (1998). *Effects of word frequency, age-of-acquisition and neighborhood density on spoken word recognition and phoneme awareness in children and adults.* Manuscript in preparation.

Garnica, O. K. (1973). The development of phonemic perception. In T. E. Moore (Ed.), *Cognitive development and the acquisition of language* (pp. 215–222). New York: Academic.

Gathercole, S. E. (1995). Is nonword repetition a test of phonological memory or long-term knowledge? It all depends on the nonwords. *Memory & Cognition, 23*(1), 83–94.

Gathercole, S. E., & Baddeley, A. D. (1993). *Working memory and language.* Hove, England: Lawrence Erlbaum Associates.

Gerken, L. (1994). Sentential processes in early childhood language: Evidence from the perception and production of function morphemes. In J. C. Goodman & H. C. Nusbaum (Eds.), *The development of speech perception* (pp. 271–298). Cambridge, MA: MIT Press.

Gleitman, L. R., & Rozin, P. (1977). The structure and acquisition of reading I. Relations between orthographies and the structure of language. In A. S. Reber, & D. L. Scarborough (Eds.), *Toward a psychology of reading.* Hillsdale, NJ: Lawrence Erlbaum Associates.

Godfrey, J. J., Syrdal-Lasky, A. K., Millay, K. K., & Knox, C. M. (1981). Performance of dyslexic children on speech perception tests. *Journal of Experimental Child Psychology, 32,* 401–424.

Goldinger, S. D., Luce, P. A., & Pisoni, D. B. (1989). Priming lexical neighbors of spoken words: Effects of competition and inhibition. *Journal of Memory and Language, 28,* 501–518.

Grosjean, F. (1980). Spoken word recognition processes and the gating paradigm. *Perception & Psychophysics, 28,* 267–283.

Hirsh-Pasek, K., Kemler Nelson, D. G., Jusczyk, P. W., Wright-Cassidy, K., Druss, B., & Kennedy, L. (1987). Clauses are perceptual units for young infants. *Cognition, 26,* 269–286.

Huttenlocher, J. (1984). Word recognition and word production in children. In H. Bouma & D. G. Bouwhuis (Eds.), *Attention and performance: Control of language processes* (pp. 447–456). Hillsdale, NJ: Lawrence Erlbaum Associates.

Ingram, D. (1979). Phonological patterns in the speech of young children. In P. Fletcher & M. Garman (Eds.), *Language acquisition* (pp. 133–148). Cambridge, England: Cambridge University Press.

Ingram, D. (1985). On children's homonyms. *Journal of Child Language, 12,* 671–680.

Jakobson, (1968). *Child language, aphasia, and phonological universals* (A. R. Keiler, Trans.). The Hague, Netherlands: Mouton.

Jusczyk, P. W. (1986). Toward a model of the development of speech perception. In J. S. Perkell & D. H. Klatt (Eds.), *Invariance and variability in speech processes* (pp. 1–33). Hillsdale, NJ: Lawrence Erlbaum Associates.

Jusczyk, P. W. (1992). Developing phonological categories from the speech signal. In C. A. Ferguson, L. Menn, & C. Stoel-Gammon (Eds.), *Phonological development: Models, research, implication* (pp. 17–64). Parkton, MD: York.

Jusczyk, P. W. (1993). From general to language-specific capacities: The WRAPSA model of how speech perception develops. *Journal of Phonetics, 21,* 3–28.

Jusczyk, P. W. (1995). Language acquisition: Speech sounds and the beginning of phonology. In J. L. Miller & P. D. Eimas (Eds.), *Speech, language, and communication* (pp. 263–301). San Diego, CA: Academic.

Jusczyk, P. W., & Aslin, R. N. (1995). Infants' detection of the sound patterns of words in fluent speech. *Cognitive Psychology, 29,* 1–23.

Jusczyk, P. W., Friederici, A. D., Wessels, J., Svenkerud, V. Y., & Jusczyk, A. M. (1993). Infants' sensitivity to the sound patterns of native language words. *Journal of Memory and Language, 32,* 402–420.

Jusczyk, P. W., Hirsh-Pasek, K., Kemler Nelson, D. G., Kennedy, L. J., Woodward, A., & Piwoz, J. (1992). Perception of acoustic correlates of major phrasal units by young infants. *Cognitive Psychology, 24,* 252–293.

Jusczyk, P. W., Luce, P. A., & Charles-Luce, J. (1994). Infants' sensitivity to phonotactic patterns in the native language. *Journal of Memory and Language, 33*, 630–645.

Jusczyk, P. W., Pisoni, D. B., Walley, A., & Murray, J. (1980). Discrimination of relative onset time of two-component tones by infants. *Journal of the Acoustical Society of America, 67*, 262–270.

Kuhl, P. K. (1993). Infant speech perception: A window on psycholinguistic development. *International Journal of Psycholinguistics, 9*, 33–56.

Kuhl, P. K., & Padden, D. (1982). Enhanced discriminability at the phonetic boundaries for the voicing feature in macaques. *Perception & Psychophysics, 32*, 542–550.

Kuhl, P. K., Williams, K. A., Lacerda, F., Stevens, K. N., & Lindblom, B. (1992). Linguistic experience alters phonetic perception in infants by 6 months of age. *Science, 255*, 606–608.

Liberman, I. Y., Shankweiler, D., & Liberman, A. M. (1989). The alphabetic principle and learning to read. In D. Shankweiler, & I. Y. Liberman (Eds.), *Phonology and reading disability: Solving the reading puzzle* (pp. 1–33). Ann Arbor: University of Michigan Press.

Liberman, I. Y., Shankweiler, D., Liberman, A. M., Fowler, C. A., & Fischer, F. W. (1977). Phonetic segmentation and recoding in the beginning reader. In A. S. Reber & D. L. Scarborough (Eds.), *Toward a psychology of reading* (pp. 207–225). Hillsdale, NJ: Lawrence Erlbaum Associates.

Lindblom, B. (1992). Phonological units as adaptive emergents of lexical development. In C. A. Ferguson, L. Menn, & C. Stoel-Gammon (Eds.), *Phonological development: Models, research, implications* (pp. 131–163). Timonium, MD: York.

Lindblom, B., MacNeilage, P., & Studdert-Kennedy, M. (1983). Self-organizing processes and the explanation of phonological universals. In B. Butterworth, B. Comrie, & O. Dahl (Eds.), *Explanations of linguistic universals.* The Hague, Netherlands: Mouton.

Locke, J. L. (1988). The sound shape of early lexical representations. In M. D. Smith & J. L. Locke (Eds.), *The emergent lexicon: The child's development of a linguistic vocabulary* (pp. 3–18). New York: Academic.

Logan, J. S. (1992). A computational analysis of young children's lexicons. *Research on spoken language processing, technical report no. 8.* Bloomington, IN: Department of Psychology, Speech Research Laboratory.

Luce, P. (1986). Neighborhoods of words in the mental lexicon. *Research on speech perception, technical report no. 6.* Bloomington, IN: Department of Psychology, Speech Research Laboratory.

Marslen-Wilson, W. D. (1987). Functional parallelism in spoken word recognition. *Cognition, 25*, 71–102.

Marslen-Wilson, W. D. (1989). Access and integration: Projecting sound onto meaning. In W. D. Marslen-Wilson (Ed.), *Lexical representation and process* (pp. 3–24). Cambridge, MA: MIT Press.

McBride-Chang, C. (1995). Phonological processing, speech perception, and reading disability. *Educational Psychologist, 30*(3), 109–121.

Menn, L. (1983). Development of articulatory, phonetic and phonological capabilities. In J. B. Gleason (Ed.), *The development of language* (pp. 61–98). Columbus, OH: Merrill.

Menn, L., & Matthei, E. (1992). The "two-lexicon" account of child phonology: Looking back, looking ahead. In C. A. Ferguson, L. Menn, & C. Stoel-Gammon (Eds.), *Phonological development: Models, research, implications* (pp. 211–247). Timonium, MD: York.

Menyuk, P., & Menn, L. (1979). Early strategies for the perception and production of words and sounds. In P. Fletcher, & M. Garman (Eds.), *Language acquisition* (pp. 49–70). Cambridge, England: Cambridge University Press.

Metsala, J. L. (1997a). An examination of word frequency and neighborhood density in the development of spoken-word recognition. *Memory & Cognition, 25*(1), 47–56.

Metsala, J. L. (1997b). Spoken word recognition in reading disabled children. *Journal of Educational Psychology, 89*(1), 159–169.

Metsala, J. L., & Brown, G. D. A. (1998). Normal and dyslexic reading development: The role of formal models. In C. Hulme & R. M. Joshi (Eds.), *Reading and spelling: Development and disorder* (pp. 235–261). Hillsdale, NJ: Lawrence Erlbaum Associates.

Metsala, J. L., & Stanovich, K. E. (1995, April). *An examination of young children's phonological processing as a function of lexical development.* Paper presented at the Annual American Educational Research Association, San Francisco, California.

Miller, J. L., & Eimas, P. D. (1994). Observations on speech perception, its development, and the search for a mechanism. In J. C. Goodman & H. C. Nusbaum (Eds.), *The development of speech perception* (pp. 271–298). Cambridge, MA: MIT Press.

Morais, J., Bertelson, P., Cary., L., & Alegria, J. (1986). Literacy training and speech segmentation. *Cognition, 24,* 45–64.

Morais, J., Cary, L., Alegria, J., & Bertelson, P. (1979). Does awareness of speech as a sequence of phones arise spontaneously? *Cognition, 7,* 323–331.

Morrison, C. M., & Ellis, A. W. (1995). Roles of word frequency and age of acquisition in word naming and lexical decision. *Journal of Experimental Psychology: Learning, Memory, and Cognition, 21,* 116–133.

Moskowitz, A. I. (1973). The acquisition of phonology and syntax. In K. K. J. Hintikka, J. M. E. Moravsik, & P. Suppes (Eds.), *Approaches to natural language* (pp. 48–84). Dordrect, The Netherlands: Reidel.

Nittrouer, S. (1992). Age-related differences in percepetual effects of formant transitions within syllables and across syllable boundaries. *Journal of Phonetics, 20,* 1–32.

Nittrouer, S., & Studdert-Kennedy, M. (1987). The role of coarticulatory effects in the perception of fricatives by children and adults. *Journal of Speech and Hearing Research, 30,* 319–329.

Nittrouer, S., Studdert-Kennedy, M., & McGowan, R. S. (1989). The emergence of phonetic segments: Evidence form the spectral structure of fricative-vowel syllables spoken by children and adults. *Journal of Speech and Hearing Research, 32,* 120–132.

Nygaard, L. C., & Pisoni, D. B. (1995). Speech perception: New directions in theory and research. In J. L. Miller & P. D. Eimas (Eds.), *Speech, language, and communication* (pp. 63–93). San Diego, CA: Academic.

Pegg, J. E., Werker, J. F., & McLeod, P. J. (1992). Preference for infant-directed over adult-directed speech: Evidence from 7-week-old infants. *Infant Behavior and Development, 15,* 325–345.

Peters, A. M. (1983). *The units of language.* Cambridge, England: Cambridge University Press.

Pisoni, D. B., Carrell, T. D., & Gans, S. J. (1983). Perception of the duration of rapid spectrum changes in speech and nonspeech signals. *Perception & Psychophysics, 34,* 314–322.

Pisoni, D., & Luce, P. (1987). Acoustic–phonetic representations in word recognition. *Cognition, 25,* 21–52.

Reed, M. A. (1989). Speech perception and the discrimination of brief auditory cues in reading disabled children. *Journal of Experimental Child Psychology, 48,* 270–292.

Reznick, J. S., & Goldfield, B. A. (1992). Rapid change in lexical development in comprehension and production. *Developmental Psychology, 28,* 406–413.

Rozin, P. (1976). The evolution of intelligence and access to the cognitive unconscious. In J. Sprague & A. N. Epstein (Eds.), *Progress in psychobiology and physiological psychology* (Vol. 6, pp. 245–280). New York: Academic.

Schwartz, R. G. (1988). Phonological factors in early lexical development. In M. D. Smith & J. L. Locke (Eds.), *The emergent lexicon: The child's development of a linguistic vocabulary* (pp. 185–218). San Diego, CA: Academic.

Seidenberg, M. S., & McClelland, J. L. (1989). A distributed, developmental model of word recognition and naming. *Psychological Review, 96*(4), 523–568.

Share, D., & Stanovich, K. E. (1995). Cognitive processes in early reading development: Accommodating individual differences into a model of acquisition. In J. S. Carlson (Ed.), *Issues in education: Contributions from psychology* (Vol. 1, pp. 1–57). Greenwich, CT: JAI.

Shvachkin, N. K. (1973). The development of phonemic speech perception in early childhood. In C. A. Ferguson & D. I. Slobin (Eds.), *Studies of child language development* (pp. 91–127). New York: Holt, Rinehart & Winston.

Smith, C. L., & Tager-Flusberg, H. (1982). Metalinguistic awareness and language development. *Journal of Experimental Child Psychology, 34*, 449–468.

Snowling, M. J., Chiat, S., & Hulme, C. (1991). Words, nonwords and phonological processes: Some comments on Gathercole, Willis, Emslie, and Baddeley. *Applied Psycholinguistics, 12*, 369–373.

Snowling, M. J., Goulandris, N., Bowlby, M., & Howell, P. (1986). Segmentation and speech perception in relation to reading skill: A developmental analysis. *Journal of Experimental Child Psychology, 41*, 489–507.

Stanovich, K. E. (1986). Mathew effects in reading: Some consequences of individual differences in the acquisition of literacy. *Reading Research Quarterly, 21*(4), 360–407.

Stoel-Gammon, C. (1991). Normal and disordered phonology in two-year-olds. *Topics in Language Disorders, 11*, 21–32.

Strange, W., & Broen, P. A. (1981). The relationship between perception an production of /w/, /r/, and /l/. *Journal of Experimental Child Psychology, 31*(1), 81–102.

Studdert-Kennedy, M. (1986). Sources of variability in early speech development. In J. S. Perkell, & D. H. Klatt (Eds.), *Invariance and variability in speech process* (pp. 58–76). Hillsdale, NJ: Lawrence Erlbaum Associates.

Studdert-Kennedy, M. (1993). Discovering phonetic function. *Journal of Phonetics, 21*, 147–155.

Suomi, K. (1993). An outline of a developmental model of adult phonological organization and behavior. *Journal of Phonetics, 21*, 29–60.

Thomas, D., Campos, J. J., Shucard, D. W., Ramsay, D. S., & Shucard, J. (1981). Semantic comprehension in infancy: A signal detection approach. *Child Development, 52*, 798–803.

Treiman, R., & Baron, J. (1981). Segmental analysis ability: Development and relation to reading ability. In G. E. MacKinnon & T. G. Waller (Eds.), *Reading research: Advances in theory and practice* (Vol. 3, pp. 159–198). New York: Academic.

Treiman, R., & Breaux, A. M. (1982). Common phoneme and overall similarity relations among spoken word syllables: Their use by children and adults. *Journal of Psycholinguistic Research, 11*, 581–610.

Vihman, M. M. (1993). Variable paths to early word production. *Journal of Phonetics, 21*, 61–82.

Walley, A. C. (1987). Young children's detections of word-initial and -final mispronunciations in constrained and unconstrained contexts. *Cognitive Development, 2*, 145–167.

Walley, A. C. (1988). Spoken word recognition by young children and adults. *Cognitive Development, 3*, 137–165.

Walley, A. C. (1993a). More developmental research is needed. *Journal of Phonetics, 21*, 171–176.

Walley, A. C. (1993b). The role of vocabulary development in children's spoken word recognition and segmentation ability. *Developmental Review, 13*, 286–350.

Walley, A. C., Flege, J. E., & Randazza, L. A. (1997). *Effects of lexical status on the perception of native and non-native vowels: A developmental study.* Manuscript in preparation.

Walley, A. C., & Metsala, J. L. (1990). The growth of lexical constraints on spoken word recognition. *Perception & Psychophysics, 47*, 267–280.

Walley, A. C., & Metsala, J. L. (1992). Young children's age-of-acquisition estimates for spoken words. *Memory & Cognition, 20*(2), 171–182.

Walley, A. C., Michela, V. L., & Wood, D. R. (1995). The gating paradigm: Effects of presentation format on spoken word recognition by children and adults. *Perception & Psychophysics, 57*(3), 343–351.

Walley, A. C., Smith, L. B., & Jusczyk, P. W. (1986). The role of phonemes and syllables in the perceived similarity of speech sounds for children. *Memory & Cognition, 14*, 220–229.

Webster, P. E., & Plante, A. S. (1995). Productive phonology and phonological awareness in preschool children. *Applied Psycholinguistics, 16*, 43–57.

Werker, J. F. (1991). The ontogeny of speech perception. In I. G. Mattingly & M. Studdert-Kennedy (Eds.), *Modularity and the motor theory of speech perception.* Hillsdale, NJ: Lawrence Erlbaum Associates.

Werker, J. F., & Pegg, J. E. (1992). Infant speech perception and phonological acquisition. In C. A. Ferguson, L. Menn, & C. Stoel-Gammon (Eds.), *Phonological development: Models, research, implications* (pp. 285–311). Timonium, MD: York.

Werker, J. F., & Tees, R. C. (1984). Cross-language speech perception: Evidence for perceptual reorganization during the first year of life. *Infant Behavior and Development, 7*, 49–63.

Zlatin, M. A., & Koenigsknecht, R. A. (1976). Development of the voicing contrast: A comparsion of voice onset time in stop perception and production. *Journal of Speech and Hearing Research, 19*, 78–92.

5

▼▼▼▼▼▼▼

The Endpoint of Skilled Word Recognition: The ROAR Model

Gordon D. A. Brown
University of Warwick

The chapters in this book represent many different perspectives on the same landscape. This landscape includes the terrain that children must negotiate in order to reach the final destination that researchers and educators are all concerned to help them reach—the state of skilled adult reading. This chapter aims to describe what this destination looks like and, more important, *why* it is the chosen destination. If beginning readers are to be provided with the best possible maps and guides to the route they must follow, an understanding of why skilled adult readers converge on a particular destination (as opposed to some other one) is essential. The present chapter focuses on the nature of skilled single-word reading, because it is there that most progress has been made in understanding the demands of the task and the different types of solution that may be possible.[1]

The chapter begins with a brief description of the rational analysis approach to human cognitive processing (Anderson, 1990) according to which mature human cognitive behavior can be understood as an adaptive reflection of the structure of the world. When applied to reading, this perspective leads to the suggestion that the cognitive abilities of skilled adult readers should have developed in such a way that performance will be statistically optimal

---

[1]It is not, of course, intended to imply that there are not many other important processes that combine to make up skilled adult reading ability. The rational analytic approach that is applied here to the case of single-word reading may eventually be applicable to other aspects of reading behavior; at present, however, single-word reading provides the most fruitful domain of application for the approach.

with respect to the structure of the English spelling-to-sound mapping system. This is the ROAR model (for rational, optimal, adaptive reading). The substantial amount of empirical evidence consistent with this suggestion is reviewed, as are the implications of the approach for learning. If the endpoint of learning to read can indeed be characterized as statistically optimal behavior, then the performance of artificial learning systems that learn statistically optimal behavior can provide important insights into the learning process. In particular, the study of such systems may lead to ways of structuring the learning process that facilitate the acquisition of a system involving both regular and irregular spelling-to-sound mappings.

THE IMPORTANCE OF THE "WHY" QUESTION

Many highly sophisticated models of reading have been developed over the past decade (e.g. Coltheart, Curtis, Atkins, & Haller, 1993; Norris, 1994; Plaut, McClelland, Seidenberg, & Patterson, 1996; Seidenberg & McClelland, 1989). Such models have been concerned to characterize the information-processing mechanisms that underlie skilled adult reading. However, this research has remained largely silent on a question that is surely of central importance: Why do skilled adult readers develop the mechanisms that they do? Indeed, the question seems often to be missed or ignored completely. To illustrate, imagine that some group of researchers developed a model of skilled adult reading that accounted for all known relevant empirical data. Let us call this "Model M." Further assume that the predictions of Model M are tested experimentally, and that no disconfirming evidence can be found. The development of Model M would not be the end of the theoretical enterprise, because the mere existence of the model would bring us no nearer the question of why Model M (rather than, say, Model P or Model Q) was the one to describe human reading. Why, in other words, does human learning lead to the development of a system that behaves like Model M? Why is Model M the best one to have?

In the first section of this chapter one possible answer to this question is proposed. It is suggested that the properties of the mechanisms used by skilled adult readers can be understood as those of a system that is optimally adapted (i.e., maximally efficient) in the light of the statistical nature of the mapping between spelling and sound in English. This is the ROAR model. According to this view, empirical phenomena, such as the use of spelling-to-sound correspondences at multiple levels, can be explained in terms of the operation of a mechanism that is optimised for the task it must perform. Such a characterization cuts across any particular implementation of the mechanisms in question—it is possible to claim that skilled adult reading is statistically optimal without commitment as to the exact nature of the mechanisms that are involved in reading.

This leads to a view of reading as statistics that is, of course, not a novel one. The approach has been implicit in connectionist models of reading dating back from the middle of the 1980s, and has more recently been made more explicit in the work of, for example, Jared, McRae, and Seidenberg (1990) and, especially, Treiman, Mullennix, Bijeljac-Babic, and Richmond-Welty (1995). In the present chapter, however, the intention is to go beyond this general claim to argue that the reading as statistics approach can be used as the basis for understanding the question posed at the beginning of this chapter, namely, why do skilled adults possess the reading system that they do (i.e., as opposed to some other one). It is one thing to show that adult reading is in some way sensitive to the statistical regularities in the English spelling-to-sound mapping system; it is quite another to explain why this should be so and, in particular, why adults should be sensitive to these regularities in the precise way that they are.

The second part of the chapter reviews empirical evidence on skilled adult reading that is consistent with the ROAR approach, and this is taken as suggestive evidence that the endpoint of reading development is indeed optimal reading in the specific sense of statistical efficiency. In the third section of the chapter the implications of the new characterization of the endpoint of reading instruction for instructional practice are considered.

A RATIONAL ANALYSIS OF READING

This section describes the approach that Brown (1996) took to describing skilled adult single-word reading as "adaptively rational" (Anderson, 1990). The suggestion is that such reading can be seen as representing optimal performance given the statistical properties of the task to be performed. This is the approach known as "rational analysis" that has been developed by Anderson (1990; Anderson & Milson, 1989) and others. A central idea of the rational analysis approach is that human psychological behavior can be understood in terms of the operation of a mechanism that is optimally adapted to its environment (Anderson, 1990), in the sense that the behavior of the mechanism is as efficient as it conceivably could be given the structure of the problem or input-output mapping it must solve. An example comes from the study of human memory, where Anderson and Milson (1989; cf. also Anderson & Schooler, 1991; Brown & Vousden, in press) showed that the rate at which information is lost from memory can be explained if it is assumed that the availability of information in memory reflects the probability that it will be necessary to access it as a reducing function of the time since the memory was last accessed.

In applying the same approach to the study of single-word reading, our aim has been to develop an understanding of why the mechanisms that skilled adults have developed for reading have the properties they do—in particular, why do they exhibit the observed forms of sensitivity to the regularity or consistency of the spelling-to-sound correspondences contained in the words to be read? Note that the question of why (or, indeed, whether) it is adaptively rational, optimal, or at least efficient for humans to have a reading system that is organized in such a way as to have the observed empirical properties is quite independent of questions concerning the actual implementation of the relevant system. For example, much debate has centred on the ability of dual-route models (e.g. Coltheart et al., 1993) or connectionist models (e.g. Brown, 1987, 1997; Norris, 1994; Seidenberg & McClelland, 1989) of reading to account for the wide range of empirical data available concerning skilled adult decoding. However, even if it were to be shown that a particular dual-route model or a particular connectionist model were to provide a complete account of the relevant experimental findings, researchers would still be no nearer an understanding of why it is that skilled adults develop a dual-route model rather than a single-route connectionist model (or vice versa). In other words, understanding the nature of the mechanism that causes or enables us to read in a particular way is just one part of the research enterprise.

The ROAR model is based on what Brown (1996) termed the *optimal reading hypothesis*. The optimal reading hypothesis states that skilled adults are reading with maximum efficiency, given the statistical structure of the mapping from orthography to phonology in English. Thus, the process of learning to read is seen, in this view, as basically a statistical process in that it requires the learner to acquire a set of associations between written word forms and their pronunciations (Brown, 1996, 1997; Brown & Loosemore, 1994, 1995; cf. also Seidenberg & McClelland, 1989; Treiman et al., 1995). In other words, they must *infer a model* (of the language) from the data to which they are exposed. If skilled adult reading is adaptively rational and statistically optimal, then the sensitivity of the adult reading mechanism to spelling-to-sound consistency should reflect optimal representation and usage of the statistical properties of the spelling-to-sound mapping system in English.

More specifically, Brown (1996) provided formal demonstrations (using Bayesian and other analyses) that the ratio of *consistent* pronunciations in the language to *all* pronunciations in the language of a given orthographic segment should be the only spelling-to-sound factor to influence skilled adult reading. In other words, if a given orthographic segment O can receive different pronunciations with probabilities p_1, p_2, p_3, and p_4, then the difficulty of assigning the pronunciation that has probability p_3 to O will be given by:

$$\frac{p_3}{p_1 + p_2 + p_3 + p_4}.$$

This will be referred to as the *consistency ratio* of an orthographic segment. In the case of the orthographic rime segment *-ave*, for example, there is only one word, *have*, with the /Av/ pronunciation (we consider here only mono-syllabic words with a frequency of at least one per million in the Kucera & Francis, 1967, count). However there are 12 words with a different pronun-ciation of the same orthographic rime segment (*save*, *cave*, *gave*, etc.). There-fore, if the consistency ratio is calculated in terms of word types, it is equal to $1/(1 + 12) = 0.08$. If word frequency is taken into account, the consistency ratio (by tokens) is equal to 0.89—a much higher value, because the token frequency of *have* is very high in relation to the summed frequency of its inconsistently pronounced neighbors. Treiman et al. (1995) examined con-sistency ratios (and other measures) by both types and tokens, and both measures are also used in the analyses reported later in this chapter.

Note that the claim that *only* the consistency ratio of an orthographic segment will determine its ease of pronunciation is not a trivial one: It excludes, for example, the possibility that the overall frequency with which an orthographic letter pattern receives a given pronunciation will inde-pendently determine pronunciation time or accuracy, and it also excludes the possibility that the overall frequency with which an orthographic pattern receives a different pronunciation to the one intended should influence proc-essing. These factors (numbers of consistent and inconsistent orthographic neighbors) should only, according to the optimal reading hypothesis, influ-ence pronunciation in so far as they contribute to the consistency ratio. Thus, the optimal reading model makes a strong prediction regarding the precise quantitative form of the relationship between reading and spelling-to-sound consistency. What the rational analysis has provided is a specific hypothesis concerning *why* and *how* skilled adult reading should reflect the statistical structure of the language. The next section focuses on evidence consistent with the account of *how* the sensitivity should manifest itself; that is, what is the precise quantitative form of the relationship between spelling-to-sound consistency and actual reading performance as assessed, for example, by word naming latency and accuracy?

EVIDENCE FOR OPTIMAL READING

The central prediction of the described approach is that single-word reading performance should be influenced by the consistency ratio of the ortho-graphic segments within a word, and not by the absolute frequencies of the orthographic or phonological rimes. An immediate problem in evaluating this prediction with respect to real empirical data is that spelling-to-sound regularities must be defined over some specific units in the language. For example, is it regularities at the level of graphemes and phonemes that matter, or the statistical relationships between larger units such as phonological rimes (e.g. the /Av/ in *have*) and the orthographic letter clusters that correspond to them (following other researchers, these are referred to as *orthographic rimes*, analogously to the concept of graphemes as the orthographic units corresponding to a single phoneme)? In line with the optimal reading hypothesis, it might be assumed that optimal readers will make use of whatever levels of spelling-to-sound correspondence are most useful (i.e., provide the most reliable guide to pronunciations). Treiman et al. (1995) adopted this perspective, and showed that, in English, the most reliable sublexical guide to the pronunciation of the vowels (where much of the inconsistency resides) of monosyllabic English words often resides in the correspondence between orthographic and phonological rimes.

Consistent with this, Treiman et al. found substantial evidence that skilled adults do indeed make use of such orthographic units, in that their single-word naming latencies and error rates are affected by spelling-to-sound consistency at the rime level independent of consistency at other levels. However, Treiman et al. also found independent effects of the consistency of other orthographic segments—such as graphemes at the beginnings of words and sometimes at the ends, as well as medial vowels. Many other studies have also found evidence of consistency at the rime level, but the Treiman et al. study is unique in its careful comparison of different levels of spelling-to-sound correspondence.

The analyses I now describe focus on spelling-to-sound consistency at the rime level, but this primarily reflects the fact that most studies that provide quantitative information on effects of different levels of spelling-to-sound consistency have focused on this particular level. As described previously, the ROAR approach predicted that naming latency and accuracy should be determined by the consistency ratio of any given orthographic segment—the ratio of *consistent* to *all* pronunciations of that orthographic segment in the language. Several studies have shown that the consistency with which an orthographic rime is pronounced affects the speed and accuracy of pronunciation of words containing that orthographic rime (e.g. Bowey, 1996; Bowey & Hansen, 1994; Brown, 1987; Brown & Watson, 1994; Coltheart & Leahy, 1992; Glushko, 1979; Jared et al., 1990; Laxon, Masterson, & Coltheart, 1991; Laxon, Masterson, & Moran, 1994; Seidenberg, Waters, Barnes, & Tanenhaus, 1984; Taraban & McClelland, 1987; Treiman, Goswami, & Bruck, 1990; Waters & Seidenberg, 1985; Waters, Seidenberg, & Bruck, 1984). Jared et al. (1990) concluded, on the basis of many studies carried out by themselves and others, that word-naming latency is determined by the relative frequencies of the consistently and inconsistently pronounced orthographic neighbours of a word (*orthographic neighborhood* here being defined in terms of other words in the language sharing the same orthographic rime unit). Consistent with this, they found larger exception effects (disadvantages for words with mainly inconsistently pronounced neighbors) for low-frequency words with few consistently pronounced neighbors. This led

Jared et al. to their suggestion that it is the *combination* of consistently and inconsistently pronounced orthographic neighbors that combines to determine word naming time.

Furthermore, they provided some evidence that it was *token* frequency (i.e., the summed frequency for all neighbors) rather than *type* frequency (number of different words in the neighborhood, ignoring frequency) that was relevant in determining pronunciation time. Thus, there is ample empirical evidence in support of the general conclusion that the consistency of pronunciation of a word's orthographic rime will determine the ease of its reading.

Treiman et al. (1995) were the first to go beyond this general claim, and they did so in two important ways. First of all, they examined the ability of a quantitative measure of consistency to predict individual word-naming latencies and error rates. Specifically, the measure they used was the ratio of consistent to all pronunciations of a given orthographic segment (note that this is exactly the consistency ratio that the rational analysis discussed earlier predicted should be influential). Second, they directly compared the ability of the consistency of different orthographic segments (at different levels) to predict latencies and accuracies. This allowed conclusions to be drawn about the size of orthographic units used by skilled readers. First of all, Treiman et al. found that the consistency ratio of orthographic rimes in monosyllabic words accounted for independent variance in both naming latency and error rate. This finding was obtained in two large analyses, each of several hundred words. They also found effects of other units (e.g., the graphemes at the beginnings and ends of words), but here the focus is on orthographic rime effects. The fact that Treiman et al. found these strong independent effects of rimes consistency ratio is highly consistent with the ROAR framework described previously.

However, further evidence could be obtained if it could be shown that this consistency ratio is the *only* spelling-to-sound measure to influence performance, as predicted by the optimal reading account. In order to attempt further evaluation of this, Brown (1996) examined the ability of the rime consistency ratio measure to account for variance in other published data. In one of their experiments, Jared et al. (1990) measured naming latency for eight different word types, varying in spelling-to-sound consistency. Both consistent and inconsistent words were used, with either high- or low-summed frequencies of consistent and inconsistent neighbors. Brown (1996) found that the simple consistency ratio was very highly correlated (around 0.95) with mean naming latency for the different word types, and also highly correlated with error rate. A simple multiple regression, with consistency ratio as the only factor, predicted every one of the eight mean naming latencies to within 4 milliseconds. Partial correlations were also carried out, to examine whether the total frequency of consistently pronounced neighbors, or the total number of inconsistently pronounced neighbors, would be related to naming latency or error rate after the effects of the consistency ratio measure were taken into account. Although the results of this analysis should be treated with considerable caution due to the small number of data points, in all cases it was found that there was no independent correlation between performance and the other measures of the spelling-to-sound characteristics of the rimes in the different word types. The comparisons between different spelling-to-sound measures are not strong evidence in themselves. However, in combination with the Treiman et al. (1995) results, the analyses do provide some evidence consistent with the optimal reading hypothesis.

In an attempt to predict a larger number of data points, Brown (1996) used the consistency ratio measure to predict the results of Jared et al.'s meta-analysis of more than 20 studies of consistency effects previously reported in the literature. All of these studies examined spelling-to-sound consistency effects at the rime level, and it was on the basis of their meta-analyses of the numbers of consistently and inconsistently pronounced orthographic neighbors of the words used in the various studies that Jared et al. concluded that the numbers of consistently and inconsistently pronounced orthographic neighbors of a word combine and conspire to determine the word's naming latency. For present purposes, the question of interest is whether the effect size can be predicted by the consistency ratios of the orthographic rimes of the stimuli used in the various experiments brought together by Jared et al.[2]

Figure 5.1 shows the effects size in 20 of the experiments described by Jared et al. as a function of consistency ratio as calculated by Brown (1996) from the data provided in Jared et al. (1990).[3] It can be seen that, consistent with the optimal reading hypothesis, there is an extremely good relation between spelling-to-sound consistency ratio and the size of the observed consistency effect. Partial correlations again found that the overall frequency of consistently or inconsistently pronounced neighbors of the word failed to correlate independently with naming latencies. This analysis therefore provides some tentative evidence consistent with the claim embodied in the ROAR model; namely, the claim that consistency ratio should be the *only* measure of spelling-to-sound consistency to account for variation in performance in skilled adult reading. Further evaluation of this claim will be important to distinguish the specific predictions of the ROAR model from the more general claim, made by a number of researchers, that the relative proportions of consistently and inconsistently pronounced orthographic neighbors will conspire in some way to determine naming latency or accuracy.

---

[2]Note that all of the experiments considered were primarily designed to examine the consistency of pronunciation of orthographic rimes, and it is therefore reasonable to assume that effects of spelling-to-sound consistency at other levels of analysis would not be a major factor in the present analyses.

[3]Three studies were excluded prior to analysis as unrepresentative; see Brown (1996) for further discussion.

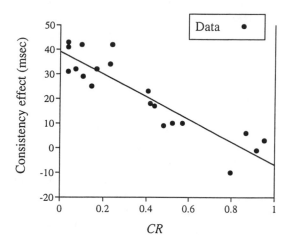

FIG. 5.1. Observed and predicted consistency effect sizes (observed and predicted effect size, analysis from Brown, 1996; data from Jared et al., 1990). *CR* = consistency ratio.

The studies and analyses described here have focused on the effect of consistency of pronunciation of orthographic rimes, because it is on that issue that most of the data are available. Such quantitative evidence as exists for skilled adult reading concerning the effects of consistency at other levels of analysis (e.g., of individual graphemes) comes mainly from the analyses carried out by Treiman et al. (1995). Such effects as were found in that study were also effects of the consistency ratio of the orthographic units examined. Thus, these results are also consistent with the predictions of the ROAR model, although they do not provide strong evidence for it. Further evidence will be necessary to compare the effects of different quantitative measures of spelling-to-sound consistency for various levels of correspondence. Brown (1996) reviewed further evidence consistent with the optimal reading analysis, and also suggested that the approach could account for the widely observed interactions between spelling-to-sound consistency and word frequency.

IMPLICATIONS FOR LEARNING

This section examines some of the implications for learning of taking seriously the view of reading as statistics described previously. If the endpoint of successful learning to read can be characterized as an internalization of the statistical regularities embodied in the English spelling-to-sound mapping system, then our understanding of the best way to attain that endpoint may be increased by examination of other learning systems that are designed to do exactly that: connectionist learning systems. Connectionist models of learning work by extracting out underlying statistical structure from a set of learned exemplars. They can be seen as performing statistical inference, in that they infer a model from a set of data (see Chater, 1995, for extensive discussion). Over the last few years, connectionist models of learning have provided us with important insights about the nature of statistical learning systems and the conditions under which different kinds of input–output mapping systems are easy or difficult to learn. This section briefly reviews some of the conclusions that have emerged from this work, because they have important potential implications for the process of learning to read. First, an important caveat: The present chapter focuses mainly on evidence relevant to the order of learning of regular and irregular words in beginning reading. In order to emphasize the issues that concern us here, motivational issues are largely ignored on the assumption that they cut across the questions addressed here. The importance of providing a rich and rewarding environment in which reading learning can take place is clear; here, the focus is on general issues concerning the learning of a system containing regular and exceptional items that may apply independent of the wider framework that is adopted.

Catastrophic Interference

Studies of associative learning in both human and connectionist learning systems have paid much attention to the phenomenon of *catastrophic interference* (Barnes & Underwood, 1959; McCloskey & Cohen 1989; Ratcliff, 1990). The phenomenon is most easily illustrated using the paradigm classically used to demonstrate it. Barnes and Underwood (1959) trained subjects to associate items from one list (List A) with items from another list (List B). When these A-B associations had been learned, a second set of associations was learned, in this case between List A items and a new set of items, List C items. The question of interest is the extent to which the more recently learned A-C associations interfere with or overwrite the first-learned A-B associations. Barnes and Underwood found gradual and incomplete forgetting of the A-B associations throughout learning of the A-C associations, and even when the A-C associations were completely learned much memory was retained for the original A-B associations. In other words, the learning of new information only partially and gradually interferes with existing stored knowledge. This phenomenon has attracted particular interest in recent years, because it appears that connectionist models of learning and memory suffered from "catastrophic interference" in that learning the new set of associations (the A-C associations) caused rapid and total forgetting of the first-learned A-B associations (e.g., McCloskey & Cohen, 1989). This is catastrophic interference.

Ratcliff (1990) further analyzed the conditions under which catastrophic interference occurs. The AB-AC paradigm, as it has become known, captures an important aspect of the task facing children as they learn to read. In this case, orthographic and phonological representations are the patterns to become associated to one another. Just as more than one item becomes associated to each List A item in the Barnes and Underwood paradigm, more than one phonological pattern may become associated to a given orthographic segment. Thus, it will clearly be undesirable if, having initially learned that the orthographic sequence -ave is pronounced /eɪv/ (as in rave, gave, save, etc.), subsequent learning that -ave is sometimes pronounced /ʌv/ as in have completely wipes out prior knowledge of the original association. In other words, it is important to ensure that catastrophic interference is avoided in learning the mapping from spelling to sound. In the connectionist modeling literature, various solutions to the problem of catastrophic interference have been proposed (e.g. French, 1992; Lewandowsky, 1991). However, of most interest to the present proposal is a kind of learning known as interleaved learning (McClelland, McNaughton, & O'Reilly, 1995).

Interleaved Learning and Gradient Descent Learning

A recent insight into connectionist learning systems concerns the need for two completely different kinds of learning to be possible (McClelland et al., 1995). On the one hand, it is necessary to be able to store distinguishable representations of (perhaps similar) events after a single exposure. On the other hand, it is by now well-established that slow incremental learning procedures, in which the weights in a network change just a small amount after presentation of each item in the set to be learned, is good for extracting underlying regularities in the mapping to be learned. In such systems, similar representations are assigned to similar items. Thus, these slow incremental learning procedures (e.g., gradient descent learning algorithms, such as back propagation in connectionist nets) are well suited to developing systems that are good at generalization. This is because the structure of the underlying system only changes by a small amount in response to each presented exemplar, and therefore a single atypical instance cannot have too great an influence on the underlying structure of the network. This leads to a system which is (a) sensitive to the underlying regularities in the mapping to be learned, and (b) good at generalization, because it has extracted what is common to all the examples with which it has been presented. It is therefore no coincidence that slow incremental learning procedures such as the back propagation or other error-correcting rules widely used in connectionist systems have provided good models of the learning of underlying regularities inherent in mappings such as the English spelling-to-sound mapping systems

(Plaut et al., 1996; Seidenberg & McClelland, 1989) or the English verb tense system (Plunkett & Marchman, 1991, 1993; Rumelhart & McClelland, 1986).

A further important characteristic of these systems is that they avoid the catastrophic interference referred to earlier because they use what McClelland et al. (1995) referred to as *interleaved learning*. This means that different example are not presented all at once, in blocks, but rather are "interleaved" (so that, e.g., irregular examples would be interspersed among regular exemplars). This has the additional consequence that the relative frequencies of different exemplars can be accurately represented in the connection strengths of the fully learned system. It remains to be seen how far such findings can be generalized to the case of learning to read. However, on the basis of computational results already established, it seems likely that interleaved learning will provide the most efficient method of ending up with a system in which both regular and irregular spelling-to-sound correspondences can be represented. Thus, for example, massed practice of regular or consistent items, followed by massed practice of irregular items, would be likely (if the previous analysis applies to real reading learning) to lead to undesirable forgetting of the originally learned regularities. Given that the final system must encode both regular spelling-to-sound correspondences and exceptions to those regularities, it seems likely that interleaved learning of regular and exceptional items will be most efficient.[4]

Little empirical investigation has been done on the issue of how to introduce regular and irregular items in children's reading, although researchers such as Kryzanowski and Carnine (1980), as well as others, found the expected general advantage for distributed versus massed practice—in one study, nearly twice as many correct posttraining naming responses were made to letters when they had been presented in distributed rather than blocked patterns (cf. also Rea & Modigliani, 1985). This study only examined responses to single letters, however, and it is possible that interleaved learning may be particularly important under conditions where multiple responses must be associated with a single input (as with ambiguously or inconsistently pronounced orthographic segments).

Thus, there is at least suggestive evidence that interleaved learning may provide the best way of avoiding catastrophic interference in leaning of input–output mapping systems such as the English spelling-to-sound map-

---

[4]One possible exception to this is provided by the phenomenon of "starting small" (Elman, 1990). In studying the acquisition of syntax, Elman showed that a system can best learn if it is initially exposed to a relatively simplified form of the grammar to be learned, thus enabling it to encode solidly the underlying regularities in the system, and then is subsequently introduced to more complex mappings (longer distance dependencies, in the case of syntax acquisition). This shows that there are some circumstances under which a connectionist learning system can most easily accommodate both exceptions and regularities if it is intially made easy for the system to encode regularities. If the system is, in contrast, given the task of learning the simple and complex regularities all at once, it may fail ever to learn the underlying regularities.

ping system, as well as extracting out the relevant underlying structural regularities that will allow generalization. It remains to be seen whether the predictions of this account can be confirmed experimentally.

Additional evidence concerning the conditions under which it is easiest for regular and exceptional items to become represented in the same system is reviewed next.

THE IMPORTANCE OF RELATIVE FREQUENCY

In studying the acquisition of verb tense learning, Plunkett and Marchman (1991) delineated some important constraints on the conditions under which exceptions and exceptions/subregularities can become represented within the same system. A complete review of this research is beyond the scope of this chapter, but for present purposes one significant conclusion may be emphasized. This is that, in a simple associative network, exceptions can only become stably represented in a system where there are underlying and conflicting regularities if the exception items are sufficiently high in frequency. If the (token) frequency of exceptional items is too low, then it is difficult or impossible for the correct output to become associated with them, for the tendency to regularize those items due to the high frequency of regular items becomes too strong. Therefore, it appears to be no accident that in language systems such as the English spelling-to-sound system or verb tense formation the irregular items tend to be high in token frequency. This appears to be a computational consequence of the need to represent exceptions and regularities in the same system.

Again this has important implications for learning. It suggests that it might be a mistake to avoid as far as possible exceptional items in the early stages of reading learning, because the irregular items will be swamped and be hard or impossible to represent if they are too low in token frequency. Again, there is a dearth of empirical evidence on this question. Although there is as yet no evidence against it, the conclusion must remain tentative, and the additional possibility remains that an early emphasis on regular items may lead to a useful focus on the levels of representation over which regularities may be defined. The importance of representations is discussed in the next section.

THE IMPORTANCE OF REPRESENTATION

Subsequent to the influential connectionist reading model of Seidenberg and McClelland (1989), much research has demonstrated that the nature of the *representations* that a connectionist model of reading is provided with has a major impact on its performance. The Seidenberg and McClelland model was criticized for its poor nonword reading performance (Besner, Twilley, McCann, & Seergobin, 1990), but improved nonword performance can be obtained if more fine-grained input and output representations are used. These allow the network to more easily capture generalizations at the level of graphemes and phonemes (e.g., Brown, 1997; Bullinaria, 1995; Norris, 1994; Plaut et al., 1996). Therefore, a model that is provided with explicit representations at many different levels will perform well (Norris, 1994; see also Phillips, Hay, & Smith, 1993). Furthermore, it has been argued that some paradoxical deficits associated with developmental dyslexia may be explained in terms of the computational capacity of a network (Brown & Loosemore, 1995; Seidenberg & McClelland, 1989) or, alternatively, in terms of the specificity of the representations given to the model (Brown, 1997; Metsala & Brown, in press). Finally, it is well-established that a network will learn more easily if it is provided with prestructured phonological output representations (Harm, Altmann, & Seidenberg, 1994; Hulme, Snowling, & Quinlan, 1991). Other extensions of the approach have been more concerned to introduce alternative routes into the model.

This evidence for the importance of representation will, of course, come as no surprise to those involved in reading instruction (see, e.g., Stahl & Murray, chap. 3, this volume; Torgesen & Burgess, chap. 7, this volume). However, the computational results described here do enable an understanding of how the importance of developing the right phonological and orthographic representations can be understood as the behavior of a system developing toward an endpoint that is characterized by statistically optimal behavior in a given cognitive domain.

DISCUSSION

The aim of this chapter has been to show that new perspectives on the nature of skilled adult reading may have important implications for our understanding of the best way to teach reading skills. Although much further research remains to be done, empirical evidence consistent with the idea that skilled adult reading involves statistically optimal or adaptively rational behavior has been reviewed. Thus, the process of learning to decode the spelling-to-sound system can be seen as just one instantiation of the general cognitive process of coming to internalise the statistical structure of the environment. This view leads naturally to an emphasis on the role of task structuring in instruction.

A consequence of this perspective is that general results obtained from the study of statistical learning become relevant to reading instruction. The final section drew attention to some results from the study of learning in connectionist systems and suggested that these results might have implications for the process of literacy instruction. Relatively little empirical work has addressed these issues. Some relevant work was conducted by Becker, Carnine, Engelmann, and their colleagues in the early 1980s as their theory of instruction. The direct instruction model (e.g., Becker, Engelmann, Carnine, & Rhine, 1981) was based on the assumption that classroom learning can be enhanced by careful engineering of students' interaction with the environment to be learned. This research program emphasized the importance of the analysis of sameness and differences among examples used in teaching. The aim was to identify, in the input to be learned, the structural basis for generalization. In general terms this fits well with the insights from computational learning described previously. As Carnine and Becker (1982) pointed out, an enormous work on stimulus generalization has been carried out under the banner of learning theory. They focused on the implications for generalization in learning to read. How does one structure a set of examples to ensure maximum generalization, and how should the design be informed on the basis of the underlying structure of sameness and difference in the examples to be used? Much of the direct instruction approach was motivated toward drawing attention to significant contrasts, by using sets of training exemplars that are only minimally different from one another (see, e.g., Carnine & Becker, 1982). On the basis of the computational results outlined earlier, it is suggested that there is ample reason to believe that learning of the English spelling-to-sound mapping system may be greatly facilitated if regular and inconsistent items are introduced in an appropriate order, with appropriate frequency, and if practice is carefully scheduled to facilitate maintenance and generalization (Rea & Modigliani, 1985; Schmidt & Bjork, 1992). There is little evidence that current educational practice approaches optimality in any of these respects.

ACKNOWLEDGMENTS

The research reported here was partially supported by a grant from the Economic and Social Research Council (U.K.), R000 23 2576. I thank Jonathan Solity for many helpful discussions. Correspondence concerning this article should be addressed to Gordon D. A. Brown, Department of Psychology, University of Warwick, Coventry, CV4 7AL, U.K. E-mail: pssac@warwick.ac.uk

REFERENCES

Anderson, J. R. (1990). *The adaptive character of thought.* Hillsdale, NJ: Lawrence Erlbaum Associates.
Anderson, J. R., & Milson, R. (1989). Human memory: An adaptive perspective. *Psychological Review, 96,* 703–719.

Anderson, J. R., & Schooler, L. J. (1991). Reflections of the environment in memory. *Psychological Science, 2,* 396–408.

Barnes, J. M., & Underwood, B. J. (1959). "Fate" of first-list associations in transfer theory. *Journal of Experimental Psychology, 58,* 97–105.

Becker, W. C., Engelmann, S., Carnine, D. W., & Rhine, W. R. (1981). Direct instruction model. In W. R. Rhine (Ed.), *Making schools more effective.* New York: Academic.

Besner, D., Twilley, L., McCann, R. S., & Seergobin, K. (1990). On the association between connectionism and data: Are a few words necessary? *Psychological Review, 97,* 432–446.

Bowey, J. A. (1996). Phonological recoding of nonword orthographic rime primes. *Journal of Experimental Psychology: Learning, Memory, and Cognition, 22,* 117–131.

Bowey, J. A., & Hansen, J. (1994). The development of orthographic rimes as units of word recognition. *Journal of Experimental Child Psychology, 58,* 465–488.

Brown, G. D. A. (1987). Resolving inconsistency: A computational model of word naming. *Journal of Memory and Language, 26,* 1–23.

Brown, G. D. A. (1996). *A rational analysis of reading: Spelling-to-sound translation is optimal.* Manuscript submitted for publication.

Brown, G. D. A. (1997). Developmental and acquired dyslexia: A connectionist comparison. *Brain and Language.*

Brown, G. D. A., & Loosemore, R. L. (1994). Computational approaches to normal and impaired spelling. In G. D. A. Brown & N. C. Ellis (Eds.), *Handbook of spelling: Theory, process and application* (pp. 9–33). Chichester, England: Wiley.

Brown, G. D. A., & Loosemore, R. L. (1995). A computational approach to dyslexic reading and spelling. In C. K. Leong & R. M. Joshi (Eds.), *Developmental and acquired dyslexia: Neuropsychological and neurolinguistic perspectives* (pp. 195–219). Dordrecht, The Netherlands: Kluwer.

Brown, G. D. A., & Vousden, J. I. (in press). Adaptive analysis of sequential behaviour: Oscillators as rational mechanisms. To appear in M. Oaksford & N. Chater (Eds.), *Rational models of cognition.* Oxford, England: OUP.

Brown, G. D. A., & Watson, F. L. (1994). Spelling-to-sound effects in single-word reading. *British Journal of Psychology, 85,* 181–202.

Bullinaria, J. D. (1995). Neural network models of reading without wickelfeatures. In J. Levy, D. Bairaktaris, J. Bullinaria, & D. Cairns (Eds.), *Connectionist models of memory and language* (pp. 161–178). London: UCL Press.

Carnine, D. W., & Becker, W. C. (1982). Theory of instruction: Generalisation issues. *Educational Psychology, 2,* 249–262.

Chater, N. (1995). Neural networks: The new statistical models of mind. In J. Levy, D. Bairaktaris, J. Bullinaria, & D. Cairns (Eds.), *Connectionist models of memory and language* (pp. 207–228). London: UCL Press.

Coltheart, M., Curtis, Atkins, P., & Haller, M. (1993). Models of reading aloud: Dual-route and parallel-distributed-processing accounts. *Psychological Review, 100,* 589–608.

Coltheart, V., & Leahy, J. (1992). Children's and adults' reading of nonwords: Effects of regularity and consistency. *Journal of Experimental Psychology: Learning, Memory and Cognition, 18,* 718–729.

French, R. M. (1992). Semi-distributed representations and catastrophic forgetting in connectionist networks. *Connection Science, 4,* 365–377.

Glushko, R. J. (1979). The organization and activation of orthographic knowledge in reading aloud. *Journal of Experimental Psychology: Human Perception and Performance, 5,* 674–691.

Harm, M., Altmann, L., & Seidenberg, M. S. (1994). Using connectionist networks to examine the role of prior constraints in human learning. *Proceedings of the Sixteenth Annual Conference of the Cognitive Science Society* (pp. 392–396). Hillsdale, NJ: Lawrence Erlbaum Associates.

Hulme, C., Snowling, M., & Quinlan, P. (1991). Connectionism and learning to read: Steps towards a psychologically plausible model. *Reading and Writing, 3*(2), 159–168.

Jared, D., McRae, K., & Seidenberg, M. S. (1990). The basis of consistency effects in word naming. *Journal of Memory and Language, 29,* 687–715.

Kryzanowski, J. A., & Carnine, D. W. (1980). Effects of massed versus distributed practice schedules in teaching sound-symbol correspondences to young children. *Journal of Reading Behavior, 8,* 225–229.

Kucera, H., & Francis, W. (1967). *Computational analysis of present-day American English.* Providence, RI: Brown University Press.

Laxon, V., Masterson, J., & Coltheart, V. (1991). Some bodies are easier to read: The effect of consistency and regularity on children's reading. *Quarterly Journal of Experimental Psychology, 43A,* 793–824.

Laxon, V., Masterson, J., & Moran, R. (1994). Are children's representations of words distributed? Effects of orthographic neighbourhood size, consistency and regularity of naming. *Language and Cognitive Processes, 9,* 1–27.

Lewandowsky, S. (1991). Gradual unlearning and catastrophic interference: A comparison of distributed architectures. In W. E. Hockley, & S. Lewandowsky (Eds.), *Relating theory and data: Essays on human memory in honor of Bennet B. Murdock* (pp. 445–476). Hillsdale, NJ: Lawrence Erlbaum Associates.

McClelland, J. L., McNaughton, B. L., & O'Reilly, R. C. (1995). Why there are complementary learning systems in the hippocampus and neocortex: Insights from the successes and failures of connectionist models of learning and memory. *Psychological Review, 102,* 419–457.

McCloskey, M., & Cohen, N. J. (1989). Catastrophic interference in connectionist networks: The sequential learning problem. In G. H. Bower (Ed.), *The psychology of learning and motivation* (Vol. 24, pp. 109–165). New York: Academic.

Metsala, J. L., & Brown, G. D. A. (in press). The development of orthographic units in reading and spelling. To appear in R. M. Joshi & C. Hulme (Eds.), *Reading and spelling: Development and disorders.* Mahwah, NJ: Lawrence Erlbaum Associates.

Norris, D. (1994). A quantitative model of reading aloud. *Journal of Experimental Psychology: Human Perception and Performance, 20,* 1212–1232.

Phillips, W. A., Hay, I. M., & Smith, L. S. (1993). Lexicality and pronunciation in a simulated neural net. *British Journal of Mathematical and Statistical Psychology, 46,* 193–205.

Plaut, D. C., McClelland, J. L., Seidenberg, M. S., & Patterson, K. E. (1996). Understanding normal and impaired word reading: Computational principles in quasi-regular domains. *Psychological Review, 103,* 56–105.

Plunkett, K., & Marchman, V. (1991). U-shaped learning and frequency effects in a multi-layered perception: Implications for child language acquisition. *Cognition, 38,* 43–102.

Plunkett, K., & Marchman, V. (1993). From rote learning to system building: Acquiring verb morphology in children and connectionist nets. *Cognition, 48,* 21–69.

Ratcliff, R. (1990). Connectionist models of recognition memory: Constraints imposed by learning and forgetting functions. *Psychological Review, 97,* 285–308.

Rea, C. P., & Modigliani, V. (1985). The effect of expanded vs. massed practice on the retention of mulitplication facts and spelling lists. *Human Learning, 4,* 11–18.

Rumelhart, D. E., & McClelland, J. L. (1986). On learning the past tenses of English verbs. In J. L. McClelland & D. E. Rumelhart (Eds.), *Parallel distributed processing: Explorations in the microstructure of cognition* (Vol. 2, pp. 216–271). Cambridge, MA: Bradford Books/MIT Press.

Schmidt, R. A., & Bjork, R. A. (1992). New conceptualizations of practice: Common principles in three paradigms suggest new concepts for training. *Psychological Science, 3,* 207–217.

Seidenberg, M. S., & McClelland, J. L. (1989). A distributed, developmental model of word recognition and naming. *Psychological Review, 96,* 523–568.

Seidenberg, M. S., Waters, G. S., Barnes, M. A., & Tanenhaus, M. K. (1984). When does irregular spelling influence word recognition. *Journal of Verbal Learning and Verbal Behavior, 23,* 383–404.

Taraban, R., & McClelland, J. L. (1987). Conspiracy effects in word pronunciation. *Journal of Memory and Language, 26,* 608–631.

Treiman, R., Goswami, U., & Bruck, M. (1990). Not all nonwords are alike: Implications for reading development and theory. *Memory & Cognition, 18,* 559–567.

Treiman, R., Mullennix, J., Bijeljac-Babic, R., & Richmond-Welty, E. D. (1995). The special role of rimes in the description, use, and acquisition of English orthography. *Journal of Experimental Psychology: General, 124,* 107–136.

Waters, G. S., & Seidenberg, M. S. (1985). Spelling-sound effects in reading: Time course and decision criteria. *Memory & Cognition, 13,* 557–572.

Waters, G. S., Seidenberg, M. S., & Bruck, M. (1984). Children's and adults' use of spelling-sound information in three reading tasks. *Memory & Cognition, 12,* 293–305.

II
▼▼▼▼▼▼▼

PROCESSES AND INSTRUCTION
FOR DISABLED READERS

6

▼▼▼▼▼▼▼

Phonological Processing
Deficits and Reading Disabilities

Linda S. Siegel
University of British Columbia

During the past 15 years, a consensus has gradually emerged in the scientific
literature that the fundamental problem underlying dyslexia or reading disability (these terms are interchangeable) is a phonological processing deficit.
In this chapter, I review the evidence for this position from a variety of
sources, including (a) a description of how a phonological deficit in dyslexia
manifests itself in a variety of tasks; (b) evidence that the phonological deficit
in dyslexia is universal and occurs in all languages, independent of their
orthographic systems; (c) the modularity of phonological processing and its
independence from general cognitive ability; and (d) the role of phonological
processing in beginning reading, especially for children who have difficulty
acquiring basic reading skills.

PSEUDOWORD READING

In an alphabetic language such as English, the best measure of phonological
processing skill is the reading of pseudowords; that is, pronounceable combinations of letters that can be read by the application of grapheme–phoneme
conversion rules, but that are, by definition, not real words in English. Examples include pseudowords such as *shum*, *laip*, and *cigbet*. Pseudowords
can be read by application of grapheme–phoneme conversion rules even
though the words are not real and have not been encountered in print or in
spoken language. Although it has been argued that pseudowords may be

read by analogy to words, some awareness of grapheme–phoneme correspondence rules and segmentation skills are necessary to read a pseudoword
correctly. For example, for a correct reading of the pseudoword *dake*, it
must be segmented into an initial letter *d* and a rime or word body *ake*; the
latter could be read by analogy to cake but the sound of *d* and the segmentation itself are, in fact, phonological processing skills.

The development of the ability to read pseudowords has been studied
extensively (e.g., Calfee, Lindamood, & Lindamood, 1973; Hogaboam &
Perfetti, 1978; Siegel & Ryan, 1988; Venezky & Johnson, 1973). Ample
evidence indicates that children with dyslexia have a great deal of difficulty
reading pseudowords. Studies such as those of Bruck (1988), Ehri and Wilce
(1983), Snowling (1980), Siegel and Ryan (1988), and Waters, Bruck, and
Seidenberg (1985) have shown that disabled readers have more difficulty
reading pseudowords than do normal readers matched on either chronological age or reading level. In a recent review, Rack, Snowling, and Olson (1992)
found that, in most of the studies, dyslexics had significantly lower scores
on pseudoword reading tasks, even when matched on reading level. For
example, Siegel and Ryan (1988) studied the development of the ability to
read pseudowords in normal and disabled readers aged 7 to 14 years old.
By the age of 9, the normal readers were quite proficient and performed
almost perfectly, reading even the most difficult pseudowords with as many
as three syllables. However, the performance of the reading-disabled children
was quite different. These children appeared to acquire such reading skills
very late in development. Even at age 14, many disabled readers performed
no better than normal readers aged 7.

In order to control, at least partially, for experience with print, Siegel and
Ryan (1988) compared disabled readers to younger normal readers matched
on reading grade level. Despite the match, the performance of the reading
disabled on a task involving the reading of pseudowords was significantly
poorer than that of the normal readers. Thus, difficulties with phonological
processing seem to be a fundamental problem of children with reading
disability, and this problem continues into adulthood. Many adults with a
reading disability become reasonably fluent readers but still have difficulty
reading pseudowords accurately or quickly (e.g., Barwick & Siegel, in press;
Bruck, 1990; Greenberg, Ehri, & Perin, in press; Shafrir & Siegel, 1994;
Siegel, 1996).

Children with reading problems have processing difficulties on a wide
range of phonological structures. To study these issues, we showed disabled
and normal readers words and pseudowords that exhibited a variety of
grapheme–phoneme conversion rules, such as consonant blends, *r*-influenced
vowels, and inconsistent vowels (Siegel & Faux, 1989). We found that complexity, as measured by the number of syllables in a pseudoword, was a
significant determinant of the difficulty of reading the pseudoword. Pseudowords

with two or more syllables were very difficult for older disabled readers (11 to 13 years), even though normal readers had become quite proficient by the age of 9 or 10. Even simple vowels and consonant blends had not been mastered by the oldest children with reading disabilities (ages 11 to 14) when they were required to read pseudowords such as *mog*, *lun*, and *spad*, although most of the 7- and 8-year-old normal readers had no difficulty with these features in words or pseudowords.

In most cases, even when the disabled readers appeared to demonstrate mastery of grapheme–phoneme conversion rules when they read a word, they were unable to read a pseudoword with the same rule. Even when they could read words with particular grapheme–phoneme correspondences in CVC words, such as *ran*, *wet*, and *sit*, they could not read pseudowords such as *han*, *fet*, and *rit*; and although they could read words involving consonant blends, such as *hunt*, *spot*, and *help*, they could not read pseudowords of a similar structure, such as *lunt*, *grot*, and *melp*.

One relatively simple rule having few exceptions in English is that a final *e* in a one-syllable word makes the vowel long. This rule had not been mastered by the older reading-disabled children at the age of 12 to 14 (Siegel & Faux, 1989). Although they could correctly read the words that reflected the rule (e.g., *like*, *cute*, *nose*), they could not read the comparable pseudowords (e.g., *rike*, *fute*, *mose*). The disabled readers had significantly lower scores than did the normal readers of the same reading age on the following tasks: reading one-syllable pseudowords at reading grade level 3, reading two-syllable pseudowords at reading grade level 4–5, reading multisyllable pseudowords at reading grade level 6, and reading pseudowords with consonant blends at grade levels 2, 3, and 6.

One possible explanation for the superiority of words over pseudowords can be understood in the context of dual-route theories of reading. Dual-route theories postulate that there are two routes to access the meaning of a presented word. One of these routes, the phonological route, involves the translation of letters or groups of letters into sounds. The other route, the direct or visual route, involves lexical access without any intermediate phonolgical processing skills. Direct lexical access might involve attempting to process each word as a picture (visual representation) retrieved from long-term memory, rather than as a series of letters with sounds. The direct route may involve visual memory, or storing partial letter-sound representations in memory (e.g., Ehri & Saltmarsh, 1995). It is possible that the reading-disabled children were using some sort of direct lexical access that worked in reading words but did not in reading pseudowords.

English orthography is characterized by variable correspondences between graphemes and phonemes. That is, when reading a given grapheme, one often cannot predict its pronunciation with certainty. Some words are regular (e.g., *paid*, *gave*, *heat*) and can be read using the rules of pronunciation of their component graphemes. Other words are irregular or exceptions, and they violate grapheme–phoneme conversion rules and have no rhymes with similar spelling patterns (e.g., *said, have, great*). Words in another category also have irregular grapheme–phoneme correspondences but, in addition, have unusual spellings that do not occur in many other words, such as *aisle, ache,* and *tongue.* Waters, Seidenberg, and Bruck (1984) found that younger normal and poor readers were sensitive to the effects of irregular spelling and irregular grapheme–phoneme correspondence and took longer to read words with these characteristics. The children also showed the effects of frequency, in that differences among regular and exception words were greater for low-frequency words, such as *pint* and *wool,* than for high-frequency words.

Other studies have shown that poor readers have difficulty with exception words (Manis & Morrison, 1985; Seidenberg, Bruck, Fornarolo, & Backman, 1985). However, still other studies have not found any difference between regular and irregular words for disabled readers (Frith & Snowling, 1983; Seymour & Porpodas, 1980; Siegel & Ryan, 1988). If regular words with regular pronunciations are not read more easily than irregular words, this suggests that grapheme–phoneme conversion rules are not being used. In addition, disabled readers are much less likely than normal readers to regularize the vowels in irregular words (Seidenberg et al., 1985). Backman, Bruck, Hebert, and Seidenberg (1984) showed good and poor readers regular words (e.g., *hope*), exception words (*said*), regular inconsistent words (i.e., words with regular pronunciations but with irregular orthographically similar neighbors; e.g., *paid* and *said*), ambiguous words (e.g., *clown* because *own* can be pronounced as in *down* or *blown*), and pseudowords constructed to test these orthographic features.

Backman, Bruck, Hebert, and Seidenberg (1984) found that beginning readers appear to be using the visual route for high-frequency words but they are also learning more about grapheme–phoneme conversion rules. Young readers and poor readers had difficulty reading homographic patterns; that is, orthographic patterns with multiple pronunciations such as *-ose* in *hose, lose,* and *dose.* Poor readers were not as skilled at using grapheme–phoneme conversion rules and had more difficulty with orthographic patterns that had multiple pronunciations. Poor readers also had more difficulty than did normal readers with the exception, inconsistent, and ambiguous words, and tended to make fewer regularization errors. Poor readers also had more difficulty with pseudowords. Under normal circumstances, as children get older they become more skilled at reading the irregular and unpredictable aspects of English orthography. Poor readers, however, continue to have difficulty with the orthographic features that are not predictable, but do well with high-frequency regular words. Young normal readers read the regular words that were of high frequency quite well, but made more errors on exception, regular inconsistent, and ambiguous words. Older good readers performed at a level comparable to high school comparison subjects.

Although most errors on the exception words involved regularizations (e.g., *come* pronounced as *coam*) rather than errors that were not (*come* pronounced as *came*), younger children made fewer regularizations than did older children and high school students. However, fewer errors involved giving regular inconsistent words an irregular pronunciation (e.g., *bone* read as *bun*, like *done*).

Seidenberg et al. (1985) also found that poor and disabled readers took longer and were less accurate in reading words with homographic patterns (e.g., *one*, as in *done* and *gone*) than normal readers. Exception words were the hardest for good readers but they read regular inconsistent, ambiguous, and regular words equally well. This pattern suggests that good readers were significantly influenced by grapheme–phoneme conversion rules because exception words, by definition, violate these rules, and these words were the most difficult to read. Poor and disabled readers made more errors on exception, regular inconsistent, and ambiguous words than on regular words.

English vowels tend to have more complex and irregular pronunciations than do English consonants, and, therefore, present a special challenge for individuals with reading problems. The grapheme–phoneme correspondences of English vowels are very unpredictable. There are more alternative vowel spellings corresponding to particular vowel phonemes than there are alternative consonant spellings for particular consonantal phonemes. Consequently, misreadings of vowels occur more frequently than do misreadings of consonants (Fowler, Shankweiler, & Liberman, 1979; Weber, 1970). Unlike consonants, which are more likely to be misread in the final than the initial position, the position of a vowel has no effect on the probability that it will be misread. Unlike consonant errors, vowel errors are unrelated to their target sound; that is, they are random in regard to phonetic features. According to Fowler, Liberman, and Shankweiler (1977), vowels are less clearly defined and are more subject to individual and dialect variation. Vowels are the foundation of the syllable and code the prosodic features, and consonants carry the information.

English vowels have the property that their pronunciation can change depending on the context. An example is the rule that an *e* at the end of a word usually makes the vowel long. The reading of vowels is *context free* if this rule is ignored and the vowel is pronounced with the short vowel sound (e.g., *cape* read as *cap*), and the reading is *context dependent* if the rule is followed (Fowler et al., 1979). Fowler et al. administered pseudowords to young normal readers and found that most of the responses to vowels were not random but were either context dependent or context free. Context-dependent responses increased with increasing age, indicating growing awareness of the relationships between spelling patterns and vowel pronunciations. Even the youngest readers, who had received only 1 year of reading instruction, could apply their knowledge of orthographic regularities to pseudowords.

As noted earlier, disabled readers are less likely to regularize the vowels in irregular words. Bryson and Werker (1989) administered a pseudoword reading task to disabled readers to determine whether they were more likely to read vowels as context dependent. As normal readers gained reading skills, they made more context dependent responses. Some of the reading-disabled children (those with significantly higher performance than verbal IQ scores) made more context-free responses than did age- and reading-level-matched controls. Some of the reading-disabled children did not make context-free errors. However, note that these children were defined on the basis of below-grade-level scores on a reading comprehension and/or text reading test. As noted earlier, children with low scores on these types of reading tests may *not* have poor word recognition or decoding skills; therefore, these children may not have been reading disabled in the sense used in the present chapter (for evidence on this point, see Siegel & Heaven, 1986; Siegel, Levey, & Ferris, 1985). Bryson and Werker also noted that poor readers and younger normal readers, when attempting to read double vowels, either sounded out the first letter and ignored the second or sounded out each individual letter. Often, the poor readers sounded out the final silent *e*, therefore adding a phoneme; they appeared to be reading letter by letter.

Seidenberg et al. (1985) found that both poor readers and clinically diagnosed dyslexic readers made more vowel than consonant errors. Most of these errors involved the incorrect lengthening or shortening of the vowel. The more severely disabled readers produced errors that involved substitution of a totally different vowel (e.g., *lake* for *like*), poor readers produced mispronunciations of the target vowel on the exception words, and good readers tended to regularize them (*come* pronounced to rhyme with *home*). The reading-disabled and poor readers were less likely to make these kinds of errors. Poor and disabled readers were less likely to regularize a pseudoword that could be pronounced like a regular or an exception word (e.g., *naid* that could be pronounced to rhyme with *said* or *paid*). Using pseudowords, Smiley, Pasquale, and Chandler (1976) also found that poor readers made more errors on vowels, especially long vowels, than did good readers. Shankweiler and Liberman (1972) conducted detailed analyses of the errors that were actually made in misreading vowels. Vowels that have many orthographic representations—such as /u/, which is represented by *u*, *o*, *oo*, *ou*, *oe*, *ew*, and *ie*—were the most difficult to read.

Guthrie and Seifert (1977) found that long vowel sounds were learned later than short vowel sounds. What they called *special rule word production*, with such vowel sounds as in *food, join,* and *bulk,* were learned even later. Typically, the poor readers' mastery of these complex rules was slower and less adequate than were the good readers'.

The increased likelihood of vowel errors does not appear to be a result of inadequate perception of sounds or difficulties with speaking. When children were asked to repeat the words that they had been asked to read, Shankweiler and Liberman (1972) found that fewer errors occurred on vowels than on consonants, and that the errors were evenly distributed between the initial and final positions.

In languages other than English, vowels have more regular patterns with fewer representations of each vowel sound. One such language is Hebrew, in which the orthography is transparent; that is, the grapheme–phoneme conversion rules are predictable. Children learning to read both English and Hebrew can be tested to compare these two very different orthographies. In a comparison of English-speaking children learning to read Hebrew as a second language, we (Geva & Siegel, in press) found that the incidence of errors in reading vowels was significantly higher in English than in Hebrew. Other children who had reading disabilities (in both languages) made many vowel errors in English but very few in Hebrew. Younger children with reading disabilities made vowel errors in both languages. However, other types of errors were more common in Hebrew. Hebrew has many visually similar letters and more errors were made involving visually confusable letters in Hebrew than in English. In addition, because Hebrew has a transparent orthography it is possible to decode it syllable by syllable and pronounce it properly, yet read the word without the proper stress. Failure to read the word with stress on the correct syllable was more common in Hebrew than in English. In English, syllable-by-syllable decoding would usually result in vowel errors (e.g., pronouncing the vowel as a short vowel when the word ends in *e* and perhaps even pronouncing the final silent *e*.) Order errors, in which a consonant was omitted or the order of the consonants was confused, were more common in English than Hebrew, possibly because Hebrew words can be decoded in a linear manner from right to left, whereas the linear strategy does not always work successfully in English.

Werker, Bryson, and Wassenberg (1989) examined the reading of consonants and found that both disabled and normal readers made more phonetic feature substitution errors than orientation reversal substitutions. Also, children with a reading disability made more consonant addition errors. Most errors were not reversal errors. Seidenberg et al. (1985) found that disabled readers make more substitution errors (*belt* for *best*) and insertion errors (*grave* for *gave*) than do normal readers.

Werker et al. noted that Seidenberg et al. confounded phonetic feature and orientation reversal substitutions by calling them both reversals (*deed* for *beed*) and inversions (*deed* for *deep*). Werker et al. studied orientation reversal errors in which one letter was read as another differing in left/right or up/down orientation, such as *b* for *d*, and phonetic feature errors in which one letter was misread as another differing in a single phonetic feature (such as voicing *b* vs. *p*) and place of articulation (*b* and *d* are both voiced but *b* is bilabial and *d* is alveolar). They found that normal and disabled readers were equally likely to make orientation reversal errors. All groups made more phonetic feature than orientation reversal errors. Therefore, errors were the result of phonetic and not visual similarities. The order of types of errors was as follows: phonetic > addition > omission > sequencing. The reading-disabled children made more errors that involved adding a consonant than did normal readers. The normal readers made more phonetic feature substitutions than any other type of error. The most common type of addition errors involved homographic errors; that is, closing a syllable with the consonant sound already existing (e.g., *ap* to *pap*). Reading-disabled, not normal readers, made these errors. Intrasyllable additions, reading *ope* as *olpe*, were less common but did occur, especially among the disabled readers and typically involved the addition of the liquids, *r* and *l*. Werker et al. speculated that errors result from knowledge of individual letters but that disabled readers have trouble knowing and retrieving the rules when they must combine letters. In addition, they may rely on articulatory information when sounding out words so that they retrieve the pronunciation of letters that are close in place of articulation to the target letter.

Smiley et al. (1976) found that disabled readers made more errors on the variable consonants (e.g., *c* and *g*). The reading-disabled group had particular difficulty with the *s* pronunciation of *c*, the *j* pronunciation of *g*, the initial *ch* sound, and two-syllable words ending in *y*. The good readers made more plausible (similar to the correct answer) errors than did the poor readers.

In summary, compared to proficient readers, people with reading problems have severe difficulties with understanding the relationships between graphemes and phonemes. Studies of English-speaking children indicate that the errors that are made by poor readers provide evidence that vowels are particularly problematic. Because the pronunciation of vowels in English is particularly unpredictable, this difficulty with vowels may be limited to the English language. Studies of other languages (e.g., Goswami, Gombert, & Barrera, in press; Sprenger-Charolles, Siegel, & Bonnet, in press) indicate that vowels do not present the same problem for disabled readers in French and Spanish.

OTHER PHONOLOGICAL SKILLS

Pseudoword reading is not the only task that distinguishes poor from normal readers. Another task is the spelling of pseudowords. Obviously, pseudowords can be spelled only by using phoneme–grapheme conversion strategies as no lexical entry exists. Disabled readers had significantly lower scores on a task that involved the spelling of pseudowords, even when the disabled readers were at the same reading level as younger normal readers (Siegel & Ryan, 1988).

Another type of evidence of phonological processing deficits comes from tasks assessing phonological recoding in short-term memory. In these tasks, rhyming (confusable) stimuli are more difficult to remember than non-rhyming stimuli. A number of studies have shown that younger poor readers are less disrupted by rhyming stimuli (e.g., Byrne & Shea, 1979; Mann, Liberman, & Shankweiler, 1980; Shankweiler, Liberman, Mark, Fowler, & Fischer, 1979; Siegel & Linder, 1984). However, Johnston (1982) and Siegel and Linder (1984) found that older dyslexic children do show phonetic confusability, although their short-term memory for letters was significantly poorer than age-matched controls. This latter finding is not surprising, because phonological recoding skills are likely to be involved in any verbal memory task and the dyslexics' poor verbal memory may be a function of inadequate phonological abilities.

Performance on a variety of phonological tasks distinguishes disabled from normal readers. Children with reading disabilities were slower than normal readers in deciding whether two aurally presented words rhymed, presumably because of inadequate use of phonological recoding in memory (Rack, 1985). Phonemic awareness, the ability to recognize the basic phonemic segments of the language, is obviously an important component of phonological processing. Difficulties with phonemic awareness predict subsequent reading problems (e.g., Bradley & Bryant, 1983; Mann, 1984; Wallach & Wallach, 1976). Poor readers also have deficits in phonological production tasks; for example, naming objects represented by multisyllable words and repeating multisyllabic words and difficult phrases with alliteration. Pratt and Brady (1988) found differences between good and poor readers on the ability to segment words into phonemes and delete sounds from words. Good readers were more accurate in judging the length of a word or pseudoword. Children with a reading disability also have difficulty recognizing the visual form of sounds (Siegel & Ryan, 1988). In the Gates McKillop test, children listen to pseudowords such as *wiskate* and are asked to select the correct version of the word from among four printed choices: *iskate, wiskay, wiskate,* and *whestit*. Poor readers had significantly lower scores on this task than did normal readers. Although this task involves skills that are relevant to spelling, aspects of it are relevant to phonological processing, including the segmentation involved in analyzing the pseudoword and in decoding the alternatives.

Most of the evidence about the nature of the core cognitive deficit in reading disabilities has been accumulated from research done with children. However, there have been some studies of reading-disabled adults who were diagnosed dyslexic as children (e.g., Felton, Naylor, & Wood, 1990; Scarborough, 1984). Deficits in phonological processing and pseudoword reading in adult dyslexics have been found (Pennington, Van Orden, Smith, Green, & Haith, 1990; Read & Ruyter, 1985; Russell, 1982; Siegel, 1996). Bruck (1992) found evidence of persistent deficits of phonological awareness in adults who had been diagnosed as dyslexic in childhood. Pratt and Brady (1988) found similar deficits in adults with poor levels of literacy skills. A number of studies have documented word recognition deficits in adults with childhood diagnoses of dyslexia (Bruck, 1990; Felton et al., 1990; Scarborough, 1984) or dyslexic adults (Russell, 1982). Greenberg et al. (in press) and Siegel (1996) found that adults with reading problems have deficits in pseudoword reading and a variety of phonological skills when compared to reading-level-matched younger normal readers. In general, the adult poor readers did not show the source deficits in orthographic skills when compared to reading-level-matched younger children.

THE UNIVERSALITY OF PHONOLOGICAL DEFICITS IN DYSLEXIA: EVIDENCE FROM OTHER LANGUAGES

Most of the studies of phonological deficits in dyslexia have been conducted in the English language. In order to test whether phonological deficits are a defining characteristic of a reading disability, it must be shown that this deficit is a characteristic of reading disabilities in all languages. We have studied phonological processing and other skills of normal readers and children with reading problems in Portuguese, Arabic, and Cantonese (a Chinese language that is spoken in Hong Kong and uses traditional Chinese characters for the written language). Portuguese and Arabic are quite regular and predictable in the correspondences between sounds and letters. Cantonese is a nonalphabetic language. These three represent languages that are orthogonal to English on two dimensions: On the dimension of regularity, English, with its variable letter sound correspondences, is on the opposite end of the continuum from Portuguese and Arabic, both of which are very regular and predictable; on the alphabetic dimension, Chinese is on the opposite end from English.

To compare English to Portuguese, we conducted a study designed to assess the reading, language, and memory skills of bilingual Portuguese-Canadian children, aged 9 to 12 years, in Toronto, Canada (da Fontoura & Siegel, 1995). The children were being educated in English in Canada but came from homes in which Portuguese was the only language spoken. They were administered parallel tasks measuring word and pseudoword reading, syntactic skills, and working memory in both English and Portuguese. From this sample of children, those who had low scores on a Portuguese word recognition test were considered reading disabled in Portuguese. They had significantly lower scores on a pseudoword reading test in Portuguese than did normal readers.

There were significant correlations among the acquisition of word and pseudoword reading, working memory, and syntactic awareness skills in the two languages. The strong relationship between pseudoword reading and word recognition across languages indicates that phonic skills are a significant component of reading of the particular alphabetic languages examined in this study. Because English and Portuguese reading, language, and memory skills were highly correlated, these relationships are suggestive of individual differences variables as the significant determinants of reading skill, rather than difficulties being language dependent. Similar problems were evident in both languages for the children who had difficulties. Phonological processing skills, as measured by pseudoword reading, are highly correlated with word recognition skills in both English and Portuguese. Disabled readers in Portuguese showed the same difficulties with phonological processing as do disabled readers in English. However, the bilingual reading-disabled children had significantly *higher* scores than the monolingual, English-speaking, reading-disabled children on the English pseudoword reading test and the English spelling task. This finding may reflect a positive transfer from the more predictable grapheme–phoneme conversion rules of Portuguese to the very opaque orthography of English.

We found similar results with a study of the reading, language, and memory skills of 56 bilingual Arab-Canadian children aged 9 to 14 (Abu Rabia & Siegel, 1996). Arabic, like Portuguese but unlike English, is characterized by regular and predictable correspondences between letters and sounds. Unlike English and Portuguese, it does not use the Latin alphabet but, instead, uses a completely different orthography. English was the main instructional language of these children, and Arabic was the language spoken at home. All children attended a Heritage Language Program in Toronto, where they were taught to read and write Arabic. The children were administered word and pseudoword reading, language, and working memory tests in English and Arabic. The majority of the children showed adequate spoken proficiency in both languages. There was a significant relationship between the acquisition of word and pseudoword reading in both languages. The poor readers in Arabic, selected on the basis of their performance on an Arabic word reading task, demonstrated poorer performance on word and pseudoword reading tasks than did the good readers.

Phonological processing skills, as measured by pseudoword reading, were highly correlated with word recognition skills in both English and Arabic. Disabled readers in Arabic showed the same difficulties with phonological processing as did disabled readers in English. The reading-disabled Arabic-English bilinguals had higher scores in the English pseudoword reading, word spelling, and some of the phonological tests than did a comparison group of monolingual, English-speaking, reading-disabled children. This finding is similar to the results from the study by da Fontoura and Siegel

(1995), in which bilingual English-Portuguese speaking reading-disabled children had higher scores in English spelling and pseudoword reading tasks than did monolingual, English-speaking, reading-disabled children. This finding may reflect a positive transfer from the more predictable grapheme–phoneme conversion rules of Arabic to the very opaque orthography of English. It is unlikely that socioeconomic factors were responsible, because the socioeconomic level of the Arab bilinguals was lower than that of the English monolinguals.

The Arabic-English bilingual children showed similar types of reading mistakes in reading Arabic and English, including errors in reading vowels and confusion of letter sounds, specifically pseudohomophones and homographs. The common types of mistakes in both languages were incorrect reading of voweled words, homophone confusions, and incorrect identification of homographs. The development of reading skills and the phonological deficit of dyslexics in Arabic seems to be identical to that of English, despite the different nature of the two orthographies.

CHINESE

The universality of phonological processing to dyslexia as a defining feature of can, perhaps, best be answered by examining how dyslexia is manifested in Chinese. Chinese is a nonalphabetic system of visual signs in which grapheme–phoneme relationships are irrelevant. However, Chinese does have some phonological features in that phonetic compounds account for over 80% of the corpus of characters (Leong, 1986; Taylor & Taylor, 1983). Phonetic compounds have two parts: a phonetic, which hints at its pronunciation; and a radical, which hints at its meaning. The phonetic is like a rhyming clue and the radical often gives an indication of the semantic domain of the word.

Chinese is a tonal language. Each character is pronounced with a particular tone, and there are four such patterns in Mandarin Chinese and nine in the Cantonese dialect. There are homophones in which the same character is pronounced with different tones depending on the meaning. We examined the correlation between phonological skills and reading skills in a sample of normally achieving and disabled readers of Chinese in Hong Kong (So & Siegel, 1997). We measured phonological skills with two tasks, a tone discrimination task and a rhyme discrimination task.

The children were also administered a task that involved the reading of an increasingly difficult series of words, and were divided into good and poor readers on the basis of performance on this task. (No standardized reading test exists in Chinese.) Tasks were also administered involving syntactic skills, vocabulary, oral language comprehension, and memory. The tone discrimination task involved four homophonic characters that were orally presented. Two of them were the same tone, whereas the other two were different. This task was used to assess the child's ability to recognize the tone differences or similarities that exist for each character used in Chinese speech.

For the rhyming discrimination task, each trial had four characters. Two of them rhymed with each other, but the other two characters did not. This task was used to assess the child's ability to recognize the phonemically similar or dissimilar characters. The child was told that the experimenter would read four characters out loud. The child's task was to listen and determine which two characters rhymed with each other.

The poor readers at each grade level performed more poorly than did the normal readers on the tone discrimination task and the rhyme discrimination task. Word recognition as measured by a reading task and phonological skills as measured by tone and rhyming discrimination tasks were all highly correlated ($r = 0.75$; $p < .001$; $r = 0.73$, $p < .001$). Similarly, there was a high correlation between tone and rhyming discrimination tasks (r = 0.86; p < .001). These are probably all related to speech decoding, which is required in order to read and speak Chinese characters.

A stepwise regression procedure was used with the outcome on the word recognition variable (reading task) as the dependent measure, and tone discrimination, sentence meaning (which is an oral comprehension task), oral cloze (a measure of syntactic skills), and working memory measures at Grades 1 to 4 as the independent variables. This procedure was used to examine the amount of variance accounted for by tone discrimination, sentence meaning, and oral cloze measures at each grade. The variables that were found to predict word reading at Grades 1 to 3 were tone discrimination and oral cloze measures. The working memory measure did not contribute significant additional variance. In contrast, sentence meaning entered first in Grade 4. The variables that entered into the equation most significantly were the tone discrimination, sentence meaning, and oral cloze measures at Grade 4. However, there were no significant differences among grades on tone and rhyming tasks dealing with phonological skills for normal readers. For the normal readers, these phonological skills may be related to phonemic awareness and may be precursors of reading skills (e.g., Stanovich, 1991). For the poor readers, only the Grade 3 or Grade 4 children had significantly higher scores than lower Grade 1 or Grade 2 children on tone and rhyming discrimination tasks, word meaning and sentence meaning tasks, and an oral cloze task, dealing with phonological, semantic and syntactic skills. In summary, in normal readers, these skills develop gradually in the 6- to 10-year-old age range. However, poor readers of Chinese showed a significant delay in the development of these skills.

In this study, we observed a relationship among children's reading ability, language skills, and working memory. Word recognition in the reading task was highly correlated with tone and rhyming discrimination tasks dealing with phonological skills, indicating that these measures may be tapping similar skills. The ability to read words may be highly correlated with the children's ability to use the system of tones to pronounce individual characters and also to distinguish the considerable number of heterographic homophones with variation in the tone (Leong, 1986). It may also be highly related to the ability of phonetic recoding in reading characters and discriminating phonetics in the initial or final part of the character (Tzeng, Hung, & Wang, 1977).

The results of stepwise regressions suggested that phonological processing is the most important aspect of reading Chinese, at least in the early stages of acquisition. Syntactic skills, as measured by the oral cloze task, were also important. In addition, sentence meaning, as predictor of reading ability at Grade 4, indicate that semantic and contextual elements become more important with the growth of reading skills.

The results of this study are similar to the studies of English (e.g., Siegel & Ryan, 1988), in which positive correlations were found among language, working memory, and reading skills, even though in Chinese the psychological mechanisms must operate on different types of orthographic units. In both languages, these skills develop gradually, approximately between 6 to 10 years of age in normal readers. However, poor readers show a significant lag in the development of these skills. As with English, phonological processing is quite significantly related to reading in Chinese. These results clearly support the significance of the phonological skills in language other than alphabetic ones. This finding is especially significant because, in Hong Kong, phonological analytic skills are not explicitly taught. In addition, poor readers in Chinese seem to experience similar difficulties to poor readers in English, in spite of the very different nature of the languages. In summary, phonological skills are very important in learning to read Chinese, and poor readers in Chinese seem to experience similar difficulties to poor readers in English in spite of the very different nature of the languages.

GENERAL COGNITIVE ABILITY
AND PHONOLOGICAL PROCESSING

The fundamental phonological deficit in dyslexia is so severe that it is found in individuals with reading problems at all IQ levels. A number of studies of adults and children have indicated that disabled readers with higher IQ scores have phonological deficits similar to those with lower IQ scores, and that dyslexics with IQ achievement discrepancies have phonological deficits similar to garden-variety poor readers who have reading difficulties but no IQ achievement discrepancies (Siegel, 1988, 1992, 1996). These studies are summarized in Toth and Siegel (1994). Phonological processing is a modular process independent of IQ scores. In one study (Siegel, 1992), I compared dyslexic children who had IQ scores at least one standard deviation higher than their reading scores with poor readers who did not show a discrepancy between IQ and reading. Although both these groups had significantly lower scores on all tasks involving phonological processing than did normal readers, there were no differences between the reading-disabled groups. Stanovich and Siegel (1994) found similar results when a reading-level match was used. This deficit is independent of general cognitive functioning, as measured by IQ, listening comprehension, language, and memory tests. This phonological deficit is an arrest, not merely a delay, because even when a reading-level match of reading-disabled adults and younger normally achieving readers was used, the phonological differences remained, even though the differences in language and memory did not.

The cognitive strengths of the dyslexics in the areas of general cognitive functioning, language, memory, visual–spatial, and listening comprehension skills do not allow them to compensate for their severe deficits in phonological skills.

BEGINNING READING

From the very beginning of the development of reading skills, phonological skills play a very important role. In this section, I briefly review some of the evidence for the significance of phonological processing skills and discuss the studies of children who have difficulty even at the beginning of reading. Reading can occur by phonological route in which graphemes are associated with their corresponding phonemes and meaning is extracted by the association of this product with a stored representation in the lexicon or by the direct, orthographic route in which the meaning is accessed directly without any intermediate phonological processing. The task of the beginning reader is to acquire these grapheme–phoneme conversion rules. The alternative is simply to memorize each word as a visual configuration and to associate a meaning with it. This type of learning may occur, but it is inefficient and makes significant demands on visual memory.

Although a great deal of evidence has accumulated about the phonological deficit of children who experience difficulties with reading, relatively little is known about the early emergence of this problem. We analyzed the reading errors of good and poor readers at the very beginning stages of reading to understand the nature of this phonological deficit (Siegel & Kerr, 1996). The subjects for this study were 67 children in Grade 1, the first year of reading instruction in Canadian schools. The children were tested in April, May, and June of Grade 1. They were administered the Wide Range Achievement Test–Revised (WRAT–R), a measure of word recognition skills, and a list of 40 high-frequency words to read. Children who scored below the 25th percentile on the WRAT–R were considered to be reading disabled; children who scored above the 30th percentile were considered to be normally achieving readers. Based on ratings of the words by experts in the field, the words were classified into three categories: regular words, whose pronunciations could be predicted from the GPC rules of English (e.g., *came, like, best*); regular inconsistent words, whose pronunciations were regular according to GPC rules but who had high-frequency neighbors with irregular pronunciations (e.g., *gave, goes, five*); and exception words, whose pronunciations violated the GPC rules of English (e.g., *have, does, give*). The three types of words were intermixed in the list.

The errors made by the children were assigned one of four categories: *regularization* errors, in which the GPC rules of English were used (e.g., *come* pronounced to rhyme with *home, said* pronounced with the same rhyme as *raid*—possible only with the exception words); *no response*, in which they did not attempt the word; *–1* errors, in which there was only one incorrect phoneme in the word; and *other*, which were responses that did not fit in any of these categories and were usually wild guesses that bore no resemblance to the target word. The –1 errors could involve consonants or vowels, and the consonant errors were scored separately from the vowel errors.

The results indicated that the normally achieving readers, not surprisingly, read significantly more words correctly than did the reading disabled. The three categories of words—regular, regular inconsistent, and exception— were all equally difficult for both groups of readers.

The percentage of errors of each type was calculated for each child. That is, the errors of each type for each child were calculated as a percentage of the total number of errors produced by that child. Significantly more of the errors of the reading-disabled children were of the no response type. In fact, most of the errors (over 86%) of the reading-disabled children were of the no response type, compared to 38.6% of the errors of the normally achieving readers. The normal readers made significantly more vowel errors than did the reading disabled (approximately 35% for the normal readers and 4% for the reading disabled). There were almost no consonant errors for either group. There were very few regularization errors, but the reading-disabled children made significantly fewer of them than did the normal readers. When compared with the normal readers, the reading-disabled children made significantly more of the "other" or wild guess errors.

These results indicate that a deficit in phonological processing exists for the children with reading problems from the very beginning of reading instruction. For the responses that were counted as vowel errors, the vowel or vowel digraphs were the only mistakes in the word. Vowel errors indicate an attempt, although an imperfect one, to use GPC rules. The normally achieving made many more of these types of errors than did the reading-disabled children, who hardly made any of these type of errors. Regularization errors indicate an attempt to use GPC rules, and the normally achieving children made many more of these errors than did the reading-disabled children, also indicating a phonological deficit in the reading-disabled children. The no response errors, more than twice as common in the reading-disabled children, indicate the absence of any attempt to apply GPC or even visual matching strategies. These data indicate that the phonological deficit is very severe in reading-disabled children, even in the earliest stages of reading.

CONCLUSION

In summary, several lines of evidence have converged to show that a reading disability involves a deficit in phonological processing. First of all, reading-disabled individuals show poorer performance than do normal readers on all tasks involving phonological processing. This difference is evident whether the comparison is basic on chronological age or reading level. This generalization appears to be supported by research on the acquisition of reading skills in other languages, even languages that have more regular GPC rules than English (e.g., Portuguese, French), languages that use a different script (e.g., Hebrew, Arabic) and nonalphabetic languages (e.g., Chinese). This generalization is true independent of the cognitive or IQ level of the poor reader or dyslexic. Other memory, syntactic, or reading skills cannot compensate, indicating a modularity of phonological processing. Finally, this generalization is supported by research on the type of errors made by beginning readers (Siegel & Kerr, 1996; Sprenger-Charolles et al., in press). In conclusion, conclusive evidence exists that reading disabilities are characterized by a core phonological deficit.

ACKNOWLEDGMENTS

This research was supported by a grant from the Natural Sciences and Engineering Research Council of Canada. The author would like to thank Letty Guirnela and Kim Kozuki for secretarial assistance.
Address for correspondence:

EPSE
University of British Columbia
2125 Main Mall
Vancouver, British Columbia
Canada V6T 1Z4
Telephone: (604) 822-1893
Fax: (604) 822-3302
e-mail: lsiegel@unixg.ubc.ca

REFERENCES

Abu Rabia, S., & Siegel, L. S. (1996). *Reading, syntactic and working memory skills of bilingual Arabic-speaking children.* Unpublished manuscript.

Backman, J., Bruck, M., Hebert, M., & Seidenberg, M. (1984). Acquisition and use of spelling–sound correspondences in reading. *Journal of Experimental Child Psychology, 38,* 114–133.

Backman, J. E., Mamen, M., & Ferguson, H. B. (1984). Reading level design: Conceptual and methodological issues in reading research. *Psychological Bulletin, 96,* 560–568.

Barwick, M. A., & Siegel, L. S. (in press). The incidence and nature of learning disabilities in homeless, runaway youths. *Journal of Research on Adolescence.*

Bradley, L., & Bryant, P. E. (1983). Categorizing sounds and learning to read: A causal connection. *Nature, 301,* 419–421.

Bruck, M. (1988). The word recognition and spelling of dyslexia children. *Reading Research Quarterly, 23,* 51–68.

Bruck, M. (1990). Word-recognition skills of adults with childhood diagnosis of dyslexia. *Developmental Psychology, 26,* 439–454.

Bruck, M. (1992). Persistence of dyslexics' phonological awareness deficits. *Developmental Psychology, 28,* 874–886.

Bryson, S. E., & Werker, J. F. (1989). Toward understanding the problem in severely disabled readers Part 1: Vowel errors. *Applied Psycholinguistics, 10,* 1–12

Byrne, B., & Shea, P. (1979). Semantic and phonemic memory in beginning readers. *Memory & Cognition, 7,* 333–341.

Calfee, R. C., Lindamood, P., & Lindamood, C. (1973). Acoustic–phonetic skills and reading: Kindergarten through twelfth grade. *Journal of Educational Psychology, 64,* 293–298.

da Fontoura, H. A., & Siegel, L. S. (1995). Reading, syntactic and memory skills of bilingual Portuguese-English Canadian children. *Reading and Writing: An Interdisciplinary Journal, 7,* 139–153.

Ehri, L. C., & Saltmarsh, J. (1995). Beginning readers outperform older disabled readers in learning to read words by sight. *Reading and Writing: An Interdisciplinary Journal, 7,* 295–326.

Ehri, L. C., & Wilce, L. S. (1983). Development of word identification speed in skilled and less-skilled beginning readers. *Journal of Educational Psychology, 75,* 3–18.

Felton, R. H., Naylor C. E., & Wood, F. B. (1990). Neuropsychological profile of adult dyslexics. *Brain and Language, 39,* 485–497.

Fowler, C., Liberman, I., & Shankweiler, D. (1977). On interpreting the error pattern in beginning reading. *Language and Speech, 20,* 162–173.

Fowler, C., Shankweiler, D., & Liberman, I. (1979). Apprehending spelling patterns for vowels: A developmental study. *Language and Speech, 22,* 243–251.

Frith, U., & Snowling, M. (1983). Reading for meaning and reading for sound in autistic and dyslexic children. *British Journal of Developmental Psychology, 1,* 329–342.

Geva, E., & Siegel, L. S. (in press). The role of orthography and cognitive factors in the concurrent development of basic reading skills in bilingual children. *Reading and Writing: An Interdisciplinary Journal.*

Goswami, U., Gombert, J. E., & Barrera, L. F. (in press). Children's orthographic representations and linguistic transparency: Nonsense word reading in English, French and Spanish. *Applied Psycholinguistics.*

Greenberg, D., Ehri, L. C., & Perin, D. (in press). Are word reading processes the same or different in adult literacy students and 3rd–5th graders matched for reading level. *Journal of Educational Psychology.*

Guthrie, J. T., & Seifert, M. (1977). Letter-sound complexity in learning to identify words. *Journal of Educational Psychology, 69,* 686–696.

Hogaboam, T. W., & Perfetti, C. A. (1978). Reading skill and their role of verbal experience in decoding. *Journal of Educational Psychology, 5*, 717–729.

Johnston, R. (1982). Phonological coding in dyslexic readers. *British Journal of Psychology, 73*, 455–460.

Leong, C. K. (1986). What does accessing a morphemic script tell us about reading and reading disorders in an alphabet script? *Annals of Dyslexia, 36*, 82–102.

Manis, F. R., & Morrison, F. J. (1985). Reading disability: A deficit in rule learning? In L. S. Siegel & F. J. Morrison (Eds.), *Cognitive development in atypical children: Progress in cognitive development research* (pp. 1–26). New York: Springer-Verlag.

Mann, V. A. (1984). Longitudinal prediction and prevention of early reading difficulty. *Annals of Dyslexia, 34*, 117–136.

Mann, V. A., Liberman, I. Y., & Shankweiler, D. (1980). Children's memory for sentences and word strings in relation to reading ability. *Memory & Cognition, 8*, 329–335.

Pennington, B. F., Van Orden, G. C., Smith, S. D., Green, P. A., & Haith, M. M. (1990). Phonological processing skills and deficits in adult dyslexics. *Child Development, 61*, 1753–1778.

Pratt, A. C., & Brady, S. (1988). Relations of phonological awareness to reading disability in children and adults. *Journal of Educational Psychology, 80*, 319–323.

Rack, J. P. (1985). Orthographic and phonetic coding in developmental dyslexia. *British Journal of Psychology, 76*, 325–340.

Rack, J. P., Snowling, M., & Olson, R. (1992). The nonword reading deficit in developmental dyslexia: A review. *Reading Research Quarterly, 27*, 28–53.

Read, C., & Ruyter, L. (1985). Reading and spelling skills in adults of low literacy. *Remedial and Special Education, 6*, 43–52.

Russell, G. (1982). Impairment of phonetic reading in dyslexia and its persistence beyond childhood—research note. *Journal of Child Psychology and Psychiatry, 23*, 459–475.

Scarborough, H. S. (1984). Continuity between childhood dyslexia and adult reading. *British Journal of Psychology, 75*, 329–348.

Seidenberg, M. S., Bruck, M., Fornarolo, G., & Backman, J. (1985). Word recognition processes of poor and disabled readers: Do they necessarily differ? *Applied Psycholinguistics, 6*, 161–180.

Seymour, P. H. K., & Porpodas, C. D. (1980). Lexical and nonlexical processing of spelling in dyslexia. In U. Frith (Ed.), *Cognitive processes in spelling* (pp. 443–473). New York: Academic.

Shafrir, U., & Siegel, L. S. (1994). Subtypes of learning disabilities in adolescents and adults. *Journal of Learning Disabilities, 27*, 123–134.

Shankweiler, D., & Liberman, I. (1972). Misreading: A search for causes. In J. Kavanaugh & I. Mattingly (Eds.), *Language by ear and by eye: The relationship between speech and reading* (pp. 293–317). Cambridge, MA: MIT Press.

Shankweiler, D., Liberman, I. Y., Mark, L. S., Fowler, C. A., & Fischer, F. W. (1979). The speech code and learning to read. *Journal of Experimental Psychology: Human Learning and Memory, 5*, 531–545.

Siegel, L. S. (1988). Evidence that IQ scores are irrelevant to the definition and analysis of reading disability. *Canadian Journal of Psychology, 42*, 201–215.

Siegel, L. S. (1992). An evaluation of the discrepancy definition of dyslexia. *Journal of Learning Disabilities, 25*, 618–629.

Siegel, L. S. (1996). *Adults with reading disabilities: The importance of phonological processing and the irrelevance of the IQ-achievement discrepancy definition.* Unpublished manuscript.

Siegel, L. S., & Faux, D. (1989). Acquisition of certain grapheme–phoneme correspondences in normally achieving and disabled readers. *Reading and Writing: An Interdisciplinary Journal, 1*, 37–52.

Siegel, L. S., & Heaven, R. K. (1986). Categorization of learning disabilities. In S. J. Ceci (Ed.), *Handbook of cognitive, social and neuropsychological aspects of learning disabilities* (Vol. 1, pp. 95–121). Hillsdale, NJ: Lawrence Erlbaum Associates.

Siegel L. S., & Kerr, A. (1996). *An analysis of the reading errors of good and poor beginning readers.* Unpublished manuscript.

Siegel, L. S., Levey, P., & Ferris, H. (1985). Subtypes of developmental dyslexia: Do they exist? In F. J. Morrison, C. Lord, & D. P. Keating (Eds.), *Applied developmental psychology* (Vol. 2, pp. 169–190). New York: Academic.

Siegel, L. S., & Linder, B. A. (1984). Short-term memory processes in children with reading and arithmetic learning disabilities. *Developmental Psychology, 20,* 200–207.

Siegel, L. S., & Ryan, E. B. (1988). Development of grammatical sensitivity, phonological, and short-term memory in normally achieving and learning disabled children. *Developmental Psychology, 24,* 28–37.

Smiley, S. S., Pasquale, F. L., & Chandler, C. L. (1976). The pronunciation of familiar, unfamiliar and synthetic words by good and poor adolescent readers. *Journal of Reading Behavior, 8,* 289–297.

Snowling, M. J. (1980). The development of grapheme–phoneme correspondence in normal and dyslexic readers. *Journal of Experimental Child Psychology, 29,* 294–305.

So, D., & Siegel, L. S. (1997). Learning to read Chinese: Semantic, syntactic, phonological and short-term memory skills in normally achieving and poor Chinese readers. *Reading and Writing: An Interdisciplinary Journal, 9,* 1–21.

Sprenger-Charolles, L., Siegel, L. S., & Bonnet, P. (in press). Reading and spelling acquisition in French: The role of phonological mediation and orthographic factors. *Journal of Experimental Child Psychology.*

Stanovich, K. E. (1991). Word recognition: Changing perspectives. In R. Barr, M. L. Kamil, P. Mosenthal, & P. D. Pearson (Eds.), *Handbook of reading research* (Vol. 2, pp. 418–452). New York: Longman.

Stanovich, K. E., & Siegel, L. S. (1994). The phenotypic performance profile of reading disabled children: A regression based test of the phonological-core variable—difference model. *Journal of Educational Psychology, 86,* 24–53.

Taylor, I., & Taylor, M. M. (1983). *The psychology of reading.* New York: Academic.

Toth, G., & Siegel, L. S. (1994). A critical evaluation of the IQ-achievement discrepancy based definition of dyslexia. In K. P. van den Bos, L. S. Siegel, D. J. Bakker, & D. L. Share (Eds.), *Current directions in dyslexia research* (pp. 45–70). Lisse, The Netherlands: Swets & Zeitlinger.

Tzeng, O. J. L., Hung, D. L., & Wang, W. S.-Y. (1977). Speech recording in reading Chinese characters, *Journal of Experimental Psychology: Human Learning and Memory, 3,* 621–630.

Venezky, R. L., & Johnson, D. (1973). Development of two letter-sound patterns in grades one through three. *Journal of Educational Psychology, 64,* 109–115.

Wallach, M. A., & Wallach, L. (1976). *Teaching all children to read.* Chicago: University of Chicago Press.

Waters, G. S., Bruck, M., & Seidenberg, M. (1985). Do children use similar processes to read and spell words? *Journal of Experimental Child Psychology, 39,* 511–530.

Waters, G. S., Seidenberg, M. S., & Bruck, M. (1984). Children's and adults' use of spelling-sound information in three reading tasks. *Memory & Cognition, 12,* 293–305.

Weber, R. (1970). A linguistic analysis of first-grade reading errors. *Reading Research Quarterly, 5,* 427–451.

Werker, J. F., Bryson, S. E., & Wassenberg, K. (1989). Toward understanding the problem in severely disabled readers. Part II: Consonant errors. *Applied Psycholinguistics, 10,* 13–30.

Consistency of Reading-Related Phonological Processes Throughout Early Childhood: Evidence From Longitudinal–Correlational and Instructional Studies

Joseph K. Torgesen
Stephen R. Burgess
Florida State University

In this chapter, we address a question of central importance in understanding individual differences in the ease with which children learn to read. We take as a starting point the widely accepted observation that the critical problem for most children with serious reading disabilities involves learning accurate and fluent word identification skills (Rack, Snowling, & Olson, 1992; Stanovich, 1988). We also take as established fact that a primary cause of variability among children in the rate at which they acquire word reading skill is variation "in the phonological component of their natural capacity for language" (Liberman, Shankweiler, & Liberman, 1989, p. 1). The question we address in this chapter is whether reading-related phonological skills display sufficient stability across the period of early reading development to qualify as a proximal cause of a learning difficulty that is as resistant to treatment as reading disabilities often prove to be.

After reviewing a large body of experimental and longitudinal–correlational research on the relationships between phonological abilities and reading growth, Share and Stanovich (1995) concluded:

> In summary, there is virtually unassailable evidence that poor readers, as a group, are impaired in a very wide range of basic cognitive tasks in the phonological domain. This applies both to reading disabled children with discrepancies from IQ and to those without such discrepancies. . . .These deficits are consistently found to be domain-specific, longitudinally predictive, and not primarily attributable to non-phonological factors such as general intelligence, semantic or visual processing. (p. 9)

The evidence to which Share and Stanovich referred has been generated by a wide variety of simple-correlational, experimental, longitudinal–correlational, and case study research. In this chapter, we supplement this evidence by reporting data from both longitudinal–correlational research and training studies that document the stability of phonological processes across the elementary school period, and also indicate that it may be very difficult to overcome phonological processing weaknesses in some children.

The chapter is organized in four sections. First, we define and discuss the nature of the three most widely studied phonological processes that are related to reading: phonological awareness, phonological coding in working memory, and rapid access to phonological information in long-term memory. Then we report several different analyses providing evidence of the stability of individual differences in phonological processing skills throughout the elementary school period. The third section considers evidence on variability in response to training in phonological awareness, and we conclude with a discussion of the implications for diagnosis and instruction that follow from the data on stability and resistance to treatment presented in earlier sections.

THE NATURE OF READING-RELATED
PHONOLOGICAL PROCESSES

Reading-related phonological processes can be defined generally as a set of mental activities or skills that are required in reading or learning to read, and that involve accessing, storing, or manipulating phonological information. The phonological processing difficulties of children with phonologically based reading disabilities can be shown on a variety of nonreading tasks that assess: awareness of the phonological structure of words in oral language (Bowey, Cain, & Ryan, 1992; Bruck, 1992; Fletcher et al., 1994); ability to represent phonological information in short-term memory (Brady, Poggie, & Rappala, 1989; Gathercole & Baddeley, 1993; Torgesen, Rashotte, Greenstein, Houck, & Portes, 1987); and rate of access to phonological information in long-term memory (Bowers & Swanson, 1991; Denckla & Rudel, 1976; Wolf, 1991). We now consider each of these skills in turn, and then present evidence about their relationships to one another in development.

Phonological Awareness

Beginning levels of phonological awareness involve sensitivity to the individual sounds in words, whereas more advanced levels involve explicit awareness of a word's full phonemic structure as well as ability to manipulate individual phonemes within words. Phonological awareness involves a certain kind of knowledge about words—that they can be divided into segments of sound smaller than a syllable. This knowledge grows from a vague awareness that words can share common ending sounds, to a knowledge of the essential distinctive features of most of the phonemes in our language. This latter kind of knowledge allows children to repeat the individual phonemes in a word (saying /m/-/a/-/n/ when given the word *man*), or to form another word by adding or subtracting a phoneme from a word (saying *fit* when asked to say *fist* without the /s/ sound). This type of knowledge about language is frequently referred to as *metalinguistic knowledge*, because it is knowledge about words that is more explicit, or conscious, than that required when words are used in speaking or listening.

Children's increasing knowledge of the unique characteristics of individual phonemes supports an increasing ability to notice, think about, or manipulate the individual sounds in words. In other words, increasing knowledge of the phonemic structure of words, and of phonemes themselves, supports increasingly complex processing of these sounds. For example, children in the first semester of first grade might be able to blend the phonemes /a/ and /t/ together to form the word *at*, but their ability to blend increasingly longer strings of sounds will improve with practice until they will be able to blend four, five, or six sounds together to form words. Similarly, children at the beginning of first grade can usually respond with the word *an* when asked to say *man* without saying the /m/ sound, but not until later in development will they be able to respond with the word *drier*, when asked to say *driver* without saying the /v/ sound.

Phonological awareness develops slowly in young children, because phonemes are not distinct from one another in the actual sounds we hear when words are spoken. For example, the word *dog* has three phonemes—it differs from *log* in the first, from *dig* in the second, and from *dot* in the third—but when it is spoken, these phonemes are merged into a single pulse of sound so that it is impossible to separate the phonemes without some articulatory distortion. Because of our natural capacity for language, it is not necessary to be consciously aware of the phonological structure of words in order to speak or understand words in oral language. The phonological processes that translate between the underlying structure of the word in the mental lexicon and its instantiation in speech operate outside of conscious awareness. However, in order to make sense of the alphabetic system we use in our written language, in order to understand that letters map to words at the phonemic level, children must become aware that words actually are composed of segments at the phonemic level.

Isabelle Liberman and her colleagues at Haskins Laboratories in New Haven, Connecticut, most completely developed the early theoretical basis for research on phonological awareness. They recognized that speech and reading both involve phonological processing, and they sought to determine why speech was so easy for most children to master with no explicit instruction, whereas at the same time reading was so hard for many children, even with explicit instruction. Their initial answer, which has been supported in subsequent research, was that reading requires an "awareness of the phonological structure of the words of the language, an awareness that must be more explicit than is ever demanded in the ordinary course of listening and responding to speech" (Liberman et al., 1989, p. 5).

Phonological Short-Term Memory

Verbal short-term memory tasks are included as measures of phonological processing ability because, when an individual is required to retain a short sequence of verbal items verbatim, these items are represented in working memory in terms of their phonological features (Baddeley, 1991). In other words, if an individual is asked to remember a brief string of digits, such as 7-4-8-9-2-6, these items are represented in memory by codes that utilize their acoustic, or phonological, features, rather than their visual or semantic features. Verbal short-term memory tasks appear to be sensitive to individual differences in the efficiency with which phonological information is represented in memory (Baddeley, 1991; Torgesen, 1995).

Children with phonological coding difficulties can be expected to have problems acquiring alphabetic reading skills because these coding difficulties make it hard to utilize knowledge of letter-sound correspondences in decoding words. Specifically, phonological coding inefficiencies make it difficult to perform the simultaneous, or rapidly sequential identification, comparison, and blending processes that are required to identify words by phonological/analytic strategies.

In fact, difficulty remembering exact sequences of verbal information over brief periods of time is one of the most frequently reported cognitive characteristics of children with severe reading disabilities (see Hulme, 1988; Jorm, 1983). The tasks most often used to demonstrate this difficulty are called *memory span tasks*. These tasks typically involve recalling sequences of random digits, words, or letters immediately after a single auditory or visual presentation. In the 1990s (Gathercole & Baddeley, 1993), another type of task has been used to assess phonological memory. This task involves the repetition of complex nonwords, such as *morphglanome*, or nonword phrases.

Rapid Automatic Naming of Verbal Material

Children's ability to easily and rapidly access phonological information that is stored in long-term memory has typically been assessed in the reading literature by rapid automatic naming tasks. This type of task was first introduced as a way of predicting and understanding individual differences in reading ability by Martha Denckla and her colleagues (Denckla & Rudel,

1976; Rudel, Denckla, & Broman, 1978), and typically requires the child to name, as rapidly as possible, a series of 30 to 50 items (digits, colors, letters, or objects) printed on a page.

Theoretically, rapid naming tasks are linked to reading because they are thought to index the speed of processes that are intrinsically involved in word identification. In utilizing alphabetic reading skills, for example, the child must rapidly access, store, and interpret strings of phonemes represented by letters in words. If access to the phonological information represented by letters occurs rapidly and easily, the entire complex string of mental operations will be facilitated. Bowers and her colleagues (Bowers, Golden, Kennedy, & Young, 1994; Bowers & Wolf, 1993) suggested that rapid automatic naming tasks may be measuring processes that are particularly critical in the formation of orthographic, or whole-word, representations that are important in fluent word reading. They argued against viewing rapid automatic naming tasks as primarily phonological in nature, and instead they emphasized the visual and speed components of these tasks. They suggested that rapid naming tasks may assess the functioning of a "precise timing mechanism," and that "slow letter (or digit) naming speed may signal disruption of the automatic processes which support induction of orthographic patterns, which, in turn, result in quick word recognition" (Bowers & Wolf, 1993, p. 70). Although empirical support for this view is still weak, it does represent an important alternative, or additional, conceptualization of the reasons why individual differences in performance on rapid naming tasks are causally related to variability in the growth of word reading skills.

We continue to believe that rapid automatic naming tasks assess an important dimension of phonological processing skill for three reasons. First, these tasks show a consistent pattern of significant correlations with other aspects of phonological skill (Wagner, Torgesen, Laughon, Simmons, & Rashotte, 1993; Wagner et al., 1997). Second, in our longitudinal research, rapid automatic naming skills show unique causal relationships with the development of *early* word reading skills, but not *later* word reading growth (Wagner et al., 1997). Current theories (Share & Stanovich, 1995) of reading skill acquisition suggest that phonological skills are more centrally involved in the growth of word reading skills in the early elementary grades (1–3) than the later grades (4–5). Finally, we have found no evidence in our longitudinal research that rapid automatic naming ability contributes uniquely to the development of orthographic representations of words (Torgesen, Wagner, Rashotte, Burgess, & Hecht, 1997). Although we assert that rapid automatic naming tasks do tap an important dimension of phonological skill, we also recognize that, when given in the serial naming format, these tasks are sufficiently complex that they may measure more than one processing skill important in reading.

Relations of Phonological Abilities to One Another
and to Reading

Considering that all the tasks just discussed require some form of processing
of the phonological features of language, it is logical to inquire whether they
are sufficiently independent of one another to be thought of as measuring
separate abilities, or whether they are better thought of as measures of a
single underlying ability. This question was directly addressed in two studies
that we reported as part of a longitudinal investigation of the relationships
between phonological processing and reading.

The first (Wagner et al., 1993) was actually a cross-sectional pilot study
in which we tested our measurement models for each type of phonological
skill and also examined their relationships to one another. In this study,
which employed 95 kindergarten and 89 second-grade children as subjects,
measures of phonological awareness were further subdivided into *analytic*
and *synthetic* tasks. Analytic measures required children to identify individual
phonemes within whole words, whereas synthetic tasks required children to
combine separately presented phonemes into words. Similarly, naming tasks
were subdivided into tasks that required the continuous naming of series of
items and others that required children to name individual items presented
one at a time on a computer screen.

Several different models of the relationships among the three measurement
domains were compared using confirmatory factor analysis to assess their fit
to the data. The results supported the view that phonological awareness,
memory, and naming are distinct yet correlated abilities. These results were
replicated in our longitudinal sample of 216 children whose phonological
abilities were assessed each year from kindergarten through fourth grade
(Wagner et al., 1997). Prior to examining developmental relationships between
phonological skills and reading, we performed tests of our measurement model
for phonological abilities. The basic model proposed correlated factors for
phonological awareness (both analysis and synthesis), memory, and rapid
naming, and this model received strong support in the data. For example, the
comparative fit index (an index that ranges from 0 for a terrible fit to 1.0 for
a near-perfect fit) ranged from .97 to .99 for the models tested at different ages.
When taken together, these studies provide strong support for conceptualizing
phonological awareness, phonological memory, and rapid automatic naming
tasks as measures of separate although correlated abilities.

The evidence that these phonological abilities are causally related to the
growth of word reading skill is strongest for phonological awareness, next
strongest for rapid automatic naming ability, and weakest for phonological
coding in working memory. The evidence for phonological awareness' role
in reading development comes from both standard and causal modeling
studies of longitudinal–correlational data (Mann, 1993; Stanovich, Cunning-

ham, & Cramer, 1984; Wagner, Torgesen, & Rashotte, 1994; Wagner et al., 1997), from comparisons of reading-disabled and normal readers using reading-level-match designs (Bowey et al., 1992), and from true experiments that show an effect of training phonological awareness on subsequent reading ability (Lundberg, Frost, & Peterson, 1988; Torgesen, Morgan, & Davis, 1992). Two of these categories of evidence are available for rapid naming's role in reading development: standard and causal modeling analyses of longitudinal–correlational data (Felton & Brown, 1990; Wagner et al., 1994, 1997; Wolf & Goodglass, 1986) and differences between normal and reading-disabled children using reading-level-match designs (Bowers et al., 1994).

Although individual differences in verbal short-term memory can be shown to predict subsequent reading development (Brady, 1991; Mann & Liberman, 1984), individual differences on these tasks do not appear to explain unique variance in reading growth beyond that explained by phonological awareness and rapid naming ability (Wagner et al., 1994, 1997). Furthermore, the evidence for special impairment of reading-disabled children on verbal short-term memory tasks from reading-level-match designs has been consistently negative (Pennington, Van Orden, Kirson, & Haith, 1991; Stanovich & Siegel, 1994). However, as Torgesen (1995) pointed out, most of the prominent case studies of phonological dyslexia in both children and adults report limitations in verbal short-term memory as one of the prominent cognitive characteristics of these subjects. Clearly, further research is required to determine what unique role, if any, problems in phonological coding in working memory play in causing reading disabilities. Although the three phonological abilities under discussion here appear to differ in their importance as unique causes of reading disabilities, because of their consistent relationships to one another, all of them are included in our discussion of stability. We turn now to an assessment of the consistency of individual differences in these abilities across development.

STABILITY OF PHONOLOGICAL ABILITIES DURING THE ELEMENTARY SCHOOL PERIOD

In all of our research on the development of reading-related phonological processes, we have employed multiple measures of each construct. This makes possible the use of latent variables in our analyses. A latent variable represents the common or shared variance among the several tests that are used to measure each construct. Because they represent only the variance common across tasks, latent variables provide relatively error-free measurement by excluding task-specific sources of error. When assessed as latent variables, reading-related phonological abilities show a high degree of stability across the elementary school period.

Stability of Phonological Abilities When Assessed
as Latent Variables

Table 7.1 (Wagner et al., 1997) presents an index of stability for each variable
(because analytic and synthetic phonological awareness were so highly correlated after second grade, they are combined into a single variable in these
analyses) from kindergarten through fourth grade. Although analagous to
correlation coefficients, these indexes are actually standardized maximum
likelihood estimates of covariances among latent variables (Bollen, 1989).
Their interpretation is very similar to standard correlation coefficients (they
can vary from 0.0 to 1.0, depending on the strength of the relationship among
constructs), and they show that individual differences in phonological skills
are more stable than those for word-level reading from kindergarten and
first grade to later grades, although they are roughly similar in stability to

TABLE 7.1
Stability of Phonological Processing Abilities and
Word-Level Reading Measured as Latent Variables

Awareness	First Grade	Second Grade	Third Grade	Fourth Grade
Kindergarten	0.83	0.62	0.64	0.63
First grade		0.89	0.83	0.86
Second grade			0.95	0.94
Third grade				0.95
Memory				
Kindergarten	1.00	0.93	0.89	0.77
First grade		1.00	0.94	0.88
Second grade			0.98	0.87
Third grade				0.86
Naming				
Kindergarten	0.84	0.64	0.60	0.55
First grade		0.87	0.77	0.72
Second grade			0.85	0.82
Third grade				0.84
Word-Level Reading				
Kindergarten	0.69	0.39	0.33	0.27
First grade		0.84	0.70	0.62
Second grade			0.96	0.87
Third grade				0.96

From: Wagner, R. K., Torgesen, J. K., Rashotte, C. A., Hecht, S. A., Barker, T. A., Burgess,
S. R., Donahue, J., & Garon, T. (1997). Changing causal relations between phonological
processing abilities and word-level reading as children develop from beginning to fluent readers:
A five-year longitudinal study. *Developmental Psychology, 33*, 468–479.

reading beginning about second grade. For example, the first- to fourth-grade stability co-efficients for phonological variables vary between .86 and .72, whereas that for word-level reading over the same period is .62. In contrast, the second- to fourth-grade stability indexes for phonological variables vary between .94 and .82, whereas that for word-level reading is .87.

Stability of Phonological Skills When Assessed as Unit-Weighted Composites

Although relationships among latent variables provide the most accurate estimate of the true degree of relationship among constructs or their true stability over time, the use of latent measures is still relatively uncommon in developmental studies of reading and related processing skills. In order to provide an estimate of the stability of phonological skills and word reading ability when they are measured as observed variables, and also to provide a comparison of their stability with a measure of general verbal ability (which could not be treated as a latent variable because we only had one measure for it), we calculated stability co-efficients among composite measures of phonological awareness, rapid naming, memory, and word-level reading skill. All composite variables were formed as an average of the standard scores for each task used to construct the composite. The tasks combined to form the measure of phonological awareness were phoneme elision, segmenting, and phoneme blending. Measures of rapid digit naming and rapid letter naming were combined to estimate rapid automatic naming ability; and digit span and verbatim memory for sentences were combined as the measure of phonological memory. The Word Identification and Word Attack subtests of the Woodcock Reading Mastery Test–Revised (Woodcock, 1987) were combined to form the measure of word-level reading ability. General verbal ability was estimated from the Vocabulary subtest of the Stanford Binet Intelligence Scale (4th ed.; Thorndike, Hagen, & Sattler, 1986). In this analysis, data was available from a final testing of the longitudinal sample when the children were in fifth grade. Two hundred and one children remained in the sample for the final testing point. The correlations of each variable with itself across the span from kindergarten to fifth grade are presented in Table 7.2. The general pattern of results from this table indicates that, over the period from kindergarten through fifth grade, individual phonological abilities are at least as stable as general verbal ability estimated by a test of vocabulary knowledge.

The values reported in Table 7.2 are very similar to those reported by Scarborough (1995) for the 6-year interval between second and eighth grades. For example, the second- to eighth-grade correlation for phonological awareness in her study was .49, for rapid naming it was .51, and for phonological memory it was .66.

TABLE 7.2
Stability of Phonological Processing Abilities
and Vocabulary Knowledge as Observed Variables

Awareness	1st Grade	2nd Grade	3rd Grade	4th Grade	5th Grade
Kindergarten	0.66	0.49	0.51	0.48	0.48
First grade		0.74	0.70	0.68	0.68
Second grade			0.77	0.76	0.74
Third grade				0.81	0.80
Fourth grade					0.84
Memory					
Kindergarten	0.77	.69	0.66	0.62	0.53
First grade		0.82	0.80	0.74	0.68
Second grade			0.84	0.73	0.73
Third grade				0.76	0.75
Fourth grade					0.74
Naming					
Kindergarten	0.76	0.59	0.58	0.51	0.41
First grade		0.82	0.75	0.70	0.58
Second grade			0.83	0.76	0.66
Third grade				0.84	0.68
Fourth grade					0.69
Word-Level Reading					
Kindergarten	0.65	0.35	0.29	0.25	0.22
First grade		0.76	0.64	0.57	0.54
Second grade			0.89	0.81	0.79
Third grade				0.92	0.90
Fourth grade					0.94
General Verbal Ability (Vocabulary)					
Kindergarten	0.65	0.46	0.54	0.56	0.44
First grade		0.55	0.62	0.68	0.56
Second grade			0.64	0.59	0.58
Third grade				0.71	0.68
Fourth grade					0.70

Consistency of Significant Disabilities in Phonological Processing and Word Reading

Thus far, we have presented evidence that individual differences in phonological abilities are very stable across the elementary school period when the full range of abilities are included in the analyses. This suggests that children who are weak in phonological skills at the beginning of school will continue to be relatively weak in these abilities in fourth or fifth grade, which increases the likelihood that children with phonologically based reading disabilities will show relatively consistent reading difficulties across grade levels in elementary school. In order to provide a more direct assessment of the stability of significant weaknesses in phonological performance across the elementary school period, we identified children in first grade and third grades who performed below the 10th percentile on each skill, and then examined their placement within the distribution of that skill 2 years later (in third and fifth grades, respectively). In other words, we examined the stability of a diagnosis of significant weakness in phonological skill and word reading ability over 2-year increments during early and late elementary school. The same composite measures of each phonological skill and word reading that were used in the previous analysis were used here. Because of slight variations in the distribution of these skills within the sample, and because of occasional tied scores at the 10th percentile cut point, the number of children identified as significantly disabled (bottom 10%) varied slightly (from 20 to 22 children) across abilities.

Table 7.3 presents the percentage of the disabled group at first and third grades that fell at each decile within the bottom half of the distribution of that skill 2 years later. For example, of the original 21 children identified as significantly weak in performance on phonological awareness tasks in first grade, 51% continued to fall in the bottom 10th percentile in third grade. Although this suggests that about half of the children who were classified as significantly disabled in their performance on phonological awareness tasks at the beginning of first grade no longer fell in this category in third grade, 75% of these children fell below the 30th percentile in third grade, and only one child achieved above-average performance. The corresponding numbers (percent of first-grade disabled children falling below the 30th percentile in third grade) for rapid automatic naming and phonological memory were very similar, 95% and 75%, respectively. The overall stability of phonological disabilities from Grade 3 to Grade 5 was very similar to that for the earlier developmental period. The stability of extremely low performance on word reading tasks was similar to that for the phonological measures, with the period from Grade 3 to Grade 5 showing particularly extreme stability.

It should be pointed out here that children in our longitudinal sample were assessed at the *beginning* of the first, second, and third grades, and at the *end* of the fourth and fifth grades. Thus, the stability estimates for the early grades encompass a 2-year span starting before the beginning of formal reading instruction. In contrast, the stability estimates for Grades 3 and 5 encompass almost 3 full school years.

The overall pattern of substantial stability in the relative performance of children with phonological weaknesses over the elementary school period is consistent with other reports of stability of reading disabilities over the same

TABLE 7.3

Stability of Significant Disabilities in Phonological Processing and Word Reading Ability Over 2-Year Periods in Early and Late Elementary School

Skill Area

Percentile Range 2 Years After Initial Assessment	Phonological Awareness		Rapid Automatic Naming		Phonological Memory		Word Reading	
	First Through Third	Third Through Fifth	First Through Third	Third Through Fifth	First Through Third	Third Through Fifth	First Through Third	Third Through Fifth
10th	51	47	60	70	50	60	36	75
20th	14	43	20	20	10	25	27	25
30th	10	5	15	0	15	0	14	0
40th	10	0	0	0	10	5	9	0
50th	10	5	0	0	15	0	9	0
Above 50th	5	0	5	10	0	10	5	0

period. Although we could not locate other studies that examined consistency of extremely poor performance on phonological processing tasks per se, there are a number of studies that have examined the stability of word reading disabilities in elementary school. For example, Juel (1988), in a longitudinal study of reading growth from first to fourth grades, reported that the probability of becoming an average reader by the end of fourth grade if a child fell within the bottom quartile in reading at the end of first grade was .13. In our sample, if we were to define *average* word reading ability as falling above the 40th percentile, then the probability of a child who is identified with severe word reading disabilities at the beginning of first grade performing in the average range at the beginning of third grade is .14. The same probability calculated for the period from the beginning of third grade to the end of fifth grade in our sample is 0.0. Thus, the conclusion from both these studies is that children who are significantly impaired in their phonological and word reading skills at one point in time during elementary school almost invariably are found to be poor or below average in these skills 2 years later. Furthermore, this stability is relatively consistent across both early and late periods of development.

This conclusion about significant stability in the diagnosis of phonologically based reading disabilities is, however, inconsistent with the results of another widely cited study (Shaywitz, Escobar, Shaywitz, Fletcher, & Makuch, 1992) that reported very little stability in the diagnosis of specific developmental dyslexia over a similar period in elementary school. These investigators, for example, reported that only 7 of 25 (28%) students diagnosed as dyslexic in first grade received the same diagnosis in third grade, and only 14 of 30 (46%) diagnosed in third grade received the same diagnosis in fifth grade. These data were widely interpreted as suggesting that specific developmental dyslexia (or phonologically based reading disabilities) is an extremely unstable disability, so that there is a high probability a child might "have it" at one point and "not have it" at another point in development.

However, there are at least two reasons to discount this interpretation within the present context, in which our concern is with the stability of phonological processing and reading levels themselves, rather than the stability of a diagnosis that involves arbitrary cutpoints in the distibution of reading skills. First, what Shaywitz and her colleagues assessed was the stability of a discrepancy definition of reading disabilities that involved a difference between measured intelligence and reading level. Difference scores, such as those used to identify discrepancies, are statistically less reliable than the scores for absolute level of reading ability or level of intelligence taken by themselves. Second, the earlier study was conducted to examine classification reliability, which can be easily influenced by small amounts of movement across the arbitrary cutpoints that are used to determine whether a child receives the diagnosis or not. In our own data, if we analyze simple classification reliability and decide that a child must perform in the bottom 10th percentile in word reading ability to be classified as reading disabled, then our results become more similar to those of Shaywitz et al. (1992). For example, only 36% of children scoring in the bottom 10th percentile in first grade do so in third grade, and 75% of children with severe reading problems in third grade continue to show the same level of impairment in fifth grade. These stability estimates are slightly higher than those reported in the Shaywitz et al. (1992) study, most probably because they used a cutpoint for discrepancy score, whereas we used a cutpoint only for reading level. However, the important point about stability is the one made in previous paragraphs: Very few of the children identified with severe reading problems in first or third grade actually achieve average reading levels in subsequent years.

Factors Related to the Stability of Phonological Processes

We began this section by suggesting that evidence confirming the stability of phonological processing across a significant developmental span would provide additional support for the theory of phonologically based reading disabilities. The cause of an academic difficulty that is as difficult to eliminate as reading disabilities should be a relatively stable characteristic of the child. Our statement is only true, however, if it is combined with evidence that early individual differences in phonological processing are more strongly related to later growth in word reading ability than the other way around. In other words, because it is relatively widely accepted that learning to read stimulates the growth of some phonological skills (phonological awareness in particular; Brady & Shankweiler, 1991), it is possible that the stability of phonological processing skills is primarily the product of stability in the distribution of word reading ability in our sample. Although there may be some truth to this argument, it cannot be the whole story, because our analyses within this same sample (Wagner et al., 1994, 1997) have consistently shown more powerful longitudinal prediction of growth from early phonological skills to later reading skills than from individual differences in reading to subsequent growth in phonological ability. In other words, our analyses of causal relationships among these variables suggest that causal influences are stronger from phonological processing to reading than from reading to phonological processing.

It also must be pointed out that the stability estimates we have reported may indicate as much about the educational environment of the children in our study as they do about the nature of phonological processes themselves. Specifically, it is possible that our data overestimate the general degree of stability in phonological abilities in young children because of a relatively weak program of instruction in word reading skills in the school district from which this sample was taken. For example, at the end of fifth grade (approximately 5.7 grade level), the average grade level score on the Word Attack subtest of the Woodcock Reading Mastery Test–Revised (Woodcock, 1987) was 4.1, and 40% of the sample achieved scores on this test that were two or more grade levels below their current grade placement. The Word Attack subtest is a direct measure of children's ability to apply "phonics" knowledge (letter-sound correspondences, phoneme blending skills) to reading novel words. This level of performance for our sample indicates either that our children as a whole had greater difficulty learning phonological skills in reading, or that they were less consistently supported in their development of these skills, than the national sample from which the test's norms were calculated. Although it is difficult to predict the precise effects that more consistent instruction and general support for the development of word-level reading skills would have on the stability of individual differences in phonological abilities, it seems likely that more effective instruction for low-ability children might reduce these estimates slightly if it were able to accelerate the development of skills in this area. We turn now to an examination of instructional effects for phonological awareness, which indicate that this core phonological skill can be significantly modified by direct instruction, but also that there are significant individual differences in response to this training.

Response to Training in Phonological Awareness

With the growing consensus about the importance of individual differences in phonological skills as causes of variation in response to early reading instruction, there has arisen the hope that early training in these skills might significantly reduce the incidence of reading disabilities in young children (Berninger, Thalberg, DeBruyn, & Smith, 1987). This hope has been supported by findings that phonological awareness, in particular, can be substantially improved in groups of kindgarten and first-grade children through direct instruction using oral language activities. For example, a recent meta-analysis of 13 phonological awareness training studies (Wagner, Torgesen, & Rashotte, 1993) found an average effect size of 1.23 standard deviation units on measures of phonological awareness after an average of only 9 hours of training. A recent study (Foster, Erickson, Foster, Brinkman, & Torgesen, 1994) using computerized activities to stimulate phonological awareness reported an effect size of 1.05 standard deviation units after only 4½ total hours of training! A number of studies (Ball & Blachman, 1991; Barker & Torgesen, 1995; Cunningham, 1990; Lundberg et al., 1988) have also demonstrated significant average effects on children's subsequent reading development following training in phonological awareness. Taken together, the data on ease of training in phonological awareness associated with subsequent improvements in reading growth provide support for hopes that early training in phonological skills may have a serious impact on the reading problems of many children.

However, a crucial question that is not consistently addressed in the training literature on phonological awareness is whether this training simply "hothouses," or accelerates, the growth of children who would be normal readers anyway, or whether it actually reduces the risk of reading failure for children with the weakest phonological abilities before training. For example, in commenting informally on his large-scale and generally successful training study using random samples of kindergarten children (Lundberg et al., 1988), Lundberg (1988) indicated that a substantial number of lower-ability children did not appear to significantly profit from the training. In our own work to develop a phonological awareness training program for kindergarten children (Torgesen et al., 1992), we found that approximately one third of a group of low-ability children did not respond (by showing meaningful growth in outcome measures) to a training program in which groups of three to four children received approximately 7 hours of training spread over 7 to 8 weeks.

Intrigued by this significant range of individual differences in response to training in phonological awareness, we conducted a study that was specifically designed to examine the child characteristics that predict growth in response to training (Torgesen & Davis, 1997). Sixty kindergarten children from two elementary schools with historically low achievement in reading were selected because of relatively low performance on a screening measure for phonological awareness. They were then provided with 16 hours of training that was spread over 12 weeks. The children were trained in small groups (three or four children), and the training focused on both analytic (recognizing and thinking about individual sounds in words) and synthetic (blending individual sounds into words) awareness skills. Children were taught to blend phonemes together to make words, to identify the positions of specific phonemes in words, and to pronounce individual phonemes in words presented as wholes. These activities were supported by the use of pictures to represent words, colored blocks to provide concrete representations of phonemes in words, and a variety of gamelike activities to maintain interest. During approximately the last 3 weeks of training, the children were taught the letters that represented a small group of the phonemes they had practiced with during their oral language training. They were then shown how to use their letter knowledge, along with their segmenting and blending skills, to read a small group of real words.

For the entire group, the effect size (compared to a no-treatment control group) for growth in analytic phonological awareness (as measured by ability to separately pronounce the individual sounds in words) was 1.35, whereas that for synthetic awareness (ability to blend separately presented phonemes into words) was 1.85. These are substantial overall training effects, and they are very consistent with average effects that are typically observed in training studies. However, 21 of the 60 children in the training group scored only 1 or 0 on the segmenting posttest; they had gained no reliable analytic skills as a result of the training. After determining that there was a significant overall training effect for both analytic and synthetic skills, our next step was to examine the individual child characteristics that best predicted response to training.

This analysis used hierarchical linear modeling to estimate a growth curve for each child in both analytic and synthetic phonological awareness. We were able to estimate only the linear component of growth, because we had available only three measures of performance: at the beginning, middle, and end of training. The slopes of these growth curves were predicted by variables from four categories: pretest levels of phonological awareness; other phonological processing skills—rapid automatic naming for digits and phonological short-term memory; beginning reading/spelling skills; and general verbal ability.

Consistent with our earlier work showing that analytic and synthetic skills are separate but correlated abilities in young children (Wagner, Torgesen, Laughon, Simmons, & Rashotte, 1993), different variables predicted growth in these two types of phonological awareness. Pretest measures of rapid automatic naming and invented spelling (a measure of both analytic awareness and letter-sound knowledge) were the best predictors of growth in blending skill, whereas measures of invented spelling and general verbal ability were the strongest predictors of growth in analytic ability.

These results indicate that children in our sample who had relative weaknesses in rapid automatic naming ability, phonological awareness, and knowledge of letter-sound correspondences were those who profited least from the training in phonological awareness. Because all of these characteristics have been associated with phonologically based reading disabilities, it seems likely that a large proportion of reading-disabled children would fall into the group of children who did not profit from the otherwise effective training provided in this study. This suggests that, if training in phonological awareness is to be successful in reducing the number of children who develop reading disabilities, it may require training procedures that go beyond those typically found in the research literature, in terms of both their explicitness and intensity. We turn now to a consideration of the practical implications, for both identification and treatment, of the research findings we have considered thus far.

Practical Applications of Research Knowledge
to Diagnoses and Intervention for Reading-Disabled Children

The information presented thus far on the stability of phonological skills during the elementary school years, as well as indications that disabilities in these areas may not be easily overcome with moderate-level interventions, has implications for practice in two important areas. First, the generally strong relationships between early individual differences in phonological processing skill and later individual differences in both phonological skills and reading suggests the possibility for advances in our ability to identify children at risk for specific reading disabilities prior to the start of reading instruction. Rather than waiting for intervention to begin once children experience reading failure in first or second grade, we now have the potential to develop theoretically and practically meaningful instruments to identify children for placement in preventive instructional programs. Second, information about the stability of phonological skills in large random samples of children, as well as resistance to treatment of phonological disabilities in low-ability children, suggest the need for a re-examination of intervention procedures for children with phonologically based reading disabilities.

Use of Phonological Measures for Early Identification

Because studies of the relationships between phonological skills and word reading growth generally indicate that phonological awareness is more strongly related to early reading growth than other types of phonological skill (Fletcher et al., 1994; Wagner et al., 1994), there have been a number of recent attempts to use early measures of phonological awareness to identify children who will later fail in reading (Catts, 1996). These studies have measured phonological awareness either during kindergarten, or at the beginning of first grade, and report overall identification accuracy's ranging from 75.6% to 99%. With the exception of two studies that measured phonological skills at the beginning of first grade, however, these studies have universally had high numbers of false positives (children who are predicted to be poor readers, but turn out to be good readers), with rates ranging from 23% to 69%. Scarborough (1996) concluded that, in order to more accurately identify specific children as at risk of reading failure, it may be useful to supplement measures of phonological awareness with measures of other phonological processes and emergent reading skills.

Using data from the longitudinal study reported on earlier in this chapter, we (Torgesen & Wagner, 1995) used a combination of three measures taken in the first semester of kindergarten to identify children at risk of being in the bottom 10% of children in word reading ability during the first semester of second grade. The predictive measures we used were letter-name knowledge (how many of the 26 uppercase letters could be named), a measure of phonological awareness (phoneme elision—"Say *mat* without saying the /m/ sound."), and rapid automatic naming ability for digits (six digits were randomly arranged in six rows for a total of 36 digits). These measures were combined together using logistic regression procedures, and 23 children were identified (of the 240 children in the sample) who had a probability greater than 50% of being in the bottom 10% in second grade. Of these 23 children, 14 actually obtained word reading scores in the bottom 10% in second grade. Of the nine "false positives" in this group, five were in the bottom 20%, two in the bottom 30%, and two were slightly above-average readers. The overall accuracy rate in this analysis was 92%, and the rate of false positives was only 4%. However, the predictive procedure we used failed to identify 10 of the 24 children who ended up in the bottom 10% of readers in second grade, which gave us a 42% false negative rate. Although this balance between false positives and false negatives was appropriate for our purpose, which was to select children for a study of instructional procedures to prevent reading disabilities, the rate of false negatives would be unacceptably high in practice. We are currently working on a different predictive equation, using a few more indicators, that will examine more completely the potential of these kinds of measures to accurately identify specific children who are most in need of supplemental instruction to prevent the early emergence of serious reading difficulties.

One issue that currently limits research on the early identification of children at risk of phonologically based reading disabilities is the lack of standardized measures in this area. There are a number of standardized (in terms of administration procedures) instruments available to measure phonological awareness, such as the *Lindamood Auditory Conceptualization Test* (Lindamood & Lindamood, 1979), the *Test of Phonological Awareness* (Torgesen & Bryant, 1994), the *Test of Awareness of Language Segments* (Sawyer, 1987), the *Phonological Awareness Profile* (Robertson & Salter, 1995), and the *Yopp-Singer Test of Phoneme Segmentation* (Yopp, 1995). However, only one of these tests includes more than one measure of phonological awareness, and none of them allow simultaneous assessment of phonological skills other than awareness. This latter constraint limits the kind of multivariate procedures recommended by Scarborough (1996) that are most likely to obtain the high identification rates that will make early screening and intervention for phonologically based reading disabilities practically feasible.

In our research program, we are currently in the processes of developing the *Comprehensive Test of Phonological Processes in Reading* (CTPPR), which will provide wide range assessment of all three areas of phonological skill discussed in this chapter. The CTPPR will contain multiple subtests to assess phonological awareness, phonological memory, and rapid automatic naming skill. We have carried out preliminary studies of the items on these subtests as well as its concurrent validity, and the test will be submitted to a national standardization during the 1996–1997 school year.

Another issue involving the use of phonological processing measures to identify children at risk for reading failure is that they are likely to identify a somewhat different group than is currently being served in programs for children with reading disabilities. We are suggesting the idea that children might be identified for special preventive instruction in reading on the basis of low performance on measures that assess a set of cognitive markers (perhaps supplemented by demographic markers) for reading disability. In contrast, procedures currently in use, and supported by a long tradition in the field of learning disabilities, identify children for special educational help in reading on the basis of a discrepancy between their general ability (as measured by a full-scale IQ test) and their reading achievement. This practice arose, in part, because of assumptions about differences between children whose reading level was discrepant versus nondiscrepant from their general intelligence, and also from a lack of knowledge about the critical cognitive factors responsible for reading disabilities in children (Torgesen, 1993). Recent research has established that the basic causes of word reading difficulties in readers of low general intelligence are indistinguishable from those responsible for reading problems in children of average and high general intelligence (Fletcher, Francis, Rourke, Shaywitz, & Shaywitz, 1992; Fletcher et al., 1994; Pennington, Gilger, Olson, & DeFries, 1992; Stanovich & Siegel, 1994). Thus, it seems appropriate that children with similar problems in acquiring word reading ability should have available similar interventions early in their schooling.

However, it is true that children whose word reading skills are discrepant versus nondiscrepant from their general intelligence will differ on cognitive skills that lie outside the word recognition module (Ellis & Large, 1987; Stanovich & Siegel, 1994). Children whose general ability is significantly higher than their ability to acquire word reading skills are likely to have higher reading comprehension levels if the basic deficit in word recognition skill can be overcome. This argument implies that children of high and low general intelligence do have a different prognosis with regard to the ultimate level of reading skill they are likely to attain, given equivalent instruction. It also implies that children of low general ability (specifically broad verbal ability) may require additional intensive instruction to acquire the general verbal knowledge and skill that supports good reading comprehension. Because of the sheer amount of knowledge and skill to be acquired, this latter deficiency is likely to be much more difficult to overcome than are problems in word reading.

The Impact of Intensive Interventions

We are currently engaged in a 5-year project to study interventions that are focused on the word reading difficulties of children with phonologically based reading disabilities. It is clear both from studies of long-term outcomes (Horn, O'Donnell, & Vitulano, 1983) for students with reading disabilities and from studies of short-term effectiveness of special education programs

(Kaufman, 1993) that public education is not currently meeting the educational needs of these children. In our own longitudinal study, for example, *none* of the children with word reading skills below the 10th percentile in third grade were reading above the 30th percentile in the fifth grade.

There are, however, scattered clinical reports indicating that appropriate instruction, if offered with sufficient intensity, can frequently produce dramatic improvements in the fundamental reading skills of children who were previously making little progress in learning to read (Clark & Uhry, 1995). These clinical reports have been recently supplemented with research evidence that it is possible to substantially improve the word reading skills of children with specific reading disabilities by using instructional programs that explicitly teach the structure of language at the word level coupled with extensive review and practice (Alexander, Anderson, Heilman, Voeller, & Torgesen, 1991; Lovett, Borden, Lea Lacerenza, Benson, & Brackstone, 1994; Olson, Wise, Johnson, & Ring, 1997).

These reports are consistent with data we have obtained from our current study of remedial instruction with reading-disabled children, in which we have found quite dramatic short-term effects on children's word reading abilities as a result of two different types of intensive intervention. This study focused on children who were already identified by their school district as learning disabled in reading, and, from this group, we selected children with the lowest scores on word-level reading skills and phonological processing measures. These selected children received 80 hours of one-on-one tutorial instruction using either of two instructional methods. One method, called the *Auditory Discrimination in Depth* (ADD; Lindamood & Lindamood, 1984) program, provides very explicit instruction in phonological awareness by helping children discover the articulatory gestures that are associated with each phoneme in the English language. This oral awareness instruction is followed by extensive practice in monitoring the number, identity, and sequence of sounds in words by using both articulatory and auditory information. The program then teaches children to apply what they have learned in the phonological awareness activities to reading and spelling words. Children received extensive decontextualized practice in reading both real and nonwords, and they were engaged in supported reading experiences with text that were phonetically controlled in the beginning.

The other instructional method is called *embedded phonics* (EP). This program provided instruction in reading that was oriented more toward the whole word and reading for meaning than the ADD program. Children spent the majority of their time reading either basal or trade books, and unusual reading vocabulary in these books was directly pretaught. Phonological awareness was stimulated during the writing of some of these words, in which the teacher encouraged the child to think about the number of sounds in the word before beginning to write. Phonics skills were directly taught, but they were not taught sequentially or drilled using decontextualized activities. During the introduction of new sight words, the phonetic patterns used in the words were introduced. Children were also explicitly taught to utilize both grapheme-based and context-based cues for the identity of words in text.

Both of these methods contained direct instruction in phonics, and they both included activities designed to stimulate phonological awareness. The fundamental contrast between them was in the degree of explicitness and amount of total instructional time focused on building phonological awareness and practicing alphabetic decoding skills.

We now have pre- and posttest outcome data for 58 students: 29 in the ADD program, and 29 who were randomly assigned to the EP method. The average age of these children when they began our program was 121 months, and their average full-scale IQ was 98, with a range from 82 to 128. There are 40 males and 18 females in the sample, with the racial balance being predominantly White. About 55% of the children have received a comorbid diagnosis of attention deficit disorder, and these children have all received stimulant medication during the intervention.

The children were assessed with a variety of reading and language measures, and their continued development will be assessed for 2 years following the end of our intervention. Measurement of short-term changes in their word reading ability using a standardized measure (Woodcock Reading Mastery Test–Revised; Woodcock, 1987) indicates substantial improvement for children receiving instruction from both methods. For example, children in the ADD group showed an average gain in the ability to apply phonics skills to reading novel words (Word Attack subtest) of 27 standard score points, with the corresponding gain for the EP group being 20 points. These gains in performance correspond to movement from the 2nd percentile to the 37th and 25th percentiles, respectively. The ADD group showed significantly more improvement on this measure than the EP group. For ability to read increasingly difficult real words (Word Identification subtest), average improvement for both groups was approximately 14 standard score points, which corresponds to movement from the 2nd to the 10th percentile. In the area of reading comprehension, the children finished at about the 27th percentile. In order to illustrate graphically the significant changes in these children's word-level reading abilities within a short time period, their average raw scores on the Word Attack and Word Identification subtests are plotted in Fig. 7.1 as a function of their age in months. The top dotted line plots data from the national standardization for the test, to indicate normal growth on these measures. These graphs assume a common starting point for all children at the beginning of first grade, and they represent pre-, mid-, and posttest data on the intervention sample during the 8 weeks of their

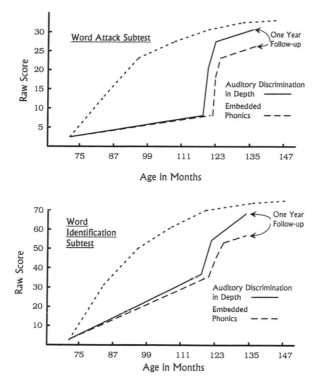

FIG. 7.1. Change in raw scores on Word Attack and Word Identification subtests as a result of intensive instructional interventions.

intervention programs. We currently have 1 year follow-up data on 34 children, and this data is also shown in Fig. 7.1.

Of course, the ultimate effectiveness of these interventions is dependent on more than short-term gains in decontextualized word reading ability. One important test is whether the children have acquired generalizable skills that will assist them to continue to grow in their reading ability after the intervention is concluded. Our preliminary answer to that question for these interventions is that the large majority (30 of 34 children for whom 1-year follow-up data is presently available) of children do continue to show improvements (measured by gains in standard scores) in Word Attack and Word Identification performance 1 year later. Equally important to the question of continued growth in word reading ability is whether growth in these skills leads to significant and continuing gains in reading comprehension and reading fluency. Although we are collecting data on this issue, they are not yet available for report. A recent review of intervention research in reading by Olson et al. (1997) suggests that the issue of growth in fluency and strong generalization of remediated word reading skills to text processing must be examined carefully in future research.

CONCLUDING COMMENTS

The major point of this chapter is that, under typical instructional conditions in elementary school, individual differences in phonological processing and word reading ability are extremely stable over the period from first through fifth grades. This stability has two important implications for professionals concerned with assisting the growth of all children in reading. First, it should be possible to utilize phonological processing measures, in combination with other measures of emergent reading skills, to accurately identify children who will require additional instructional support to avoid early failure in learning to read. Although the question is still open for additional research, it seems likely at this point that these children will require instruction that is more explicit, more intensive, and more supportive than is currently available in most school settings (Torgesen, 1996). This second implication derives from the fact that children with the lowest abilities in the phonological domain do not easily respond to conventional levels of intensity and explicitness of instruction in the skills required to accurately identify words in text. However, several recent research reports do indicate that a number of different approaches can be effective in significantly enhancing word-level reading skills in children with phonologically based reading disabilities if they are offered with sufficient intensity. Our immediate next goals should be to explore ways of delivering the "special education" these children need within the school setting along with continued development of this instruction, so that it leads to broadly functional reading skills.

ACKNOWLEDGMENTS

The research reported in this manuscript was supported by grant numbers HD23340 and HD30988 from the National Institute of Child Health and Human Development, and by grants from the National Center for Learning Disabilities and the Donald D. Hammill Foundation.

REFERENCES

Alexander, A., Anderson, H., Heilman, P. C., Voeller, K. S., & Torgesen, J. K. (1991). Phonological awareness training and remediation of analytic decoding deficits in a group of severe dyslexics. *Annals of Dyslexia, 41*, 193–206.
Baddeley, A. D. (1991). *Human memory: Theory and practice*. London: Allyn & Bacon.

Ball, E. W., & Blachman, B. A. (1991). Does phoneme awareness training in kindergarten make a difference in early word recognition and developmental spelling? *Reading Research Quarterly, 26*, 49–66.

Barker, T. A., & Torgesen, J. K. (1995). An evaluation of computer-assisted instruction in phonological awareness with below average readers. *Journal of Educational Computing Research, 13*, 89–103.

Berninger, V., Thalberg, T., DeBruyn, I., & Smith, R. (1987). Preventing reading disabilities by assessing and remediating phonemic skills. *School Psychology Review, 16*, 554–565.

Bollen, K. A. (1989). *Structural equations with latent variables.* New York: Wiley.

Bowers, P., Golden, J., Kennedy, A., & Young, A. (1994). Limits upon orthographic knowledge due to processes indexed by naming speed. In V. W. Berninger (Ed.) *The varieties of orthographic knowledge I: Theoretical and developmental issues* (pp. 173–218). Dordrecht, The Netherlands: Kluwer.

Bowers, P. G., & Swanson, L. B. (1991). Naming speed deficits in reading disability: Multiple measures of a singular process. *Journal of Experimental Child Psychology, 51*, 195–219.

Bowers, P. G., & Wolf, M. (1993). Theoretical links betwen naming speed, precise timing mechanisms and orthographic skill in dyslexia. *Reading and Writing: An Interdisciplinary Journal, 5*, 69–85.

Bowey, J. A., Cain, M. T., & Ryan, S. M. (1992). A reading-level design study of phonological skills underlying fourth grade children's word reading difficulties. *Child Development, 63*, 999–1011.

Brady, S. A. (1991). The role of working memory in reading disability. In S. A. Brady & D. P. Shankweiler (Eds.), *Phonological processes in literacy* (pp. 129–152). Hillsdale, NJ: Lawrence Erlbaum Associates.

Brady, S., Poggie, E., & Rapala, M. M. (1989). Speech repetition abilities in children who differ in reading skill. *Language and Speech, 32*, 109–122.

Brady, S., & Shankweiler, D. (1991). *Phonological processes in literacy: A tribute to Isabelle Y. Liberman.* Hillsdale, NJ: Lawrence Erlbaum Associates.

Bruck, M. (1992). Persistence of dyslexics' phonological awareness deficits. *Developmental Psychology, 28*, 874–886.

Catts, H. (1996, March). *Phonological awareness: A key to detection.* Paper presented at conference titled The Spectrum of Developmental Disabilities XVIII: Dyslexia, at the Johns Hopkins Medical Institutions, Baltimore, MD.

Clark, D. B., & Uhry, J. K. (1995). *Dyslexia: Theory and practice of remedial instruction* (2nd ed.). Baltimore: York.

Cunningham, A. E. (1990). Explicit versus implicit instruction in phonemic awareness. *Journal of Experimental Child Psychology, 50*, 429–444.

Denckla, M. B., & Rudel, R. (1976). Naming of object drawing by dyslexic and other learning disabled children. *Brain and Language, 3*, 1–16.

Ellis, N., & Large, B. (1987). The development of reading: As you seek so shall you find. *British Journal of Psychology, 78*, 1–28.

Felton, R., & Brown, I. S. (1990). Phonological processes as predictors of specific reading skills in children at risk for reading failure. *Reading and Writing: An Interdisciplinary Journal, 2*, 39–59.

Fletcher, J. M., Francis, D. J., Rourke, B. P., Shaywitz, S. E., & Shaywitz, B. A. (1992). The validity of discrepancy-based definitions of reading disabilities. *Journal of Learning Disabilities, 25*, 555–561.

Fletcher, J. M., Shaywitz, S. E., Shankweiler, D. P., Katz, L., Liberman, I. Y., Stuebing, K. K., Francis, D. J., Fowler, A. E., & Shaywitz, B. A. (1994). Cognitive profiles of reading disability: Comparisons of discrepancy and low achievement definitions. *Journal of Educational Psychology, 86*, 6–23.

Foster, K. C., Erickson, G. C., Foster, D. F., Brinkman, D., & Torgesen, J. K. (1994). Computer administered instruction in phonological awareness: Evaluation of the *DaisyQuest* program. *Journal of Research and Development in Education, 27*, 126–137.

Gathercole, S. E., & Baddeley, A. D. (1993). Phonological working memory: A critical building block for reading development and vocabulary acquisition? *European Journal of Psychology of Education, 8*, 259–272.

Horn, W. F., O'Donnell, J. P., & Vitulano, L. A. (1983). Long-term follow-up studies of learning disabled persons. *Journal of Learning Disabilities, 16*, 542–555.

Hulme, C. (1988). Short-term memory development and learning to read. In M. Gruneberg, P. Morris, & R. Sykes (Eds.), *Practical aspects of memory: Current research and issues. Vol. 2. Clinical and educational implications* (pp. 234–271). Chichester, England: Wiley.

Jorm, A. F. (1983). Specific reading retardation and working memory: A review. *British Journal of Psychology, 74*, 311–342.

Juel, C. (1988). Learning to read and write: A longitudinal study of 54 children from first through fourth grades. *Journal of Educational Psychology, 80*, 437–447.

Kaufman, J. M. (1993). How we might achieve the radical reform of special education. *Exceptional Children, 60*, 6–16.

Liberman, I. Y., Shankweiler, D., & Liberman, A. M. (1989). The alphabetic principle and learning to read. In D. Shankweiler & I. Y. Liberman (Eds.), *Phonology and reading disability: Solving the reading puzzle* (pp. 1–33). Ann Arbor: University of Michigan Press.

Lindamood, C. H., & Lindamood, P. C. (1979). *Lindamood auditory conceptualization test.* Austin, TX: PRO-ED.

Lindamood, C. H., & Lindamood, P. C. (1984). *Auditory discrimination in depth.* Austin, TX: PRO-ED.

Lovette, M. W., Borden, S. L., Lea Lacerenza, T. D., Benson, N. J., & Brackstone, D. (1994). Treating the core deficits of developmental dyslexia: Evidence of transfer of learning after phonologically- and strategy-based reading training programs. *Journal of Educational Psychology, 30*, 805–822.

Lundberg, I. (1988). Preschool prevention of reading failure: Does training in phonological awareness work? In R. L. Masland & M. W. Masland (Eds.), *Prevention of reading failure* (pp. 163–176). Parkton, MD: York.

Lundberg, I., Frost, J., & Peterson, O. (1988). Effects of an extensive program for stimulating phonological awareness in pre-school children. *Reading Research Quarterly, 23*, 263–284.

Mann, V. A. (1993). Phoneme awareness and future reading ability. *Journal of Learning Disabilities, 26*, 259–269.

Mann, V. A., & Liberman, I. Y. (1984). Phonological awareness and verbal short-term memory. *Journal of Learning Disabilities, 10*, 592–599.

Olson, R. K., Wise, B., Johnson, M., & Ring, J. (1997). The etiology and remediation of phonologically based word recognition and spelling disabilities: Are phonological deficits the "hole" story? In B. Blachman (Ed.), *Foundations of reading acquisition and dyslexia* (pp. 305–326). Mahwah, NJ: Lawrence Erlbaum Associates.

Pennington, B. F., Gilger, J. W., Olson, R. K., & DeFries, J. C. (1992). The external validity of age-versus IQ-discrepancy definitions of reading disability: Lessons from a twin study. *Journal of Learning Disabilities, 25*, 562–573.

Pennington, B. F., Van Orden, G., Kirson, D., & Haith, M. (1991). What is the causal relation between verbal STM problems and dyslexia? In S. A. Brady & D. P. Shankweiler (Eds.), *Phonological processes in literacy: A tribute to Isabelle Y. Liberman* (pp. 173–186). Hillsdale, NJ: Lawrence Erlbaum Associates.

Rack, J. P., Snowling, M. J., & Olson, R. K. (1992). The nonword reading deficit in developmental dyslexia: A review. *Reading Research Quarterly, 27*, 29–53.

Robertson, C., & Salter, W. (1995). *Phonological awareness profile.* East Moline, IL: LinguiSystems.

Rudel, R. G., Denckla, M. B., & Broman, M. (1978). Rapid silent response to repeated target symbols by dyslexic and nondyslexic children. *Brain and Language, 6*, 52–62.

Sawyer, D. J. (1987). *Test of awareness of language segments.* Austin, TX: PRO-ED.

Scarborough, H. S. (1995, April). *Long-term prediction of reading skills: Grade 2 to grade 8.* Paper presented at annual meetings of the Society for Research in Child Development, Indianapolis, IN.

Scarborough, H. S. (1996, March). *Phonological awareness: Just a piece of the puzzle.* Paper presented at conference titled The Spectrum of Developmental Disabilities XVIII: Dyslexia, at the Johns Hopkins Medical Institutions, Baltimore, MD.

Share, D. L., & Stanovich, K. E. (1995). Cognitive processes in early reading development: A model of acquisition and individual differences. *Issues in Education: Contributions From Educational Psychology, 1*, 1–57.

Shaywitz, S. E., Escobar, M. D., Shaywitz, B. A., Fletcher, J. M., & Makuch, R. (1992). Evidence that dyslexia may represent the lower tail of a normal distribution of reading ability. *The New England Journal of Medicine, 326*, 145–150.

Stanovich, K. E. (1988). Explaining the differences between the dyslexic and the garden-variety poor reader: The phonological-core variable-difference model. *Journal of Learning Disabilities, 21*, 590–604.

Stanovich, K. E., Cunningham, A. E., & Cramer, B. B. (1984). Assessing phonological awareness in kindergarten children: Issues of task comparability. *Journal of Experimental Child Psychology, 38*, 175–190.

Stanovich, K. E., & Siegel, L. S. (1994). The phenotypic performance profile of reading-disabled children: A regression-based test of the phonological-core variable-difference model. *Journal of Educational Psychology, 86*, 24–53.

Thorndike, R. L., Hagen, E. P., & Sattler, J. M. (1986). *Guide for administering and scoring, the Stanford-Binet Intelligence Scale: Fourth edition.* Chicago: Riverside.

Torgesen, J. K. (1993). Variations on theory in learning disabilities. In R. Lyon, D. Gray, N. Krasnegor, & J. Kavenagh (Eds.), *Better understanding learning disabilities: Perspectives on classification, identification, and assessment and their implications for education and policy* (pp. 153–170). Baltimore: Brookes.

Torgesen, J. K. (1995). A model of memory from an information processing perspective: The special case of phonological memory. In G. Reid Lyon (Ed.), *Attention, memory, and executive function: Issues in conceptualization and measurement* (pp. 157–184). Baltimore: Brookes.

Torgesen, J. K. (1996). Thoughts about intervention research in learning disabilities. *Learning Disabilities: An Interdisciplinary Journal, 7*, 55–58.

Torgesen, J. K., & Bryant, B. (1994). *Test of phonological awareness.* Austin, TX: PRO-ED.

Torgesen, J. K., & Davis, C. (1997). Individual difference variables that predict response to training in phonological awareness. *Journal of Experimental Child Psychology, 63*, 1–21.

Torgesen, J. K., Morgan, S. T., & Davis, C. (1992). Effects of two types of phonological awareness training on word learning in kindergarten children. *Journal of Educational Psychology, 84*, 364–370.

Torgesen, J. K., Rashotte, C. A., Greenstein, J., Houck, G., & Portes, P. (1987). Academic difficulties of learning disabled children who perform poorly on memory span tasks. In H. L. Swanson (Ed.), *Memory and learning disabilities: Advances in learning and behavioral disabilities* (pp. 305–334). Greenwich, CN: JAI.

Torgesen, J. K., & Wagner, R. K. (1995, May). *Alternative diagnostic approaches for specific developmental reading disabilities.* Manuscript prepared for the National Research Council's Board on Testing and Assessment. Presented at a Workshop on IQ Testing and Educational Decision Making, Washington, DC.

Torgesen, J. K., Wagner, R. K., Rashotte, C. A., Burgess, S., & Hecht, S. (1997). The contributions of phonological awareness and rapid automatic naming ability to the growth of word reading skills in second to fifth grade students. *Scientific Studies of Reading, 1,* 161–185.

Wagner, R. K., Torgesen, J. K., & Rashotte, C. (1993, April). *The efficacy of phonological awareness training for early reading achievement: A meta-analysis.* Symposium presented at annual meetings of the American Educational Research Association, Atlanta, GA.

Wagner, R. K., Torgesen, J. K., Laughon, P., Simmons, K., & Rashotte, C. A. (1993). The development of young readers' phonological processing abilities. *Journal of Educational Psychology, 85,* 1–20.

Wagner, R. K., Torgesen, J. K., & Rashotte, C. A. (1994). The development of reading-related phonological processing abilities: New evidence of bi-directional causality from a latent variable longitudinal study. *Developmental Psychology, 30,* 73–87.

Wagner, R. K., Torgesen, J. K., Rashotte, C. A., Hecht, S. A., Barker, T. A., Burgess, S. R., Donahue, J., & Garon, T. (1977). Changing causal relations between phonological processing abilities and word-level reading as children develop from beginning to fluent readers: A five-year longitudinal study. *Developmental Psychology, 33,* 468–479.

Wolf, M. (1991). Naming speed and reading: The contribution of the cognitive neurosciences. *Reading Research Quarterly, 26,* 123–141.

Wolf, M., & Goodglass, A. (1986). Dyslexia, dysnomia, and lexical retrieval: A longitudinal investigation. *Brain and Language, 28,* 154–168.

Woodcock, R. W. (1987). *Woodcock reading mastery tests–revised.* Circle Pines, MN: American Guidance Service.

Yopp, H. K. (1995). A test for assessing phonemic awareness in young children. *The Reading Teacher, 49,* 20–29.

8

▼▼▼▼▼▼▼

Interactive Computer Support for Improving Phonological Skills

Barbara W. Wise
Richard K. Olson
Jerry Ring
Mina Johnson
University of Colorado

A book about beginning literacy usually focuses on children in kindergarten to second grade, yet some children fail to learn to read during these years because of specific reading disabilities. If these children are fortunate, they acquire their fundamental literacy skills later, in remedial programs. Less fortunate children with reading disabilities continue to struggle all their lives with reading, writing, and academic pursuits. The issues in the field of remedial instruction are similar to those in initial reading instruction: How can programs establish foundation skills in phonological and orthographic processing, and how can they ensure that the processes are integrated and applied in reading in context in a fluent and flexible manner? These questions fit well within the framework of this book, and they have long been the focus of our studies in Colorado using talking computers for reading remediation.

This chapter begins with theoretical and empirical information about the nature and causes of specific reading disability (SRD), or dyslexia. This background information guided the design of our programs using talking computers to study the remediation of the problems in SRD. Our first study's program, discussed in the next section, provided decoding and speech support for difficult words in the context of interesting stories. The section after that discusses a study that compared two contrasting training strategies used prior to and concurrent with the story-reading work. The study's results suggest that structured skills work helps most poor readers improve in phoneme awareness and phonological decoding, although by the study's end, many children were not yet applying the skills with fluency and flexibility. The chapter closes with ideas for future research to encourage better transfer of the skills into long-term fluent reading.

THEORETICAL BACKGROUND

In this chapter, *specific reading disability (SRD)* and *dyslexia* are used synonymously, as in the recent NIH working definition of dyslexia (Lyon, 1995). Although children with SRD certainly have problems comprehending text, those are secondary to their problem of slow and inaccurate word recognition. Their reading comprehension suffers for two reasons. First of all, comprehension will be confused when a child misidentifies a word in a text. Second, if the child decodes the words correctly but laboriously, few attentional resources will be left for comprehension.

When children with SRD are compared to age-matched average readers, they score lower than their age mates on many measures (Olson, Wise, Conners, Rack, & Fulker, 1989). They are behind in reading and frustrated by most tests related to it. However, researchers can look for causal patterns by matching children on the basis of reading word recognition instead of age: matching older children with SRD to younger average readers at the same reading level (RL) for isolated words. The older children with SRD have the advantage of more experience with school and language, so they score higher on vocabulary, listening comprehension, and reading comprehension (Conners & Olson, 1990). If they score lower than do younger RL-matched controls on a test, despite their experiential advantages, it suggests a causal role for that skill.

Older children with SRD usually score higher than do younger RL matches on reading comprehension (Conners & Olson, 1990). Their higher-level thinking skills and greater experience with story structures and context probably lead to this advantage. Word recognition thus apparently plays a causal role in reading comprehension difficulties, rather than the other way around. Perfetti (1985) presented other evidence about the causal nature of word recognition difficulties for reading comprehension.

Older children with SRD tend to score lower than do younger RL-matched controls on analytic language skills, suggesting a causal role for these skills (Olson et al., 1989; Olson, Forsberg, & Wise, 1994; Rack, Snowling, & Olson, 1992; Wise, 1991). One of these abilities is "phonological decoding," the ability to translate print into sound, measured in our studies by reading pronounceable nonwords (e.g., *niss, framble*). Children with SRD also perform worse than do the RL controls in phoneme awareness—awareness of speech sounds inside syllables—measured by deleting or manipulating sounds within spoken syllables.

Other lines of evidence also suggest that children with SRD have problems in analytic language skills. Neuropsychological MRI and brain flow studies show differences in children with SRD relative to normally reading children in areas of the brain that relate to analytic language (Hynd, Semrud-Clike-man, & Lyytinen, 1991). Nonword reading and phoneme awareness show strong heritability in twin studies (Olson et al., 1994), and phoneme awareness is the strongest predictor of reading ability throughout the school years (Calfee, Lindamood, & Lindamood, 1973). One very hopeful line of evidence that supports a causal role for phoneme awareness in reading disabilities comes from training studies. Many studies demonstrate that training in phoneme awareness and phonological analysis prior to and concurrent with reading instruction improves later reading in both early and remedial readers (Ball & Blachman, 1991; Bradley & Bryant, 1983; Byrne & Fielding-Barnsley, 1993; Hatcher, Hulme, & Ellis, 1994; Lundberg, Frost, & Peterson, 1988). Thus, even though deficits in phoneme awareness and phonological decoding have been shown to have an organic base in many children with SRD, studies suggest they can be changed with specific intervention designed to remedy the underlying deficit.

THE DECODING-IN-CONTEXT STUDY

Background for the Decoding-in-Context Study

In the 1980s, computers obtained the power of high-quality synthetic speech (our studies use DECtalk). "Talking computers" provided one good way to conduct research on the remediation of reading disabilities. These computers can provide immediate feedback for difficult words or parts of words, in stories or in isolated skills exercises, whenever a student requests help. One problem in field research of teaching is control of method; a good teacher will usually modify a method if he or she thinks it is not the best one for a particular child. This is perfectly appropriate for teaching, but it makes research about the effectiveness of methods difficult. A computer program has no preconceived ideas about methods, and it will continue to deliver a method as long as it is programmed to do so; thus, a researcher can compare benefits over a given time.

In our original study with talking computers (Olson & Wise, 1992), children did all their word decoding in the context of reading stories, with no isolated skills work. We thought that this would prove engaging, and Ehri (1980) discussed how reading words in context enriches children's syntactic and semantic associations for the words. Also, centering our program within a rich literature context fit well with the whole language orientation of the Boulder schools where we do our research. We called our program ROSS, for Reading with Orthographic and Special Segmentation.

Design and Method

Stories were arranged into grade-level directories from primer to sixth grade, based on average length of words in the sentences. Each directory had between 20 and 40 stories in it. Students chose stories of interest to them to read silently when reading independently, or orally when reading with a trainer. Whenever a student encountered a word that he or she found difficult, the student "targeted" that word by clicking on it with a mouse, and the computer gave decoding assistance by segmenting the word and pronouncing and blending the segments. At logical breaks in the story, the program asked a multiple-choice comprehension question, and at the end of the session, the program tested the student on 15 of the words targeted that day, or filled in with long words from that day's reading if fewer than 15 words had been targeted.

The point of the study was to see whether supported reading in context with immediate speech and segmentation support would prove to be a remedy for deficits in word recognition and phonological decoding. The study also compared different types of segmentation support: whole words, syllables, or subsyllables of onset and rime (e.g., *pl/ant*). When students targeted a word with a mouse, the computer first highlighted the segments sequentially in reverse video, and then highlighted and pronounced the segments. We hypothesized that support with segmentation at syllable or onset-rime levels would benefit decoding skills more than would the whole word support.

Second- to fifth-grade students were referred by teachers for being in the lower 10% of the class for word recognition difficulties, and were screened with the Wide Range Achievement Test (Jastak & Jastak, 1978) to confirm this difficulty. All students had normal intelligence, English as their first language, and no other primary sensory or emotional problems. Children were pre- and posttested on word recognition, nonword reading, phoneme awareness, and reading comprehension, and given a questionnaire concerning interests and attitudes about school and reading.

The children came to the computer room for 30 minutes per day during reading or language arts time. This kept the general reading instruction time the same for experimental subjects as for matched untrained controls back in class. Trained students read with the computer 3 or 4 days a week for 1 semester. A trainer from our laboratory taught the students to use the programs. Whenever the trainer read with the student, the student read aloud, and the trainer encouraged the student to target any word with which the child struggled. If the student reached the end of a sentence and had not targeted a misread word, the trainer pointed to that word and asked the child to target it. Trainers were present only 2 days per week. The other days, students were to come and read independently. This arrangement was designed partly to reduce staffing requirements and partly to see how well the students would respond to the computer without adult supervision. Not surprisingly, it led to substantial attendance problems on days when the trainer was not present.

Results

The study of decoding in context lasted 5 semesters, with different students each semester. At the end of each semester, students had read 10 to 14 hours with the computer. Trained students averaged about twice the gains in word recognition, compared to the untrained controls who spent that time back in the classroom: .6 compared to .3 grade levels gain on the Peabody Individualized Achievement Test (PIAT; Dunn & Markwardt, 1970), which was used to see grade-level gains. This was not an exceptional gain in 1 semester, but significantly greater than for controls (see Table 8.1). The trained students gained about four times as much (gaining about 10 percentage points) on nonword reading, and changed significantly more toward a positive attitude about reading relative to the matched untrained controls. However, no reliable differences occurred between training conditions: Children with whole word support gained as much in real and nonword reading as did those who had received speech support for word segments.

In all conditions, children's initial skill and their gains in real and nonword reading correlated with their initial skill in phoneme awareness (see Table 8.2). That is, children with lower initial phonemic awareness started lower and gained less than did students who started with relatively higher awareness. This is a typical but rather discouraging result in most training studies. Stanovich (1986) called this the "Matthew effect," in which children who start with the lowest abilities in reading do not just lag behind the others—they consistently gain less and, thus, fall further and further behind. The correlation of initial phoneme awareness with gain scores appeared even stronger in the onset-rime condition, suggesting that children with the lowest levels of phoneme awareness were having more difficulty than were other

TABLE 8.1
Gains in Reading With Decoding-in-Context Study:
Nonword Reading and Word Recognition

Group	Whole	Syllable	Onset-Rime	Control
N	41	46	51	46
Nonword reading (% correct)				
Pretest	40.7	37.7	43.2	45.2
Gain	9.1	11.3	9.4	2.5; $p < .01$
Time-limited word reading (number correct)				
Pretest	93.0	85.4	80.4	100.8
Gain	17.0	15.4	18.4	9.8; $p < .01$
Untimed word reading (PIAT grade equivalent)				
Pretest	2.7	2.7	2.7	2.7
Gain	.6	.6	.6	.3; $p < .05$

Note. Adapted from Olson and Wise (1992).

TABLE 8.2
Phoneme Deletion Correlations in Decoding-in-Context Study

	Nonword Pretest	Nonword Gain	Word Recognition Pretest	Word Recognition Gain
All subjects				
Pretest				
Phoneme deletion	.58	.27	.42	.32
Subjects in onset-rime condition				
Pretest				
Phoneme deletion	.68	.47	.46	.71

Note: All correlations significant at the $p < .01$ level. Table adapted from Olson and Wise (1992).

children in blending segmented words. We decided to change our agenda and no longer do all skills work in the context of stories.

THE STRATEGY TRAINING STUDY

Background for Strategy Study

In the next study, one group of children spent half their training time on structured and sequenced work to improve phoneme awareness in isolated exercises, and then they practiced the skills when reading stories. We wanted to see whether computer-based practice could improve children's phonemic awareness skills, and whether this would improve their gains with the story-reading programs. We hoped to reduce the Matthew effect, so that children with the initially lowest skills would gain at nearly the rate of those who started relatively stronger in phonemic awareness.

Design of the Study

We compared two very different supplemental strategies that we hoped would aid different aspects of reading: an experimental phonological analysis condition (PA) training, and a "control" comprehension strategy condition (CS).

Similarities in the Two Training Strategies Conditions

The methods had many planned similarities. Both methods had theoretical and research support (Lyon, 1995; Montgomery, 1981; Palincsar & Brown, 1984; Wise, Olson, & Lindamood, 1993). Both used a guided discovery, or teaching by questioning, approach. Finally, both methods were purported to improve children's error detection. In our previous studies, children did not know when they needed to ask for computer help on a word. We had major training efforts just to get them to ask for help even half as frequently when they read independently as when they read with a trainer.

We also planned many similarities in how we used the methods. Both training groups were given equivalent time in small-group instruction in their strategies and in individualized computer instruction in which they practiced using the strategies. Group sessions were interspersed with independent practice time on the computer. When working with the computer, children in both conditions worked independently for 2 of 3 days, and worked with the trainer on the third day.

For story reading in both conditions, the computer showed targeted words with segments written against blue and green backgrounds. Children in both conditions were asked to make an attempt for every segment before clicking the mouse again to hear the speech support. This was done to encourage all children into more active attempts to sound out words. One-syllable words were segmented into onsets and rimes (e.g., *pl/ant*), and multisyllable words were segmented into syllables (e.g., *bas/ket*). Syllables were segmented according to Spoehr and Smith's (1973) phonologic patterns, such that the orthography could be used to predict the sound of the vowel (e.g., *holping* vs. *hop/ping*; and *rec/ord* vs. *re/cord*).

Main-idea comprehension questions came at logical breaks in the story. Children also took tests at the end of the session on 15 of the words that they had targeted that day. In the test, each word was first presented in colored segments (without speech support) and the child attempted to read it. Then the child clicked the mouse to hear the word's proper pronunciation. Students scored themselves on independent days and were scored by a trainer on monitored days. Forty of these tested words were retested at the end of each month and at the end of the training period, always scored by the trainer. Trainers also tested children on nonwords that were constructed by the program to be analogous to words from the child's monthly and year-end tests. Onsets and rimes of items were swapped to create nonwords (e.g., *farmer* and *plant* yielded *pant* and *plarmer*).

Children attended in sets of three, with the trainer present every day. We balanced conditions for ability, first by matching sets of three students on age, word recognition, and nonword reading scores, and then by randomly assigning the sets to training condition. We controlled for trainer and school effects, by having both methods taught in each school and by each trainer. This way method, trainer, and school effects would not confound each other.

The Two Strategy Conditions: Planned Differences

There were two major planned differences in the methods. The first planned difference was in the type of strategy: phonological analysis (PA) versus comprehension strategy (CS). The second planned difference was in the amount of reading in context. When doing individualized work with the computer, students in the PA condition spent about half of their time in analytical skills work with isolated words and nonwords, and the other half of their time reading stories with speech and segmentation support. In contrast, children in the CS condition spent all of their individualized computer time reading stories, with the speech and segmentation support for difficult words.

The Phonological Analysis Treatment

The phonological analysis (PA) condition included initial work in articulatory awareness concepts from the Auditory Discrimination in Depth Program (ADD; Lindamood & Lindamood, 1975). It continued with other programs designed in Colorado to encourage manipulation and comparison of sounds in word and nonword reading and spelling exercises. In the ADD programs, the teacher selected items for the children to practice. The Colorado exercises automatically increased or decreased in difficulty depending on the child's performance. We chose the ADD method because of its theoretical base (Liberman, Shankweiler, & Liberman, 1989; Montgomery, 1984), and because of a reanalysis of data from a study done by the Lindamoods suggesting that children with especially low phoneme awareness gained at least as much from this program as did children who started with higher phonological skills (Wise, Olson, & Lindamood, 1993). The method appeared to help children who had failed to succeed with other methods, in reports of evidence from reading clinics without control group comparisons (Alexander, Anderson, Voeller, & Torgesen, 1991; Truch, 1994).

In the PA small-group instruction, children learned to feel the mouth and voicing actions that produced different sounds. They also learned to associate these feelings with sounds, letters, and articulatory labels and pictures to help them analyze similarities and differences among sounds. For instance, children used mirrors to discover that their lips made a popping action for the "brother pair" sounds of /p/ and /b/. They associated these with both the labels "quiet and noisy lip poppers" and a picture showing the lips coming together, with a puff of air for the "pop" of these stop consonants. They learned to distinguish the "quiet from the noisy brother" by touching their necks to feel their vocal cords vibrating, or by covering their ears and comparing the sounds. Small-group instruction was interspersed with computer exercises with programs under development at Lindamood-Bell Learning Processes, where the children practiced associating the pictures, sounds, letters, and labels.

When children were about 80% successful with the consonant concepts and had at least three vowels sounds—"ee," "o" (ah), and "oo"—they practiced in small groups manipulating mouth pictures to represent changes in simple two- and three-phoneme syllables (e.g., for "If this is *op* show me *pop*," the child would add a picture of a lip popper at the front of a picture of an open vowel followed by a lip popper). They then started working individually with programs developed at Colorado with synthetic speech support for analyzing and manipulating sounds within syllables, which were designed to be compatible with the ADD concepts and methods.

The PAL (phonological analysis with letters) program asked children to build a simple syllable, and then to change letter-sound symbols to match single sound changes that the program said, for example, "Show me *eef*." The child found the appropriate letter symbols, and compared how the program pronounced them to how it pronounced what they were supposed to spell. Then the program said, "If that says *eef*, show me *meef*," and the child made changes to match the changes made by the program.

Letter symbols matched those taught in the ADD program, and were arranged on the screen in terms of "brother pairs, cousins, and vowels" to match the organization of sounds taught in the ADD program. Trainers used positive questioning, based on children's responses, to help them check their attempts at spelling with the symbols. The PAL program advanced and retreated in 16 levels of difficulty from levels that included consonant vowel (CV) up to levels with items containing up to three-consonant clusters (CCCVCCC).

Children also did another program (Non), designed at the University of Colorado, in which they chose one of four nonwords to match one pronounced by the program. The nonwords used regular English orthographic patterns, as opposed to the Lindamood symbols; for example, *ae, th* (unvoiced) versus *th* (voiced). Words were pronounced and scored as the children chose them, and children received more points for choosing the correct nonword on the first try. The Non program automatically advanced and retreated in difficulty depending on the child's performance for 15 levels that included CV to multisyllable levels.

When children were 80% successful at a CVC level with the PAL program, they started spending about half their computer time reading stories, as in the earlier ROSS reading-in-context studies, and half their time on the phonological analysis programs described previously. After success at the next CVC level (using more vowels), Spello (a spelling exploration program) was introduced. With Spello, children could manipulate letters and sounds to explore real English spelling patterns. Spello also advanced and retreated in difficulty from CVC to multisyllable words in 20 levels, according to the child's performance (see Wise & Olson, 1992, for a description of this program).

Word decoding in stories was generally the same in the PA condition as in the CS condition, except when a child failed to target a misread word. Children in both conditions were asked to "use the colors to help you sound out the word" whenever they encountered a word that was difficult or of which they were unsure. If a child in the PA condition reached the end of a sentence without targeting a misread word, the trainer asked the child to compare his or her pronunciation with what was on the page. This was done by first covering the word and asking, "Now, when you say (the error as the child pronounced it), what do you feel (at the point of contrast with the correct pronunciation)?" Next the trainer let the child see the word and make an attempt at correction, and the child then listened to the speech to confirm the word. This feedback resembles that used in traditional Lindamood training to encourage self-correction.

The Comprehension Strategy Treatment

The trained control condition used a comprehension strategy (CS) approach based on reciprocal teaching (Palincsar & Brown, 1984). Children began with small-group instruction, learning the strategies that "good" readers use: predicting, generating questions, clarifying, and summarizing. The trainer discussed how and why children would learn to become their own teachers and would learn how and when to apply the above strategies in reading. The trainer discussed why he or she would be trading the role of teacher, so children could learn to use the strategies in their independent reading. Later, the trainer defined and explained how to use a strategy like prediction. For instance, this was done by discussing what a prediction is and why and when we make predictions in real life and in reading. Then the trainer modeled leading the group using this strategy, and later traded the role of discussion leader, guiding the children as they learned to lead discussions using the strategy. The other strategies were gradually introduced and added. The children practiced leading discussions of group story reading, first of stories on paper and then of stories on the computer. The student leader chose readers and asked students in the group to use particular strategies and to justify why a particular strategy might best be used at different times to aid comprehension. In our version of reciprocal teaching we used a wooden "teaching apple" to designate who was acting as leader of the group, to make the method work in our small groups or in our one-on-one reading (it is usually practiced in groups of five or more).

In this condition, as in the PA condition, small-group instruction was interspersed with individualized computer instruction. However, in the CS condition, all the computer instruction involved reading in context, with segmentation and speech support for difficult words. Students marked a chart to show places where they used the strategies in independent reading with the computer. During monitored reading, teachers engaged students in discussions about the content of the stories. Trainer and child would trade the apple to be clear who was in charge of leading the discussion about the text. Children enjoyed trading roles, and discussions were often quite lively. However, the method was more difficult to use with some second-grade groups than with the older children.

During story reading, when students reached the end of a sentence without targeting a misread word in the CS condition, the trainer pointed to the word and asked the student to use the colors to help him or her sound out the word.

Results of the Strategy Study

Subjects

Two hundred and one second- to fifth-grade students participated in the strategy study over 2 years, with 103 students the first year and 98 the second year. Students were from eight different schools. Students were selected and screened as being in the lower 10% to 15% on word recognition, as in the earlier story-reading studies (see Table 8.3).

Hours. After pretesting on reading and language measures, children in both conditions received 14 sessions (7 hours) of small-group instruction in their metacognitive strategy. Children in both conditions averaged 18 hours in individualized computer time.

Gain Scores

Both groups made larger gains in non- and real-word reading and in comprehension than in the decoding-in-context study (see Tables 8.2 and 8.4). These differences were probably due in part to the increased engagement and longer training times brought about by the presence of a trainer every

TABLE 8.3
Strategy Training Study: Subject Characteristics and Pretests

Training Group	CS	PA
N	91 (36 F/55 M)	110 (46 F/64 M)
Age (at pretest)	8.92	8.95
Grade	3.2	3.2
Severity of deficit*	.74	.73
Pretest scores:		
Phoneme awareness		
Number correct on LACii	5.0	5.1
Percentage correct Phodel	32.6	31.4
Nonword reading (percentage correct)	25.8	26.4
Untimed word reading		
PIAT GE	2.4	2.4
WRAT GE	2.5	2.5
Time-limited word reading (number correct)	23.5	23.5

*Severity of deficit is a ratio of word recognition score compared to national norms; thus, 1 = at national grade level. The ratio for average readers in Boulder is 1.25.

TABLE 8.4
Strategy Training Study: Gain Scores

Training Group	CS	PA
Phoneme awareness		
(LACii number correct)	1.8	4.5 ($p < .001$)
Phodel percentage correct	7.0	19.1 ($p < .001$)
Nonword reading (percentage correct)	12.6	26.3 ($p < .001$)
Untimed recognition		
PIAT GE	.9	1.1 ($p < .1$)
WRAT GE	.9	1.1 ($p < .05$)
Timed recognition (number correct)	15.8	12.9 ($p < .05$)

day. Differences were also due in part to the use of strategies and the extra motivation and social interaction with groups of three children.

Gains in Phonological Skills. The PA training led to very large gains in all tests of nonword reading, our measure of phonological decoding (see Table 8.4). Even the CS students gained a few percentage points here more than in the previous studies, probably due to increased engagement and training time. However, the PA students gained more than twice as much as did the earlier students and the CS students, on three different measures of nonword reading where all students read the same nonwords, and on all the individualized tests of nonwords created by the program to be analogous to words they had studied (see Table 8.5).

PA students also made substantial and significant gains in phoneme awareness relative to the CS students. Phoneme awareness gains were measured by the Lindamood Auditory Conceptualization (LAC) Test (Lindamood & Lindamood, 1979), which uses colored blocks to represent sound changes, and by a phoneme deletion task. We used the raw score on the second half of the test as a more sensitive measure of phoneme awareness, because this is the only part that has to do with the ability to be aware of sounds within syllables. The LAC test has a slight confound in our study,

TABLE 8.5
Strategy Training Study: Daily Reading Behavior

Training Group	CS	PA
Target ratio	65%	69% $p < .05$
Words monitored	80%	88% $p < .05$
Monthly word check	61%	73% $p < .05$
Monthly comprehension	95%	93% $p < .05$
Independent comprehension	87%	88%
End of year		
Studied words	76%	83% $p < .05$
Nonword analogs	47%	60% $p < .05$

because many students noticed that the task is quite similar to our PAL letter-sound manipulation program (although no blocks are used in our training). However, the phoneme deletion task did not resemble anything done in training, and the PA children made substantially and significantly stronger gains on this test than did the CS children.

Gains in Word Recognition. Differences in the gains in word recognition between the PA and CS conditions were not nearly as marked as were the differences in the gains in phonological skills. The only standardized measure that showed a significant difference between the two trained conditions was the untimed Wide Range Achievement Test (WRAT; Jastak & Jastak, 1978). Although significant, the differences between conditions were much smaller on this test of real-word reading than on any test of nonword reading. The PA students also showed a consistent but nonsignificant trend of an advantage on the PIAT test of untimed word recognition (Dunn & Markwardt, 1970). However, the CS students actually did better on our time-limited test of word recognition (2 second exposure; Wise & Olson, 1995). Yet, on all measures of word recognition taken from words that each child had targeted while reading his or her stories, the PA children outperformed the CS children by significant and fairly substantial amounts (8, 12, and 7 percentage point differences in the groups on daily, monthly, and end-of-year tests of words studied in the stories; see Table 8.5).

Comprehension

There were no differences between the groups on any standardized reading comprehension measures, nor on measures of comprehension in independent daily reading. However, on the days that the children read with the trainer, children in the CS condition scored significantly higher on comprehension questions than did children in the PA condition (see Table 8.5). Children in the CS condition were often prompted to use their comprehension strategies while reading with their trainer.

DISCUSSION

Children in the strategy training study made greater gains than did children in the decoding-in-context study. Besides the greater gains in word recognition and nonword reading, anecdotal evidence supports this claim. The students themselves, their teachers, and their parents enthusiastically reported gains in reading at home and at school far more in the strategy training study than in the earlier study. This suggests benefits of the increased presence of the trainer, the extended training, and the increased engagement with the stories by attempting to apply instructed strategies compared to the relatively passive use of computer support in the decoding-in-context study.

PA children in the strategy study made much larger gains in all tests of phonological skills than did the CS children. They also performed better on word recognition in all tests of words studied on the computer, but on only one of the standardized measures. This difference was much smaller and lower in significance than for the nonword reading tests. The CS students showed a small but significant advantage on time-limited word recognition.

Share's (1995) self-teaching hypothesis suggests that over time, students whose deficient phonological skills have improved should gain more in word recognition than those whose phonological skills remain poor. Did our PA students need more time for their improved phonological skill to transfer into independent, time-limited word recognition? In results from 1-year follow-up testing of the first-year students (Olson, Wise, Ring, & Johnson, 1997), PA students maintained their advantage in nonword reading, and caught up to the CS children in time-limited word recognition. No differences occurred between the groups on either the PIAT untimed test (Dunn & Markwardt, 1970) or our own time-limited test of word recognition.

Why Gains Were Smaller on Standardized Tests Than on Tests of Studied Words

Why did the impressive gains in phoneme awareness and nonword reading not transfer more strongly into word recognition, or why did they do so only in the daily, monthly, and end-of-year word recognition tests of words studied earlier in the story reading? We have been investigating possible reasons for the different patterns of gains.

There are reasonable hypotheses for why PA children showed lesser relative benefits of their training on standardized tests than on our computerized tests of words from the stories. For one thing, the tests of words from the stories were never timed, and children were encouraged to use the same strategies, in the same computer context, that they had used in reading. Thus, the generalization of context would encourage more transfer of the analytic techniques to these tests. Also, the PA students probably spent more time and energy when studying the words in context than the CS students did, because all their training when not reading stories encouraged this kind of strategy.

We checked whether the reason also related to our segmentation of words. In all tests of words from the stories, the words appeared segmented against alternating blue and green backgrounds as they were in the stories, although no speech support was given in the tests. The ROSS program segments words in such a way that segments can be consistently used to predict vowel sounds: In an "open" syllable that ends in a vowel, the vowel "says its name" ("long" sound) (e.g., ba/sic; ho/ping); in a closed syllable with one vowel followed by consonants, the vowel "says its (short) sound" (e.g., bas/ket; hop/ping). PA children were instructed about how "open or closed syllables" influenced vowel pronunciation, and were encouraged to use this information when sounding out the segments.

PA children were never instructed in how to divide syllables by themselves, nor in how to try different sounds for a vowel or different stress patterns if a word attempt was unsuccessful. This was because we had limited group instruction time, in order to leave plenty of time for individual practice with the computers.

A child who reads the real word *bind* to rhyme with *pinned* is following phonics regularities. The child must vary the vowel and try the other likely sound for the letter *i* to decode that word correctly. Given our lack of instruction in how to segment words and vary vowel pronunciations without the computer's help, it is not very surprising that PA students showed stronger advantages from their training in the "segmented" computer tests than in time-limited or rapidly presented tests of unsegmented real words. The training strategies that they had learned were more helpful with nonwords, because any rule- or analogy-based vowel pronunciation is accepted as correct for nonwords (thus, *drind* could rhyme with the noun *wind* or the verb *wind*).

There was one training difference, not previously discussed, that occurred for half the students in the second year only. In that year, half the PA and half the CS children received whole-word feedback as they read stories. These children did not gain as much on daily and end-of-year test of words from the stories as did children who received segmented word support (segmented feedback 79% compared to 76.4% for whole word for the end-of-year test, $p = .20$; and 84.1% vs. 80.9% on daily monitored tests, $p = .07$). However, there were no differences on the monthly tests of words from the stories (66% compared to 66.8%). This does not support the hypothesis that the children depended on segmentation to encourage them to use their phonological strategies. In both the decoding-in-context and the strategy studies, the presence or absence of segmentation during reading stories in context had little or no effect. Thus, it seems more likely to be the similar context of the testing that led to the more marked difference between conditions on tests of words studied in the stories compared to the smaller differences on standardized tests of word reading.

Why There Were Differences in Patterns of Gains on Tests of Words Not Studied

Could other aspects of tests be encouraging or discouraging the children from using their strategies and taking advantage of their improved phonological skills? Our test of time-limited word recognition apparently did not allow our relatively slow decoders to use their skills to the same advantage that they showed on the untimed tests, and actually worked to their disadvantage. Yet, neither the PIAT nor the WRAT are time limited. The PA children showed a small but significant advantage over the CS students on the WRAT, but a nonsignificant advantage on the PIAT.

We compared items from the PIAT and the WRAT on ratings of word frequency, number of consonant clusters, number of syllables, and ratings of regularity that are tied to the phonics concepts we teach in our small-group sessions. The codes were as follows:

1 = Taught early and practiced much (e.g., the "bossy e" and name/sound distinctions as in *hop* and *hope*).

2 = Taught later and practiced a little (e.g., "two vowels go walking" as in *rain*, and "open syllable" as in *ho/ping*).

3 = Predictable but not taught by us (e.g., *right* and *-tion*).

4 = Least predictable (e.g., *though* and *move*).

Results of these analyses indicate interesting differences between the tests. In the first 30 words on each test, the PIAT has words with significantly lower frequency ratings [$t(1, 29) = 5.44$, $p < .001$], with significantly more consonant clusters [$t(1, 29) = 3.63$, $p < .001$], and with less predictable vowel sounds than either of the other two tests. Thus, children may be more successful applying their strategies on the WRAT, with its tendency toward words that are higher in frequency, lower in number of clusters, and more predictable in their vowels' pronunciations.

Why the Differential Gains Do Not Increase With Time

Training differences in general were maintained at the 1-year follow-up, but the rate of gain was much less when children were no longer receiving the support of small-group instruction and individualized computer instruction (Olson et al., in press). Note that we did not get all children to grade level, nor to where they could find and correct all their own errors by the end of the year's training. Unfortunately, our studies always terminate training after 1 year, so we can train enough students to look for individual differences in treatment. We hypothesize that more students will retain their skills and achieve continuing rates of growth more similar to their classmates' if they finish the program when they are self-correcting their own errors at or above their grade level.

Interestingly, other studies are also finding that children receiving intense phonological training make larger gains in nonword reading beyond those of trained controls, and yet smaller or nonsignificant gains over trained controls in word recognition in training periods of similar duration. Torgesen and his colleagues (Torgesen, Wagner, Rashotte, Alexander, & Conway, in press) reported this pattern of results after 1 year of training in a study that uses the full version of the ADD program. (In a personal communication, Torgesen related that he is finding word recognition differences in the second year of training the same subjects.) Lovett et al. (1995) also reported a similar pattern of results (relative to her *trained* controls). They found a small but significant differential word recognition gain only on tests of words created to be like those used in training and on the WRAT reading test, just as we found. Lovett et al.'s trained children did better in word recognition relative to controls who received less reading instruction, as we also found with the untrained controls in the decoding-in-context study (see Table 8.1). We did not measure an untrained control group in our strategy training study.

Differential gains in comprehension have also been lacking in our and the others' studies. CS children showed an advantage on daily comprehension with the computer word-recognition support, but only on the days when reading with the trainer and engaging in the rich reciprocal teaching interactions. Trends actually favored the PA children on standardized posttests of the PIAT and the *Gates-MacGinitie Reading Tests* (1989). It is notoriously hard to establish differential training gains on standardized comprehension tests. Testing time limits the amount of material to be read and questions to be asked, and differences in children's prior knowledge of different passages are hard to control. Yet, ultimately, differential benefits in independent word recognition and comprehension are surely what we all want most to demonstrate.

Before we discuss how to strengthen the gains in fluent independent word recognition, we first want to reemphasize the significance of what these studies have already shown. What we, Lovett et al. (1995) and Torgesen et al. (in press), have established is very important: Children with reading disabilities can improve greatly in phonological skills with intensive training that teaches the children to become aware of the order of sounds in syllables and of English orthography and phonology. All three studies are notable and unusual because they train children with demonstrated deficits, and they compare two good training methods, not just results to untrained controls. Our study adds two more important contributions. First, we have demonstrated that computer instruction can help support and extend work on phonological skills and reading. But second, and probably more important, our study is one of few where training method is not confounded by differences in schools or trainers. In our study, both methods were implemented in all schools and by all trainers. This does not deny the results of studies in which different methods are taught by different teachers, in different schools, or on different islands (as in the famous Lundberg et al., 1988, study), but it is important to have a study to confirm these results in an unconfounded situation.

These studies have demonstrated some ways to remedy significant deficits in phonological skills, building a foundation on which to build strong, flexible, and fluent word recognition to be used in independent reading. This is very important and hopeful. Yet, we can apparently not expect children with reading disabilities to transfer these skills automatically into reading just because we encourage them and support them in using the skills in reading in context. Our strategy study showed that direct, structured instruction was needed to get large and lasting changes in phonological decoding. We should not be surprised to discover that we will need to add direct and structured practice in extending these skills into flexible, fluent, and auto-matized word recognition skills that can be used both in isolation and in the context of reading stories. In our future studies, we hope to increase training time, to assist better transfer into story reading. We also plan to add training for some of the students that includes direct training in syllabication, in learning flexibility with vowel sounds, and in automaticity. How many of these we will manipulate as experimental variables has not yet been decided, because we are also interested in which aspects of the phonological training are most important for different children, the articulatory awareness or the letter–sound manipulation.

SUMMARY

How do our computer-supported studies inform the question of whether it is better to try to remedy phonological deficits in isolated structured exercises or in a literature-rich engaging context? In the decoding-in-context study, all training occurred in a literature-rich environment. Students gained in real and nonword reading and attitude about reading relative to untrained con-trols. However, gains were not large enough to help these children catch up with the other readers in their classes. Our strategy training study used intensive, structured phonological skills work. It definitely improved the children's phonological skills substantially beyond the earlier study and be-yond the trained controls in ways that remained stable after a year. However, the 30 minutes a day training time for 25 hours during a semester was not enough to bring most of the children completely up to reading and self-cor-recting their errors at or above grade level.

We demonstrated that expecting the children to apply these skills in reading is not enough, even though half of their training time was spent applying these skills in supported reading with the computers. The children made very good gains relative to trained controls with words from the computer study. These gains were substantial with previously decoded words, even when they appeared weeks or months later with orthographic segmen-tation and without speech support. However, the skills were not strong enough or flexible enough in 25 hours' time to transfer strongly to time-lim-ited or independent reading without the decoding support.

How amiable—our work supports a balanced answer to the question. It demonstrates strong advantages for beginning with direct, structured instruc-tion to remedy phonological deficits and lay a strong foundation for future work. The lesser transfer of these skills to independent reading (beyond what was gained by the other children with computer-supported reading) is also informative. It suggests that we continue the structured support and practice in flexibility and fluency in real reading, gradually reducing support as children gain in confidence and independence. Hopefully, our future studies will confirm these ideas of how this can be done.

ACKNOWLEDGMENTS

We thank principals, staff, and students of four schools in the Boulder Valley Schools for this study. We thank our trainers Heidi Gilman, John Green, Sally Moody, Beverly Peterson, Laura Rogan, Joanne Trombley, and Kate Wise; programmer Jennifer Restrepo; and research assistants Laura Kriho and Bonnie Houkal. We thank consultants Pat Lindamood and Beverly Peterson for help with ADD training, and Leigh Kirkland and Michael Meloth for help with Reciprocal Teaching. We thank NICHD for supporting the research with grants No. HD 11683 and HD 22223 to Richard K. Olson and Barbara W. Wise.

REFERENCES

Alexander, A., Anderson, H., Voeller, K., & Torgesen, J. (1991). Phonological awareness training and remediation of analytic coding deficits in a group of severe dyslexics. *Annals of Dyslexia, 31*, 193–207.

Ball, E., & Blachman, B. A. (1991). Does phoneme awareness training in kindergarten make a difference in early word recognition and developmental spelling? *Reading Research Quarterly, 26*, 49–66.

Bradley, L., & Bryant, P. (1983). Categorizing sounds and learning to read: A causal connection. *Nature, 301*, 419–421.

Byrne, B., & Fielding-Barnsley, R. (1993). Evaluation of a program to teach phoneme awareness to young children: A 1-year follow-up. *Journal of Educational Psychology, 85*, 104–111.

Calfee, R., Lindamood, P., & Lindamood, C. (1973). Acoustic–phonetic skills and reading: Kindergarten through twelfth grade. *Journal of Educational Psychology, 64*, 293–298.

Conners, F., & Olson, R. K. (1990). Reading comprehension in dyslexic and normal readers: A component skills analysis. In D. A. Balota, G. B. Flores d'Arcais, & K. Rayner (Eds.), *Comprehension processes in reading* (pp. 557–579). Hillsdale, NJ: Lawrence Erlbaum Associates.

Dunn, L. M., & Markwardt, F. C. (1970). *Peabody individual achievement test.* Circle Pines, MN: American Guidance Service.

Ehri, L. C. (1980). The role of orthographic images in learning printed words. In J. Kavanaugh & R. Venezky (Eds.), *Orthography, reading, and dyslexia* (pp. 155–170). Baltimore: University Park Press.

Hatcher, P. J., Hulme, C., & Ellis, A. W. (1994). Ameliorating early reading failure by integrating the teaching of reading and phonological skills: The phonological linkage hypothesis. *Child Development, 65*, 41–57.

Hynd, G., Semrud-Clikeman, M., & Lyytinen, H. (1991). Brain imaging in learning disabilities. In J. Obrzut & G. Hynd (Eds.), *Neuropsychological foundations of learning disabilities* (pp. 475–512). New York: Academic.

Jastak, J., & Jastak, S. (1978). *The wide range achievement test—revised.* Wilmington, DE: Jastak Associates.

Liberman, I. Y., Shankweiler, D., & Liberman, A. M. (1989). The alphabetic principle and learning to read. In I. Y. Liberman & D. Shankweiler (Eds.), *Phonology and learning to read* (pp. 102–124). Ann Arbor: University of Michigan Press.

Lindamood, C., & Lindamood, P. (1975). *Auditory discrimination in depth.* Columbus, OH: Science Research Associates Division, MacMillan/McGraw-Hill.

Lindamood, C., & Lindamood, P. (1979). *Lindamood auditory conceptualization test (LAC).* Hingham, MA: Teaching Resources Corporation.

208   WISE ET AL.

Lovett, M., Borden, S., DeLuca, T., Lacerenza, L., Benson, N., & Brackstone, D. (1994). Treating the core deficits of development dyslexia: Evidence of transfer-of-learning following strategy and phonologically-based reading training programs. *Developmental Psychology, 30*(6), 805–822.

Lundberg, I., Frost, J., & Peterson, O. (1988). Effects of an extensive program for stimulating phonological awareness. *Reading Research Quarterly, 23*, 263–284.

Lyon, G. R. (1995). Toward a definition of dyslexia. *Annals of Dyslexia, 15*, 3–30.

MacGinitie, W. H., & MacGinitie, R. K. (1989). *Gates–MacGinitie reading tests, 3rd Ed.* Chicago: Riverside Publishing.

Montgomery, D. (1981). Do dyslexics have difficulty accessing articulatory information? *Psychological Research, 43*, 235–243.

Olson, R. K., Forsberg, H., & Wise, B. W. (1994). Genes, environment, and the development of orthographic skills. In V. Berninger (Ed.), *The varieties of orthographic knowledge I: Theoretical and developmental issues* (pp. 27–71). Dordrecht, The Netherlands: Kluwer.

Olson, R. K., & Wise, B. W. (1992). Reading on the computer with orthographic and speech feedback. *Reading and Writing, 4*, 107–144.

Olson, R. K., Wise, B. W., Conners, F., Rack, J., & Fulker, D. (1989). Specific deficits in component reading and language skills: Genetic and environmental influences. *Journal of Learning Disabilities, 22*, 339–348.

Olson, R. K., Wise, B. W., Ring, J., & Johnson, M. (1997). Computer-based remedial training in phoneme awareness and phonological decoding: Effects on post-training development of word recognition. *Scientific Studies of Reading, 1*(3), 235–253.

Palincsar, A. S., & Brown, A. L. (1984). Reciprocal teaching of comprehension-fostering and comprehension-monitoring activity. *Cognition and Instruction, 2*, 117–175.

Perfetti, C. (1985). *Reading ability.* New York: Oxford University Press.

Rack, J., Snowling, M., & Olson, R. (1992). The nonword reading deficit in developmental dyslexia: A review. *Reading Research Quarterly, 27*, 28–53.

Share, D. L. (1995). Phonological recoding and self-teaching: *Sine qua non* of reading acquisition. *Cognition, 55*, 151–218.

Spoehr, K. T., & Smith, E. E. (1973). The role of syllables in perceptual processing. *Cognitive Psychology, 5*, 71–89.

Stanovich, K. (1986). Matthew effects in reading: Some consequences of individual differences in acquisition of literacy. *Remedial and Special Education, 5*, 11–19.

Torgesen, J. K., Wagner, R. K., Rashotte, C. A., Alexander, A. W., & Conway, T. (in press). Preventive and remedial interventions for children with severe reading disabilities. *Learning Disabilities: A Multi-Disciplinary Journal.*

Truch, S. (1994). Stimulating basic reading processes using *Auditory Discrimination in Depth. Annals of Dyslexia, 24*, 218–233.

Wise, B. (1991). What reading disabled children need: What is known and how to talk about it. *Learning and Individual Differences, 3*, 307–321.

Wise, B. & Olson, R. (1992). Spelling exploration with a talking computer improves phonological coding *Reading and Writing, 4*, 145–156.

Wise, B., W., & Olson, R. K. (1995). Computer-based phonological awareness and reading instruction. *Annals of Dyslexia, 45*, 99–122.

Wise, B., Olson, R., & Lindamood, P. (1993, April). *Training phonemic awareness: Why and how in computerized instruction.* Paper delivered at the annual meeting of the American Educational Research Association, Atlanta, GA.

9

▼▼▼▼▼▼▼

A Beginning Literacy Program
for At-Risk and Delayed Readers

Irene W. Gaskins
Benchmark School

Children come to school with different strengths and weaknesses. They come from environments with varying degrees of print richness and literacy values. Nevertheless, most learn to read despite differences in their strengths and weaknesses, home environments, and school programs. The students at Benchmark School, a school for struggling readers in Grades 1 through 8, have had opportunities for print experiences that are similar to those of other students who learn to read. Yet, despite their having at least average learning potential, our students have not succeeded in learning to read. They are children who, parents tell us, would not sit still to hear a story read to them and did not pick up pencil and paper to experiment with words during their preschool years. They showed little interest in the magnetic alphabet letters on the refrigerator door and did not voluntarily look at books and pretend to read. When they entered kindergarten and first grade, teachers labeled them "not ready" for formal instruction.

By the time they reach Benchmark School, they have failed in kindergarten or first grade, and they have lost any view of themselves as capable learners. Commonly they appear as either inattentive, passive, nonpersistent, impulsive, inflexible, or a combination of these personal styles, especially with respect to print activities. Our goal has been to create a beginning literacy program that is structured to capture their attention; to keep them actively and meaningfully engaged with print; to reward reflective attention to letters, sounds, words, and connected text; and to scaffold success in their responding to print flexibly. Meeting these needs is a challenge we face each day. At

Benchmark School, the best determiner of students' ultimate success in literacy has not been their specific intellectual strengths or their home environments, but rather our ability to actively engage them in print activities. This chapter is the story of a continually evolving beginning reading program to help the children we teach grapple with and come to master their interaction with print.

THEORY AND RESEARCH

Knowledge of the form and function of words is characteristic of children who become capable readers (Adams, 1990; Venezky, 1970). Such knowledge includes knowledge of the printed and spoken forms of words, knowledge of word meanings, and knowledge of how words function in context. One reason why some children are delayed in learning to read is that they have gaps in their knowledge of the form and function of words. In the section that follows I discuss the different kinds of word knowledge that the Benchmark staff believes are necessary for learning to read. Next, I describe how our students fall short in their word reading. Then, I develop a theoretical framework for instruction that is designed to fill gaps that exist in our students' knowledge of the form and function of words.

Knowledge About Words

One way that children build a foundation for becoming capable readers is by attending to print (Ehri, 1980). As toddlers, they may notice differences among the letters in their own names. They may point out other words that begin with the same letters as their names do. For example, at the age of 2, my grandson Will said, "Let's go to Wendy's, Grandma. It starts like Will. McDonald's does, too, but it's upside down." My granddaughter Lindsay, at 3, used the magnetic alphabet letters on the refrigerator door to write, "PHONE NOTES"; then turned to her mother and asked, "What does that say?" Lindsay had carefully studied and reproduced the words on the pad next to the phone in her play kitchen. Will and Lindsay notice the forms that differentiate words in our writing system on a regular basis. They study books about trucks and Winnie the Pooh and ask about the words that label the pictures that interest them. They exhibit the beginnings of print awareness. By the time they enter kindergarten they will have logged hundreds of hours looking at print. They also know that the white spaces before and after words signal where words begin and end. They have developed the concept of word.

Visual knowledge about print is essential for learning to read. This knowledge results from being attentive to print. If children have not attended to print prior to reading instruction, then the program for teaching them to read must be structured in such a way that they will become attentive to print (Stanovich, 1992).

To become capable readers, children must also attend to the sounds in spoken words (Bradley & Bryant, 1983; Wagner & Torgesen, 1987). As a 2-year-old, Helen loved to have the nursery rhyme "Old Mother Hubbard" read to her time and time again. When it was read, she insisted on saying the last word on each page. For example, I would read, "Old Mother Hubbard went to the market to get some bread, when she came back the old dog was. . . ." Helen would chime in with the rhyming word, "dead." As she got older, she liked to play the consonant game while riding in the car. She'd say, "I see a cow. Can you see something that starts like cow?" I usually responded, "I see a cat." However, on occasion, I would say a word with the wrong beginning sound. Immediately Helen would gleefully correct me and announce that I lost a point. Helen liked playing with the sounds of language. At age 4, she liked to segment words into sounds and use invented spelling to write those sounds, although she showed little interest in reading back what she had written. Helen was developing knowledge about the written and spoken forms of words. She was aware of beginning sounds in words and rhyming words, and she could segment words into sounds. Attention to the sounds in spoken language and awareness that these sounds are represented by letters provides a critical foundation for learning to read (Ehri & Wilce, 1983). These are essential elements of any beginning reading program.

Children who become capable readers are aware that spoken and written words carry meaning. They experiment with the new words they hear and are tuned to the reaction of their audience regarding the appropriateness of a word's use. I remember making coffee with one of my grandchildren and saying that I love the "aroma" of coffee. Audrey later told her father that she loved "aroma," just like Grandma did. Children who have an interest in words, pay attention to word meanings, and remember words have a distinct advantage over those who are less attentive. A beginning reading program that dealt only with sounds and letters, but not with meanings of words, would be deficient.

Finally, children who become capable readers are aware of the contexts in which words are embedded. They know the language of stories from having been read to frequently, and can detect immediately when the reader reads something that does not make sense. They want the stories they write and the stories they hear to make sense. They pay attention to meaning and syntax. They are anxious to read on their own and become constructors of meaning. One of our staff members babysits once a week for 5-year-old Allison and 7-year-old Nathan. Both of them love the books that their babysitter brings to read to them. After storytime with the babysitter, they go to bed with their favorite books. One week Allison called the babysitter back to her bedroom quite panic-stricken: Allison had been pretend reading a book when she discovered that a page was missing. Although she could not read the words, the meaning she was constructing as she pretend read was interrupted by the missing page. Meaningful reading and writing are the focal points of a beginning literacy program. These acts provide the rationale for learning about letters, sounds, and words.

Knowledge about the written and spoken forms of words and letters, the meanings of words, and the way words function in context are all crucial to becoming a reader (Adams, 1990; Venezky, 1970). Whereas many pre-schoolers appear to acquire this knowledge by writing and interacting with print in their environment, some children like those who attend Benchmark do not pay much attention to letters and sounds in words. As a result, they miss opportunities to gain basic knowledge about words that other children have gathered during several years prior to formal schooling. They also miss opportunities to develop interconnections among words, letters, sounds, and meaning. Our job as teachers at Benchmark is to help these students fill gaps in their knowledge of written and spoken forms of words, meanings of words, and meaningful contexts in which words function, and to help students develop interconnections between these kinds of knowledge.

Instruction to Develop Knowledge About Words

Each year in planning the program for our beginning readers, we begin by immersing them in a print-rich environment and teaching diagnostically to assess their knowledge about the form and function of words. Once we are aware of their gaps in knowledge, we structure activities not only to help students fill these gaps and to help them build on what they know about language, but also to help them eliminate maladaptive habits, such as poor attention.

The profile that typifies beginning readers who enter our program has been quite consistent during recent years. Typically, they can identify some, but not all, of the letters of the alphabet; they are inconsistent in producing words that rhyme; they may be able to segment spoken words into onset and rime; and they have very little awareness of the phonemic significance of letters or visual awareness of where one word ends and another begins in print. They also tend to have difficulty recalling words they attempt to learn as sight words, often recognizing five or fewer sight words upon entry to the program. On the other hand, they typically have a meaning vocabulary that is average or above average for their age and, contrary to reports that they do not like to have stories read to them, are easily engaged in a good story, although it is not uncommon for attention to wander. When attention is adequate, comprehension is generally a strength.

We believe that the reading instruction these children receive should capitalize on their interest in challenging words and on their love of a good story. It should also structure their experiences so that they attend to the order and identities of sounds and letters within words, so that they think actively about letter-sound relationships, and so that they discover consistencies and common patterns in written language. Students should be given opportunities to share their discoveries about language, and these discoveries should be applauded as each is expressed in the child's natural language. Rote rules and abstract language about letters and sounds, such as "short," "silent," and "soft," should be discouraged. We have observed that when beginning readers are left on their own to learn sight words they often rely on faulty strategies, such as using selective visual cues or a few sound-letter correspondences (Ehri, 1992). Beginning readers need to be taught how to learn words as sight words. They also need to be provided with a reliable means of independently decoding words. Once acquired, knowledge about words should be put to use immediately in reading and writing connected text.

For Benchmark's beginning readers, the key to achieving these goals is guiding students to an awareness of the individual sounds in spoken words and how these sounds are represented by letters in printed words (Ehri, 1994; Gaskins, Ehri, Cress, O'Hara, & Donnelly, 1996). Once this awareness is developed, students will be able to capitalize on the systematic nature of the relationship between sounds and letters in our written language. One way children develop this awareness of the relationship between sounds and letters is through thoughtful, active efforts to learn sight words in a fully analyzed way (Ehri, 1992; Perfetti, 1991). In learning sight words, students should be taught to match the sounds they hear in the sight word to the letters they see. Once the letters of words become bonded to the sounds and meanings already present in memory, students will discover that these fully analyzed words are more easily recalled than are words they have attempted to learn by such methods as looking at a few distinctive letters, visualizing the shape of the word, or using partial sound-letter cues (Ehri, 1992). When the sounds and letters of a word are consolidated as a unit in memory, students can use that word to decode unknown words with the same spelling pattern. This application of knowledge about common letter units to decoding (analogizing) is the way most mature readers decode unknown words. Mature readers recognize patterns in words and use these known parts to decode unknown words (Cunningham, 1975; Ehri, 1994). This is what we want our students to be able to do.

Reading, of course, is much more than sounds, letters, and decoding words; students must be provided with opportunities to see the interconnectedness between their knowledge of the word form and their knowledge of the function of words in text (Adams, 1990). For this to occur, students need ample practice applying their word knowledge to reading and writing connected text. It is these experiences with connected text that make instruction about sounds, letters, and words relevant and sensible. This is especially true for our students.

During reading instruction, strategies for becoming self-regulated readers who actively monitor and construct meaning should be explicitly explained and modeled for students (Gaskins, Anderson, Pressley, Cunicelli, & Satlow, 1993; Pressley et al., 1992). Teacher-led discussions of stories and books that students have read should provide opportunities for students to discuss patterns and inferences in text and should encourage students to respond personally to what was read (Pearson, 1993). To make these accomplishments a reality, instruction about sounds, letters, words, and text must be designed to foster sustained attention and to enhance time on task. Activities in which every pupil is expected to respond simultaneously (every-pupil-response activities, or EPRs) should be commonplace as a way of supporting students' attention to the form and function of words. The remainder of this chapter describes the program of instruction we have built for beginning readers.

THE BENCHMARK BEGINNING LITERACY PROGRAM

Beginning readers at Benchmark spend over 4 hours a day engaged in literacy activities. To prepare for each day's events, they complete homework the previous night that includes listening to a parent read a book, reviewing high-frequency words, and reading for 30 minutes. Daily instruction in literacy is divided into six time blocks. During the first 40-minute time block, students write a response to the previous evening's parent-read-aloud book, review a personal word ring containing high-frequency words from basal readers, and discuss the library books or books in bags that were read at home the previous evening. A second time block of 40 minutes is for reading independently in preprimer books and writing sentence responses about the books. During the next 40-minute block, students participate in a small reading group in which new words are introduced and decoded, active reader strategies are taught, and students read and discuss a selection in a basal reader. Mid-morning, students are given a 20-minute break to participate in activities in the gym. The next block is 80 minutes in duration and is devoted to word identification—a time for making discoveries about words and applying those discoveries to reading connected text. After lunch, and between participation in math and other special subjects, there is a 40-minute block devoted to process writing instruction during which students plan, draft, revise, and publish original pieces. Also during the afternoon there is a time for listening to children's literature.

In the remainder of this chapter I describe the learning activities that take place during these time blocks. Because understanding and applying how words work tends to be our students' greatest weakness, I emphasize this aspect of our program. I begin with a description of the activities that take place during the word identification block (the third block in the sequence). The concepts taught during this block are reviewed and reinforced throughout the other literacy blocks.

Word Identification Block

The word identification instructional block is one of our students' favorite times during the day. They enjoy the variety of every-pupil-response activities that are part of each lesson, including choral, echo, and partner reading of stories with difficult but decodable words. They love the challenge and success they feel as they read what they consider to be "college" words, for example, *shenanigans*. They also like being word detectives and making discoveries about how our language works, sometimes even making discoveries that their parents and teachers have not made. For each strategy or activity that is presented, the teacher provides a rationale, explaining how it will help students become better readers. The teacher also discusses when the skill or strategy students are learning can be used. Next, the teacher explains how to do the task and, using self-talk, models how it should be completed. The focal point of each week's lessons is learning three or four sight words that contain high-frequency spelling patterns (the vowel and what comes after it in a one-syllable word); we call these words *key words*. Reinforcement for learning these key words and using them to decode unknown words takes many forms throughout the week. (See Gaskins et al., 1988, 1996; Gaskins, Gaskins, Anderson, & Schommer, 1995, for information about the development of the word identification program, the selection of the key words, and revisions that have been made in the program.)

Building a Word Wall. Each week, when new key words are introduced, they are written on rectangular pieces of colored paper and attached to the chalkboard with magnets. At the end of the week, the words are placed in alphabetical order on the word wall above the chalkboard. Here they remain during the school year to serve as a resource for comparison to other words. If students cannot retrieve from memory a key word to use in decoding an unknown word with the same spelling pattern, they can scan the word wall.

Writing a Structured Language Experience Story. During the early weeks of the school year, students as a class compose structured language experience stories using the key words that are introduced for that week. The teacher capitalizes on the writing of language experience stories to acquaint students with the structure of stories and to teach students how to plan their writing. We call these stories "structured" because teachers guide students in the writing of them by providing a framework and helping students plan and rehearse ideas to include in the class story. The framework that students see posted on the chalkboard is: characters, setting, story problem, and resolution of the story problem. Students, with teacher guidance, flesh out the details of these story elements before they begin composing their story. They particularly enjoy using their classmates as characters in their story. After the story is planned, the students suggest sentences for the story and critique one another's suggestions. Once written, the story is typed and students are given copies to read throughout the week.

Generating and Reading Rhyming Words. When the key words for the week are introduced, students as a class generate rhyming words for each key word. When a child suggests a word that has the same spelling pattern as a key word, it is written under the key word. Should a child suggest a rhyming word that is spelled differently from the key word, the word is written on the chalkboard away from the rhyming lists, so that the child can see how it is spelled differently from the key word. For example, in supplying rhyming words for *slide*, Sue suggested *lied*. The teacher praised her for contributing a rhyming word and placed *lied* on the chalkboard as an example of another way the sounds in the spelling pattern in *slide* could be represented. Students may be reminded about the importance of being flexible in dealing with English spellings that can vary in structure. Once students have generated rhyming words for the key words, they read each one as the teacher points to it. The teacher selects successive words with different spelling patterns (e.g., those rhyming with *ride, hit, got*) so that students are required to perform processing that is deeper than reading down a rhyming list of words (*side, ride, hide*). Students use the form, "If this is _____ (saying the key word), then this is _____ (saying the rhyming word)."

Spelling Chant and Check. From the first day that students learn to read key words, they also practice writing them. In spelling these words each day, they are encouraged to get the words from their heads, but they are allowed to copy the correct spelling from the chalkboard or word wall if they need that support. Early in the week, students write only the key words featured that week, but as the week progresses, any word on the word wall, or its rhyme, is fair game for the 3- to-10-word spelling "test." After students have completed writing the words that the teacher dictates, they chant the spellings together, putting a small dot beneath each letter as it is said, and crossing out and rewriting any words they have misspelled.

Playing Ready-Set-Show. We have included special word games to help students develop awareness of rhyming sounds and beginning sounds in words. One of the students' favorites is Ready-Set-Show. During this game, the teacher discusses the concept of rhyme and models how to play Ready-Set-Show. Students have a card on their desk with a smiling face on one side and a frowning face on the other side. The teacher says a pair of words. If the words rhyme, students hold the smiling face toward the teacher after he or she says, "Ready-set-show." The game is played similarly for recognizing words that sound the same or different at the beginning. The teacher is careful to give students ample time to reflect before saying, "Ready-set-show." Furthermore, he or she models what should be going on in the students' heads as they compare the two words they have heard. For example, the teacher might say, "*bell, talk*—hmmmm, do those words sound alike at the end? Let's see, *ell, alk*, hmmm." One advantage of this game is that the teacher can scan the face cards and very quickly see which children are processing sounds correctly and which are not. For those who are not, the teacher may quickly move to their desks and individually say the words again, emphasizing the end sounds, or he or she may make a mental note of those who may need some additional practice.

Reading Tongue Twisters. To help students develop an awareness of the relationship between initial consonant sounds and the letters that represent them and to help them develop the concept of word, students echo read while pointing to the words in a sentence in which most words begin with the same letter. For example, early in the school year students echo read, "Sitting silently, Susie's sister sipped seven sodas." Echo reading is conducted by the teacher first reading a sentence as students point to each word, and then the students read the sentence with the teacher, again pointing to each word as they read. Reading three or four tongue twisters is usually followed by playing Ready-Set-Show featuring the same consonant sounds. As the year progresses, students graduate to reading tongue twister sentences in which all the words begin with the same consonant digraph or consonant blend.

Completing a Rhyming Word Sort. To perform a word sort, students are given a worksheet with a list of words printed in a box (word bank) at the bottom of the page. The words have the same spelling patterns as the three or four key words for the week, which are printed across the top of the page. Words in the box are in random order and students are told to rewrite each word from the box beneath the key word with the same spelling pattern. For example, during the week that *it, not,* and *slide* were introduced, the word bank contained: *dot, bit, hide, fit, got, ride*, and so on. If a student were writing *dot* from the word bank, he or she would look for the key word with the same vowel-consonant pattern and write *dot* beneath that key word—in this case, *not*. Once all the word-bank words are rewritten, students read the words listed under the key words to the teacher, or to one another, in random order saying, "If this is _____ (reading the key word), then this is _____ (reading the word-bank word)." This activity accomplishes several learning objectives: practice in discriminating between spelling patterns, practice in applying the compare/constrast strategy to decode words, and awareness of the sounds associated with each spelling pattern.

Playing What's in My Head. In this game, the teacher presents in succession five clues leading to the identity of a key word. After each clue is given, students write a key word that fits the clue. For example, if the first clue is, "My word has three sounds," students could write any key word on the word wall with three sounds and be correct. The second clue might be, "My word begins with the sound I hear at the beginning of *coat.*" Again, this is not a very helpful clue for pinpointing the word, but it does narrow down the possible word wall words to those that begin with *c* or *k*. Students might write *king*, an acceptable response to the clue. The next clue might be, "My word ends with the sound that I hear at the beginning of *name.*" If students have been keeping track of the clues, they will know that only one word on the wall fits all three clues they have heard—*can*. However, they are given two more clues to either find or confirm the correct response. Students love this game and listen well to clues about words in the hope that they will predict the correct word sooner than their classmates. When the game is concluded, four or five students read the words that they wrote for each clue. This activity draws students attention to fully analyzing words and noting individual sound-letter matches.

Completing a Compare/Contrast Worksheet. The compare/contrast worksheet contains 10 sentences, each with an underlined word that has the same spelling pattern as one of the key words for the week. For example, the sentence might be: "My goal is to become very strong." Students circle the spelling pattern in the underlined word, then, on the line below the underlined word, they write the key word (*long*) that has the same spelling pattern. When students have written a key word for each underlined word, they practice using the compare/contrast (analogy) approach to decode the underlined word. After they have practiced decoding each word, the teacher "checks out" each student. The teacher reads each sentence, hesitating at the underlined word. When the teacher hesitates, the student says, "If I know _____ (saying the key word), then I know _____ (saying the underlined word). Once a student has been checked out, the teacher will often let that student check out other students.

Fully Analyzing Words. During the first 7 weeks of the word identification program, primary emphasis is placed on establishing routines for the word identification activities, scaffolding success with rhyming and initial consonant activities, and reading key words in the context of structured language experience stories. It is a time for diagnosing the gaps and strengths that each student has with respect to word knowledge. In the eighth week, we begin teaching students the process of fully analyzing each key word. For example, the teacher introduces the key word *right* by saying it. With the teacher's voice leading the way, students stretch out the sounds in *right*—/r/, /i/, /t/—and put up a finger for each sound they hear. The teacher asks, "How many sounds do you hear in *right*?" The response is "three." Next, the word card for *right* is put on the chalkboard. The teacher asks, "How many letters do you see?" Most students are amazed to discover that the word they just stretched with three sounds has five letters. The next job for students is to match the sounds they hear in *right* to the letters they see. In the process, students conclude that it takes three letters, *i-g-h*, to represent the vowel sound in *right*, and that *r* and *t* each represent one sound. A chart posted on the board reminds students about the steps involved in fully analyzing a word:

Talk-to-Yourself Chart

1. The word is _____.
2. Stretch the word.
   I hear _____ sounds.
3. I see _____ letters because _____.
4. The spelling pattern is _____.
5. This is what I know about the vowel: _____.
6. Another word on the word wall with the same vowel sound is _____.

In following the cues on the chart to fully analyze *right*, students would say: "The word is *right*, /r/ /i/ /t/. I hear three sounds and I see five letters because it takes *i-g-h* to represent the *i* sound. The spelling pattern is *i-g-h-t*. This is what I know about the vowel—the vowel is the only vowel in the word and it says its own name. Another word on the word wall with the same vowel sound is *slide*." Next the class stretches out the word one more time, then as they say each sound, they write the letter or letters that represent that sound. The students have now fully analyzed *right*. Using this new process, the students' first contact with key words is not a visual one; instead, the first exposure students have to a new key word is by hearing it pronounced by the teacher. We discovered that it is easier for students to segment words into sounds if they do not already have a visual image of the word.

Writing Words in Elkonin Boxes. To consolidate the match between sounds in a key word and the letters that represent the sounds, students write the key words they have fully analyzed in Elkonin boxes (Elkonin, 1973). On each student's spelling sheet next to each number there are six boxes, with extra boxes not needed for the word crossed out. For example, for the key word *skate*, there are four empty boxes. The teacher has crossed out the remaining two boxes because *skate* has only four sounds. In writing *skate* on the spelling sheet, the student says the word by stretching out the sounds, then writes the letter or letters that represents each sound in a separate box. Thus the student would write *S, K, A,* and *T* in the four boxes. There would be no box for *E* because it does not represent a sound. We teach students to write a small *e* in the same box with the *T* to indicate that the *e* is part of the spelling pattern, *A*-consonant-*e*, in which *e* marks the *A* saying its own name, but *e* does not represent a sound. Thus, when written in boxes the word appears: *S K A Te.* The word *right* would have three boxes and would be written: *R IGH T.* We have found that placing letters in boxes that represent the number of sounds in words helps our students remember how letters are matched to the sounds in words. Once students are taught to fully analyze words, they write their spelling words in Elkonin boxes for the first two spelling "tests" of the week Then later in the week they spell the words without the structure provided by Elkonin boxes. This activity follows the chant and check procedure described earlier.

Reading Predictable Rhymes. The most pleasurable part of the program for me has been writing the predictable-rhyme stories. These are stories that students read in order to practice the compare/contrast decoding strategy. Each story features words with the same spelling patterns as the key words for the week, as well as words with spelling patterns that have been introduced previously, plus high-frequency words that students are encountering in their preprimers. Initially, the vocabulary of the stories is limited because the students have been introduced to only a few spelling patterns. However, as the year progresses and more spelling patterns are introduced, stories can be written that students find far more interesting and challenging than those usually found in basal readers. For example, during the fourth month of the program, students read a story about a young boy's room that concludes: "Just ask William—he'll tell you, his room is magnificent. It's a place where he doesn't need consent to make a mess of great proportionment." Students who were once deemed poor readers feel good about themselves when they can dazzle their parents and grandparents by reading words such as *magnificent* and *proportionment.*

The teacher introduces these predictable rhymes to the class just as he or she would introduce any good story. The title is read and predictions are made about the story. The pictures are examined and further predictions are made. Next, students set purposes for listening to the story, and then the teacher reads it aloud, pausing occasionally to ask students if they can predict what the next word will be based on the rhyme and rhythm of the previous words. For example, after reading, "There's even a tent in William's room! The tent is round, but, it can't always be . . . ," the teacher might ask what they expect the next word to be based on what they have learned about

William's messy room. Next, the teacher reads the story again as students complete a response sheet by writing the missing consonants for 10 to 15 selected words in the story. For example, *skate, grate*, and *plate* are words in the story. The spelling pattern *-ate* is written on the response sheet three times and students fill in *sk, gr*, and *pl* as each of these words is read in the story. Finally, students are given their copies of the story. As the teacher reads *William's Room* one more time, students point to each word and chime in with the teacher on words they recognize or remember. The little book *William's Room* is added to each student's plastic bag of predictable rhyme books to be read at home each evening. A one-page copy of the story is also placed in the students' word identification folders at school and is read at school throughout the week.

Being Word Detectives and Keeping a Language Log. On the first day of the eighth week of school, our students begin their training as word detectives. Their job is to look for clues that give them information about how our language works. Students are encouraged to look for consistencies in the way that sounds correspond to letters, and to analyze letters surroundings the matches for clues that might alert them to expect a specific sound. As a result of noticing the match between combinations of letters and sounds, students begin to share their theories about how our language works. For example, one theory that students advance early in the year is, "Consonant letters seem to have one sound, but vowel letters have more than one sound in different words." It is usually not too long after this theory is advanced that students discover that the words *she* and *he* both have two sounds, but *she* has three letters. Our word detectives then proclaim, "Sometimes it takes two consonants to represent one sound." The next discovery may be that *cat* and *king* sound the same at the beginning, but the sound is represented by two different letters. By the time the students have encountered *city, can, cent, cut*, and even *cyclone* in the many little books that they read, they suggest such theories as: "Some consonants can have more than one sound," "*C* doesn't have a sound of its own—it takes the sound of *k* or *s*," or "I think the letter that comes after *c* has something to do with its sound."

Each evening, as students read their predictable rhyme books to their parents, they are on the lookout for patterns in their language that might explain why sounds and letters are matched in the way they are. When they notice these patterns, they dictate them to a parent who records the discovery in a language log. For example, after reading in the little book *William's Room* that William's toys were "In his bed, on the floor, even piled high in a chair," one child dictated: "The *i* in *high* works the same way the *i* does in *right* and in both words the *i* is followed by *g-h*." Another child shared with her mother, "In the word *his*, the *s* sounds like a *z*." These beginning readers enjoy being word detectives and sharing their discoveries with the class the next day. The additional benefit of analyzing the words in the predictable rhymes is that, for those students who take their role as word detectives seriously, these stories are not just rotely memorized. They have really looked at each word and are able to recognize most of the words in or out of the little books—this is especially true of the words the students consider "college words." This activity proves valuable to students with respect to both increased awarness of sound-letter matches they can apply in reading and improved spelling.

Self-Assessing Word Knowledge.   Each day students self-assess what they remember about a few of the key words they have learned. On some days, they self-assess their knowledge of the words for the week. On other days, they self-assess to see how much they remember about a word on the wall. The procedure works as follows. Students are instructed to select a word that they know they have a hard time calling to mind when they need it for decoding or spelling. Then, just as they did in the original full analysis of the word, they stretch the word, count the sounds they hear, match the sounds they hear to the letters they see, talk to themselves about the vowel and spelling pattern, and find a word on the wall that is like the word they are analyzing either with respect to sound or sound and spelling pattern. Finally, without looking at the word, they stretch the word, and as they stretch the sounds in the word, they write the letters that represent each sound that they hear. In self-assessing the word *king*, a student would follow the Talk-to-Yourself Chart and say: "The word is *king*. Stretch the word—/k/ /i/ /ng/. I hear three sounds. I see four letters because *ng* makes one sound. The spelling pattern is *i-n-g*. This is what I know about the vowel. The vowel is between two consonants and is the only vowel in the word. Another word on the word wall with the same vowel sound is *will*."

Sharing With a Partner.   Three times a week, after students have fully analyzed a word, they are given the opportunity to share what they know about a word with a partner. On each occasion they write the word they will share on a card that they show to their partner as they tell their partner about the word. On one day they share the information listed on the Talk-to-Yourself Chart. Another day they follow a Partner-Sharing Chart, which says: "My word is _____. My word wall word is _____. The words are alike because _____. Do you agree?" After one partner shares, the other has a turn sharing his or her word. A partner share might sound like this: "My word is *pig*. My word wall word is *it*. The words are alike because they both have one vowel, *i*, followed by a consonant, and both *is* say /i/. Do you agree?" The partner would agree with that information, and then would share about the word on his or her card.

The students' favorite partner-share activity is making a word. The chart for this activity says: "My word is _____. My new word is _____. I made this word because I know _____. Do you agree?" A partner share might sound like this: "My word is *treat*. My new word is *trot*. I made this word because I know that in *treat* it takes two letters to make the vowel sound, so I took out the two letters and put in an *o*. I know that when an *o* is between two consonants it will probably have the same sound as in *not*. The new word also has the same spelling pattern as the key word *not*. Do you agree?"

Going on a Word Hunt. The day after the predictable rhyme is introduced, students go on a word hunt. They search through the predictable rhyme and look for words they can decode, either because they know a key word with the same spelling pattern or because they have discovered something about their language that will help them figure out the word. Students are given a one-page copy of the text of the predictable rhyme book that features the key words for the week. They circle the spelling patterns in the words they can decode because the words have the same spelling pattern as the key words for the week. They also look for additional words they can decode because they know the words on the wall. These words are underlined. After about 5 minutes, the teacher calls a stop to the word hunt and, moving through the story verse by verse, gives students the opportunity to share the words they can read. Students respond in the form: "I can read _____ because I know _____." For example, a student said after looking through *William's Room*, "I can read *grate* because I know *skate*." Another student said, "I can read *consent* because I know *on* and *tent*."

Participating in Echo Reading. To provide students with further practice reading words with the same spelling patterns as the key words for the week, I have written a second set of books. These books are more like nursery rhymes than stories, and work very well for echo reading. The books often contain some dialogue, and students love taking parts and reading their roles with expression. We divide the class into two or three heterogenous reading groups for echo reading, with each led by an adult. Echo reading is an activity that students and adults enjoy, so it is usually not hard to convince a library aide, parent, or supervisor to join us for 15 minutes of echo reading. The adult leader introduces the book to the group by surveying the title and pictures, asking students for predictions, and setting a purpose for listening to the book. The adult reads the story once to the students. He or she mental models his or her thought process by describing them as he or she reacts to the story line and words. The adult's self-talk for the first echo reading book, *Ferdinand's Commands*, might sound something like this: "Dublin, hmmmm. I wonder if that is the city in Ireland or a city in the United States." "This boy is pretty demanding—I wonder why he is asking for such a lot of different things." "Stirrups—I'm having a hard time picturing exactly what they look like, maybe I can ask someone to explain exactly what they look like."

After the adult leader finishes reading the story, students comment on the story line and discuss unfamiliar words. The adult leader asks if the students noticed any patterns in the story. Next, students are given their own copies of the book. They point to the words as the adult leader reads the first sentence, then the students echo the first line, pointing to each word as they read. The adult leader reads the second line and students again echo that line as they point to each word. This procedure is continued for the entire book, with occasional pauses to talk about rhymes and spelling patterns in words. Students like to point out words with familiar spelling patterns after having read a page.

The echo reading book *Ferdinand's Commands* features the spelling patterns *in, and*, and *up*. The teacher reads, "A boy who's almost nine is who this tale's about." Students echo the line. The teacher then reads, "He lives in Dublin and he loves to shout." The students echo the line, followed by the teacher reading and students echoing: "Get me teacups, pickups, I want lots of cups. Get me stirrups, too—I think I'll saddle up." After echo reading the book, the students choral read the book, then parts are often assigned for the third reading of the book. The echo reading book is sent home in the students' homework folders to be practiced with parents.

Looking Through Words. It is common for our beginning readers to glance only at initial letters in reading words, or to guess words from context. To impress on students the necessity for looking at every single letter in a word, we designed the activity Looking Through Words. Students are shown a column of several words and pseudowords headed by a key word. Each word in the list differs from the one preceding it by just one letter. This activity is introduced during the eighth week of school when students are introduced to the key words *in, and*, and *up*. The first column of words on the Looking Through Words page is composed of *in, ip*, and *dip*. Students place an index card under the first word in the first list. The teacher calls on a student to read the first word. Cards are moved down and placed under the second word or pseudoword and a student is asked to tell how the second word is different from the first. The reply would be, "The *n* was taken off and a *p* was put in its place. The new word is *ip*." Cards are moved down again and another child is asked to tell what is different this time. The child would say, "*D* has been added to the front of the word. The new word is *dip*." After several simple lists like *in-ip-dip*, students read: *and, an, am, amp, ramp, tramp*. In several weeks, students are reading columns that end with words such as *thermometer*. By this time they are beginning to believe that, given enough time, they can figure out any college word.

Reading to a Partner. As a special treat, on Fridays of each week students spend about 15 minutes reading to each other their predictable rhyme and echo-reading books. The texts for all these books are arranged in four-line verses. One student reads and points to a verse while the partner follows and points in his or her copy of the text. Then, for the next verse, the roles are reversed. Students are asked not to supply a word for a partner; rather, if the partner miscalls or cannot read a word, the student gives cues just as a teacher would. For example, in *Ferdinand's Commands* a partner was stuck on *martins*. The student asked how many chunks he thought the word had. Once the word was divided into two parts, the student coached his partner to think of the key words for the spelling patterns *a-r* and *i-n*.

Summarizing What I Know About My Language. Each day the word identification block ends with the teacher asking students what they have discovered about how their language works. Sometimes the teacher asks specific students to share a discovery made during reading group. Students put forth their discoveries as theories or hypotheses, and other students are encouraged to look for words that support or run contrary to the theory. Teachers accept students' language in describing their observations, rather than try to formalize students' observations by making them into abstract rules. For example, our beginning readers have never heard of "*r*-controlled vowels," yet they do observe and talk about them. They notice that when there is a vowel between two consonants and the consonant after the vowel is an *r*, the vowel doesn't have the sound you would normally expect it to have. In fact, we find students saying things like: "When there is an *r* after a vowel, the *r* talks so loud you can't hear the vowel" or "*r* is such a loudmouth that the vowel can't be heard even though it is trying to say something" or "When there is an *r* after a vowel, the vowel just makes a peep."

It is not uncommon for students to observe some aspect of a predictable rhyme that has gone completely unnoticed by the teacher and the author of the story. For example, when reading *Frog Ball*, Jeff noticed the words *old* and *stroll* and commented that he was surprised that the vowel didn't have the sound that *o* usually has when it is the only vowel followed by a consonant. He said that when he noticed the vowel saying its name in *old*, he just assumed it was a word that didn't fit a pattern. However, when he read *stroll* he noticed that the *o* in that word also said its name, and that the *o* in both words is followed by an *l*. The theory he suggested was that maybe when there is the *ol* pattern, the *o* will say its name. He went on to suggest that *l* might hold power over other vowels, too, because the *a* in *ball* didn't sound like the *a* in *cat* and *can*. Another child entered the discussion at this point to remind the class that he had shared a few weeks earlier his discovery that the *i* in *child* was the only vowel in the word and was followed by a consonant, but it didn't have the expected sound. Now he realized that *child* fit the same pattern as *stroll, old,* and *ball*. There is no doubt that these students are very alert word detectives!

Individualized Instruction Block

During this block the teacher meets individually with as many children as he or she can. Then, on the following days, she meets with different children until all the children have been seen individually. Once she has worked with each child, the cycle begins again. The purpose of this individual time is both to diagnose needs and to provide individual instruction to meet these needs.

Parent-Read-Aloud Book Report. At home the previous night, parents read aloud to children a book above the child's reading level that the child has selected from the classroom library of read-aloud books. The books differ for each child. Every school day begins with children writing a response to the book their parents read to them. To write this response, children follow the book report format that is posted on the chalkboard. For fiction this includes: the title of the book, who the characters are, the story problem and resolution, and the child's favorite part. Students must explain why they found this part interesting.

Before arriving at school for the day, children may have discussed the read-aloud book as many as three times with their parents: once during the reading of the book, then after reading the book, and again in the car on the way to school. The children then review the information again with the teacher before writing their summaries and reactions to the book. Even with this support, at the beginning of the year most students are able to write only one or two sentences using the crudest of invented spellings. However, 3 months into the school year, most of the children are writing thorough and well-planned summaries of their books. Adults in the classroom interact with the students about their writing and encourage them to use what they know about their language to spell words. Drawing a picture about the book is saved for after the satisfactory completion of the book report.

Word Ring Practice. Because our beginning readers have virtually no sight vocabulary, and because many exposures to words are required for them to be able to read them correctly, the high-frequency words found in their basal preprimers and primers are introduced 3 to 5 days before they will need them. When these words are introduced in reading group, students are directed to look at every single letter and talk about what they know about the sounds represented by those letters. After discussion of two or three words, these words are placed on each child's word ring. The word is written in isolation on one side of the card and in the context of a sentence on the reverse side. Children practice reading these words as part of their nightly homework, then they read them for an adult at school the next day. When children have five check marks on the card indicating that they have read the word automatically as a sight word, the word is placed in their file box of known words. When the teacher reviews the word ring with each child, he or she reinforces the application of what has been learned about how language works.

Book Discussion. After listening to a student read the words on his or her word ring, the teacher conducts a book conference about at least one of the five little Wright Group and Rigby books that were read at home. The teacher typically asks the student to pick a favorite book and tell about the characters, setting, story problem, and problem resolution. Students keep track of the number of books they read, and each week this number is added to the book-reading chart at the front of the classroom. No matter what the child's level of readiness for learning to read in the fall, we almost always find that the child who reads the most books during the year is also the child who makes the most progress in reading.

Independent Reading and Response

While the teacher is conducting reading groups, some students are at work at their desks. In the Benchmark program, time spent working independently is devoted to reading and responding to books. At the beginning level, students read stories written with the corpus of words they have learned in reading group. Initially, these beginning readers look for answers to concrete questions about text they have read independently. Later, we expect students to write about the inferences made while reading. Students are taught to write a sentence answer by using words in the question for the first part of the answer. For example, if the question asked, "Where do the children go to play?" students would write, "The children go to play at _____ ." A teaching assistant supervises students during their independent work. He or she interacts with students about the stories they are reading and guides them as they construct written responses. When the children ask how to spell a word, they are guided to look in the book, in the question, at the word wall for a key word, or on their word ring. Upon completing written responses to a story, students independently check their response sheet by using a checklist: name and date, pages to read underlined, capitals and periods, full sentences, and spelling. After students have evaluated themselves, the teaching assistant and student discuss the story and answers on the response sheet. Words that the students misspell that should have been caught are underlined by the teaching assistant, and students are asked to use their spelling strategies to correct the misspellings.

Reading Group

Each day children meet in small groups to read and discuss basal reader stories. One goal is to teach students strategies for active involvement in their reading.

Words. As discussed previously, new words are introduced several days ahead of the time students will encounter them in their basal reader stories. For example, one of the words children needed to know for an upcoming story was *noodle.* The teacher placed the word on the chalkboard in a sentence and asked the students how they would decode the word. The children concluded that the context did not help them and that they would have to look at every letter and think about words they knew with the same letter patterns as *noodle.* One child said that the word ended like *little,* so they could use the end sound of *little* to get the end sound of *noodle.* Others suggested that maybe the two *o*s would have the sound you hear in *zoo* or *look,* so students concluded that they would have to be flexible and try both sounds. Using those clues, the students were able to decode *noodle.* This is typical of the discussions held each day in reading group, as two to four new words are introduced. Even if students are able to figure out the word based on context, the teacher asks them to explain to the rest of the class how they might have decoded the word using what they know about language.

Strategies. Several comprehension strategies are taught explicitly to beginning readers:

1. Reading must make sense, so if the words do not make sense I must reread them to determine why the passage is not making sense.
2. Active readers survey, predict, and set purposes.
3. Stories are composed of four major elements—characters, setting, story problem, and resolution of the story problem.
4. I can summarize a story using the story elements.

The pacing of strategy instruction is drawn out over the entire year in such a way that one strategy is introduced and practiced for months before another is introduced. For example, during the entire 6 weeks of summer school, students focused on "reading must make sense." From the beginning of the school year until the beginning of March, students learned and practiced the strategies of survey, predict, and set a purpose. Finally, in March and April, story elements were introduced in reading group as a strategy for guiding comprehension. During the last month of school, students learned to use the story elements to summarize a story as one way of monitoring comprehension.

Each day before reading, the strategy is discussed. In introducing or reviewing a strategy, the teacher tells the students *what* strategy they are learning, *why* it will be useful, *when* it can be used, and *how* the strategy is implemented. Next, he or she models how to implement the strategy using a simple text, usually one of the Wright Group little books. For example, the teacher might say:

Today we are going to learn how to stay actively involved in what we are reading. It is important to stay actively involved because if you drift off and don't pay attention to the meaning of what you are reading, the story won't make sense and you won't be able to contribute to the discussion. The strategy I'm going to teach you for staying actively involved can be used any time you read something. This is how you do it. You read the title of the story or book and think about what it might be about. Then, you survey the story looking at the pictures, again making predictions about what you think the story is about. As you survey and predict, you are building an outline in your head of what will probably happen in the story. This will help you make sense of the story, as well as let you know when the story isn't making sense. The third thing you do that will keep you actively involved is to set a purpose for reading. This means you tell yourself what you want to find out when you read the story. Let me model what I might be thinking as I survey, predict, and set a purpose for this story I will read to you.

After modeling how to implement the strategy, the teacher asks students to read the title and make some predictions by asking themselves: Who are the characters? Where does the story take place? What will the characters be doing? These questions guide students to make predictions that are connected to the story and do not simply rely on personal background information. Next, the children share their purposes for reading the selection. On subsequent days, the teacher may begin the strategy portion of the reading group block by asking students what they can do to stay actively involved in their reading. Students then describe how to survey, predict, and set purposes.

After the strategy discussion and a review of the unfamiliar words, students read all or part of the story silently. For beginning readers, this means that they whisper read, thus making it easy for the teacher to monitor how the students are doing and to intervene when someone gets off track. Some students finish reading the selection before others, so the teacher has a pencil and paper handy and asks the early finishers to jot down some notes about the characters, setting, problem, and solution, or a personal response to the story that they would like to share. Writing these notes often alerts students to the fact that they need to reread to clear up some fuzzy spots in their understanding.

Discussion.   When all of the students have read the selection, the teacher asks them to make some comments about their predictions, purposes for reading, and personal responses to the story. Teachers try to make their discussions with students genuine rather than formulaic. Interactional patterns in which the teacher *i*nitiates with a question, a student *r*esponds, and the teacher *e*valuates the answer—known as an IRE (Cazden, 1988)—tend to stifle discussion. Instead of an IRE, the Benchmark teacher tries to get members of the group to respond to one another. For example, Bill might say, "I thought the problem in the story was going to be solved by _____, but it didn't turn out that way. I would have liked the story better if it had turned out as I predicted." The teacher's response to this might be, "Bill wasn't satisfied with the way the problem was solved. What do the rest of you think?" Discussions among our students are always lively, with students often returning to the text to read several sentences to prove a point.

Process Writing

The goals of the writing program for beginning readers at Benchmark are to convince our students that they have a lot to share, that others are interested in hearing their ideas, and that getting their ideas on paper using invented spelling is perfectly acceptable. Spelling only needs to be correct on the final draft. Each day the teacher discusses and models an element of the writing process. For example, it might be writing an "attention-grabbing" first sentence, or using "juicy" words. Students next rehearse their ideas, then begin or continue a piece in their writing journal. They usually write on every other line. Early in the year we find that the teacher needs to ask most students to read back their sentences so that the teacher can write them on the line above what the students have written. This enables students to read back what they have written when it is time to share. As students master more sound-letter correspondences, they rely less on teacher support to get their ideas on paper so that they can read them back. Most of the students' early writing consists of personal experience stories, although students also write poems, biographies, thank-you notes, personal letters, and expository pieces. The process that is stressed is always the same: plan, draft, revise, publish. A favorite time during the writing period is the author's chair. One student sits in the author's chair and shares his or her piece, and the other students respond with praise and suggestions.

Literature

The goal of the literature program is to introduce students to a variety of genres and to make them aware of the characteristics that differentiate among genres. Typically, these young children are read literature in the following categories: realistic fiction, fanciful fiction, historical fiction, folk tales, fables, biographies, and myths. The characteristics of each genre are discussed before each group of books is read to the class by the teacher. It is not unusual for the teacher, as well as parents, to read the same genre to children for 3 or 4 weeks. During discussions, students are regularly asked to compile a list of the characteristics that make the stories alike. They love showing off their knowledge of story genre when surveying a story in their basal reader and predicting which genre it will fit.

CONCLUDING COMMENT

There is much agreement among the authors of chapters in this volume about how children process words. This agreement is rooted in solid research on which beginning reading programs can be based. Although Ehri may emphasize fully analyzing words and Goswami learning words by analogy, we have discovered at Benchmark that each is describing an important aspect of the process of learning to read. Both fully analyzing words and analogizing are crucial aspects of becoming mature readers. Many of the authors of chapters in this book speak of the predictability of children's growth paths based on early indicators, such as phonemic awareness. Although agreeing in principle, Calfee, Pressley, and Torgesen in their chapters portray an optimistic future for those early poor performers who receive intense interventions. These intense interventions, if characterized by explicit instruction about the word-learning process, can in fact alter children's growth paths. This is the kind of program we have attempted to develop at Benchmark School.

By employing all of the activities described in this chapter, Benchmark teachers have succeeded in helping beginning readers not only become attentive to print, but also become amazingly knowledgeable about how our language is constructed. In addition, these at-risk-for-failure and delayed readers acquire confidence in their ability to understand challenging text and in their ability to become immersed in a good book. Like other capable readers, they are knowledgeable about the form and function of words, and they are constructors of meaning. We feel we have succeeded in creating a beginning literacy program that is structured in such a way that it captures the attention of beginning readers; keeps them actively and meaningfully engaged with print; rewards reflective attention to letters, sounds, words, and connected text; and scaffolds success in flexibly responding to print. However, we will continue searching for even better ways to help at-risk and delayed readers become successfully engaged in literacy.

ACKNOWLEDGMENTS

Correspondence may be sent to the author at 2107 N. Providence Rd., Media, PA 19063. The phone number is 610-565-3741; the fax number is 610-565-3872.

REFERENCES

Adams, M. J. (1990). *Beginning to read: Thinking and learning about print.* Cambridge, MA: MIT Press.

Bradley, L., & Bryant, P. E. (1983). Categorizing sounds and learning to read—a causal connection. *Nature, 301,* 419–421.

Cazden, C. B. (1988). *Classroom discourse: The language of teaching and learning.* Portsmouth, NH: Heinemann.

Cunningham, P. M. (1975). Investigating a synthesized theory of mediated word identification. *Reading Research Quarterly, 11,* 127–143.

Ehri, L. C. (1980). The development of orthographic images. In U. Frith (Ed.), *Cognitive processes in spelling* (pp. 311–338). London: Academic.

Ehri, L. C. (1992). Reconceptualizing the development of sight word reading and its relationship to recoding. In P. Gough, L. Ehri, & R. Treiman (Eds.), *Reading acquisition* (pp. 107–143). Hillsdale, NJ: Lawrence Erlbaum Associates.

Ehri, L. C. (1994). Development of the ability to read words: Update. In R. Ruddell, J. Ruddell, & H. Singer (Eds.), *Theoretical models and processes of reading* (4th ed., pp. 323–358). Newark, DE: International Reading Association.

Ehri, L. C., & Wilce, P. C. (1983). Development of word identification speed in skilled and less skilled beginning readers. *Journal of Educational Psychology, 75,* 3–18.

Elkonin, D. B. (1973). U.S.S.R. In J. Downing (Ed.), *Comparative reading* (pp. 551–559). New York: Macmillan.

Gaskins, I. W., Anderson, R. C., Pressley, M., Cunicelli, E. A., & Satlow, E. (1993). Six teachers' dialogue during cognitive process instruction. *The Elementary School Journal, 93,* 277–304.

Gaskins, I. W., Downer, M., Anderson, R. C., Cunningham, P., Gaskins, R., Schommer, M., & the Teachers of Benchmark School. (1988). A metacognitive approach to phonics: Using what you know to decode what you don't know. *Remedial and Special Education, 9,* 36–41.

Gaskins, I. W., Ehri, L. C., Cress, C., O'Hara, C., & Donnelly, K. (1996). Procedures for word learning: Making discoveries about words. *The Reading Teacher, 50,* 312–327.

Gaskins, R. W., Gaskins, I. W., Anderson, R. C., & Schommer, M. (1995). The reciprocal relationship between research and development: An example involving a decoding strand for poor readers. *Journal of Reading Behavior, 27,* 337–377.

Pearson, P. D. (1993). Teaching and learning reading: A research perspective. *Language Arts, 70,* 502–511.

Perfetti, C. A. (1991). Representations and awareness in the acquisition of reading competence. In L. Rieban & C. A. Perfetti (Eds.), *Learning to read: Basic research and its implications* (pp. 33–44). Hillsdale, NJ: Lawrence Erlbaum Associates.

Pressley, M., El-Dinary, P. M., Gaskins, I. W., Schuder, T., Bergman, J. L., Almasi, J., & Brown, R. (1992). Beyond direct explanation: Transactional instruction of reading comprehension strategies. *The Elementary School Journal, 92,* 513–555.

Stanovich, K. E. (1992). Speculations on causes and consequences of individual differences in early reading acquisition. In P. Gough, L. Ehri, & R. Treiman (Eds.), *Reading acquisition* (pp. 307–342). Hillsdale, NJ: Lawrence Erlbaum Associates.

Venezky, R. L. (1970). *The structure of English orthography.* The Hague, Netherlands: Mouton.

Wagner, R. K., & Torgesen, J. K. (1987). The nature of phonological processing and its causal role in the acquisition of reading skills. *Psychological Bulletin, 101*(2), 192–212.

III

WORD RECOGNITION
IN CONTEXT

10

▼▼▼▼▼▼▼

The Impact of Print Exposure
on Word Recognition

Anne E. Cunningham
University of California, Berkeley

Keith E. Stanovich
University of Toronto

THE IMPACT OF PRINT EXPOSURE
ON WORD RECOGNITION

The role that experiential factors play in determining variation in children's cognitive growth has been at the heart of much theorizing in developmental psychology. Multiple factors have been cited as contributing to children's cognitive development. For example, individual differences in home and family environment play a large role in children's cognitive growth (e.g., Dickinson & Tabors, 1991; Hewison & Tizard, 1980; Iverson & Walberg, 1984; Payne, Whitehurst, & Angell, 1994).

When speculating about variables in people's ecologies that could account for cognitive variability, we should focus on variables that have the requisite potency to perform their theoretical roles. A class of variables that might have such potency would be one that has long-term effects because of its repetitive and/or cumulative action. Schooling is obviously one such variable (Cahan & Cohen, 1989; Ceci, 1990, 1991; Morrison, 1987). In this chapter we argue that exposure to print is another experiential factor that, like schooling, has long-term cumulative effects.

Reading is a very special type of interface with the environment, providing the child with unique opportunities to acquire declarative knowledge. Furthermore, the processing mechanisms exercised during reading receive an unusual amount of practice. Certain microprocesses of reading that are linked to words or groups of words are repeatedly exercised. For example, from the time of at least fifth grade, an avid reader is seeing literally millions of words a year (Anderson, Wilson, & Fielding, 1988). Thus, whatever cognitive processes are engaged over word or word-group units (phonological coding, semantic activation, parsing, induction of vocabulary items) are being exercised hundreds of times a day. It is surely expected that this amount of cognitive muscle flexing will have some specific effects. Differential participation in such a process should result in large individual differences, not only in reading ability but in other cognitive skills as well.

Indeed, Biemiller (1977–1978) found large ability differences in exposure to print within the classroom as early as midway through the first-grade year. Convergent results have been obtained by Allington (1984). In his first-grade sample, the total number of words read during a week of school reading group sessions ranged from a low of 16 for one of the children in the less-skilled group to a high of 1,933 for one of the children in the skilled reading group. The average skilled reader read approximately three times as many words in the group reading sessions as did the average less-skilled reader. Nagy and Anderson (1984) estimated that, regarding in-school reading, "The least motivated children in the middle grades might read 100,000 words a year while the average children at this level might read 1,000,000. The figure for the voracious middle grade reader might be 10,000,000 or even as high as 50,000,000. If these guesses are anywhere near the mark, there are staggering individual differences in the volume of language experience, and therefore, opportunity to learn new words" (p. 328). There are, of course, also differences in the volume of reading outside of the classroom that are linked to reading ability (Fielding, Wilson, & Anderson, 1986), and these probably become increasingly large as schooling progresses.

It is these individual differences in out-of-school reading volume and their resulting effects that we have attempted to model in our research program. It has been shown that cognitive processes influence children's ability to read, yet very little attention has been focused on what might be considered a form of reciprocal causation—that is, on the possibility that differences in exposure to print affect the development of cognitive processes and growth of knowledge.

The effect of reading volume on cognitive processes and declarative knowledge bases, combined with the large skill differences in reading volume, could mean that a "rich-get-richer" or cumulative advantage phenomenon is almost inextricably embedded within the developmental course of reading progress (see Stanovich, 1986). For example, we can see these rich-get-richer (and their converse poor-get-poorer) effects in vocabulary development. The very children who are reading well and have good vocabularies will read more, learn more word meanings, and hence read even better. Children with inadequate vocabularies—who read slowly and without enjoyment—read less, and as a result have slower development of vocabulary knowledge, which inhibits further growth in reading ability.

These educational sequences, in which early achievement spawns faster rates of subsequent achievement, were termed *Matthew Effects* (Stanovich, 1986; see also Walberg & Tsai, 1983). The term *Matthew Effects* derives from the Gospel according to Matthew—"For unto every one that hath shall be given, and he shall have abundance: but from him that hath not shall be taken away even that which he hath" (XXV:29)—and refers to rich-get-richer and poor-get-poorer effects embedded in the sociodevelopmental context of schooling. Reading comprehension provides an example of this effect—children who are already good comprehenders may tend to read more, thus spurring further increases in their reading comprehension abilities and increasing the achievement differences between them and their age-mates who are not good comprehenders and not avid readers (Chall, Jacobs, & Baldwin, 1990; Juel, 1988; Share, McGee, & Silva, 1989; Share & Silva, 1987; Stanovich, 1986; van den Bos, 1989).

We attempt to examine these reciprocal effects in children's early reading development and evaluate their subsequent cognitive growth in a series of studies reported on in this chapter. Our first investigation delineates the relation between first-grade literacy environment and the development of children's orthographic and phonological skills. Our second study describes the growth of phonological and orthographic processing in students from first through third grade, and examines the covariance structure of many tasks purporting to measure orthographic knowledge. In our third study, we go beyond the word level to discuss the effects print exposure has on reading comprehension for older third- and fifth-grade readers. In our last study, we explore the reciprocal effects of a lifetime of print exposure. We followed a first-grade group of students, and 10 years later assessed their level of reading volume as well as verbal intelligence and reading comprehension. In this longitudinal investigation, we were able to observe the widening achievement disparities and the relative contribution of print exposure in explaining these differences. Aside from their current level of reading comprehension ability, we explored whether the speed with which children attain reading fluency in their early years predicts how engaged with print they will be as adolescents. We provide evidence that early success in reading acquisition is one of the keys that unlocks a lifetime of reading habits.

Assessing Literacy Environment Through Print Exposure

For the past several years, our research group has attempted to develop and validate measures of individual differences in print exposure (Cunningham & Stanovich, 1990, 1991; Stanovich, 1992; Stanovich & Cunningham, 1992, 1993; Stanovich & West, 1989; West & Stanovich, 1991). We first examined the relation between print exposure and cognitive growth among adults (Stanovich & West, 1989), and later among children (e.g., Cunningham &

Stanovich, 1990, 1991). In our methodology, we attempt to correlate differential engagement in reading with various cognitive outcomes that have been associated with the acquisition of literacy (Cunningham & Stanovich, 1990, 1991; Stanovich & Cunningham, 1992, 1993; Stanovich & West, 1989; West & Stanovich, 1991; West, Stanovich, & Mitchell, 1993). However, such a logic, if not supplemented with additional methodological controls, is subject to the same problem that has plagued historical investigations of literacy's effects—the problem of spurious correlation. The argument is that degree of print exposure is correlated with various reading skills, such as word decoding, and with cognitive abilities generally. Simply and obviously, individuals with superior reading skills read more. This correlation is problematic because it raises the possibility that an association between amount of print exposure and any criterion ability, skill, or knowledge base might arise not because of the unique effects of print exposure, but instead because of individual differences in general ability or in specific reading subskills such as decoding.

Consider vocabulary as an example. The counterargument to the claim that print exposure is a major mechanism determining vocabulary growth (Hayes, 1988; Nagy & Anderson, 1984; Stanovich, 1986) is that superior decoding ability leads to more print exposure and that decoding abilities are themselves related to vocabulary development, because better decoding ensures an accurate verbal context for inducing the meanings of unknown words. Thus, according to this argument, vocabulary and print exposure are spuriously related via their connection with decoding ability: Good decoders read a lot and have the best context available for inferring new words. Decoding ability could also, in part, reflect the efficiency of the phonological short-term memory, which Gathercole and Baddeley (1989) argued is critical to early oral vocabulary acquisition. Finally, vocabulary and print exposure could be spuriously linked through general cognitive abilities that are associated with both print exposure and the ability to induce meaning from context (Sternberg, 1985).

We have utilized a regression logic to deal with this problem. In the analyses here, we first statistically control for the effects of general ability before examining the relationship between print exposure and criterion variables. This procedure of reducing possible spurious relationships by first partialing out relevant subskills and abilities and then looking for residual effects of print exposure has been used in our earlier investigations. For example, in previous work we demonstrated that, independent of decoding ability, variation in print exposure among adults predicts spelling ability and orthographic knowledge (Stanovich & West, 1989). Similarly, in a previous study of children's performance (Cunningham & Stanovich, 1990), we found that after partialing out IQ, memory ability, and phonological processing abilities, print exposure accounted for additional variance in orthographic knowledge and word recognition. The logic of our analytic strategy is quite conservative, because we partial out variance in abilities that are likely to be developed by print exposure itself (Stanovich, 1986). Yet even after print exposure is robbed of some of its rightful variance, it remains a unique predictor.

Assessing Print Exposure

In this chapter, we report further data on three recognition measures of print exposure—the author recognition test (ART), the magazine recognition test (MRT), and the title recognition test (TRT)—that have proven to be robust predictors in earlier studies (Allen, Cipielewski, & Stanovich, 1992; Cunningham & Stanovich, 1990, 1991; Stanovich & Cunningham, 1992, 1993; Stanovich & West, 1989; West & Stanovich, 1991).

When employing the TRT with much younger students, such as those in first through third grades, the measure could be viewed as a proxy for the general literacy environment in the home or, alternatively, as a measure of the child's own print exposure. It is obviously not intended to measure absolute levels of print exposure, as are diary studies of students's activities. Instead, the TRT and ART were designed as measures reflecting relative individual differences in exposure to print. The interested reader is referred to our earlier papers (e.g., Allen, Cipielewski, & Stanovich, 1992; Cunningham & Stanovich, 1990, 1991; Stanovich & Cunningham, 1992, 1993; Stanovich & West, 1989; West & Stanovich, 1991) for a more in-depth discussion of the recognition measures and their relation to other indices of print exposure.

EXPERIENTIAL CORRELATES OF PHONOLOGICAL AND ORTHOGRAPHIC PROCESSING

An enormous amount of research has indicated that there are critical linkages between the development of phonological abilities and the acquisition of word recognition skills (Juel, 1988, 1994; Liberman & Shankweiler, 1985; Perfetti, 1985; Share, 1995; Share & Stanovich, 1995; Stanovich, 1986, 1988a, 1988b; Vellutino & Scanlon, 1987). Nevertheless, despite the importance of phonological variables in explaining variance in the acquisition of word recognition skill, it is possible that another class of factors could explain additional variance. Although the correlations between phonological processing skill and word recognition ability are quite high, they still probably leave some reliable word recognition variance unaccounted for (Stanovich, Cunningham, & Cramer, 1984; Wagner, 1988; Wagner & Torgesen, 1987; Yopp, 1988). In addition, some investigators have argued that the development of a minimal level of phonological sensitivity is a necessary but not sufficient condition for the development of efficient word recognition processes (Juel, Griffith, & Gough, 1986; Tunmer & Nesdale, 1985).

Recently, theoretical attention has centered on orthographic processing abilities as a potential second source of variance in word recognition ability (see Stanovich & West, 1989). However, isolating individual differences in orthographic processing is problematic, because there is little doubt that the development of orthographic processing skill must be somewhat dependent on phonological processing abilities (Barron, 1986; Ehri, 1984, 1987, 1992; Jorm & Share, 1983). The critical question for research is whether the development of the orthographic lexicon is entirely parasitic on the operation of phonological processes. In a study employing adult subjects, Stanovich and West (1989) obtained data that answered this question in the negative. They found that even after the considerable variance associated with phonological processing had been partialed out, orthographic processing skills explained significant additional variance in reading and spelling ability.

In further analyses, Stanovich and West (1989) found that differences in amount of exposure to print were linked to orthographic processing variance after phonological abilities had been partialed out. This was no trivial finding, because it is quite possible that print exposure differences could have been entirely parasitic on phonological processing abilities. The problem is that even if differences in orthographic processing abilities had as their proximal cause differences in exposure to print, reading practice may simply be determined by how skilled the reader is at phonological coding. This conjecture yields the prediction that print exposure differences should not account for variance in orthographic processing efficiency once the influence of phonological skill has been removed. It is just this prediction that was falsified. In the following review of studies, we discuss the linkages among these same relationships in younger, beginning readers.

Study 1: First-Grade Students' Orthographic and Phonological Processing

With the exception of the seminal work of Maclean, Bryant, and Bradley (1987) on knowledge of nursery rhymes, there has been very little work on the experiential correlates of early phonological and orthographic processing skill. We addressed this issue in our first investigation by examining whether children's phonological and orthographic processing skill is differentially related to our index of children's home literacy environment—an index that is probably an indirect indicator of individual differences in exposure to print.

Twenty-six first-grade children were recruited. All testing took place in March through May of the school year. We relied primarily on three tasks to partial out phonological processing variance. The first one was a deletion task that required the students to delete the initial consonant from a monosyllabic word and pronounce the embedded word. In the second deletion task, the students were required to delete the initial phoneme from a series of 10 beginning consonant blends and pronounce the embedded word or wordlike segment that remained. The second part of this task required the students to delete the final phoneme from a series of 10 final consonant blend words, and provide the remaining sounds. Our third measure was a phoneme transposition task. Essentially, the students were required to switch the beginning and ending phoneme of a monosyllabic word to create a new word (e.g., *top* → *pot*).

In addition to the spelling subtest of the Stanford Achievement Test, two other tasks served as measures of orthographic processing skill. The first task was taken in part from the spelling study of Mann, Tobin, and Wilson (1987). Target words contained at least one of the following attributes: a letter name within the word, a short vowel, a nasal, a liquid, or a consonant represented with a digraph. The words were chosen so as to "increase the likelihood that subjects would invent preconventional spellings that could easily be distinguished from conventional spellings" (Mann, Tobin, & Wilson, 1987, p. 126). To spell these items conventionally, an orthographic representation must be consulted, so that accuracy on the items becomes, at least in part, a measure of the quality of the early-developing orthographic lexicon.

The third orthographic processing measure was a letter-string choice task in which we employed stimuli provided by Rebecca Treiman. The students were presented with 16 pairs of three- to seven-letter strings on a sheet of paper, and instructed to circle the one word that looked most like it could be a real word. The students were told that neither string was an actual word, but that one letter string was more like a word. One member of each pair (e.g., *beff-ffeb*) contained an orthographic sequence that either never occurs in English or that occurs with extremely low frequency. The student's score is the number of times that the nonword without the illegal or low-frequency letter string was chosen. Although this task undoubtedly implicated phonological coding to some extent, the coding of frequent and infrequent orthographic sequences in memory should have been a substantial contributor to performance.

Finally, a standardized reading achievement test—the word reading subtest from the Stanford Achievement Test—was employed to assess students' word reading and spelling performance.

Our proxy measure of children's literacy environment, the TRT, was group administered within the classroom. Twenty-six titles of children's books that were not read in the classroom were interspersed with eight foils (names of books that were fabricated). The titles were read out loud to the students, and the students were instructed to underline only the names of books that they knew were actual books. The students were told that guessing could easily be detected, because some of the titles were not the names of actual books. The TRT took approximately 5 minutes to administer.

Can Orthographic Processing Ability Account for Unique
Variance in Word Recognition?

By utilizing the logic of hierarchical multiple regression, we addressed the
question of whether there is variance in word recognition that can be reliably
linked to orthographic processing skill once variance due to phonological
processing has been partialed out. Table 10.1 presents the results of two such
analyses. The three phonological processing tasks were entered first and
collectively achieved a multiple R with Stanford word reading of .504. However, when the letter-string choice task was entered fourth, it accounted for
a substantial proportion of additional variance (30.1%). Similarly, when the
score on the experimental spelling test was entered as the fourth variable in
the equation, it accounted for 29.1% of the variance in word reading scores.
Thus, there does seem to be variation in orthographic processing skill that
is linked to word recognition ability and is independent of phonological
processes. The analyses reported here are at least a tentative indication that
phonological and orthographic processing skills are separable components
of variance in word recognition during the very earliest stages of reading
acquisition. That is, the development of print-specific knowledge is not entirely parasitic on phonological processing skill among beginning readers.

Can Variance in Orthographic Processing Ability
Be Linked to Print Exposure Differences That
Are Independent of Phonological Processing Skill?

The latter conclusion shifts attention to the question of what factors determine variation in orthographic processing abilities and, in particular, whether
print exposure is related to orthographic processing skill. In exploring this
relationship it is important to partial out phonological processing ability,

TABLE 10.1
Unique Orthographic Processing Variance in Word Recognition
After Phonological Processing Variance Is Partialed Out

	Multiple R	R^2 Change
Phoneme deletion 1	.401	.161*
Phoneme deletion 2	.490	.079*
Phoneme transposition	.504	.014
Letter-string choice	.742	.301*
Phoneme deletion 1	.401	.161*
Phoneme deletion 2	.490	.079*
Phoneme transposition	.504	.014
Experimental spelling	.738	.291*

$*p < .001$.

because even if differences in orthographic processing abilities had as their proximal cause differences in exposure to print, reading practice may simply be determined by how skilled the child is at phonological processing. If this is the case, then print exposure would not serve as a unique source of orthographic variance once phonological processing skill was partialed out.

The hierarchical regression analyses presented in Table 10.2 address this question. The criterion variable in the first analyses is the score on the letter-string choice task. Entered first are the three phonological processing tasks that attain a multiple R of .480. Entered last is the score on the TRT, and it accounts for an additional 8.5% of the variance. However, probably due to the modest size of the sample, this unique proportion of variance explained did not reach statistical significance. The second hierarchical regression was conducted with the experimental spelling test performance as the criterion variable. The three phonological tasks attained a multiple R of .595 when entered as the first three steps. When entered as the last step, the TRT accounted for a statistically significant 21.2% of the variance.

The third hierarchical regression was conducted with Stanford spelling subtest scores as the criterion variable. This task was assumed to contain substantial orthographic processing variance, because it is a spelling recognition test and because it displayed substantial correlations with performance on the letter-string choice task and the experimental spelling test. The three phonological tasks had a multiple R of .365 with performance on the spelling subtest. When entered as the fourth step, the TRT accounted for a substantial

TABLE 10.2
Unique Print Exposure Variance After Phonological
and Orthographic Processing Variance Is Partialed Out

Dependent Variable	Predictors	Multiple R	R² Change
Letter-string choice	Phoneme deletion 1	.020	.020
	Phoneme deletion 2	.435	.169*
	Phoneme transposition	.480	.042
	Title recognition test	.563	.085
Experimental spelling	Phoneme deletion 1	.432	.432*
	Phoneme deletion 2	.576	.245*
	Phoneme transposition	.595	.042
	Title recognition test	.753	.212*
Stanford spelling	Phoneme deletion 1	.224	.224*
	Phoneme deletion 2	.227	.001
	Phoneme transposition	.365	.083
	Title recognition test	.753	.432*
Stanford word reading	Phoneme deletion 1	.401	.401*
	Phoneme deletion 2	.490	.079
	Phoneme transposition	.504	.010
	Title recognition test	.777	.349*

*$p < .01$.

43.2% of additional variance. Thus, in two of the three analyses reported here, exposure to print (as measured by the TRT) accounted for significant variance in orthographic processing variance once individual differences in phonological processes had been statistically controlled. The orthographic processing knowledge or processing skill that is separable from phonological processes appears to be linked to individual differences in the student's experiential history of literacy activities.

The final hierarchical regression displayed in Table 10.2 simply illustrates that performance on the TRT also accounts for significant variance in Stanford Word Reading scores after phonological abilities have been partialed out. In summary, this study demonstrates that it is possible to separate variance in orthographic processing skill from variance in phonological processing ability very early in the reading acquisition process.

Voluminous evidence exists on the importance of phonological processing in early reading, but less is known about how orthographic processing skill and/or the buildup of an orthographic lexicon interacts with the early stages of reading acquisition. This study has linked at least part of this variance in orthographic structures and/or processes to variation in students' literacy environments, which can be measured with a very simple indicator. The study has demonstrated, in the orthographic domain, how reading might itself develop skills and knowledge bases that then serve to enable more efficient subsequent reading.

What Is the Relation Between Phonological Processing Skill and Print Exposure?

One unusual finding of potential theoretical significance concerns the different magnitudes of the correlations involving the print exposure measure. Although the TRT correlated strongly with both subtests of the Stanford Achievement Test and moderately with both orthographic processing measures, it failed to correlate with any of the phonological processing tasks. This finding at first might seem odd, because it would seem that exposure to print should facilitate phonological processes as well as orthographic processing ability. It would be natural to consider the current finding an anomaly had it not recurred in several previous studies. For example, in a study of third- and fourth-grade children, Cunningham and Stanovich (1990) found that the TRT displayed nonsignificant correlations of −.04 with a phoneme deletion task and .12 with a phonological choice decoding task. In a study of fifth-grade children, Cipielewski and Stanovich (1992) found that the phonetic analysis (decoding) subtest of the Stanford Achievement Test displayed correlations of .31 and .17 with two different measures of print exposure (the latter correlation not statistically significant). Finally, in a study of adult subjects (Stanovich & West, 1989), two measures of print exposure displayed correlations of .35 and .06 with pseudoword naming ability and correlations of .27 and .07 with performance on a phonological choice decoding task, only one correlation attaining significance in each case.

Thus, across a variety of ages, the correlations between measures of print exposure and measures of phonological processing skills remain quite modest. It is not the case that the print exposure indicators are insensitive: They displayed some high correlations with the word recognition, spelling, and orthographic tasks in the current study, and in other investigations they have displayed very strong correlations with vocabulary and other verbal abilities (Cunningham & Stanovich, 1991; Stanovich, 1993; Stanovich & Cunningham, 1992; West & Stanovich, 1991).

Study 2: A Longitudinal Study of First Through Third Grade

We extended our investigation of the contribution of phonological and orthographic processing to variation in word recognition skill by conducting a longitudinal study of first- through third-grade students. In addition to asking some of the same basic questions regarding the link between these variables, this study contains multiple measures of orthographic processing that were reliable enough to examine the patterns of covariance among the tasks. This is a timely investigation for the field. Although there has been great interest in the covariance structures of various phonological tasks (Wagner, Torgesen, & Rashotte, 1994; Yopp, 1988), a literature to which we ourselves have contributed (e.g., Stanovich, Cunningham, & Cramer, 1984), there has been less work on the relationships of the various tasks that we call measures of orthographic processing. In this study, we focused as well on the issue of task convergent validity and comparability. We asked the question of whether the several tasks in the literature that are labeled orthographic are measuring the same thing. We initially tested 62 first-grade students. Thirty-nine of these children remained when we tested the same children in third grade.

The students completed four phonological awareness tasks that varied in difficulty in Grade 1. The first task was Bradley and Bryant's (1985) oddity task. Four words were presented to the students, and they were required to choose which one sounded different in either the initial, final, or medial position (e.g., *rock, sock, pop, knock*). In the second task, phoneme deletion 1, the students were required to delete the initial phoneme of a word and pronounce the embedded word that remained. The stimuli were all words in which the initial consonant formed the entire onset (e.g., *pink, told, man, nice*). In phoneme deletion 2, the students were required to delete the initial phoneme from a series of 10 beginning consonant blend words (e.g., *stop, trick, spark, globe*). Phoneme deletion 3 was more difficult, and required the child to delete the final phoneme from a series of 10 final consonant blend words (e.g., *best, lift, just, craft*).

In second grade, the students completed a battery of tasks purportedly designed to assess orthographic coding skill. We chose six commonly employed tasks of orthographic processing. Our first task was the spelling subtest of the Peabody Individual Achievement Test (PIAT). Fifty words (plates 13 through 62) were used as stimuli. This task was individually administered using standardized procedures and instructions. In the Spelling subtest, the student is required to recognize which of four alternatives represents the correct spelling of a word. Because the alternatives are minimally different (e.g., *time, teim, tihm,* and *tiem*), performance is facilitated if the student has an accurate and complete orthographic representation of the stimulus stored in memory. The experimenter pronounced each word, used it in a sentence, and then pronounced the word again. The raw score on the test was used in the analyses that follow.

Five other measures of orthographic processing were group administered on a different day to the students. Three letter-string choice tasks were followed by a orthographic-choice and homophone-choice task. The first letter-string choice task (LSC1) with 16 pairs of three- to seven-letter strings was the same stimuli provided by Rebecca Treiman and employed in our previously discussed first-grade study. Two additional letter-string choice tasks were employed (see Siegel, Share, & Geva, 1995; Stanovich & Siegel, 1994). Letter-string choice task 2 (LSC2) contained 17 pairs of four-letter strings (e.g., *gwup-gnup, nitl-nilt, clid-cdil*) and letter-string choice task 3 (LSC3) contained 18 pairs of four- to five-letter strings (e.g., *fim-phim, booce-buice,* and *lerst-lurst*).

The orthographic choice task was adapted from the work of Olson and colleagues (e.g., Olson, Forsberg, & Wise, 1995; Olson, Wise, Conners, Rack, & Fulker, 1989). The students viewed pairs of letter strings that sounded alike (e.g., *rain-rane* and *boal-bowl*) and indicated which one was spelled correctly. Because the two strings sound the same when decoded, differences in phonological decoding ability cannot be the sole cause of performance differences on this task (indeed, it is possible that it is an interfering factor). Although students might still use phonological recoding to determine into what word the two strings map, the task requires a lexical representation be examined. Thus, the task to some extent reflects the accessibility and quality of the orthographic entries in the lexicon. Twenty-three pairs of phonologically similar letter strings were presented to the students on a sheet of paper. The experimenter told the students that each pair of letter strings contained one word that was spelled correctly and one that was spelled incorrectly. Students were then instructed to circle the correctly spelled word.

The homophone choice task was developed by Stanovich and West (1989). Seventeen pairs of phonologically identical but orthographically different words were presented to the students. The students were instructed to listen carefully to the experimenter, who would be reading short sentences (four to six words in length) to them. Each sentence was in the form of a question (e.g., Which is a part of the body?) that the students were instructed to answer by circling which of the two words was spelled correctly, according to the way it was used in the sentence (e.g., *feet* or *feat*). Each item was preceded by a question in this manner.

A new version of the TRT was developed for the third-grade students. It contained a total of 36 items: 23 actual children's book titles and 13 foils. The TRT was developed in conjunction with the classroom teachers and school librarian, and thus eliminated most books read in school. When administering the TRT, the same procedures used in earlier studies were employed.

An achievement test of reading and spelling ability—the Metropolitan Reading Achievement Test (MAT6), Elementary level—was administered in May of the third-grade year. The Elementary level of the MAT6 consists of vocabulary, word recognition, reading comprehension, and spelling tasks. The total raw score was used in the analyses discussed.

Is There Task Convergent Validity and Comparability Among the Orthographic Processing Tasks?

One of the central questions of this study was whether the tasks we call *orthographic knowledge* tasks are measuring the same thing. This question was answered in the affirmative. Interrelationships among the orthographic tasks were all significant at the .05 level with the exception of LSC1 and LSC2. The correlations were moderate in size and ranged from .32 to .73. The correlations were particularly strong between the PIAT and the other measures. LSC2 and LSC3 were highly correlated (.70), but less so with LSC1. The uniformly moderate correlations suggest that the several tasks in the literature we have labeled *orthographic* measures do indeed seem to be tapping the same construct.

We examined the relation between our orthographic measures assessed in second grade and the student's reading and spelling performance on the Metropolitan Achievement Test in third grade. All six of the orthographic tasks displayed significant correlations of moderate strength with later reading ability (LSC1 .57, LSC2 .62, LSC3 .67, orthographic choice .64, homophone choice .67, PIAT .74 with Metropolitan Achievement Test, $p < .01$). Some idea of the relative magnitude of the difference in performance on the orthographic tasks between readers of different abilities is provided in Table 10.3. Thirty-eight students who were assessed in the third grade were split into a group of 20 less-skilled readers and a group of 18 skilled readers based on their score on the Metropolitan Reading Test. The mean grade equivalent of the less-skilled group was 2.4, and the mean grade equivalent of the skilled

TABLE 10.3
Performance on Orthographic Tasks in Second Grade and TRT
in Third Grade as a Function of Third-Grade Reading
Ability on Metropolitan Achievement Test

Task	Skilled	Less Skilled	t
Letter-string choice1	11.06	9.25	−3.04*
Letter-string choice2	11.78	9.90	−3.42*
Letter-string choice3	13.56	10.85	−5.13*
Orthographic choice	19.56	16.00	−3.24*
Homophone choice	13.72	11.20	−3.84*
PIAT spelling	26.06	18.20	−5.23*
Title recognition	.32	.08	−5.74*

*$p < .01$.
Note. Median split on Metropolitan total reading (skilled group $N = 18$, less-skilled group $N = 20$).

group was 5.4. The scores of the two groups on these orthographic tasks and TRT were significantly different at the .01 level.

Can Orthographic Processing Ability Account for Unique Variance in Word Recognition?

As in the previous study, we sought to examine whether there is variance in word recognition that can be reliably linked to orthographic processing skill once variance due to phonological processing has been partialed out. Table 10.4 presents the results of four hierarchical regression analyses. The four phonological processing tasks from first grade were entered first, and collectively achieved a multiple R with Metropolitan Reading Test in third grade of .655. Next, we conducted a series of analyses in which each of the orthographic measures were forced in at the fifth step. We combined the

TABLE 10.4
Unique Variance in Third-Grade Metropolitan Performance
Predicted by Orthographic Processing After
Phonological Processing Variance Is Partialed Out

Step	Variable	R	R^2 Change	Partial r
Forced entry				
1.–4.	Phoneme 1, 2, 3, 4	.655	.429**	—
5.	Orthographic choice	.737	.115**	.488**
5.	Homophone choice	.701	.062*	.329*
5.	PIAT	.736	.113**	.445**
5.	LSC composite	.711	.076*	.365*

*$p < .05$, ** $p < .01$.

letter-string choice tasks into one composite score for these analyses. When the orthographic choice task was entered fifth, it accounted for a substantial 11.5% of additional variance. Similarly, when the score on the homophone choice test was entered as the fifth variable in the equation, it accounted for 6.2% of the variance in word reading scores ($p < .05$). The third hierarchical regression showed a basically similar result; when the PIAT was entered at the fifth step it also accounted for a substantial 11.3% additional variance. And, finally, when we entered the composite score of the three letter-string choice tasks in the fifth step after the four phonological measures it accounted for 7.6% additional variance in third-grade reading and spelling performance.

Thus, the linkage between orthographic processing ability and word recognition skill seems not to be the result of spurious linkages between orthographic processing skill and phonological abilities. Once again, we see there does seem to be variation in orthographic processing skill that is independent of phonological processes and that is linked to word recognition ability. The data reported in this study and our earlier one provide at least a tentative indication that phonological and orthographic processing skills are separable components of variance in word recognition during the beginning stages of reading acquisition. The findings are consistent with our investigations of the performance of older students and adults (Cunningham & Stanovich, 1990, 1991; Stanovich & West, 1989) and those of others (e.g., Barker, Torgesen, & Wagner, 1992; Bryant & Impey, 1986; Freebody & Byrne, 1988; Treiman, 1984) and thus provide converging evidence that orthographic processing skills are not entirely parasitic on the operation of phonological processes.

This, however, remains a controversial point in the literature. Nevertheless, any processing model of these relations that is eventually adopted will have to explain the reliable empirical finding reported here (and in other cross-sectional research with older students)—that tasks stressing orthographic processing predict variance in reading skill independent of phonological processing factors.

The Role of Print Exposure in the Buildup of the Orthographic Lexicon

Although exposure to print is related to both orthographic and phonological processes in early development, there have been some indications in the literature that it is more strongly related to orthographic processes (Barker et al., 1992; Olson et al., 1995). These empirical facts are consistent with Juel's (1994) conclusions that print exposure is related to getting a precise representation in the lexicon, but only indirectly related to phonological knowledge. In her longitudinal study of first- through fourth-grade students, Juel (1994) observed that although both orthographic and phonological knowledge develop from exposure to print, its effect on phonological (or cipher) knowledge will not be felt until a prerequisite amount of phonemic awareness is present. Thus, only after this milestone is achieved does print exposure foster quick application of the spelling-sound correspondences of the cipher, as well as word-specific lexical knowledge. As Juel (1994) pointed out:

> Most children do not appear to gain cipher knowledge merely by seeing lots of words. First-grade teachers must make sure that children learn to read the words in their readers. Sheer coverage of stories will not compensate for, nor remediate, poor decoding skill. Quality of word recognition in first grade (i.e., being able to recognize words) is more important than quantity of exposure to words. On the other hand, once there is high quality word recognition, then and only then does quantity of reading become critical. (1994, p. 124)

That print exposure's primary role at the beginning stages of word recognition may be more strongly related to the buildup of the orthographic lexicon and thus play a more indirect role in the development of phonological processing is supported by our studies and others (e.g., Barker et al., 1992). As discussed, we have consistently observed nonsignificant relationships between phonological processing and print exposure (e.g., Cipielewski & Stanovich, 1992; Cunningham & Stanovich, 1990; Stanovich & West, 1989) across a variety of ages. Thus, there is a growing consensus that print exposure's role in word recognition may have very specific effects in the development of word recognition skills.

Study 3: The Effects of Print Exposure in Predicting Reading Comprehension

We have been discussing the role of print exposure at the word level; however, there is reason to believe that print exposure is also implicated in comprehension growth. To go just briefly beyond the word, we discuss the results of a study (Cipielewski & Stanovich, 1992) showing that exposure to print predicted growth in reading comprehension over a period of 2 years.

Ninety-eight children were recruited for the study. Scores were available from the school's third-grade administration of the reading comprehension subtest of the Iowa Tests of Basic Skill, and from the school's fifth-grade administration of the reading comprehension subtest of the Iowa Tests of Basic Skills. In the fifth-grade year, the school also administered the Stanford Diagnostic Reading Test, and scores on the reading comprehension and phonetic analysis subtests were available.

We administered two measures of print exposure. The title recognition test (TRT) consisted of a total of 38 items: 25 actual children's book titles and 13 foils. The TRT was administered and scored just as the other TRTs. The author recognition test (ART) was a children's version of a measure used in previous adult studies of print exposure (Stanovich & West, 1989). Authors on the measure were chosen using the same procedures employed for the versions of the TRT. There were 40 names on the test: 25 actual children's authors and 15 foil names. Directions and scoring on the ART were the same as those on the TRT, with suitable alterations for content.

In the hierarchical regressions reported in Table 10.5, third-grade reading comprehension scores on the Iowa test are entered first, followed by the print exposure measures, as predictors of fifth-grade comprehension. These analyses thus determine whether the measures of print exposure can predict individual differences in growth in reading ability between third and fifth grade.

The results of the analyses indicate that, in the case of the fifth-grade Stanford reading comprehension scores, both measures of print exposure accounted for significant variance after third-grade reading comprehension is partialed out (11.0% and 8.1% unique variance for the TRT and ART, respectively). The TRT was also a significant unique predictor of fifth-grade Iowa reading comprehension scores (7.4% unique variance), but the ART was not.

With one exception (ART as a predictor of Iowa comprehension), the print exposure measures predicted individual differences in third- to fifth-grade growth in reading ability. The single exception occurs in the most

TABLE 10.5
Hierarchical Regressions Predicting Fifth-Grade Reading Ability

Step	Variable	R^2	R^2 Change	F to Enter
	Fifth-Grade Stanford Reading Comprehension			
1.	Iowa comprehension (third)	.416	.416	54.06*
2.	Title recognition test	.526	.110	17.38*
	Fifth-Grade Stanford Reading Comprehension			
1.	Iowa comprehension (third)	.349	.349	34.89*
2.	Author recognition test	.430	.081	9.02*
	Fifth-Grade Iowa Reading Comprehension			
1.	Iowa comprehension (third)	.297	.297	33.78*
2.	Title recognition test	.371	.074	9.25*
	Fifth-Grade Iowa Reading Comprehension			
1.	Iowa comprehension (third)	.236	.236	20.95*
2.	Author recognition test	.253	.017	1.56

*$p < .01$.

Note. The four regressions are based on Ns of 78, 67, 82, and 70, respectively. The dependent variables for the regression analyses are indicated by the spanner headings.

conservative analysis—one in which the Iowa comprehension test was both the criterion and the first predictor. Because these two tests share method variance, it is possible that the third-grade Iowa comprehension test partials too much variance from the fifth-grade criterion.

A second set of hierarchical regression analyses were run in order to include an additional control for spurious correlations between print exposure and comprehension growth. Decoding skill, as measured by the phonetic analysis subtest of the Stanford, was examined as a possible third variable mediating the linkage between reading experience and comprehension growth. This linkage might come about if, for example, good decoding skills support growth in reading comprehension and, at the same time, make reading more enjoyable, thus leading to greater print exposure. The analyses displayed in Table 10.6 controlled for decoding skill by entering performance on the phonetic analysis subtest into the regression equation prior to third-grade reading comprehension scores. The print exposure measures were entered last as predictors of the fifth-grade measures of reading ability.

The results of the hierarchical regression analyses displayed in Table 10.6 were analogous to the results displayed in Table 10.5. Both the TRT and

TABLE 10.6
Hierarchical Regressions Predicting Fifth-Grade Reading Ability

Step	Variable	R^2	R^2 Change	F to Enter
	Fifth-Grade Stanford Reading Comprehension			
1.	Stanford phonetic analysis	.101	.101	8.47**
2.	Iowa comprehension (third)	.454	.353	47.81**
3.	Title recognition test	.543	.089	14.11**
	Fifth-Grade Stanford Reading Comprehension			
1.	Stanford phonetic analysis	.072	.072	4.98*
2.	Iowa comprehension (third)	.393	.321	33.27**
3.	Author recognition test	.459	.066	7.55**
	Fifth-Grade Iowa Reading Comprehension			
1.	Stanford phonetic analysis	.093	.093	7.70**
2.	Iowa comprehension (third)	.339	.246	27.57**
3.	Title recognition test	.387	.048	5.72*
	Fifth-Grade Iowa Reading Comprehension			
1.	Stanford phonetic analysis	.041	.041	2.77
2.	Iowa comprehension (third)	.260	.219	18.56**
3.	Author recognition test	.269	.009	0.77

$*p < .05$, $** p < .01$.
Note. The four regressions are based on Ns of 77, 66, 77, and 66, respectively. The dependent variables for the regression analyses are indicated by the spanner headings.

ART were significant unique predictors of Stanford comprehension, but only the TRT was a significant predictor of fifth-grade Iowa comprehension scores after third-grade comprehension skill and decoding ability were partialed out.

Thus, in three of four analyses, individual differences in reading comprehension growth were reliably linked to differences in print exposure. These results were obtained even when decoding skill was partialed out from the analyses. That the TRT and ART survive as predictors of fifth-grade comprehension in most such analyses in this study is certainly suggestive of a role for print exposure in developing comprehension ability. Print exposure appears to be both a consequence of developed reading ability and a contributor to further growth in that ability.

Study 4: A Longitudinal Investigation of Early Reading Acquisition and Its Relation to Reading Experience

In the next study, we explore the reciprocal effects of a lifetime of reading. We examined the performance of a sample of students who had been tested as first graders (see Stanovich, Cunningham, & Feeman, 1984). About half of this sample were available 10 years later for testing as eleventh graders. Thus, we were able to go beyond contemporaneous correlations, extending the logic of the previous study, and track the growth of word recognition and comprehension ability with our cumulative indicator of variance in reading volume.

In first grade, we had administered a battery of tasks to 56 students that included measures of intelligence (Otis-Lennon School Ability Test and Raven Progressive Coloured Matrices, 1962), vocabulary (Peabody Picture Vocabulary Test, PPVT) and reading achievement (Gates-MacGinitie Reading Tests, 1978; Metropolitan Reading Achievement Test, 1978; Wide Range Achievement Test, 1978). The cognitive performance of the children was tracked during the subsequent 10-year period. Standardized test scores from the intervening period were available, and we discuss performance on the Metropolitan Achievement Test (1978) in third and fifth grades. In the latter part of this study, we assessed the students' reading comprehension (Nelson-Denny Reading Test), intelligence (Raven Advanced Progressive Matrices, 1962), and vocabulary (Peabody Picture Vocabulary Test, PPVT) in eleventh grade. We also assessed their level of print exposure via two high school versions of the ART and MRT. We combined the two measures to create a composite variable of print exposure labeled ARTMRTZ. Twenty-seven eleventh-grade students remained from our earlier sample. The 27 students who were available for testing did not differ significantly from the 29 students who were not available for testing on any of the first-grade tasks.

Predicting Growth in Comprehension Ability
From a Retrospective Measure of Print Exposure

The variance in performance on the recognition checklist measures of print exposure is presumably reflecting not just reading activities in the contemporaneous time period, but is also indexing engagement in literacy activities from several years before. It is this characteristic that led us to characterize the measure as a retrospective indicator of reading experiences occurring some time before the measure was administered. However, the actual retrospective reach of the instrument is unknown. In a series of analyses, we examined whether our indicator of print exposure in the eleventh grade could predict the growth of reading comprehension ability at earlier points in time.

Table 10.7 presents the results of these analyses. The first forced entry regression analysis illustrates the basic logic. First-grade performance on the Metropolitan Achievement Test (MAT) is entered first as a predictor of third-grade performance on the MAT and accounts for 49.5% of the variance. By entering ARTMRTZ as the second step in the equation we are asking whether print exposure, as assessed by these instruments in the eleventh grade, can predict individual differences in growth in reading comprehension ability between first and third grades. In this case, the answer is in the affirmative.

TABLE 10.7
ARTMRTZ as a Predictor of Reading
Comprehension Growth at Earlier Points in Time

Step	Variable	R	R^2 Change	F to Enter	Final Beta	Final F
		Criterion Variable: Grade 3 Metropolitan Reading Percentile Rank				
1.	Grade 1 MAT	.704	.495	20.58**	.445	6.03*
2.	ARTMRTZ	.770	.097	5.01*	.405	5.01*
		Criterion Variable: Grade 5 Metropolitan Reading Percentile Rank				
1.	Grade 1 MAT	.531	.282	8.64**	.193	0.93
2.	ARTMRTZ	.679	.178	7.27*	.541	7.27*
		Criterion Variable: Grade 5 Metropolitan Reading Percentile Rank				
1.	Grade 3 MAT	.689	.475	19.01**	.444	4.74**
2.	ARTMRTZ	.735	.066	3.02	.355	3.02
		Criterion Variable: Grade 10 Metropolitan Reading Percentile Rank				
1.	Grade 5 MAT	.640	.410	13.90**	.325	2.82
2.	ARTMRTZ	.734	.128	6.12*	.478	6.12*

$*p < .05, ** p < .01.$
Notes.   ARTMRTZ = Composite index of print exposure.
         MAT = Reading Comprehension subtest of the Metropolitan Achievement Test.

ARTMRTZ accounted for 9.7% ($p < .05$) of the variance in third-grade reading comprehension after first-grade comprehension ability had been partialed out. Thus, in this analysis we have an indication that an indicator of print exposure can track the generation of individual differences in comprehension during a period 7 or 8 years earlier.

The next regression equation indicates that the same was true when reading comprehension growth was measured from first to fifth grades. Individual differences in ARTMRTZ accounted for 17.8% ($p < .025$) of the variance in growth in comprehension ability from first to fifth grades. The next regression indicates that ARTMRTZ was not a significant predictor of changes in individual differences in comprehension between third and fifth grades (6.6% variance explained, $.05 < p < .10$). However, the last analysis indicates that ARTMRTZ was a significant predictor of changes in individual differences in comprehension between fifth and tenth grades (12.8% variance explained, $p < .05$). Taken collectively, these analyses indicate that an indicator of exposure to print administered in the high school years can predict the amount of growth in reading comprehension skill during the elementary school years and beyond.

Does Rapid Acquisition of Reading Skill in the Early Elementary Years Predict Proclivity Toward Reading in Adolescence?

So far, the analyses conducted have treated exposure to print as a predictor variable of criterion abilities such as reading comprehension. However, it is generally agreed that comprehension ability and exposure to print are in a reciprocal relationship (Anderson et al., 1988; Stanovich, 1986, 1993). Thus, it is equally important to ask the question: What cognitive variables predict the reading habits of adolescents?

We focus here on an even more specific question: Aside from their current level of reading comprehension ability, does the speed with which children attain reading fluency in their early years predict how engaged with print they will be as adolescents and adults? The regressions displayed in Table 10.8 provide data on this issue. Entered first in the hierarchical regression is eleventh-grade reading comprehension ability (Nelson-Denny performance) in order to remove the direct association between print exposure and contemporaneous reading ability. Listed next in Table 10.8 are alternative second steps in the regression equation. All three measures of first-grade reading ability (MAT, Gates, and WRAT) predicted significant variance (slightly over 10%) in eleventh grade print exposure even after eleventh-grade reading comprehension ability had been partialed out!

Table 10.8 indicates that the two measures of cognitive ability administered in first grade (Raven and PPVT) did not account for unique variance

TABLE 10.8
Hierarchical Regression Analysis Predicting Exposure
to Print in the Eleventh Grade

Step	Variable	R	R² Change	F to Enter	Partial r
Forced entry					
1. Grade 11 ND Comp		.604	.364	13.74**	—
2. Grade 1 MAT		.696	.121	5.61*	.435
2. Grade 1 Gates		.681	.100	4.45*	.396
2. Grade 1 WRAT		.686	.106	4.78*	.408
2. Grade 1 Raven		.632	.035	1.39	.234
2. Grade 1 PPVT		.641	.047	1.89	.270
2. Grade 3 MAT		.765	.221	11.09**	.588
2. Grade 5 MAT		.719	.153	6.72*	.484
2. Grade 11 Raven		.621	.022	0.40	.131
2. Grade 11 PPVT		.672	.088	3.82†	.371

*$p < .05$, **$p < .01$, †$p < .10$.
Notes. ND Comp = Nelson-Denny reading comprehension test.
MAT = Reading comprehension subtest of the Metropolitan Achievement Test.
Gates = Gates-MacGinitie reading comprehension subtest.
WRAT = Wide Range Achievement Test administered in Grade 1.
Grade 1 Raven = Raven's Colored Progressive Matrices.
PPVT = Peabody Picture Vocabulary Test.
Grade 11 Raven = Raven's Advanced Progressive Matrices.

in print exposure once eleventh-grade reading comprehension ability had been partialed out (and neither did the eleventh-grade administration of these tasks). Thus, an early start in reading is important in predicting a lifetime of literacy experience—and this is true regardless of the level of reading comprehension ability that the individual eventually attains. Finally, third- and fifth-grade measures of reading ability account for even more variance in print exposure than do the first-grade measures.

Several interesting linkages between the first-grade reading/cognitive measures and eleventh-grade outcomes were demonstrated in this study. First, the speed of initial reading acquisition, as operationalized by early test performance on the Gates (or MAT or WRAT, both of which produced highly convergent results) is at least moderately related to reading comprehension (.59) and vocabulary (.40) in Grade 11. We found through hierarchical analyses that early reading ability largely maintains its ability to predict these eleventh-grade cognitive outcomes even when the variance accounted for by two first-grade measures of general cognitive ability (Raven and PPVT) was partialed out.

When exposure to print is considered as a criterion variable (see Table 10.8), early reading acquisition in the first grade (as measured by either the Gates, MAT, or WRAT) can predict variance even after eleventh-grade comprehension ability is partialed out. This is a strong finding because it indicates that, regardless of the student's level of reading comprehension in the eleventh grade, if the student got off to a fast start in reading (as indicated by their first-grade reading ability score) then he or she is more likely to engage in more reading activity. Thus, a fast initial start at reading acquisition might well help to develop the lifetime habit of reading, irrespective of the ultimate level of reading comprehension ability that the individual attains.

In several analyses of the results of this study (see Table 10.7) we interpreted the print exposure measures administered in the eleventh grade as cumulative indicators of individual differences in reading habits that had been exercised for several years prior to the administration of the print exposure measures. The analyses displayed in Table 10.7 illustrate that, on such an interpretation, individual differences in exposure to print can predict differences in the growth in reading comprehension ability throughout the elementary grades and thereafter.

Obviously, any theoretical and/or practical implications drawn from these data must be highly tentative, because the attrition in our sample over the 10-year period resulted in a small sample size for the final investigation and, of course, our study was correlational. However, with these caveats clearly in mind, we would attempt the following extrapolation. Combining the implications of the outcomes illustrated in Tables 10.7 and 10.8, we can sketch a view of the reciprocal influences of print exposure and early reading acquisition as determinants of later reading comprehension and other cognitive outcomes. Early success at reading acquisition is one of the keys that unlocks a lifetime of reading habits. The subsequent exercise of this habit serves to further develop reading comprehension ability in an interlocking positive feedback logic (Juel, 1988; Juel et al., 1986; Snow, Barnes, Chandler, Goodman, & Hemphill, 1991; Stanovich, 1986, 1993). Our longitudinal analyses have provided us with a window on the past literacy experiences of our first-grade sample and provided some empirical clues to the cause of their subsequent divergences in verbal abilities.

CONCLUSIONS

Our first question—whether orthographic processing ability accounts for word recognition skill independent of phonological processing skill—was answered in the affirmative. We saw that orthographic knowledge is not completely parasitic on phonological processes. This is, however, a controversial point in the literature, because we know the development of orthographic processing skill must be somewhat dependent on phonological processing. Nevertheless, we argue that any processing model of these relations that is eventually adopted will have to explain the reliable empirical finding reported here (and in other cross-sectional research with older students)—that tasks stressing orthographic processing predict variance in reading skill independent of phonological processing factors.

We turned next to the question: Can these orthographic processing differences that are independent of phonological processing be linked to differences in children's literacy environment? Although correlational, the results of the studies presented in this chapter lend further support to the hypothesis that early word recognition ability plays a significant role in shaping one's later literacy environments. We can say that the rich appear to get richer not only in terms of absolute levels of reading ability, but in their levels of print exposure as well. Such rich-get-richer and their converse (poor-get-poorer) effects are becoming of increasing concern to educational practitioners (Adams, 1990; Chall, 1989) and are playing an increasingly prominent role in theories of individual differences (Anderson et al., 1988; Chall et al., 1990; Hayes, 1988; Hayes & Ahrens, 1988; Juel, 1988; Nagy & Anderson 1984; Siegel, 1989; Stanovich, 1986, 1988, 1993; van den Bos, 1989). Several authors have emphasized that, both in and out of school, readers of higher ability are progressively exposed to more print than are their less-skilled peers, thus leading to an increasing divergence in the performance of skilled and less-skilled readers (Allington, 1980, 1983, 1984; Anderson et al., 1988; Biemiller, 1977–1978; Juel, 1988; Nagy & Anderson, 1984; Nagy, Herman, & Anderson, 1985; Stanovich, 1986).

Although it is difficult to tease apart, we have attempted in this chapter to model the increasing divergence in children's reading ability as well as other cognitive outcomes, by examining both sides of the important role of reciprocal causation. Our longitudinal studies have permitted us to observe these effects, whereby children who get out of the gate quickly—who crack the spelling-to-sound code early on—appear to enter into a positive feedback loop. One of the benefits of these reciprocating effects may be a level of participation in literacy activities that leads to a lifetime habit of reading and thus sets the stage for future opportunities—opportunities not enjoyed by children who enter into this feedback loop more slowly. Fortunately, research is converging on an increasingly explicit model of these effects (see Adams, 1990; Share, 1995; Share & Stanovich, 1995) that might address the pressing social problem of the widening achievement disparities between between the educational haves and have-nots.

REFERENCES

Adams, M. J. (1990). *Beginning to read: Thinking and learning about print.* Cambridge, MA: MIT Press.

Allen, L., Cipielewski, J., & Stanovich, K. E. (1992). Multiple indicators of children's reading habits and attitudes: Construct validity and cognitive correlates. *Journal of Educational Psychology, 84*, 489–503.

Allington, R. L. (1980). Poor readers don't get to read much in reading groups. *Language Arts, 57*, 872–876.

Allington, R. L. (1983). The reading instruction provided readers of differing reading abilities. *The Elementary School Journal, 83*, 548–559.

Allington, R. L. (1984). Content coverage and contextual reading in reading groups. *Journal of Reading Behavior, 16*, 85–96.

Anderson, R. C., Wilson, P. T., & Fielding, L. G. (1988). Growth in reading and how children spend their time outside of school. *Reading Research Quarterly, 23*, 285–303.

Barker, K., Torgesen, J. K., & Wagner, R. K. (1992). The role of orthographic processing skills on five different reading tasks. Reading *Research Quarterly, 27*, 334–345.

Barron, R. (1986). Word recognition in early reading: A review of the direct and indirect access hypothesis. *Cognition, 24*, 93–119.

Biemiller, A. (1977–1978). Relationships between oral reading rates for letters, words, and simple text in the development of reading achievement. *Reading Research Quarterly, 13*, 223–253.

Bradley, L., & Bryant, P. E. (1985). *Rhyme and reason in reading and spelling.* Ann Arbor: University of Michigan Press.

Brown, J., Bennett, J., & Hanna, G. (1981). *The Nelson-Denny Reading Test.* Lombard, IL: Riverside.

Bryant, P., & Impey, L. (1986). The similarities between normal readers and developmental and acquired dyslexics. *Cognition, 24*, 121–127.

Cahan, S., & Cohen, N (1989). Age versus schooling effects on intelligence development. *Child Development, 60*, 1239–1249.

Ceci, S. J. (1990). *On intelligence . . . more or less: A bio-ecological treatise on intellectual development.* Englewood Cliffs, NJ: Prentice-Hall.

Ceci, S. J. (1991). How much does schooling influence general intelligence and its cognitive components? A reassessment of the evidence. *Developmental Psychology, 27*, 703–722.

Chall, J. S. (1989). Learning to read: The great debate 20 years later. *Phi Delta Kappan, 70*, 521–538.

Chall, J. S., Jacobs, V. A., & Baldwin, L. E. (1990). *The reading crisis: Why poor children fall behind.* Cambridge, MA: Harvard University Press.

Cipielewski, J., & Stanovich, K. E. (1992). Predicting growth in reading ability from children's exposure to print. *Journal of Experimental Child Psychology, 54*, 74–89.

Cunningham, A. E., & Stanovich, K. E. (1990). Assessing print exposure and orthographic processing skill in children: A quick measure of reading experience. *Journal of Educational Psychology, 82*, 733–740.

Cunningham, A. E., & Stanovich, K. E. (1991). Tracking the unique effects of print exposure in children: Associations with vocabulary, general knowledge, and spelling. *Journal of Educational Psychology, 83*, 264–274.

Dickinson, D. K., & Tabors, P. O. (1991). Early literacy: linkages between home, school and literacy achievement at age five. *Journal of Research in Childhood Education, 6*(1), 30–46.

Dunn, L. M., & Dunn, L. (1981). *Peabody Picture Vocabulary Test-Revised.* Circle Pines, MN: American Guidance Service.

Ehri, L. C. (1984). How orthography alters spoken language competencies in children learning to read and spell. In J. Downing & R. Valtin (Eds.), *Language awareness and learning to read* (pp. 119–147). New York: Springer-Verlag.

Ehri, L. C. (1987). Learning to read and spell words. *Journal of Reading Behavior, 19*, 5–31.

Ehri, L. C. (1992). Reconceptualizing the development of sight word reading and its relationship to recoding. In P. Gough, L. C. Ehri, & R. Treiman (Eds.), *Reading acquisition* (pp. 107–145). Hillsdale, NJ: Lawrence Erlbaum Associates.

Fielding, L., Wilson, P., & Anderson, P. (1986). A new focus on free reading: The role of the trade books in reading instruction. In T. Raphael & R. Reynolds (Eds.), *Contexts of literacy* (pp. 149–160). New York: Longman.

Freebody, P., & Byrne, B. (1988). Word-reading strategies in elementary school children: Relations to comprehension, reading time, and phonemic awareness. *Reading Research Quarterly, 23*, 441–453.

Gathercole, S. E., & Baddeley, A. D. (1989). Evaluation of the role of phonological STM in the development of vocabulary in children: A longitudinal study. *Journal of Memory and Language, 28*, 200–213.

Gates-MacGinitie reading tests (primary level A). (1978). Boston: Houghton-Mifflin.

Hayes, D. P. (1988). Speaking and writing: Distinct patterns of word choice. *Journal of Memory and Language, 27*, 572–585.

Hayes, D. P., & Ahrens, M. (1988). Vocabulary simplification for children: A special case of "motherese"? *Journal of Child Language, 15*, 395–410.

Hewison, J., & Tizard, J. (1980). Parental involvement and reading attainment. *British Journal of Educational Psychology, 50*, 209–215.

Iverson, B. K., & Walberg, H. J. (1984). Home environment and learning: A quantitative synthesis. *Journal of Experimental Education, 7*, 144–151.

Jastak, J. & Jastak, S. (1978). *The Wide Range Achievement Test-Revised.* Wilmington, DE: Jastak Associates.

Jorm, A., & Share, D. (1983). Phonological recoding and reading acquisition. *Applied Psycholinguistics, 4*, 103–147.

Juel, C. (1988). Learning to read and write: A longitudinal study of 54 children from first through fourth grades. *Journal of Educational Psychology, 80*, 437–447.

Juel, C. (1994). *Learning to read and write in one elementary school.* New York: Springer-Verlag.

Juel, C., Griffith, P. L., & Gough, P. B. (1986). Acquisition of literacy: A longitudinal study of children in first and second grade. *Journal of Educational Psychology, 78*, 243–255.

Liberman, I. Y., & Shankweiler, D. (1985). Phonology and the problems of learning to read and write. *Remedial and Special Education, 6*, 8–17.

Maclean, M., Bryant, P., & Bradley, L. (1987). Rhymes, Nursery-rhymes, and reading in early childhood. *Merrill-Palmer Quarterly, 33*, 255–281.

Mann, V. A., Tobin, P., & Wilson, R. (1987). Measuring phonological awareness through the invented spelling of kindergarten children. *Merrill-Palmer Quarterly, 33*, 365–391.

Metropolitan achievement tests–primary. (1978). New York: Psychological Corporation.

Morrison, F. J. (1987, November). *The "5-7" shift revisited: A natural experiment.* Paper presented at the meeting of the Psychonomic Society, Seattle, WA.

Nagy, W. E., & Anderson, R. C. (1984). How many words are there in printed school English? *Reading Research Quarterly, 19*, 304–330.

Nagy, W. E., Herman, P. A., & Anderson, R. C. (1985). Learning words from context. *Reading Research Quarterly, 20*, 233–253.

Olson, R., Forsberg, H., & Wise, B. (1995). Genes, environment and the development of orthographic skills. In V. W. Berninger (Ed.), *The varieties of orthographic knowledge I: Theoretical and developmental issues* (pp. 27–72). Boston: Kluwer.

Olson, R., Wise, B., Conners, F., Rack, J., & Fulker, D. (1989). Specific deficits in component reading and language skills: Genetic and environmental influences. *Journal of Learning Disabilities, 22*, 339–348.

Otis-Lennon school ability test (primary 1). (1979). New York: Psychological Corporation.

Payne, A. C., Whitehurst, G. J., & Angell, A. L. (1994). The role of home literacy environment in the development of language ability in preschool children from low-income families. *Early Childhood Research Quarterly, 9*, 427–440.

Perfetti, C. A. (1985). *Reading ability.* New York: Oxford University Press.

Raven, J. C. (1962). *Standard colored progressive matrices (Set I).* London: H. K. Lewis.

Raven, J. C. (1962). *Advanced progressive matrices (Set II).* London: H. K. Lewis.

Share, D. L. (1995). Phonological recoding and self-teaching: Sine qua non of reading acquisition. *Cognition, 55*, 151–218.

Share, D. L., McGee, R., & Silva, P. (1989). IQ and reading progress: A test of the capacity notion of IQ. *Journal of the American Academy of Child and Adolescent Psychiatry, 28*, 97–100.

Share, D. L., & Silva, P. A. (1987). Language deficits and specific reading retardation: Cause or effect? *British Journal of Disorders of Communication, 22*, 219–226.

Share, D. L., & Stanovich, K. E. (1995). Cognitive processes in early reading development: Accommodating individual differences into a model of acquisition. *Issues in Education: Contributions From Educational Psychology, 1*, 1–57.

Siegel, L. S. (1989). IQ is irrelevant to the definition of learning disabilities. *Journal of Learning Disabilities, 22*, 469–478.

Siegel, L. S., Share, D., & Geva, E. (1995). Evidence for superior orthographic skills in dyslexics. *Psychological Science, 6*, 250–254.

Snow, C. E., Barnes, W. S., Chandler, J., Goodman, I., & Hemphill, L. (1991). *Unfulfilled expectations: Home and school influences on literacy*. Cambridge, MA: Harvard University Press.

Stanovich, K. E. (1986). Matthew effects in reading: Some consequences of individual differences in the acquisition of literacy. *Reading Research Quarterly, 21*, 360–407.

Stanovich, K. E. (Ed.). (1988a). *Children's reading and the development of phonological awareness*. Detroit, MI: Wayne State University Press.

Stanovich, K. E. (1988b). The right and wrong places to look for the cognitive locus of reading disability. *Annals of Dyslexia, 38*, 154–177.

Stanovich, K. E. (1992). Are we overselling literacy? In C. Temple & P. Collins (Eds.), *Stories and readers: New perspectives on literature in the elementary classroom* (pp. 209–231). Norwood, MA: Christopher-Gorder.

Stanovich, K. E. (1993). Does reading make you smarter? Literacy and the development of verbal intelligence. In H. Reese (Ed.), *Advances in child development and behavior* (Vol. 24, pp. 133–180). Orlando, FL: Academic.

Stanovich, K. E., & Cunningham, A. E. (1992). Studying the consequences of literacy within a literate society: The cognitive correlates of print exposure. *Memory & Cognition, 20*, 51–68.

Stanovich, K. E., & Cunningham, A. E. (1993). Where does knowledge come from? Specific associations between print exposure and information acquisition. *Journal of Educational Psychology, 85*, 211–229.

Stanovich, K. E., Cunningham, A. E., & Cramer, B. (1984). Assessing phonological awareness in kindergarten children: Issues of task comparability. *Journal of Experimental Child Psychology, 38*, 175–190.

Stanovich, K. E., Cunningham, A. E., & Feeman, D. J. (1984). Intelligence, cognitive skills and early reading progress. *Reading Research Quarterly, 19*, 278–303.

Stanovich, K. E., & Siegel, L. (1994). Phenotypic performance profile of children with reading disabilities: A regression-based test of the phonological-core variable-difference model. *Journal of Educational Psychology, 86*(1), 24–53.

Stanovich, K. E., & West, R. F. (1989). Exposure to print and orthographic processing. *Reading Research Quarterly, 24*, 402–433.

Sternberg, R. J. (1985). *Beyond IQ: A triarchic theory of human intelligence*. Cambridge, England: Cambridge University Press.

Treiman, R. (1984). Individual differences among children in reading and spelling styles. *Journal of Experimental Child Psychology, 37*, 463–477.

Treiman, R., & Baron, J. (1983). Phonemic-analysis training helps children benefit from spelling-sound rules. *Memory & Cognition, 11*, 382–389.

Tunmer, W. E., & Nesdale, A. R. (1985). Phonemic segmentation skill and beginning reading. *Journal of Educational Psychology, 77*, 417–427.

van den Bos, K. P. (1989). Relationship between cognitive development, decoding skill, and reading comprehension in learning disabled Dutch children. In P. Aaron & M. Joshi (Eds.),

Reading and writing disorders in different orthographic systems (pp. 75–86). Dordrecht, The Netherlands: Kluwer.

Vellutino, F., & Scanlon, D. (1987). Phonological coding, phonological awareness, and reading ability: Evidence from a longitudinal and experimental study. *Merrill-Palmer Quarterly, 33*, 321–363.

Wagner, R. K. (1988). Causal relations between the development of phonological processing abilities and the acquisition of reading skills: A meta-analysis. *Merrill-Palmer Quarterly, 34*, 261–279.

Wagner, R. K., & Torgesen, J. K. (1987). The nature of phonological processing and its causal role in the acquisition of reading skills. *Psychological Bulletin, 101*, 192–212.

Wagner, R. K., Torgesen, J. K., & Rashotte, C. A. (1994). The development of reading-related phonological processing abilities: New evidence of bi-directional causality from a latent variable longitudinal study. *Developmental Psychology, 30*, 73–87.

Walberg, H. J., & Tsai, S. (1983). Matthew effects in education. *American Educational Research Journal, 20*, 359–373.

West, R. F., & Stanovich, K. E. (1991). The incidental acquisition of information from reading. *Psychological Science, 2*, 325–330.

West, R. F., Stanovich, K. E., & Mitchell, H. R. (1993). Reading in the real world and its correlates. *Reading Research Quarterly, 28*, 34–50.

Yopp, H. K. (1988). The validity and reliability of phonemic awareness tests. *Reading Research Quarterly, 23*, 159–177.

11

▼▼▼▼▼▼▼

Home Experiences Related to the Development of Word Recognition

Linda Baker
Sylvia Fernandez-Fein
Deborah Scher
Helen Williams
National Reading Research Center
and
University of Maryland Baltimore County

Researchers have documented many aspects of the home environment that seem to be important for optimal literacy development (for reviews, see Guthrie & Greaney, 1991; Morrow, 1989; Snow, Barnes, Chandler, Goodman, & Hemphill, 1991; Sonnenschein, Brody, & Munsterman, 1996; Sulzby & Teale, 1991). In this chapter we focus specifically on the role of home experiences in promoting the development of word recognition skills, a topic that has not been systematically explored either empirically or theoretically.

Other chapters in this volume have made it clear that phonological processing and grapheme–phoneme knowledge play critical roles in the development of word recognition (e.g., Ehri, chap. 1; Metsala & Walley, chap. 4). What role does the family play in the development of such skills? In the first section, we present descriptive evidence about children's home experiences that might be relevant to the development of word recognition. We consider home experiences relevant to the development of print knowledge and phonological awareness, based on information from parental reports, home observations, and analyses of parent–child interactions during book reading. Given the well-documented evidence of differences in the reading attainment of low-income and minority children, many researchers have looked to differential home experiences as contributing factors. Accordingly, we discuss available evidence of sociocultural differences in experiences related to word recognition to shed light on this issue. In the second section, we examine relations between children's home experiences and their emergent competencies in areas relevant to beginning reading. The chapter concludes with a discussion of the implications of the research for providing sound guidance to parents.

WHAT KINDS OF EXPERIENCES DO CHILDREN
HAVE AT HOME THAT MIGHT FACILITATE
THE DEVELOPMENT OF WORD RECOGNITION?

Children's Everyday Home Experiences Involving Print

Virtually every study of home influences on children's literacy development includes surveys, questionnaires, or interviews designed to acquire information about children's home experiences with print. Some studies also include qualitative examinations of children's experiences involving print, relying on direct observations of home literacy activities or parental diaries. One home literacy activity—shared storybook reading—has garnered particular attention. We discuss relevant data in the sections that follow.

Parents' Responses to Questionnaires and Rating Scales. A major source of information about children's home experiences is an ongoing longitudinal study directed by Linda Baker, Susan Sonnenschein, and Robert Serpell. It focuses on the development of literacy in urban children, both African American and European American, low income and middle income, and it includes a broad array of measures of home experiences, parental beliefs, and children's competencies (see Baker, Sonnenschein, et al., 1996; Baker, Serpell, & Sonnenschein, 1995; Baker, Sonnenschein, Serpell, Fernandez-Fein, & Scher, 1994; Serpell et al., 1997; Sonnenschein, Baker, Serpell, Scher, Fernandez-Fein, & Munsterman, 1996; Sonnenschein et al., 1997). Throughout this chapter we refer to the study as the *Early Childhood Project.* When children participating in the project were in prekindergarten, their mothers were questioned about children's participation in specific activities with the potential to foster the development of knowledge and competencies associated with early reading (see Baker et al., 1994, for details). The parent indicated the frequency of the child's participation in each activity using a four-point scale: 0—never; 1—rarely, less than once a week; 2—occasionally, at least once a week; and 3—often, almost every day. Within the area of reading, writing, or drawing activities, the parent rated engagement with the following specific types of books: educational (e.g., ABC books), picture books (i.e., books without a printed story), storybooks, and nonfiction books, as well as other printed material (e.g., magazines, comics); drawing; writing; and looking at books on his or her own.

All children participated regularly in experiences relevant to the development of knowledge about print. They had frequent experiences with storybooks; the overall mean rating was 2.39. No other types of books had mean frequency ratings above 2.0. The mean frequency rating for the child looking at books independently was 1.75, and the mean rating for writing was 2.39. The percentages of parents who reported that their child interacted with at least one type of book every day or almost every day differed as a function of income level; 90% of the middle-income parents reported daily book reading activity, whereas 52% of the lower-income parents did so. Income-related differences were also evident in reported frequency of visits to the library, favoring middle-income families.

Additional information about home literacy experiences relevant to the development of print knowledge comes from studies by Raz and Bryant (1990), Chaney (1994), Marvin and Mirenda (1993), and Elliott and Hewison (1994). Of particular interest in these studies, as in the Early Childhood Project, was whether there were sociocultural differences in the nature of children's experiences. In the Raz and Bryant study, low-income and middle-income parents of British preschoolers reported that their children looked at books on their own with comparable frequencies, but middle-income parents reported more frequent reading to their child, more books owned by the child, and more visits to the library. In Chaney's study, parents of 3-year-olds from a range of socioeconomic backgrounds reported that their children received some exposure to print. However, middle-class families routinely provided abundant exposure to a wide variety of literacy experiences, whereas the quantity of literacy experiences varied more among poorer and less well-educated families.

Marvin and Mirenda (1993) compared the home literacy experiences of low- and middle-income children using a mailed parent survey. Over 80% of all parents reported their children had access to picture or storybooks at home, 63% said the child used some type of reading material at home at least once a day, and 60% said their child practiced writing letters. Children also did not differ in their independent experiences with print. However, middle-income children reportedly went to the library more frequently and had more adult literacy materials in their homes.

Elliott and Hewison (1994) examined the home literacy activities of a somewhat older sample, 7-year-old British children from middle- and low-income families. Middle-income parents reported more frequent reading stories to their children, using flashcards to help children learn words, hearing children read, having books and magazines in the home, and having children experiment with the creation of words and sentences using flashcards.

We cannot compare the findings from these studies directly because of differences in the instruments and differences in the participant samples. Nevertheless, the general consensus is that children from various sociocultural groups have many relevant home literacy experiences, but middle-income children tend to have more frequent and/or more varied experiences of one sort or another.

It is often difficult to draw conclusions from the broader literature about the opportunities children have for learning skills related to word recognition in particular, because data are often aggregated across questions. Thus, researchers might ask parents whether they teach children letters of the alphabet and whether they play games with rhymes, but then the researchers create a composite measure of home literacy experience that incorporates responses to these questions along with questions about storybook reading and environmental print.

Interpretation of parental reports must always be made cautiously, especially when sociocultural differences are indicated. It may be that middle-income parents are more sensitive to societal expectations and thus more likely to respond based on social desirability. Senechal, LeFevre, Hudson, and Lawson (1996) recently argued that frequency ratings are subject not only to social desirability bias but also to variations in parents' interpretations of the questions and their difficulties in determining frequency reliably.

Observations and Parent Diaries. Reliance on ratings scales provides a limited picture of what is really going on in children's everyday lives. Observational and ethnographic studies have demonstrated that children in low-income and minority families do indeed have many experiences with print in their everyday lives, albeit not necessarily the conventional middle-class storybook reading (Anderson & Stokes, 1984; Goldenberg, Reese, & Gallimore, 1992; Heath, 1983; Taylor & Dorsey-Gaines, 1988; Teale, 1986). For example, Teale (1986) observed everyday home literacy experiences of low-income children of various ethnicities. He categorized the experiences into the following domains: daily living, entertainment, school or work related, religion, interpersonal communication, getting information, and literacy for the purpose of teaching the child. Few of the families engaged in frequent literacy activities for this latter purpose, nor did they read for pleasure; most reading was done for functional purposes.

Parents of children in the Early Childhood Project kept a diary documenting all of the activities that the child engaged in during the course of 1 week. The parents were not informed that our primary interest was in literacy, so their records were unlikely to be biased in this direction. A coding scheme for characterizing the reported experiences with print was devised, influenced in part by Teale (1986) and Goldenberg et al. (1992). We identified three main uses of literacy in the activities involving print, corresponding to three broad cultural themes: literacy is a source of entertainment; literacy consists of a set of skills that should be deliberately cultivated; and literacy is an intrinsic ingredient of everyday life, figuring prominently in daily living routines. Within the entertainment category were the following activities: joint book reading; independent reading; play involving print; incidental exposure to print; and visits to libraries. Within the skills category were homework and practice (Baker et al., 1994).

Table 11.1 shows the percentages of parents of prekindergarteners and first graders spontaneously reporting activities in each category as a function of income level. Consider first the prekindergarten data. The only significant income difference was in the entertainment domain; more middle-income parents than low-income parents reported that children interacted with books independently or of their own initiative (78% vs. 34%). Income differences were also evident in the proportion of print-related activities reported in the diaries that fell into each of the three broad domains. For the middle-income parents, the categorical distribution was 70% entertainment, 11% skills, and 20% daily living; whereas the distribution for the lower-income parents was 47% entertainment, 36% skills, and 17% daily living. These data suggest that middle-income families tend to show greater endorsement of the cultural theme of literacy as a source of entertainment than do low-income families, whereas low-income families tend to give more attention to the theme of literacy as a skill to be deliberately cultivated.

Consider now the diaries of the parents of first graders. Middle-income parents again reported that their children interacted with books independently or on their own initiative more frequently than the low-income parents reported concerning their own children (62% vs. 10%). Middle-income parents reported at least one instance of a daily routine involving literacy, whereas only 70% of the lower-income parents did. With respect to the proportion of print-related activities reported in the diaries that fell into each of the three broad domains, more than half of the references to literate activity reflected entertainment uses, whereas almost one third dealt with the

TABLE 11.1
Percentages of Parents Spontaneously Reporting Children's Print
Related Experiences in Various Domains at Least Once in Diaries

| | Type of Comparison | | | |
| | Prekindergarten | | First Grade | |
	Low Income (n = 31)	Middle Income (n = 10)	Low Income (n = 20)	Middle Income (n = 13)
Entertainment				
Joint book reading	59	67	50	62
Independent reading	34	78*	10	62*
Play involving print	41	67	65	85
Incidental print	45	22	65	92
Bookstore/library visits	3	22	0	23
Cultivation of literacy skills				
Homework	48	44	60	77
Practice	41	11	20	15
Daily routines	59	67	70	100*

*Comparisons of the two means immediately to left of asterisk were significant at $p < .05$.

cultivation of literacy skills. There were no significant income differences with respect to the skill theme as there were for children who were 2 years younger, perhaps because first graders were receiving explicit instruction in learning how to read in school.

The value of the diaries as a source of information about experiences relevant to the development of word recognition can best be revealed through the parents' own words. A mother of a prekindergartner illustrated the child's attention to words during storybook reading: "Him and daddy will read a book. He likes to listen to you when you read to him and then he likes to tell you the words you told him, so that makes it likes he's reading the book to you, but he's just memorizing the words."

Another mother described her prekindergarten child's independent inter-actions with a book (he read three "Spot" books): "He likes to lift the flags. Also, they are short and words are big, so he memorizes them very easily and pretends—or actually thinks—he's reading."

In one family, the prekindergarten child was so interested in print that she asked about letters on piano music books: "She was asking what letters on music were—she would point to a letter and I would tell her what it was; she would point to another letter, trace it with her finger . . . and when she finished with saying the words, she went back over it and say it. . . . She seemed to remember the letters as we came along them when we go to one she remembered, she would say it before I would say it."

Diaries of parents of the first graders included somewhat different expe-riences than did those of the prekindergarteners, although joint book reading was still a popular event. However, the interactions surrounding the book readings seem to have changed: "After reading her the story we discussed it to try to identify the characters and see if she understood what was read." The first-grade children appeared to be fascinated by the mechanics of reading and writing: "He sat next to me on the couch, asking, of course, many questions and he's intrigued by spelling words, so he'll spell them and I have to tell him what they are." The children also spent a lot of time playing school: "[Child], [brother], and [friend] went up to her room to play school. She was the teacher and she had a blackboard and chalk and was giving [brother] and [friend] homework." There was evidence that children were trying to read on their own and they were getting help from parents and siblings: "He is really starting to get in to reading alot. We all take turns helping but [older sister] must get alot [sic] of created [credit]. He likes to read to her more cause she makes a game out of it by playing school with him."

Parents of both prekindergarteners and first graders made many references to encouraging writing and reading through homework or practice of skills. Among the prekindergarten parents, one mentioned making her child "some dots of his name, address, and phone number to trace." Another parent mentioned she was "teaching her [child] how to spell and to identify the letters in her name using paper and pencils and flashcards." Many parents mentioned that their children were learning their ABCs through various means. One child was "playing with ABC magnets on refrigerator and singing ABCs." Another child was "learning how to write her ABCs and numbers." One mother observed that her child "traces ABCs from plastic to paper." Homework also facilitated learning the alphabet: "homework was the letter *R*, tracing the letter *r*, cutting out pictures that begin with the letter *r*." A parent of a first grader noted that her child "comes home from school and shows me her list of words for the upcoming week. We take 10 minutes to have her point and say different words."

References to attention to print in daily experiences most frequently focused on the child picking out items in grocery stores. A parent of a prekindergartener wrote, "unloaded groceries. He has a good time spelling every cereal box . . . draws on chalkboard with cereal box to copy letters."

As with rating scales, there are limitations to the diary approach in acquiring information about children's home experiences with print. Parents varied greatly in the amount of information they provided us, and failure to mention particular activities does not necessarily mean that they did not occur. However, the diaries are important because they show what parents *choose* to reveal about their children's everyday lives. The parents' values, as well as their perceptions of what the researchers really wanted to know, undoubtedly influence the content that gets recorded. The fact that middle-income parents wrote more about reading for entertainment than did low-income parents provides an indication that the middle-income parents view literacy as a source of pleasure, even if we must be cautious in inferring true differences in children's experiences. Another facet of the Early Childhood Project that assessed parents' beliefs about reading provided converging evidence that this sociocultural difference is real (Sonnenschein et al., 1997).

Shared Storybook Reading. As Snow (1994) argued, storybook reading may be construed less as an event in itself but rather as a microenvironment in which relevant experiences occur. Thus, it is not only the act of reading that is important, but also the kinds of conversations that reader and child have with one another during the reading session, the affective quality of those interactions, the print-related discussions that might ensue, and so on. This suggests that frequency measures alone are not very informative; qualitative analyses of what goes on during book reading interactions are also needed. This is especially true when the goal is to identify aspects of storybook reading that may be conducive to the development of word recognition. Even qualitative analyses have not proved very informative to date, because few researchers have examined the nature and degree of print-related talk during the book readings; the focus is typically on content-related questions and commentary, and talk about nonimmediate events (e.g., Bus & van

IJzendoorn, 1995; Dickinson, DeTemple, Hirschler, & Smith, 1992; Pellegrini, Perlmutter, Galda, & Brody, 1990). On the other hand, as we see later in our discussion, the few studies addressing this issue have reported minimal attention to print during storybook reading (Bus & van IJzendoorn, 1988; Munsterman & Sonnenschein, 1997; Phillips & McNaughton, 1990; Yaden, Smolkin, & Conlon, 1989).

Phillips and McNaughton (1990) asked 10 middle-income New Zealand parents to read researcher-supplied narrative storybooks with their 3- and 4-year-old children over a period of 4 or 6 weeks. They coded the types of "insertions" (comments and questions) made by the reader or the child as to whether they were print related (references to letters, words, pages, and book handling), narrative related, or other. Only 3.3% of the total insertions were print related, whereas 85% were narrative related. Despite this lack of attention to print during storybook reading, the children knew an average of 13 letters, 2 words, and 5 concepts about print.

Similar lack of speech about print was evident in analysis of dyadic storybook reading within the Early Childhood Project (Munsterman & Sonnenschein, 1997). Kindergarten children were observed during shared book reading with the person they were most likely to read with at home, usually either the mother or an older sibling. There were 30 dyads, 25 of whom were low-income. All parents reported at least occasional shared storybook reading; only 3 said this occurred less than once a week. Each dyad read one unfamiliar storybook supplied by the researcher and, if available, one familiar book from the child's home library. Munsterman and Sonnenschein coded the utterances into the categories of content-related immediate speech, content-related nonimmediate speech, story structure/organizational speech, and print/skills related speech. Examples in this latter category are: "N is also in your name" and "What's that word? Spell it." Print/skills-related and nonimmediate content-related utterances occurred least frequently and did not differ from one another; content related-immediate talk was most frequent. Only 6.3% of total speech was skills/print related, and the mean frequency of such speech was .82 utterances per book. However, print-related talk was more common with certain types of books, such as rhyming, alphabet books or predictable language books. Fifteen percent of the familiar books read were of this type. The percentage of skills comments during readings of these types of books was 64%, with a frequency of 5.75 per book, in contrast to the percentage of skills comments for all familiar books of 11%, with an average of only 1.48 utterances per book. Parent and sibling readers did not differ significantly in the extent of print-related speech.

Bus and van IJzendoorn (1988) systematically compared interactions across the two genres of books: storybooks and ABC books. They found that mothers of 3- and 5-year-old children engaged in more talk about the print in the ABC book than that in the storybook. Moreover, the children engaged in more "protoreading" behaviors with the ABC book; for example, they tried to spell words and identify letters.

The child's own contribution to the book reading interaction is perhaps more important than the parent's. Information that the child solicits may be processed more deeply because it is of greater interest to the child than is unsolicited information provided by the parent or questions asked by the parent that disrupt the child's own engagement in the story. As Yaden et al. (1989) noted, there has been much anecdotal evidence that children ask questions about the print they encounter, but not much systematic investigation. Durkin (1966) asked parents whether early readers asked about letters, words, sounds, and other aspects of books. Durkin found that they did, but most research suggests that the majority of questions asked by preschoolers focus on illustrations rather than print.

Yaden et al. (1989) explored the kinds of questions preschool children spontaneously asked during storybook reading at home with parents over the course of 1 or 2 years. Questions included those about (a) graphic form (letter configuration, letter name, letter sound, punctuation, written word form, written word name, spelling, form of multiple word arrays, name of multiple word arrays); (b) word meanings; (c) oral (story) text; (d) illustrations; and (e) book conventions. Children asked the most questions about illustrations, followed by questions about story text; there were far fewer questions about graphic form, although all children did ask such questions. The percentages of total questions about graphic form ranged from 3% to 24% (mean = 8.4). The child who addressed 24% of his questions to print was reported by his mother to be asking about other print in his environment and seemed to be trying to decode on his own. Consistent with findings discussed previously, questions about print were more likely with certain types of books, such as alphabet books and a book with big speech balloons. Perhaps when print is more salient in a book, children's attention is more likely to be directed toward it.

The familiarity that occurs with repeated readings of a book also leads children to focus more attention on print, as shown in a school-based study by Morrow (1988). Morrow suggested there may be a developmental transition in the kinds of things children talk about during storybook reading; the earliest appearing focus is on illustrations, then story meaning, and only later on print. Bus and van IJzendoorn (1995) proposed a similar developmental model.

Information relevant to learning about print through shared storybook reading comes not only from analyses of interactions when parents read to children, but also when children read to parents. Elliott and Hewison (1994) observed 7-year-old children in Britain from various sociocultural groups read aloud to their parents, and analyzed the kinds of corrections that parents provided. Working-class families put a strong emphasis on phonics when correcting (e.g., sound it out), whereas the middle-class mothers put more emphasis on strategies oriented around comprehension. In many of the lower-income families, the overall orientation tended to be on reading as an exercise, rather than reading for meaning; there was an emphasis on accuracy rather than comprehension and interest. Similar emphasis on print was observed by Goldenberg et al. (1992) in the storybook interactions of low-income Hispanic kindergartners and their parents. Parents gave little attention to the meaning inherent in the storybooks; rather, they focused on the associations of written symbols with their corresponding oral sounds.

It is clear that the majority of experiences children have during shared storybook reading do not involve discussion of the print. This is not meant to imply that storybook reading is of little value for beginning word recognition, but rather that its influence is likely to be more indirect, as in fostering vocabulary knowledge and an interest in learning to read.

Experiences With Educational Books.   Use of explicitly educational books, such as ABC books, is likely to promote skills directly related to word recognition. However, use of these books is relatively infrequent. Phillips and McNaughton (1990) asked parents to keep a diary of book reading with their children over the course of 28 days. Only 4.8% of the books that were read were classified as educational (e.g., alphabet books, labeling books, number books). Within the Early Childhood Project, storybooks were read with much greater frequency than were educational books (Baker et al., 1994). Sociocultural differences in the availability of such books were reported by McCormick and Mason (1986): 47% of parents receiving public assistance said they had no alphabet books in the home, whereas only 3% of professional families said they had none.

Summary.   Preschool children growing up in literate societies such as the United States have frequent experiences with print. Storybook reading is a common occurrence, especially among middle-income families. However, there is relatively little attention to print during shared storybook reading. More attention occurs when books are read repeatedly or when ABC books are used. In most families, however, ABC books are not used very often in comparison to other types of books. Nevertheless, observations and diary reports of everyday activities show that children have other opportunities to learn about print. These include talking about the print encountered through daily routines such as grocery shopping and practicing writing letters of the alphabet. Parents differ in the relative emphases they place on reading as a source of entertainment and reading as a set of skills to be cultivated; these differing perspectives affect the kinds of literacy opportunities they make available to their children.

Children's Everyday Home Experiences Involving Rhyme

In addition to providing children with useful knowledge about print, a variety of home experiences might foster the development of phonological awareness. Many people have suggested that children develop phonological awareness through exposure to books with rhymes, to poems, to rhyming verses and songs, and to rhyming language play (e.g., Hannon, 1995; Treiman, 1991). We now consider empirical evidence of such experiences.

Children's Experiences Involving Rhyme. In the Early Childhood Project, parents of prekindergartners rated frequency of participation in singing, word games, and hand-clap games—activities likely to include rhyme. Parents of all sociocultural groups reported high frequencies of engagement in singing, with a mean rating of 2.44 out of 3. Participation in word games and hand-clap games was relatively infrequent (mean ratings = .83 and 1.02 respectively; Baker et al., 1994).

Sociocultural differences in home experiences related to rhyme have been reported in several different studies. Fernandez-Fein and Baker (1997) found that middle-income families reported that their preschool children had more frequent engagement in word games (usually involving rhyme) than low-income families reported. Marvin and Mirenda (1993) compared the home literacy experiences of low- and middle-income children using a parent survey, and found that a high percentage of all families reported they sang children's songs (82%), but a higher percentage of parents of children in the middle-income group reported reciting rhymes, poems, or other jingles than did those in the low-income group. Similarly, Elliott and Hewison (1994) found that British middle-class parents of 7-year-olds reported more frequent teaching of nursery rhymes and songs than did working-class parents. In contrast, Raz and Bryant (1990) found no reported differences in exposure to rhymes among low-income and middle-income British preschoolers.

Children are also exposed to rhymes in books, although it does not seem to be a high-frequency event. Parents in the Early Childhood Project were asked whether their children interacted with books that contain rhyme, and 67% noted that, at least occasionally, their child did so. Dickinson et al. (1992) asked mothers of 4-year-old low-income children to read a familiar favorite book to their child, and found that nursery rhyme books were selected just 10% of the time and rhyming/predictable narratives 5%.

Diaries and Observations. Young children often produce rhymes in their own poems and songs. Dowker (1989) studied rhyme and alliteration in poems elicited from a group of socioculturally diverse children between 2 and 6 years of age. She found that 42% of their poems contained rhyme and

26% contained alliteration. Evidence of preschoolers' language play also comes from Heath's (1983) ethnographic study. Heath reported that preschool girls in Trackton, a mill town with a large African American population, engaged in older girls' playsong games. Playsongs included jump-rope songs, hand-clap songs, as well as "made-up" playsongs that accompanied a wide variety of activities. When the older girls read books to their younger siblings (which they did only rarely), they chose alphabet books or nursery rhyme books that lent themselves to sing-song performance. For boys in the community, clever language play involving rhyme and alliteration was highly valued.

Fernandez-Fein and Baker (1997) characterized the rhyme and alliteration experiences of prekindergarten children within the Early Childhood Project as well as a larger sample of middle-income children. Children from diverse sociocultural backgrounds tended to be familiar with a similar set of rhyming routines and songs. Children were not as familiar with tongue twisters, routines that contain alliteration.

The diaries of parents of prekindergarten children in the Early Childhood Project revealed participation in activities that might promote phonological awareness. The most common oral language activity mentioned in the diaries was singing. Another oral activity mentioned by a number of parents was reciting the ABCs. Rhyming activities were specifically mentioned by 10% of the families. These activities involved saying rhyming words, saying or reading nursery rhymes, and reciting poems. In most of these cases, the child initiated the rhyming activity.

Summary. Although we must again be cautious in the conclusions we draw from data based on parental reports, it seems clear that children have frequent exposure to rhyme through singing. However, learning a song that contains rhyming words does not require the same conscious reflection on the sounds of the language as does playing games that require the child to produce rhyming words or words that start with a particular letter of the alphabet. These activities are less common, and there is some evidence from frequency ratings that low-income children experience them less frequently than do middle-income children. On the other hand, ethnographic observations reveal that language play is common among diverse sociocultural groups.

HOW DO CHILDREN'S HOME EXPERIENCES RELATE TO THE DEVELOPMENT OF WORD RECOGNITION SKILLS?

In the previous sections, we presented descriptive information about children's experiences at home that have the potential to promote the skills needed for word recognition, either directly or indirectly. In this section we consider the effects of specific kinds of experiences on children's emergent competencies in relevant areas, such as phonological awareness and orthographic knowledge, as well as word recognition per se.

Relations Between Knowledge of the Letters of the Alphabet and Beginning Reading

Many parents believe that part of their role in helping children learn to read is teaching them the letters of the alphabet, and thus they engage in direct instruction of letter names and letter-sound correspondences. Sonnenschein, Baker, and Cerro (1992) asked middle-income mothers of 3- to 5-year-olds to identify specific skills in any domain of development that they were teaching their children at home. The most frequently mentioned skills were emergent literacy skills, which included letter recognition, spelling-sound correspondences, reading, writing letters of the alphabet, and writing; overall, 90% of the mothers mentioned one or more of these skills. The mothers took advantage of the informal educational opportunities afforded by their homes, reporting that they used street signs and food containers to teach the alphabet.

What is the impact of such direct instruction? Not unexpectedly, children who receive instruction from parents in letter naming score higher on tests of letter recognition than do those who have not received such instruction (Hess, Holloway, Price, & Dickson, 1982). Crain-Thoreson and Dale (1992) reported that exposure to instruction in letter-sound correspondences predicted knowledge of print conventions and invented spelling of 4½-year-olds. According to parental reports obtained by Burns and Collins (1987), gifted kindergartners who were early readers had more exposure at home to discussions of letter-sound correspondences, letter names, and word identification experiences than did those who were not early readers.

There is ample evidence that knowing the letters of the alphabet is important for beginning reading, but it is also clear that just teaching children to name the letters of the alphabet is not sufficient (Adams, 1990). What does seem to be important, as Ehri (1984) suggested, is that letter names help children learn to associate phonemes with printed letters. In support of Ehri's position, children's letter knowledge in the Early Childhood Project in prekindergarten was significantly correlated with their performance on rhyme detection and rhyme production measured concurrently (Sonnenschein, Baker, Serpell, Scher, Fernandez-Fein, & Munsterman, 1996). In addition, Wagner, Torgesen, and Rashotte (1994) determined that letter-name knowledge exerted a modest causal influence on phonological processing abilities in a longitudinal study of 244 children from kindergarten to second grade. Accuracy of letter naming is not the only important variable; ease or fluency of naming is also important. Walsh, Price, and Gillingham

(1988) found that children's speed of letter naming in kindergarten was strongly related to later progress in reading.

Exposure to Environmental Print
and Beginning Word Reading

Does exposure to environmental print facilitate the development of reading? Mason (1980) suggested that reading failure may occur if children do not have experiences with environmental print during the preschool years that help them learn to recognize and name letters. However, there is little empirical evidence of a direct connection. According to parental reports obtained by Burns and Collins (1987), intellectually gifted kindergarten readers and nonreaders had statistically comparable amounts of exposure to environmental print. Masonheimer, Drum, and Ehri (1984) concluded that children who were experts at "reading" environmental print did not pay much attention to the print itself.

It appears that exposure to environmental print alone is unlikely to foster knowledge of individual letters and words unless parents and others explicitly discuss letters and words with children. Rather, environmental print may be valuable in orienting children to print, to the notion that print is meaningful and serves a specific function.

Relations Among Exposure to Rhyme,
Phonological Awareness, and Early Reading

It is often assumed that language play helps children develop their rhyme and alliteration skills. Some empirical evidence is available in support of this view (Fernandez-Fein & Baker, 1997; MacLean, Bryant, & Bradley, 1987), but other studies have yielded conflicting evidence (Chaney, 1994; Raz & Bryant, 1990). MacLean et al. (1987) demonstrated in a longitudinal study that there is a relation between children's knowledge of nursery rhymes and their phonological awareness, as measured by rhyme and alliteration detection and production tasks. Furthermore, knowledge of nursery rhymes and of rhyme and alliteration was related to early reading measured 15 months later. Bryant, Bradley, Maclean, and Crossland (1989) reported that the relations found after 15 months continued to apply over a 3-year period, even after accounting for differences in social background. The authors provided evidence that nursery rhymes enhance children's sensitivity to rhyme, which in turn helps them learn to read. Although Bryant et al. did not specifically ask parents about their role in fostering knowledge of nursery rhymes, they implied that home experiences were responsible.

Fernandez-Fein and Baker (1997) more directly examined preschool children's sensitivity to rhyme and alliteration in relation to home experiences as well as nursery knowledge. Participants included 39 prekindergartners in the Early Childhood Project and 20 additional African American and European American middle-income children. Five tasks adapted from MacLean et al. (1987) assessed phonological competencies: rhyme detection, rhyme production, alliteration detection, alliteration production, and nursery rhyme knowledge. Parents provided information about the frequency of their child's exposure to activities that might foster rhyme and alliteration sensitivity, including word games; hand-clap games; singing; and interactions with storybooks, picture books, educational books, and nonfiction books.

Frequency of participation in word games was significantly correlated with performance on the rhyme detection task ($r = .39$), the rhyme production task ($r = .47$), and the nursery rhyme knowledge task ($r = .32$), suggesting that word games may be important in the development of rhyme sensitivity. Frequency of engagement with books, as indexed by a composite score, was also related to these phonological measures: rhyme detection ($r = .47$), rhyme production ($r = .45$), and nursery rhyme knowledge ($r = .38$). Multiple regression analysis showed that nursery rhyme knowledge accounted for 39% of the variance in sensitivity to rhyme, consistent with the findings of MacLean et al. (1987) and Bryant et al. (1989). Frequency of participation in word games accounted for a significant amount of additional variance (5%), but experiences with books did not.

Information about later progress in word recognition was available for those students who were also participants in the Early Childhood Project (Baker & Mackler, 1997). During prekindergarten as well as kindergarten, children were given the four assessments of phonological awareness as well as the test of nursery rhyme knowledge. They also were given tests of their lowercase and uppercase letter knowledge. In the spring of their second grade year, the Woodcock-Johnson Word Identification test and the Word Attack test were administered to the children as part of a larger assessment battery. We first determined whether prekindergarten or kindergarten performance on the various competency measures was a better predictor of Grade 2 performance on the two outcome measures. The strongest significant predictors on the nursery rhyme tasks, the letter tasks, the rhyme tasks, and the alliteration tasks were then entered into a regression equation. For Word Attack, the predictors were kindergarten nursery rhyme knowledge, kindergarten lowercase-letter knowledge, prekindergarten alliteration detection, and prekindergarten rhyme detection. Nursery rhyme knowledge was the strongest predictor, accounting for 36% of the variance; letter knowledge accounted for an additional 11% of the variance, and alliteration detection 10%. The predictors for Word Identification were kindergarten nursery rhyme knowledge, kindergarten lowercase-letter knowledge, prekindergarten rhyme production, and kindergarten alliteration detection. Once again, nursery rhyme knowledge was the strongest predictor, accounting for 48% of the variance, and letter knowledge contributed an additional 18%.

Interestingly, nursery rhyme knowledge was not a significant predictor of second-grade word recognition when it was assessed in first grade in a different group of children just recruited into the project. Rather, alliteration detection and uppercase-letter knowledge were significant predictors. Nursery rhyme knowledge is based at least in part on children's home experiences, and other research has suggested that home experiences become less important as children progress through school (Chall, Jacobs, & Baldwin, 1990). These findings are also consistent with the large literature showing the importance of letter knowledge on beginning word recognition.

Chaney (1994) examined relations of home experiences to phonological awareness among 3-year-old children. Family literacy, based on a composite score, was significantly correlated with phonological awareness scores ($r = .31$), but it did not account for any of the variance in phonological awareness once child age and language development scores were controlled. It is not clear, however, that controlling for language development is appropriate in this context. Moreover, use of a composite measure that included book reading, child interest, library use, and other measures may have masked specific contributions of experiences with rhymes.

Raz and Bryant (1990) examined relations between home experiences, phonological awareness, and early reading. Four- and five-year-old British children from middle-income and low-income families were tested over a period of 18 months, and their mothers were interviewed. Multiple regression analyses using sensitivity to rhyme as the criterion variable and measures of the children's home experiences as predictor variables revealed that none of the home variables contributed significantly to phonological awareness. That one of the home measures was similar to the word games measure used by Fernandez-Fein and Baker (1997) reflects a failure to replicate. Children's phonological awareness scores predicted later reading up to 18 months later. Middle-income children were more successful at reading than were low-income children, but the difference between the groups on word recognition were eliminated once differences in phonological awareness were controlled.

Methodological differences among the studies reviewed in this section make it difficult to generalize, but there is at least some evidence that children's home experiences involving rhyme, including exposure to nursery rhymes and language play, influence children's sensitivity to rhyme. These experiences are related, either directly or indirectly, to children's early reading skills.

Relations of Home Reading Activity
to Word Recognition Skills

Many studies of home influences on literacy development have explored the effects of shared storybook reading. The government-sponsored report, *Becoming a Nation of Readers* (Anderson, Hiebert, Scott, & Wilkinson, 1985), emphasized the importance of home storybook reading, with the widely quoted assertion that reading is the single most important thing parents can do to help prepare their children for reading. Indeed, this position goes back as far as the turn of the century, when Huey (1908) wrote, "The secret of it all lies in the parents reading to and with the child" (p. 32).

Two recent syntheses of the literature on the effects of storybook reading concluded that storybook reading accounts for approximately 8% of the variance in outcome measures such as vocabulary development, reading achievement, and emergent literacy (Bus, van IJzendoorn, & Pellegrini, 1995; Scarborough & Dobrich, 1994). Interestingly, Bus et al. interpreted their data as indicative of positive support for the value of storybook reading, whereas Scarborough and Dobrich interpreted their data as indicating that storybook reading really does not contribute as much as has been assumed. Bus et al. were critical of some aspects of the Scarborough and Dobrich synthesis, as were Dunning, Mason, and Stewart (1994) and Lonigan (1994), but all of the researchers concurred that the evidence is not as compelling as one might think given the degree to which storybook reading is promoted.

Relations Between a Focus on Print During Shared Book Reading and Emergent Competencies.   Does storybook reading help children develop an understanding of grapheme–phoneme correspondences? Goodman (1986) suggested that with repeated joint storybook reading experience, children come to pay closer attention to the print, noticing correspondences between the words the caregiver is reading and the letters on the page. However, Wells (1986) suggested that the role of storybook reading in enhancing awareness of print and speech may be overestimated. We consider here the evidence related to this issue.

It has proven difficult to detect relations of print-related speech during storybook reading with outcome measures, because so little such speech seems to occur, as we discussed previously. For example, Munsterman and Sonnenschein (1997) were unable to test their hypothesis that the frequency of print-related utterances would predict children's phonological awareness and knowledge about print because so little such talk occurred. However, Bus and van IJzendoorn (1988) found that the extent to which children focused on print in an ABC book was positively correlated with a variety of emergent literacy measures, including letter-name knowledge, conventions of print, functions of print, and word construction. Attention to the print in the storybook was correlated only with the measure of letter-name knowledge. The extent to which mothers focused on meaning in the ABC book was *negatively* associated with these emergent literacy measures.

Can knowledge of print be acquired from any story reading experience, or only from story reading interactions that target the print directly? Given that so few interactions do target print directly, the source of such learning must be either incidental or it must occur through other avenues. It is easier to credit incidental learning about the conventions of print (e.g., book handling, directionality) than it is specific knowledge of letters and spelling-sound correspondences. Correlations have been reported between book reading and preschool measures of orthographic knowledge and general concepts about print (e.g., Wells, 1986), but these "may be explained by the fact that families that practice storybook reading also engage in a number of other literacy activities, some of which may be more closely related to these print skills" (Phillips & McNaughton, 1990, p. 211).

Relations Between Frequency of Book Reading and Skills Related to Word Recognition. Relatively few studies have specifically linked home reading activity to word recognition, focusing instead on emergent literacy skills or global reading achievement (Bus et al., 1995; Scarborough & Dobrich, 1994). With respect to component skills, Chaney (1994) found that a composite measure of family literacy predicted 3-year-old children's alphabet concepts. In the Early Childhood Project, frequency of storybook reading in kindergarten predicted performance on a composite measure of orientation toward print (including letter knowledge, concepts about print, knowledge of the functions and uses of print materials), but not a composite measure of phonological awareness (including rhyme detection, rhyme production, alliteration detection, alliteration production, and nursery rhyme knowledge) assessed in kindergarten (Sonnenschein, Baker, Serpell, Scher, Goddard-Truitt, & Munsterman, 1996). Using an entirely different approach to measuring book reading by first graders, Cunningham and Stanovich (1993) found that print exposure was related to orthographic processing but not phonological awareness (see Cunningham & Stanovich, chap. 10, this volume).

With respect to global reading achievement, Williams and Silva (1985) found that the number of books read to children when they were aged 3 and 5 predicted their reading achievement at age 7, and a similar predictive pattern was reported by Wells (1986). Within the Early Childhood Project, composite measures of total book reading in prekindergarten and kindergarten were significantly correlated with the CTBS comprehension and vocabulary tests in first grade.

Evidence regarding effects of storybook reading on word recognition per se comes from Crain-Thoreson and Dale (1992), who found a relation between frequency of story reading in the home at age 2½ and early word recognition at age 4½. In the Early Childhood Project, reported frequencies of experience with various types of print materials in prekindergarten and kindergarten, including storybooks, were significantly correlated with children's second-grade scores on the Woodcock-Johnson Word Attack and Word Identification subtests (Baker & Mackler, 1997). However, frequency of looking at educational ABC type books in prekindergarten was the strongest predictor of later scores on both subtests, accounting for 33% and 39% of the variance, respectively. It appears that experience with the more explicitly skills-based books may have greater influence on the development of children's word recognition skills than does storybook reading. Home experiences with books in Grade 1 were not significant predictors of Grade 2 Word Identification and Word Attack skills, providing additional support for the idea that home experiences have less impact on reading as children grow older.

Summary

Although the database is not abundant, there is evidence that children's home experiences involving print do help to prepare them for learning to read words in school. Letter names are often explicitly taught by parents, and it is clear that letter knowledge is strongly related to word recognition. When parents and children attend to print during book reading, children show increased knowledge of print. Phonological processing skills are not typically facilitated through direct instruction at home, but reading nursery rhymes to children and playing language games with them help children develop phonological sensitivity.

Storybook reading contributes less than is generally thought to literacy development, probably because initial growth in reading is so heavily dependent on knowledge of letters and phonological awareness, which are not developed by storybook reading. Experience with ABC books is a better predictor of development of skills related to word recognition than storybook reading. However, reading stories to children is important nonetheless, because it affects other dimensions relevant for learning to read, such as fostering interest in reading, vocabulary development, knowledge of story structure, knowledge of the world, and familiarity with the conventions of written language (Baker, in press; Baker et al., 1995).

Caution is needed in interpreting the evidence showing positive effects of storybook reading, because it is usually correlational. As Arnold and Whitehurst (1994) suggested, perhaps shared book reading at home is just a marker of parental values or some other factors and the benefits do not come from the book reading itself. For example, the parents may be more educated, they may read more themselves, they may use more sophisticated vocabulary, and so on. As noted earlier, there is considerable evidence of more frequent storybook reading among middle-income families than low-income families, but there are also associated differences in material resources and cultural capital (Lareau, 1989).

Most children, of course, do not learn to read at home, regardless of how much storybook reading parents do with them. It is most common for children to learn to read through formal instruction in school. One reason may be that parents do not engage children in the kinds of activities that move them into independent reading, such as teaching children all of the letter names and promoting phonological awareness through language play. Another reason may be that learning to read in English is not easy. The grapheme–phoneme mapping relations between English print and speech are not transparent, making it difficult for children to discover these on their own.

CONCLUSIONS AND IMPLICATIONS

A concluding recommendation in *Becoming a Nation of Readers* (Anderson et al., 1985) is: "Parents should read to preschool children and informally teach them about reading and writing. Reading to children, discussing stories and experiences with them, and—with a light touch—helping them learn letters and words are practices that are consistently associated with eventual success in reading" (p. 117).

Anderson et al. recognized that more than storybook reading is desirable in helping promote reading development at home. However, the key phrase "with a light touch" indicates that they are not recommending a heavily didactic drill-and-practice routine. The phrase "helping them learn" also implies a softer touch; the recommendation is not to teach, but rather to assist the child in what he or she may already have some interest. Parents who see that children are interested in letters and words can provide opportunities for the children to learn more about them in informal playful settings rather than formal schoollike lessons. Middle-income parents are more comfortable with this playful orientation than are lower-income parents (Baker et al., 1995; Baker, Scher, & Mackler, 1997).

Intervention programs that teach low-income and minority parents how to help their children with reading have met with some success (Edwards, 1994). For example, Whitehurst et al. (1988) demonstrated that teaching low-income parents to ask their children questions that extend the meaning of the story is beneficial to children's vocabulary development. However, many researchers stress the importance of developing reading intervention programs that mesh with parents' preexisting beliefs (e.g., DeBaryshe, 1995; Goldenberg et al., 1992). This would suggest that home literacy materials and activities should be meaningful to parents within the frames of reference they use to understand how children learn (Baker, Allen, et al., 1996; Thompson, Mixon, & Serpell, 1996).

If storybook reading does not contribute greatly to what children know about letters and sounds, as the available evidence suggests, how then do they acquire this knowledge? Preschoolers frequently ask about signs, labels, and print in the environment. Mere exposure to environmental print does not seem to play a role, as Masonheimer et al. (1984) demonstrated, but children's questions about environmental print may well be a powerful signal that they are attending to the relevant graphic cues. Another avenue may be in children's play activities involving print, as when they play with magnetic letters of the alphabet or play "school" with older siblings. Data collected in the Early Childhood Project when the children were in prekindergarten indicate that such activities occur regularly in many families. Writing also is a powerful mechanism for learning letter-sound correspondences and is also a common recurrent activity. And, of course, direct instruction of alphabet letter names and sounds is a potent avenue of learning.

What, then, should be the role of parents regarding early literacy? Should they teach their children to read? Might their efforts interfere with rather than facilitate children's development as readers? Parents who emphasize the skills that are important to word recognition at the expense of enjoyable storybook reading focused on meaning may convey a picture of reading as dull and lifeless that stays with the child long after school entry. There are many things parents can do to prepare children for the instruction they will receive in school that stop short of reading instruction per se. They can regularly read books to their children and they can illustrate through their own actions that reading is useful and enjoyable. They can teach children to name and write letters in a playful manner, drawing on educational toys, television, and computer software if such resources are available. They can play with sounds in words in ways that promote sensitivity to rhyme, alliteration, and phonemic awareness. Parents should not try to teach their child to read unless the child leads the way.

ACKNOWLEDGMENTS

Preparation of this chapter and some of the research described in it was supported in part by the National Reading Research Center of the Universities of Georgia and Maryland and the National Institute of Child Health and Human Development (principal investigators Linda Baker, Susan Sonnenschein, and Robert Serpell), and by a National Science Foundation graduate fellowship to Sylvia Fernandez-Fein. We deeply appreciate the contributions of our other colleagues on the Early Childhood Project: Robert Serpell, Susan Sonnenschein, Hibist Astatke, Evangeline Danseco, Marie Dorsey, Victoria Goddard-Truitt, Linda Gorham, Susan Hill, Kirsten Mackler, Tunde Morakinyo, Kim Munsterman, Diane Schmidt, and Sharon Teuben-Rowe. Any opinions, findings, conclusions, or recommendations expressed in this chapter are those of the authors and do not necessarily reflect the views of the National Reading Research Center, the Office of Educational Research and Improvement, the National Institute of Child Health and Human Development, or the National Science Foundation.

REFERENCES

Adams, M. J. (1990). *Beginning to read: Thinking and learning about print.* Cambridge, MA: MIT Press.

Anderson, R. C., Hiebert, E. H., Scott, J. A., & Wilkinson, I. A. (1985). *Becoming a nation of readers: The report of the commission on reading.* Champaign, IL: National Academy of Education, Center for the Study of Reading.

Anderson, A. B., & Stokes, S. J. (1984). Social and institutional influences on the development and practice of literacy. In H. Goelman, A. A. Oberg, & F. Smith (Eds.), *Awakening to literacy* (pp. 24–37). London: Heinemann.

Arnold, D. S., & Whitehurst, G. J. (1994). Accelerating language development through picture book reading: A summary of dialogic reading and its effects. In D. K. Dickinson (Ed.), *Bridges to literacy: Children, families, and schools* (pp. 103–128). Cambridge, MA: Blackwell.

Baker, L. (in press). Opportunities at home and in the community that foster reading engagement. In J. T. Guthrie & D. E. Alvermann (Eds.), *Engagement in reading: Processes, practices, and policy implications.* New York: Teachers' College Press.

Baker, L., Allen, J. B., Shockley, B., Pellegrini, A. D., Galda, L., & Stahl, S. (1996). Connecting school and home: Constructing partnerships to foster reading development. In L. Baker, P. Afflerbach, & D. Reinking (Eds.), *Developing engaged readers in school and home communities* (pp. 21–41). Mahwah, NJ: Lawrence Erlbaum Associates.

Baker, L., & Mackler, K. (1997, April). Contributions of children's emergent literacy skills and home experiences to Grade 2 word recognition. In R. Serpell, S. Sonnenschein, & L. Baker (Chairs), *Patterns of emerging competence and sociocultural context in the early appropriation of literacy.* Symposium presented at the meeting of the Society for Research in Child Development, Washington, DC.

Baker, L., Scher, D., & Mackler, K. (1997). Home and family influences on motivations for reading. *Educational Psychologist, 32*, 69–82.

Baker, L., Serpell, R., & Sonnenschein, S. (1995). Opportunities for literacy learning in the homes of urban preschoolers. In L. M. Morrow (Ed.), *Family literacy: Connections in schools and communities* (pp. 236–252). Newark, DE: International Reading Association.

Baker, L., Sonnenschein, S., Serpell, R., Fernandez-Fein, S., & Scher, D. (1994). *Contexts of emergent literacy: Everyday home experiences of urban pre-kindergarten children* (Research Report #24). Athens, GA: National Reading Research Center, Universities of Georgia and Maryland.

Baker, L., Sonnenschein, S., Serpell, R., Scher, D., Fernandez-Fein, S., Munsterman, K., Hill, S., Goddard-Truitt, V., & Danseco, E. (1996). Early literacy at home: Children's experiences and parents' perspectives. *The Reading Teacher, 50*, 70–72.

Bryant, P. E., Bradley, L., MacLean, M., & Crossland, J. (1989). Nursery rhymes, phonological skills and reading. *Journal of Child Language, 16*, 407–428.

Burns, J. M., & Collins, M. D. (1987). Parents' perceptions of factors affecting the reading development of intellectually superior accelerated readers and intellectually superior nonreaders. *Reading Research and Instruction, 26*, 239–246.

Bus, A. G., & van IJzendoorn, M. H. (1988). Mother–child interactions, attachment, and emergent literacy: A cross-sectional study. *Child Development, 59*, 1262–1272.

Bus, A. J., & van IJzendoorn, M. H. (1995). Mothers reading to their 3-year-olds: The role of mother–child attachment security in becoming literate. *Reading Research Quarterly, 30*, 998–1015.

Bus, A. G., van IJzendoorn, M. H., & Pellegrini, A. D. (1995). Joint book reading makes for success in learning to read: A meta-analysis on intergenerational transmission of literacy. *Review of Educational Research, 65*, 1–21.

Chall, J. S., Jacobs, V. A., & Baldwin, L. E. (1990). *The reading crisis: Why poor children fall behind.* Cambridge, MA: Harvard.

Chaney, C. (1994). Language development, metalinguistic awareness, and emergent literacy skills of 3-year-old children in relation to social class. *Applied Psycholinguistics, 15,* 371–394.

Crain-Thoreson, C., & Dale, P. S. (1992). Do early talkers become early readers? Linguistic precocity, preschool language, and emergent literacy. *Developmental Psychology, 28,* 421–429.

Cunningham, A. E., & Stanovich, K. E. (1993). Children's literacy environments and early word recognition subskills. *Reading and Writing: An Interdisciplinary Journal, 5,* 193–204.

DeBaryshe, B. D. (1995). Maternal belief systems: Linchpin in the home reading process. *Journal of Applied Developmental Psychology, 16,* 1–20.

Dickinson, D. K., DeTemple, J. M., Hirschler, J. A., & Smith, M. W. (1992). Book reading with preschoolers: Coconstruction of text at home and at school. *Early Childhood Research Quarterly, 7,* 323–346.

Dowker, A. (1989). Rhyme and alliteration elicited from young children. *Journal of Child Language, 16,* 181–202.

Dunning, D. B., Mason, J. M., & Stewart, J. P. (1994). Reading to preschoolers: A response to Scarborough and Dobrich (1994) and recommendations for future research. *Developmental Review, 14,* 324–339.

Durkin, D. (1966). *Children who read early.* New York: Teachers' College Press.

Edwards, P. A. (1994). Responses of teachers and African American mothers to a book reading intervention program. In D. K. Dickinson (Ed.), *Bridges to literacy: Children, families, and schools* (pp. 175–208). Cambridge, MA: Blackwell.

Ehri, L. C. (1984). How orthography alters spoken language competencies in children learning to read and spell. In J. Downing & R. Valtin (Eds.), *Language awareness and learning to read* (pp. 119–147). New York: Springer-Verlag.

Elliott, J. A., & Hewison, J. (1994). Comprehension and interest in home reading. *British Journal of Educational Psychology, 64,* 203–220.

Fernandez-Fein, S., & Baker, L. (1997). Rhyme and alliteration sensitivity and relevant experiences in preschoolers from diverse backgrounds. *Journal of Literacy Research, 29,* 433–459.

Goldenberg, C., Reese, L., & Gallimore, R. (1992). Effects of literacy materials from school on Latino children's home experiences and early reading achievement. *American Journal of Education, 100,* 497–536.

Goodman, Y. (1986). Children coming to know literacy. In W. H. Teale & E. Sulzby (Eds.), *Emergent literacy: Writing and reading* (pp. 1–14). Norwood, NJ: Ablex.

Guthrie, J., & Greaney, V. (1991). Literacy acts. In R. Barr, M. L. Kamil, P. Mosenthal, & P. D. Pearson (Eds.), *Handbook of reading research* (Vol. II, pp. 68–96). New York: Longman.

Hannon, P. (1995). *Literacy, home, and school.* Bristol, PA: Falmer.

Heath, S. B. (1983). *Ways with words: Language, life, and work in communities and classrooms.* Cambridge, England: Cambridge University Press.

Hess, R. D., Holloway, S., Price, G. G., & Dickson, W. P. (1982). Family environments and acquisition of reading skills: Toward a more precise analysis. In L. M. Laosa & I. Sigel (Eds.), *Families as learning environments for children* (pp. 87–113). New York: Plenum.

Huey, E. B. (1908). *The psychology and pedagogy of reading.* NY: Macmillan.

Lareau, A. (1989). *Home advantage: Social class and parental intervention in elementary education.* London: Falmer.

Lonigan, C. J. (1994). Reading to preschoolers exposed: Is the emperor really naked? *Developmental Review, 14,* 303–323.

MacLean, L., Bryant, P., & Bradley, L. (1987). Rhymes, nursery rhymes, and reading in early childhood. *Merrill-Palmer Quarterly, 33*(3), 255–281.

Marvin, C., & Mirenda, P. (1993). Home literacy experiences of preschoolers enrolled in Head Start and special education programs. *Journal of Early Intervention, 17*, 351–367.

Mason, J. (1980). When do children begin to read?: An exploration of four-year-old children's letter and word reading competencies. *Reading Research Quarterly, 15*, 203–227.

Masonheimer, P. E., Drum, P. A., & Ehri, L. C. (1984). Does environmental print identification lead children into word reading? *Journal of Reading Behavior, 16*, 257–271.

McCormick, C. E., & Mason, J. M. (1986). Intervention procedures for increasing preschool children's interest in and knowledge about reading. In W. H. Teale & E. Sulzby (Eds.), *Emergent literacy: Writing and reading* (pp. 90–115). Norwood, NJ: Ablex.

Morrow, L. M. (1988). Young children's responses to one-to-one story readings in school settings. *Reading Research Quarterly, 23*, 89–107.

Morrow, L. M. (1989). *Literacy development in the early years.* Englewood Cliffs, NJ: Prentice-Hall.

Munsterman, K. A., & Sonnenschein, S. (1997, April). Qualities of storybook reading interactions and their relations to emergent literacy. In R. Serpell, S. Sonnenschein, & L. Baker (Chairs), *Patterns of emerging competence and sociocultural context in the early appropriation of literacy.* Symposium presented at the meetings of the Society for Research in Child Development, Washington, D.C.

Pellegrini, A. D., Perlmutter, J. C. Galda, L., & Brody, G. H. (1990). Joint book reading between black Head Start children and their mothers. *Child Development, 61*, 443–453.

Phillips, G., & McNaughton, S. (1990). The practice of storybook reading to preschoolers in mainstream New Zealand families. *Reading Research Quarterly, 25*, 196–212.

Raz, I. T., & Bryant, P. (1990). Social background, phonological awareness and children's reading. *British Journal of Developmental Psychology, 8*, 209–225.

Scarborough, H. S., & Dobrich, W. (1994). On the efficacy of reading to preschoolers. *Developmental Review, 14*, 245–302.

Senechal, M., LeFevre, J., Hudson, E., & Lawson, E. P. (1996). Knowledge of storybooks as a predictor of young children's vocabulary. *Journal of Educational Psychology, 88*, 520–536.

Serpell, R., Sonnenschein, S., Baker, L., Hill, S., Goddard-Truitt, V., & Danseco, E. (1997). *Parental ideas about development and socialization of children on the threshold of schooling* (Reading Research Report #78). Athens, GA: Universities of Georgia and Maryland, National Reading Research Center.

Snow, C. E. (1994). Enhancing literacy development: Programs and research perspectives. In D. K. Dickinson (Ed.), *Bridges to literacy: Children, families, and schools* (pp. 267–272). Cambridge, MA: Blackwell.

Snow, C. E., Barnes, W. S., Chandler, J., Goodman, I. F., & Hemphill, L. (1991). *Unfulfilled expectations: Home and school influences on literacy.* Cambridge, MA: Harvard University Press.

Sonnenschein, S., Baker, L., & Cerro, L. (1992). Mothers' views on teaching their preschoolers in everyday situations. *Early Education and Development, 3*, 1–22.

Sonnenschein, S., Baker, L., Serpell, R., Scher, D., Fernandez-Fein, S., & Munsterman, K. A. (1996). *Strands of emergent literacy and their antecedents in the home: Urban preschoolers' early literacy development* (Reading Research Report #48). Athens, GA: Universities of Georgia and Maryland, National Reading Research Center.

Sonnenschein, S., Baker, L., Serpell, R., Scher, D., Goddard-Truitt, V., & Munsterman, K. (1996, August). *The relation between parental beliefs about reading development and storybook reading practices in different sociocultural groups in Baltimore.* Paper presented at the biennial meeting of the International Society for the Study of Behavioral Development, Quebec City.

Sonnenschein, S., Baker, L., Serpell, R., Scher, D., Goddard-Truitt, V., & Munsterman, K. (1997). Parents beliefs about ways to help children learn to read: The impact of an entertainment or a skills perspective. *Early Child Development and Care, 127–128*, 111–118.

Sonnenschein, S., Brody, G., & Munsterman, K. (1996). The influence of family beliefs and practices on children's early reading development. In L. Baker, P. Afflerbach, & D. Reinking (Eds.), *Developing engaged readers in school and home communities* (pp. 3–20). Mahwah, NJ: Lawrence Erlbaum Associates.

Sulzby, E., & Teale, W. (1991). Emergent literacy. In R. Barr, M. L. Kamil, P. Mosenthal, & P. D. Pearson (Eds.), *Handbook of reading research* (Vol. II, pp. 727–758). New York: Longman.

Taylor, D., & Dorsey-Gaines, C. (1988). *Growing up literate: Learning from inner city families.* Portsmouth, NH: Heinemann.

Teale, W. H. (1986). Home background and young children's literacy development. In W. H. Teale & E. Sulzby (Eds.), *Emergent literacy: Writing and reading* (pp. 173–205). Norwood, NJ: Ablex.

Thompson, R., Mixon, G., & Serpell, R. (1996). Engaging minority students in reading: Focus on the urban learner. In L. Baker, P. Afflerbach, & D. Reinking (Eds.), *Developing engaged readers in school and home communities* (pp. 43–63). Mahwah, NJ: Lawrence Erlbaum Associates.

Treiman, R. (1991). Phonological awareness and its roles in learning to read and spell. In D. J. Sawyer & B. J. Fox (Eds.), *Phonological awareness in reading: The evolution of current perspectives* (pp. 159–189). New York: Springer-Verlag.

Wagner, R. K., Torgesen, J. K., & Rashotte, C. A. (1994). The development of reading-related phonological processing abilities: New evidence of bi-directional causality from a latent variable longitudinal study. *Developmental Psychology, 30*, 73–87.

Walsh, D. J., Price, G. G., & Gillingham, M. G. (1988). The critical but transitory importance of letter naming. *Reading Research Quarterly, 23*, 108–122.

Wells, G. (1986). *The meaning makers: Children learning language and using language to learn.* Portsmouth, NH: Heinemann.

Whitehurst, G. J., Falco, F. L., Lonigan, C. J., Fischel, J. E., DeBaryshe, B. D., Valdez-Menchaca, M. C., & Caulfield, M. (1988). Accelerating language development through picturebook reading. *Developmental Psychology, 24*, 552–559.

Williams, S. M., & Silva, P. A. (1985). Some factors associated with reading ability: A longitudinal study. *Educational Research, 27*, 159–168.

Yaden, D. B., Smolkin, L. B., & Conlon, A. (1989). Preschoolers' questions about pictures, print conventions, and story text during reading aloud at home. *Reading Research Quarterly, 24*, 188–213.

12

▼▼▼▼▼▼▼

Why Spelling? The Benefits of Incorporating Spelling Into Beginning Reading Instruction

Rebecca Treiman
Wayne State University

Reading and spelling are often treated as separate subjects, with reading considered to be more important than spelling at the early elementary school level. Today, in many U.S. first- and second-grade classrooms, reading is taught at one time of day and with one set of materials. Spelling, if formally covered at all, is taught at a different time of day and with different materials than those used for reading. Is this an optimal approach? No, say the many children for whom spelling means dreary memorization of lists of words and boring workbook exercises. No, say those advocates of skill-based approaches who propose that spelling instruction be better integrated with reading and vocabulary study (Templeton, 1991). No, say advocates of whole language instruction, who recommend that the language arts be integrated by bringing reading and writing together and who further recommend that children not be pushed to spell correctly during the early grades (Bergeron, 1990). In this chapter, I review the research basis for these claims. I ask whether there are benefits to be gained by emphasizing writing and spelling at the early elementary school level. I also ask whether writing should be integrated with reading in instruction and, if so, how. The research to be reviewed suggests that writing has an important role to play in the early grades and that it should be coordinated with reading. However, contrary to the claims of whole language advocates, skill in spelling does not always arise naturally and automatically as a result of reading. Spelling needs to be taught, but in a manner that is more sensitive to the natural course of spelling development than are many traditional methods.

Because the focus of this chapter is on how English-speaking children learn to spell, thc chapter begins by reviewing the nature of the English writing system. I discuss how children learn about this system and the types of errors they make along the way. Next, I show that spelling skill does not always emerge as a by-product of reading. Becoming a good speller typically requires experiences above and beyond those provided by the reading of connected text. Even though learning to read does not automatically make children good spellers, learning to spell does benefit their reading. It does so, in part, by improving children's ability to focus on the individual sounds or phonemes within spoken words. Other research suggests that young children find it easier to use an alphabetic strategy in writing than in reading. Thus, children may be able to use spelling as an entry point into the writing system. Children's spellings also provide an excellent window onto their knowledge of phonology and orthography. Teachers can use children's spellings to group them for instruction, to predict future progress, and to shed light on any problems that they may be experiencing. In the last section of the chapter, I review various approaches toward spelling that have been used with children in the early elementary grades. I ask whether children should be encouraged to invent their own spellings for words with minimal guidance and correction, as proponents of the whole language approach maintain, or whether children need some type of direct teaching to become good spellers.

THE ENGLISH SPELLING SYSTEM AND THE
NATURAL COURSE OF SPELLING DEVELOPMENT

The English spelling system is the butt of many jokes. How irregular it is, we complain, how illogical! How can children ever be expected to master such a system except through brute force memorization? In fact, the English writing system is not as irregular as often thought. Although one cannot always spell an unknown word correctly, one can usually produce a readable approximation if one knows the rules and patterns that are embodied in the writing system.

The phonemic structure of a word is the major constraint on its spelling. We know that the word *seat* could alternatively be spelled as *sete* or *seet*, but we know that it could not be spelled as *seab* or *vaim*. A person who is able to segment spoken words into phonemes and who knows which graphemes (i.e., letters or letter groups) may represent each phoneme has an excellent start on spelling. Our prospective writer will do even better if he or she knows something about the contexts in which particular graphemes may occur. For example, *ck* may be used in the middle of a word (as in *packet*) or at the end of a word (as in *pack*), but may not occur at the beginning of a word. A speller who knows this orthographic pattern might spell *soccer* as *socker* but will not spell *can* as *ckan*. As another example, the /ɛ/ ("short e") sound is sometimes spelled as *ea* when it occurs before *d*, as in *dead* and *head*, but is rarely spelled as *ea* when it occurs before *p*.

The morphological structure of a word (i.e., whether the word is made up of smaller meaningful parts) also influences its spelling. In many cases, a spelling that would be anticipated on the basis of phoneme–grapheme correspondences is overridden by morphological considerations. For example, one would normally expect *health* to be spelled as *helth*. The *a* in the conventional spelling reveals the relationship to *heal*. As another example, the English writing system does not represent the difference between the final /t/ sound of *jumped* and the final /d/ sound of *hemmed*. Both words are spelled with final *ed* to indicate that both are past tense verbs.

Even when phonological, orthographic, and morphological patterns are considered, the spellings of English words are not totally predictable. For example, *sword* is an irregular spelling for present-day speakers who no longer include a /w/ when pronouncing this word. The *i* in *plaid* is likewise unexpected. When multiple sources of information are taken into account, however, the English writing system is more reasonable and more logical than often believed.

Given the complexity of the English spelling system and the fact that it encodes several different types of information, one would expect mastery of the system to require a long time. Indeed, it does. Learners take years to become accurate and automatic spellers, and they make many mistakes along the way. Importantly, however, children's spelling errors do not typically involve the random substitution and omission of letters. Nor, for the most part, do early spelling errors arise for visual reasons, as with confusions between *v* and *w*. Rather, children's misspellings reflect their linguistic knowledge. The errors are often logical and reasonable given the knowledge that children possess.

A brief history of the acquisition of spelling is in order at this point. Preschoolers may begin to "write" by making marks with a crayon or pencil. Although these early productions may not include any conventional letters, they often reveal some understanding of the gross visual features of writing, such as its linearity. Gradually, children learn the letters of the alphabet and begin to relate letters in spellings to the sounds that they hear in words. When asked to spell, young children may represent a whole word or a whole syllable with a single letter. Children gradually represent more and more of the sounds in words, moving from spellings like B for *beat* to spellings like BT and BET. (Children's spellings of words will be printed in capital letters throughout this chapter.) Children's spellings reveal that their analyses of the sounds in words do not always match those embodied in conventional English. For example, first graders may represent the first sound of *drum* with *g* rather than *d* or the second sound of *spider* with *b* rather than *p*. They may spell the middle sound of *city*, which is called a *flap*, with *d* rather than with *t*. Even though these spellings are unconventional, they are reasonable from a phonetic viewpoint. Other common errors, such as SIK for *sink* and BED for *bread*, involve a failure to represent one phoneme of a consonant cluster. These errors reveal children's difficulties in apprehending consonant clusters as sequences of individual phonemes. It tends to be the second phoneme of a two-consonant initial cluster (e.g., the /r/ of *bread*) and the first phoneme of a two-consonant final cluster (e.g., the /ŋ/ *of sink*) that is omitted. Still other errors, such as BR for *bar*, suggest a difficulty in analyzing certain vowel + consonant units, along with a tendency to spell these units with the letters that have the corresponding names. In the case of BR, a child spells the phoneme sequence /ar/ with *r*, the letter that has this name.

The kinds of spelling errors that I have described gradually abate as children improve in their ability to segment spoken words into phonemes and as their phonemic analyses become more conventional. In addition, children gain a knowledge of the contexts in which particular spellings may occur and of the morphological underpinnings of English spelling. For example, they learn that *ck* may occur in the middles or at the ends of words but not at the beginnings. They learn that the past tense ending is spelled as *ed*, regardless of its pronunciation. In addition, children learn the conventional spellings of words whose spellings cannot be fully determined from their linguistic forms. For example, they learn about the *i* in *plaid* and the *w* in *sword*. For a more detailed discussion of children's spelling than I am able to provide here, see Adams, Treiman, and Pressley (1998), Read (1986), or Treiman (1993).

Two major theoretical approaches have been taken in explaining the course of spelling development. The first approach is that of *stage theories* (Ehri, 1986; Gentry, 1982; Henderson, 1985). Stage theorists propose that children pass through a series of qualitatively different stages in the course of learning to spell. During the early stages of spelling development, children draw on their knowledge of letter names and their knowledge of phonology in order to spell words. During later stages, additional sources of information come into play, including knowledge of orthographic patterns and morphological relationships among words. These latter types of knowledge are said to be unavailable to beginning spellers. Thus, stage theorists propose that different stages in the development of spelling are marked by reliance on qualitatively different types of information.

The second theoretical approach proposes that spelling development is more continuous. Rather than using certain types of information at some points in time and other types of information at later points in time, children use a variety of strategies from the beginning. This second approach may be called the *strategy approach*. Support for the strategy approach comes from findings suggesting that even young children can use orthographic patterns and morphological relationships among words to aid their spelling. Thus, even first graders appear to have picked up that *ck* does not occur at the beginnings of English words and do not often use this orthographic pattern (Treiman, 1993). With regard to morphology, first graders begin to be able to spell the flap of *dirty* with *t* rather than *d* based on the relationship between *dirty* and *dirt* (Treiman, Cassar, & Zukowski, 1994). Although the ability to use orthographic and morphological information improves over time, it emerges earlier than expected under stage theories of spelling development (Cassar & Treiman, in press). Stage theories further predict a degree of consistency among a child's spellings at a given point in time. During the so-called letter-name stage, for example, children should spell *bar* as BR and *mess* as MS, using their knowledge of letter names in both cases. Researchers who have looked for such consistency have not always found it, however (Treiman, 1994; Varnhagen, McCallum, Burstow, Pawlik, & Poon, 1997).

At some level, the question of whether spelling development takes place through movement from one stage to another or through the gradual accumulation of more sophisticated strategies is not critical for the questions being addressed in this chapter. What is critical is that children make progress. How can we help children to move from primitive spellings like S or SD for *sword* to more sophisticated spellings like SORD and eventually to the correct SWORD? Is it enough to have children read good literature and trust that their knowledge of reading will transfer to spelling? Or is direct instruction in spelling necessary? These questions are addressed in the following sections.

LEARNING TO SPELL DOES NOT COME ABOUT JUST THROUGH READING

If learning to spell were a natural by-product of learning to read, our task would be simple. Teach children to read, let them read a lot of good literature, and they will become skilled spellers. Experience suggests that the situation is not so simple. If spelling were an automatic by-product of reading, why would this writer have to pause over the spelling of *occasional* when she has read the correctly spelled word thousands of times? Research findings confirm that spelling, for most people, requires something above and beyond experience with reading.

There *are* correlations between the ability to read and the ability to spell (see Ehri, chap. 1, this volume). In a study of second graders, for example, Shanahan (1984) found a correlation of .66 between performance on a spelling test and performance on a test of phonetic abilities in reading. This correlation is moderate but is far from perfect. Shanahan suggested on the basis of such results that reading and writing consist of both dependent and independent abilities, and that reading instruction does not suffice to teach writing. Further support for the claim that ability to read a word does not guarantee ability to spell it comes from the fact that some children (as well as some adults) are good readers but poor spellers (e.g., Bruck & Waters, 1990; Frith, 1980). The opposite pattern is much less common. Moreover, dyslexic individuals who as a result of intensive instruction have reached normal levels in reading often continue to be poor spellers (Boder, 1973; Critchley, 1975).

Research shows that the type of reading experience recommended by whole language advocates—the reading of connected, meaningful text—is less effective than is the reading of isolated words as a way to learn words' spellings. In one study, Ehri and Roberts (1979) worked with first graders who had experienced between 7 and 8 months of reading instruction. The children were taught to read 16 words, such as *which* and *witch*. Half of the children studied the words in sentences and the other half of the children studied isolated printed words. Each child completed three sessions of word training during which he or she read each word a total of 16 times. Those children who studied single words showed a larger gain from pretest to posttest on a spelling recognition test than did those children who studied words in context. Also, the first group of children got more letters correct on a spelling production test. In a follow-up study, Ehri and Wilce (1980a) compared first graders' ability to learn grammatical words such as *might* and *enough* in sentences and in lists. Again, children learned more about the words' spellings when they studied the words in nonmeaningful lists than when they read them in sentences. Thus, it is experience with words taken out of context that is most helpful in learning to spell.

Research further suggests that children need to read a word many times before their ability to spell that word begins to improve. The younger the children, the more reading experience is required (see Bosman & Van Orden, 1997). In one study, Dutch children with 10 months of formal literacy instruction made equal numbers of errors in spelling words they had read six times and words they had read just twice. Only when words had been read at least nine times did the children's spelling performance began to improve through reading. The Dutch results reviewed by Bosman and Van Orden further show that tasks that require a child to focus on the exact spelling of a word—whether copying the word, spelling it out loud, or forming the word using letter tiles—are superior to reading as a means of learning the word's spelling. If these results generalize to English, as I suspect they would, this would support the view that reading experience does not always transfer to spelling.

The claim that reading knowledge does not always transfer to spelling should not be taken to imply that transfer never occurs. For example, as mentioned earlier, first graders who were taught primarily by whole language methods tended to avoid using *ck* at the beginnings of words. This was true even though the children were not explicitly taught that *ck* may not occur in this position (Treiman, 1993). The children must have picked up this orthographic pattern through reading. However, this type of learning takes time. It stands to reason that it would be more effective with patterns that are found in a large number of words than with patterns that occur in just a few words. For example, many English words have *ck* in the middle or at the end and none have *ck* at the beginning. Exposure to this entire body of words should help children learn the pattern. *Sword* is one of the few words that a child will see in which /s/ is spelled with *sw*, and so the correct spelling of this word should be learned more slowly through reading experience.

Why does the ability to read a word not always guarantee that a child will be able to spell that word? Beginners have been reported to read words *logographically*, by means of visual clues (Byrne; 1992; Frith, 1985; Gough, Juel, & Griffith, 1992). Ehri (chap. 1, this volume) referred to this strategy as *prealphabetic reading*. Children who use this approach may identify *dog* by virtue of the "tail" at the end of the word rather than by linking the letters in the printed word to the sounds in the spoken word. A child who uses a logographic strategy to recognize printed words does not focus on all of the words' letters and so may be unable to remember and reproduce the full spelling. Even when children begin to link words' spellings to their sounds, they do not do so completely. Instead, children may read by means of partial clues, connecting some of the letters in a word's spelling to its pronunciation but ignoring other letters (Ehri, 1992, chap. 1, this volume; Perfetti, 1992). This approach will sometimes allow children to read words correctly. For example, a young child may identify *bar* in reading by connecting the letter *b* to the phoneme /b/ and the letter *r* to the phoneme sequence /ar/. Because the child has not linked the letter *a* to a separate phoneme in the spoken word, the child may not remember this letter when attempting to spell the word and may therefore produce the error BR.

LEARNING TO SPELL BENEFITS READING AND PHONEMIC AWARENESS

The evidence just reviewed suggests that most children need to do more than read a lot in order to become good spellers. Children need experiences that encourage them to focus directly on individual words and their spellings. Exactly what these experiences might be is discussed in more detail later in this chapter. The point that I wish to make in this section is that learning to spell, in addition to its effects on spelling, also benefits children's reading.

The benefits of writing are both motivational and cognitive. With regard to motivation, Chomsky (1979) suggested that having young children generate their own stories and using these stories as reading material gives children a sense of ownership. Children may be more willing to try to read something they have written themselves than something that is unfamiliar. In addition, spelling appears to have cognitive benefits. It encourages children to analyze words into smaller units of sound and to link these sounds to letters. In this way, children practice their phonemic segmentation skills. Through writing, children learn to see spellings as maps of phonemic content rather than as arbitrary sequences of letters. Practice in using the alphabetic strategy to spell helps children transfer this strategy to reading and go beyond strategies involving logographic reading or partial clues.

Support for the cognitive benefits of spelling claims comes from both correlational and experimental studies. Cataldo and Ellis (1988) used causal modeling to suggest that, early on, knowledge gained from spelling is transferred to reading more than the reverse. However, their study was an exploratory one involving a relatively small number of children. In a larger study of Dutch children, Mommers (1987) found direct effects of spelling ability on word decoding speed after children had received 3 to 4 months of first-grade instruction.

More definitive are the results of training studies. One such study, reported by Ehri and Wilce (1987), involved kindergartners. Children in the experimental group received several hours of one-on-one training over a 1-month period in segmenting spoken syllables into phonemes and representing the phonemes with letter tiles. Children in the control group practiced matching letters to isolated sounds but did not learn to spell words. After the training, children were given seven trials to learn to read a list of 12 words. These words had not been taught during the training period but were composed of the taught letters. The children in the experimental group performed better on this word learning task than did the children in the control group, although neither group of children mastered the full set of words. However, the spelling-trained children seemed to have a better handle on alphabetic reading than did the control children, in that their errors showed a closer phonetic relationship to the presented stimuli. The spelling-trained children also outperformed the control children on a test of phonemic segmentation. Ehri and Wilce suggested that the experimental group's better performance in reading reflected their improved segmentation skills. Supporting this suggestion, research shows that training in phonemic segmentation contributes to reading acquisition, especially when phonemic awareness is taught in conjunction with alphabet letters (Ball & Blachman, 1991; Bradley & Bryant, 1985; Hatcher, Hulme, & Ellis, 1994).

Uhry and Shepherd (1993) followed up on Ehri and Wilce's (1987) study by working with first graders rather than kindergartners and by extending the length of training and the variety of posttest reading measures. In Uhry and Shepherd's study, first graders from a classroom that used primarily (but not exclusively) a whole language approach received 40 minutes per week of supplemental small-group instruction over the course of 6½ months. For the children in the experimental group, this instruction involved breaking spoken words into phonemes and representing the phonemes with letter tiles. The children practiced spelling the same lists of words that were used for regular classroom reading instruction. The children in the experimental group also played spelling games on the computer. The children in the control group practiced reading the same words used by the experimental children, reading the words out of context rather than in stories. However, the control children did not segment or spell the words. The children in the control group also played reading games on the computer. At the end of training, the children in the experimental group outperformed the control children on measures of nonsense word reading, timed word reading, and timed oral passage reading. Group differences in silent reading comprehension were not significant, although the researchers suggested that such differences may have emerged if the children had been followed for longer. The experimental children also outscored the controls on oral segmentation and blending tests. Uhry and Shepherd's findings suggest that segmentation and spelling training that is coordinated with classroom reading instruction leads to better performance in reading than additional reading practice itself. These results suggest that it is important to include segmentation and spelling instruction in first-grade classrooms. They also suggest that spelling and reading instruction should be integrated with one another.

Bosman and Van Orden (1997) objected that the training methods used by Ehri and Wilce (1987) and Uhry and Shepherd (1993) allowed the children time to practice reading the words. The additional reading practice, they argued, could explain the experimental group's superior performance in reading. However, the control group in the Uhry and Shepherd study had even more time for reading practice than did the experimental group, yet did more poorly than the experimental group on reading posttests. Thus, Bosman and Van Orden's counterargument does not seem to be supported.

Learning to spell not only raises children's level of phonemic awareness but also shapes their conceptions of phonemes. As discussed earlier, young children do not always analyze spoken words the same way that literate adults do and the same way that the conventional English writing system does. For example, children may consider the first sound of *drum* to be /dʒ/ (as in the first sound of "George") rather than /d/. They may consider the second sound of *spider* to be /b/ rather than /p/ and the middle consonant of *city* to be /d/ (Treiman, 1985a, 1985b, 1993). As children learn the conventional spellings of words, their judgments about phonemes become more conventional. Support for this claim comes from a study by Ehri and

Wilce (1986), which focused on flaps such as the middle sound of *city*. Flaps are often spelled as *t* in conventional English even though they sound more similar to /d/. Teaching second graders the spellings of flaps affected the children's conceptions of the flaps' sounds, as assessed through a rhyming task. These and other results (e.g., Ehri & Wilce, 1980b) suggest that learning to spell gradually brings children's representations of sounds in line with those assumed by the conventional writing system.

The ability to spell a word may not guarantee the ability to read it. Indeed, as discussed in the next section, some young children are able to spell certain words but unable to read them. The point that I have tried to make in this section is that learning to spell words benefits children's reading down the line by giving them practice in segmenting spoken words into phonemes and in relating phonemes to graphemes.

CHILDREN MAY BE ABLE TO USE THE ALPHABETIC PRINCIPLE IN SPELLING BEFORE THEY CAN DO SO IN READING

As I have mentioned, many researchers believe that children initially approach reading as a paired-associate learning task. They read not by connecting letters in printed words to sounds in spoken words, but by connecting salient visual characteristics of words to the words' pronunciations or meanings (see Ehri, chap. 1, this volume). Evidence for this claim comes from experimental work (e.g., Byrne, 1992) and classroom studies (Seymour & Elder, 1986). For example, children who have learned to read both *fat* and *bat* may perform at chance levels when asked whether *fun* says "fun" or "bun" (Byrne, 1992). Apparently, these children have not linked the *f* of *fat* to the sound /f/ and so cannot deduce that *fun* must correspond to "fun." Although some researchers suggest that not all English-speaking children go through a logographic stage in learning to read (e.g., Stuart & Coltheart, 1988), the proposal has enjoyed a good deal of popularity. In contrast, children are thought to use a sound-based approach in spelling from an early age. It has been suggested that spelling acts as the pacesetter for reading early in the course of development, with children employing an alphabetic strategy in spelling before they are able to use this strategy in reading (Frith, 1985; Goswami & Bryant, 1990).

Support for the idea that children systematically relate print and sound in spelling before they do so in reading comes from several sources. Researchers such as Read (1975) and Chomsky (1979) described preschool children who begin to spell before they are able to read. Often, these children cannot read back what they have written or are not interested in doing so. They are more concerned with the activity of spelling than with the end result. If these children do wish to check what they have written, they do not read it back as an older child or adult would do. Instead, they start again from the pronunciation and make sure that they have chosen the appropriate letters. It has been suggested that young children have a writing mode and a reading mode and that they sometimes operate in one mode only, without recourse to the other (Chomsky, 1979).

Results of a study by Burns and Richgels (1989) confirm that preschoolers who can invent plausible sound-based spellings can not always read words when presented in isolation. These researchers identified 16 gifted pre-schoolers who could produce phonetically reasonable spellings for one-syllable words. The inventive spellers were compared with a group of 16 nonspellers from the same program for gifted children. Seven of the 16 inventive spellers could read some isolated words. However, the other nine inventive spellers performed poorly on the reading tasks, no better than the nonspellers. Burns and Richgels concluded that, early in literacy development, "Word reading appears to be a very separate ability from word writing or spelling" (p. 13).

Other studies have examined children who learn to read and write at school rather than children who begin on their own at home. Huxford, Terrell, and Bradley (1991) studied British children in their first year at school, beginning when the children were 4 and 5 years old. The researchers compared children's ability to read and spell simple nonwords such as *zep*. The children spelled by using plastic letters. Testing was carried out at 8-week intervals, stopping when the children performed almost perfectly on both the reading and the spelling test (at an average age of about 5½). Throughout the series of tests, the children's spelling scores were consistently higher than their reading scores. In another study, which looked at older British children aged about 7 years, most children were better at reading than at spelling (Bryant & Bradley, 1980). However, there were still some items—phonetically regular words and simple nonwords—that children could spell but could not read (Bryant & Bradley, 1980; but see Gough et al., 1992 for some questions about these claims).

There are several reasons why children may find it easier to use an alphabetic strategy in spelling than in reading. For one thing, spelling places fewer demands on memory. Children can write down phonemes as they come to them in analyzing a word, rather than holding them in memory until the end of the word and then blending them together to form a unified pronunciation. Supporting this claim, Stahl and Murray (1994) found that digit span, a test of short-term memory, did not account for any additional variance in spelling ability above and beyond that explained by phonological awareness. In contrast, digit span made a small but significant additional contribution to word recognition.

Another reason that children may use a phonological approach for spelling before they do for reading is that the alternative logographic or prealphabetic strategy is easier to use in reading. Children easily learn to relate the golden arches in the McDonald's logo to the word *McDonald's*. Having experienced some success at "reading" this and other environmental print, they may be reluctant to go beyond a logographic approach in reading. In contrast, memorizing the entire spelling of a word with no alphabetic support is so hard that children are led to look for some principled way of remembering the spelling of a word based on its sound.

CHILDREN'S SPELLINGS PROVIDE AN EXCELLENT WINDOW ONTO THEIR KNOWLEDGE OF PHONOLOGY AND ORTHOGRAPHY

Children may begin to produce spellings like B or BT for *beat* before they can read very much, if at all. By carefully examining a child's spellings, one can gain insight into where the child is in the process of literacy acquisition. For example, a child who spells *beat* as BT is farther along than a child who spells the word with a random string of letters and numbers or a child who mixes up the letters of his or her own name.

The quality of children's invented spellings in kindergarten or at the beginning of first grade is a good predictor of later reading achievement (Mann, 1993; Mann, Tobin, & Wilson, 1987; Morris & Perney, 1984). For example, Mann (1993) gave a spelling task to groups of children at the end of kindergarten. About a year later, the children were given standardized measures of word identification and word attack skills. A measure of the phonological quality of the kindergarten spellings predicted between 37% and 47% of the variance in first-grade reading achievement. This measure was more successful than other measures of spelling that assessed children's ability to approximate the overall shape of a word or their tendency to reverse letters such as *s* and *p*. Mann's findings suggest that teachers can use a short group-administered spelling test at the end of kindergarten to pick out children who may have problems learning to read in first grade.

In the study by Mann (1993), the invented spelling task was a better predictor of first-grade reading achievement than was a phonemic awareness task focusing on initial consonants. Other studies suggest that spelling may actually be an easier measure of phonemic awareness than many oral phonemic awareness tasks, at least for children who know the basic correspondences between phonemes and graphemes. For example, Stahl and Murray (1994) found that children who produced spellings like LESTR for *lap*, in which the first phoneme is correctly represented but the rest of the word is not, often failed to master an oral task that involved separating onsets from rimes. That is, these children seemed to show an implicit ability to divide onsets from rimes in spelling but not in oral segmentation. Duighuisen,

Kerstholt, and van Bon (1990, cited in van Bon & Duighuisen, 1995), working with Dutch children who had about three months of formal reading and spelling instruction, also found that spelling is sometimes easier than oral segmentation. The same discrepancy was reported among Dutch 8-year-olds who were poor spellers (van Bon & Duighuisen, 1995). Spelling tests may be more sensitive to phonological knowledge than many oral phonemic awareness tasks because spelling places fewer demands on short-term memory. Children can write down segments as they encounter them rather than having to hold the sound segments in memory. In addition, spellers can check and modify their responses without relying solely on phonological memory.

Spelling tasks provide a good basis for grouping children for reading instruction and word study. Bear and Barone (1989) argued that an assessment of children's spelling can provide more information than a standardized reading test. Morris and Perney (1984) drew similar conclusions. For example, why drill a child on beginning and ending consonant sounds if the child consistently represents these sounds in spelling? Why teach the distinction between "short" and "long" vowels to a child who cannot yet spell the initial consonants of simple words?

To take advantage of the information in children's spellings, teachers must go beyond looking at the spellings simply as correct or incorrect. They need to have an understanding of the nature of the English writing system, the sound system of the spoken language, and the normal course of spelling development. If teachers are not given the opportunity to acquire such knowledge, they may fail to appreciate why it is reasonable for a child to begin *drum* with a *g* or *spider* with *sb*. They might not understand why a child would omit the *r* of *bread* or the *n* of *sink* when spelling these words. Unfortunately, many teachers do not receive adequate training in phonemic awareness, linguistics, and the nature of written English (Moats, 1994). Teachers' difficulty in thinking about the sounds of words as distinct from their spellings arises, in large part, *because* teachers are good readers. As discussed previously, learning to read shapes people's conceptions of sounds, making their ideas about sounds similar to those embodied in the conventional orthography. Phonemic sensitivity may actually decline after reading has become skilled and automatic (Scarborough, 1995). The phonemic segmentation skills of literate adults can be improved through instruction. Teachers must be given the opportunity to receive such instruction so that they can interpret and respond to students' spelling errors, pick the best examples for use in instruction, and sequence teaching in an optimal manner. Moats (1995) and Treiman (1993, chap. 1) outlined some information about phonology and orthography that may be useful for teachers.

As I have argued in this section, there are a number of advantages to be gained by analyzing the spelling errors that children produce and tailoring instruction accordingly. Analyses of children's reading errors can provide some of the same benefits (see Siegel, chap. 6, this volume). However, young children are often more willing to try writing a word than to try reading it. Even kindergartners will typically attempt to spell a word when told to spell it as it sounds and not to worry about being right or wrong. When asked to read a word, the same children may say that they cannot read or that they do not know what the word says. In addition, spellings are easier to analyze than are oral reading responses because they are concrete and permanent. Teachers can collect their students' writings and analyze them later, rather than listening to children read and making quick judgments about the quality of their errors. In addition, as discussed earlier in this chapter, young children's alphabetic knowledge may reveal itself more clearly in their spelling than in their reading. For all these reasons, it is not enough to focus on reading miscues. One can get a fuller picture of children's progress and potential by also looking at their spellings.

HOW SHOULD SPELLING BE APPROACHED AT THE EARLY ELEMENTARY SCHOOL LEVEL?

I have reviewed a number of reasons for including spelling as one component of literacy instruction at the early elementary school level. What types of writing experiences should young children have and how should teachers deal with the misspellings that are bound to occur? In this section, I discuss a variety of approaches that have been proposed and evaluate these approaches in light of research.

One approach is to begin literacy instruction with writing rather than with reading (Chomsky, 1979; Montessori, 1964). This approach is motivated by some of the findings discussed earlier in this chapter. As I discussed, some children start to write at an early age even before they begin to read. Those children who do not begin to write on their own before they go to school may use the alphabetic principle earlier in spelling than in reading. The idea of approaching reading through invented spelling fits with the view that children learn best if they construct a system on their own rather than having it handed to them by an adult (e.g., Piaget, 1972). Chomsky described a first-grade classroom in which children begin by writing, using invented spelling, and later use the books they have written, recopied in standard spelling, as reading material.

One problem with the "write first, read later" approach lies in what to do about children who cannot write words or who produce spellings that have no relationship to the intended word. Should we wait until these children begin to spell on their own, letting them draw pictures or engage in other activities while their classmates write stories? Alternatively, should we provide these children with experiences that will help them to spell on their own?

As I discuss later in this section, instruction in phonemic awareness and in how phonemes relate to letters can be very helpful for such children.

A related approach to writing and spelling is advocated by proponents of the whole language approach to literacy instruction. Although these individuals do not necessarily believe that children should begin to write before they read, they recommend that writing be an integral part of early literacy instruction. Children are encouraged to write from an early age and there is little stress on the correctness of their spellings. In some classrooms, like the one studied by Treiman (1993), children are not told the standard spellings of words, even if they ask. The idea is that learning to spell is a developmental process and that children will move toward conventional spelling on their own with little or no direct teaching. The main type of input that is required for learning to spell, in the whole language view, is experience with print. Children will get this experience through their reading and so spelling need not be directly taught.

Some of the research reviewed earlier in this chapter casts doubt on aspects of the whole language approach. As I discussed, children do not always become good spellers by doing a lot of reading. Moreover, children learn to spell better if they study words in isolation than if they read them in context. The whole language approach, by eschewing presentation of isolated words and isolated sounds, may not give children the kinds of experiences that they need in order to become good spellers. A similar problem applies to the "write first, read later" approach, if it is assumed that children will learn to spell as a result of reading their own stories in conventional print.

Castle, Riach, and Nicholson (1994) reported an empirical evaluation of the whole language approach as applied to spelling. In New Zealand, where they conducted the study, literacy instruction begins at the age of 5 and follows a whole language approach. As one feature of this approach, children are encouraged to write stories and invent their own spellings. Castle and her colleagues identified 30 school beginners who started out low in phonemic awareness. Half of these children were assigned to the experimental group. These children worked with an experimenter twice weekly for 20 minutes each session over a 10-week period. The children engaged in a variety of activities that were designed to foster phonemic awareness and knowledge of sound-letter associations. The other half of the children were assigned to the control group. These children spent the same amount of time writing stories and inventing spellings. The children in the experimental group showed more improvement in phonemic awareness from pretest to posttest than did the children in the control group. In addition, the experimental group made larger gains on a standardized real-word spelling test and an experimental spelling test. The experimental group was particularly good at spelling pseudowords, suggesting that the training they received improved their ability to segment novel words into phonemes and represent these phonemes with letters. The superiority of the experimental group is especially noteworthy given that the control group actually engaged in more story writing and inventive spelling than did the experimental group.

The results of Castle et al. (1994) suggest that, for children who enter school with poor phonological awareness, grasping the alphabetic principle requires more than writing using invented spelling. Such writing should be supplemented with phonemic awareness training and training in sound-letter associations. These findings concur with other findings showing that, for children who are initially low in phonemic awareness, instruction that is directed toward improving these skills improves later spelling (Bradley & Bryant, 1985; Lie, 1991; Lundberg, Frost, & Petersen, 1988; Tornéus, 1984). The gains appear to be most pronounced when the phonemic awareness instruction is integrated with instruction about the relationships between phonemes and letters, as in the study by Castle and colleagues (Ball & Blachman, 1991; Bradley & Bryant, 1985; Hatcher et al., 1994). That is, children should be taught not only how to analyze spoken words into phonemes but also how to represent the phonemes with letters.

If phonemic awareness instruction and instruction in letter-sound corre-spondences are provided, then encouraging children to invent their own spellings during free writing assignments may be helpful. Evidence for this claim comes from a study by Clarke (1988). Clarke studied four first-grade classrooms, two in which children were expected to invent spellings for unknown words during their creative writing periods and two in which children were expected to use traditional spellings. The children in both the invented spelling classrooms and the traditional spelling classrooms also learned letter sounds, generally in isolation, and followed a basal reading program. All of the children were taught phonics as a part of their language arts instruction using a variety of oral drills and worksheets. Clarke found that children whose teachers encouraged invented spelling wrote longer sto-ries containing a greater variety of words than did children whose teachers expected correct spelling. Clarke also reported that the inventive spellers spent more time during a writing session actually engaged in writing or in reading what they had written. The traditional spellers spent more time asking or telling classmates how to spell words or copying spellings from dictionaries or wall charts. When these children asked the teacher for help, they spent time in unproductive waiting if the teacher was busy with another child.

A possible drawback of invented spelling that is suggested by the results of Clarke's (1988) study is that the first graders who were encouraged to invent spellings did not improve in usage of correct spellings over the course of the study. The percentage of correct spellings for this group increased from 70% in November to 73% in December, but decreased over the next 3 months to 60% in March. In contrast, the children using traditional spelling were over 90% correct throughout the course of the study . However, another study of first graders who followed a similar approach as the children in the invented spelling classrooms studied by Clarke found that children's spellings did become more correct over the course of the school year (Treiman, 1993). Perhaps Clarke would have found improvement had she followed the children for longer.

The most important result of Clarke's (1988) study is that the invented spelling group performed significantly better than did the traditional spelling group on a standardized spelling test and a spelling test involving low-frequency regularly spelled words. The inventive spellers also outperformed the traditional spellers on single-word reading tests, although not on passage comprehension. Importantly, the benefits of invented spelling were only significant for the children who had lower levels of alphabet knowledge, spelling skill, and reading skill at the beginning of first grade. For children who performed well on these measures at the start of first grade, there were no reliable differences in outcome between the invented spelling group and the traditional spelling group. Thus, Clarke's results suggest that encouraging children to invent spellings while they are engaged in creative writing helps them to appreciate the alphabetic principle. Once children have grasped this principle, inventive spelling is no longer superior to traditional spelling.

It is important to keep in mind that the inventive spellers in Clarke's study did not follow a strict whole language approach to reading and writing. These children were learning about phonics and letter-sound associations as well as doing creative writing. It is not clear whether a superiority for inventive spelling over traditional spelling would have been found among children who did not receive any phonics instruction.

Clarke's (1988) results help to alleviate a fear that is commonly voiced by opponents of invented spelling—that young children who are encouraged to invent their own spellings will come to believe that these spellings are correct and will get "stuck" producing incorrect spellings. If this were so, then the children in Clarke's invented spelling classrooms should have performed worse on the spelling posttests than the children in the traditional spelling classrooms. As discussed earlier, young children do not always read back what they have written. Even when they do, children must read a word many times in order to learn its spelling. Because the children in the invented spelling classrooms spelled a large variety of words, they probably did not produce any single error often enough to encode the error as correct. Supporting this line of reasoning, Ehri, Gibbs, and Underwood (1988) found that second and third graders who invented spellings for novel words did no worse when later learning the words' correct spellings than children who did not invent spellings. Also, Bradley and King (1992) found that exposure to misspellings did not hurt the spelling accuracy of most fifth graders. Although production of or exposure to misspellings seems to have negative effects on some fifth graders (Bradley & King, 1992) and adults (Brown, 1988; Jacoby

& Hollingshead, 1990), it does not appear to hurt early elementary school children.

The results reviewed so far suggest that first graders can and should write at some time during the school day. During this creative writing period, it is probably a good idea to encourage children to invent spellings for unknown words if they cannot readily recall or locate the correct spelling. This policy will mean that children spend more time writing and less time waiting for a teacher's help. It will allow children to write more interesting and engaging stories than if they were limited to a small set of known words. By inventing spellings, children will gain practice breaking words into phonemes and representing these phonemes with letters. However, creative writing using invented spelling should not be the only type of writing experience that children receive. To make most progress in learning to spell, children need instruction in phonemic awareness if they are initially lacking in these skills. They also need some type of direct instruction in spelling. Clarke's (1988) findings suggest that, as children become better spellers, there are fewer benefits to be gained from inventive spelling. As time goes on, children should be encouraged to spell words correctly, for example by looking for words in a dictionary or a personal word bank, rather than inventing their own spellings.

If children need some type of direct instruction in spelling above and beyond experience with writing and inventive spelling, what kind of instruction is most useful? One possibility is to embed spelling instruction into each child's independent writing experiences. Using this approach, the teacher selects certain invented spellings for consideration and helps the child to understand how the spellings can be improved. This approach may be called *guided invented spelling*. Because it is integrated into the context of writing, it is an example of what Tracey and Morrow (chap. 14, this volume) called *authentic instruction*.

Currently, many teachers who encourage invented spelling do not offer children much guidance on how to improve their spellings. For example, the teachers in the invented spelling classrooms studied by Clarke (1988) seem not to have commented on the correctness of the children's spellings or helped children to improve their spellings. The children usually read their stories to the class, the teachers commented on the content of the stories, and this marked the end of the writing process. In the classroom studied by Treiman (1993), the teacher wrote the conventional spellings of the words on the child's paper but did not discuss how the child's spellings differed from the conventional ones and did not help the child to improve his or her spellings.

Guided invented spelling would seem to be very helpful if well and sensitively done. This is because the instruction is tailored to individual children, giving them feedback on the errors they have just made and teaching them what they need to know at that particular time. However, there is as yet no body of research systematically addressing the effectiveness of guided invented spelling.

The research does suggest a number of techniques by which guided invented spelling could be carried out. For certain types of errors, it may be helpful to focus on phonemic awareness, helping children to divide problematic parts of spoken words into phonemes. For example, a child who spells *bread* as BED can be helped to analyze the /br/ cluster into /b/ followed by /r/. The child can be shown that each part of the cluster can be represented with a separate letter, yielding *br*. If the child then spells the word as BRED, the teacher might say that this is an excellent attempt, not mentioning at this time that the word actually contains an *a*. Another way to guide invented spelling is to focus on reading. For instance, a teacher may have the child read BED and help the child to realize that this printed word corresponds to *bed*, not *bread*. Confronted with the fact that they have spelled two different-sounding words alike, children sometimes change their spellings. Indeed, this happened about 40% of the time among the first graders studied by Treiman (1991). This rate may be increased by teaching children how to use reading to check their spelling. Such an approach should help children learn to integrate reading and spelling, which, as I have discussed, are not always well connected in young children.

Teachers can offer guidance, as well, on the use of orthographic and morphological spelling strategies. For example, a child who spells *can* as CKAN can be shown known words that end with *ck* and words that have *ck* in the middle and can be led to the generalization that *ck* appears in these positions of words but not at the beginnings. Teachers can also help children use morphologically related words to guide their spelling. For example, a child who represents the flap sound of *dirty* with *d* rather than with the conventional *t* can be helped to think of *dirt* and use it as a guide. As another example, the child who omits the /n/ of *rained* can be taught to think of the stem *rain*. Children can learn to use not only morpheme units but other subword units in spelling. For example, a child who has spelled *tight* as TITE but who is familiar with the *ight* pattern in *might* and *light* could be taught that /ait/ is often spelled as *ight* (see Goswami, chap. 2, this volume).

Teachers using guided invented spelling must sometimes admit to children that certain letters in the conventional spelling of a word do not make good sense on the basis of sound. For example, there is no separate /I/ ("short i") sound in *girl*. The word instead contains a *syllabic* /r/ that takes the place of a vowel. If a child spells *girl* as GRL, as many first graders do (Treiman, 1993; Treiman, Berch, Tincoff, & Weatherston, 1993), a teacher may say that this is a good attempt to capture the word's sound but that the word happens to contain an *i* before the *r*. The teacher may use this opportunity to point out the orthographic generalization that all written syllables contain a vowel letter.

Although guided invented spelling would appear to offer many benefits, there are some potential problems with this approach. Teachers need time to interact with individual students based on the errors that each student has made in his or her writing. With many students, there may be little time for this type of individual teaching. In addition, guided invented spelling requires a large degree of skill on the part of teachers. They must be aware of the reasons behind children's errors and of what children are ready to learn next. Unfortunately, as discussed earlier, many teachers do not have the opportunity to acquire the linguistic knowledge that they need in order to guide children's spelling in the most effective manner. For instance, it would be counterproductive to tell a child that he or she should be able to hear an /ɪ/ sound in the spoken word *girl*. Telling a child that there is such a sound when there in fact is not could cause the child to doubt his or her ability to analyze words phonemically. Finally, because guided invented spelling takes place spontaneously, in response to a particular need, it may not be systematic enough to teach children what they need to know.

Given the limitations of guided invented spelling, this approach needs to be supplemented with group instruction. As discussed earlier (Bear & Barone, 1989; Morris & Perney, 1984), children can be placed in groups on the basis of their spelling and reading skills and spelling instruction can take place in these settings. Useful suggestions for such instruction may be found in the chapters in this volume by Goswami (chap. 2), Calfee (chap. 13), and Gaskins (chap. 9), as well as in Templeton (1991) and Brown, Sinatra, and Wagstaff (1996). For example, children can play games that involve analyzing spoken words into phonemes. They can sort printed words into categories, for example words beginning with single consonants versus those beginning with consonant clusters. They can learn to form new words by substituting one letter for another, forming *cat* and *mat* from *rat*. They can learn strategies for spelling new words based on familiar words and word parts, using *dirt* to spell *dirty* and *ight* to spell *tight* and *sight*. Instruction should be grounded on knowledge of spelling development and of the errors that children typically make. For example, given many first graders' difficulties in spelling consonant clusters, it would be useful to teach this skill directly. One cannot assume that a child who can use *b* at the beginning of *bed* and *r* at the beginning of *red* will necessarily be able to use *br* at the beginning of *bread* (Treiman, 1991). Some programs assume that children will be able to do this and so do not offer explicit teaching about the spelling of consonant clusters (Cronnell & Humes, 1980).

Memorization of spelling words and weekly spelling tests can be one component of spelling instruction. This type of activity is particularly useful for common but difficult-to-spell words such as *said* and *would*. However, children need to understand that the spellings of many words make sense on the basis of linguistic principles and that patterns like the *ai* of *said* are a special case. By placing too much stress on the rote memorization of unusual words, particularly during the early stages, teachers may give children the idea that the English spelling system is irregular and illogical. Thus, such study should not begin until children have grasped the alphabetic basis of the English writing system and have begun to read comfortably. Templeton (1991) suggested that the second half of first grade is a good time to begin the systematic study of word lists. The lists should be short, about five or six words, and should be made up of words that children already know how to read. Through spelling study, children critically examine the words and learn the details of their spellings. Several authors (Cunningham & Stanovich, 1990; Woloshyn & Pressley, 1995) have offered useful suggestions for strategies that children may be taught to use in memorizing words.

How should spelling instruction be integrated with reading? One way is to focus on the same or similar words in reading and in spelling. The results of Mason, McDaniel, and Callaway (1974) suggest that children who are taught to spell words from their reading program, whether through direct instruction or as they use the words in composition, progress more rapidly than do children who are taught to spell words that are not in their readers. Another way of integrating spelling and reading is to teach children to use reading to check their spelling. Although this strategy seems obvious to adults, young children do not always read back what they have written. Activities involving spelling and word study can form a common core that links the domains of reading and writing (Templeton, 1991). Through such activities, children are led to examine and analyze the words that they know how to read. They learn to use the knowledge extracted from these analyses as a foundation for reading and spelling new words.

CONCLUSIONS

Advocates of phonics-based instruction and advocates of whole language instruction, although they disagree on many things, agree on at least one point. Specifically, both think that writing is important. Both are interested in children's early invented spellings, if for somewhat different reasons. Advocates of direct instruction in phonics believe that spelling helps strengthen children's phonics skills by giving them practice in segmenting spoken words into phonemes and relating phonemes and graphemes. These individuals are impressed by the knowledge of phonology and language structure that children bring with them to the spelling task and by the role that spelling can play in furthering this knowledge. Whole language advocates, although they place primary stress on higher-level writing skills, are struck by the fact that some children who have received no formal reading or spelling instruction can make up their own spellings for words. They encourage all children to invent spellings for words when writing, and they believe that children will move toward correct spelling on their own as they learn to read. Whole language advocates further stress the importance of integrating writing and reading and the need to make both activities interesting and motivating for children.

Both of the positions outlined here have some merit. The research reviewed in this chapter shows that spelling helps children master the alphabetic principle and also has a positive impact on reading. Proponents of the whole language approach are thus correct in suggesting that writing not be put off until the middle or late elementary grades but should begin much earlier. However, contrary to the belief of whole language advocates, the research shows that children will not automatically become good spellers as a result of reading a lot. One cannot count on transfer from reading to teach spelling. Children should certainly read good literature, but they should also spend time focusing on individual words. These experiences can be provided through individual instruction—what I have called guided invented spelling—through group activities, or, ideally, through both. Although children need to spend some time studying isolated words and sounds, this study should not be meaningless or boring. Fortunately, there are a number of interesting and motivating activities through which children can learn about words and their spellings. Memorization of word lists may be one part of such instruction, but it should by no means be the only part. Indeed, the systematic study of words—their spellings, meanings, and derivations—provides an important foundation for all of reading and writing.

ACKNOWLEDGEMENTS

Preparation of this chapter was supported by NSF Grant SBR-9408456. I thank Usha Goswami, Kira Rodriguez, Marie Cassar, and the editors for their helpful comments.

REFERENCES

Adams, M. J., Treiman, R., & Pressley, M. (1998). Reading, writing, and literacy. In W. Damon (Editor-in-Chief), I. E. Sigel & K. A. Renninger, (Vol. Eds.), *Handbook of child psychology, 5th ed. Vol. 4* (pp. 275–355). New York: Wiley.

Ball, E. W., & Blachman, B. A. (1991). Does phoneme awareness training in kindergarten make a difference in early word recognition and developmental spelling? *Reading Research Quarterly, 26,* 49–66.

Bear, D. R., & Barone, D. (1989). Using children's spellings to group for word study and directed reading in the primary classroom. *Reading Psychology: An International Quarterly, 10,* 275–292.

Bergeron, B. S. (1990). What does the term whole language mean? Constructing a definition from the literature. *Journal of Reading Behavior, 22,* 301–329.

Boder, E. (1973). Developmental dyslexia: A diagnostic approach based on three atypical reading–spelling patterns. *Developmental Medicine and Child Neurology, 15*, 663–687.

Bosman, A. M. T., & Van Orden, G. C. (1997). Why spelling is more difficult than reading. In C. A. Perfetti, L. Rieben, & M. Fayol (Eds.), *Learning to spell: Research, theory, and practice across languages* (pp. 173–194). Hillsdale, NJ: Lawrence Erlbaum Associates.

Bradley, J. M., & King, P. V. (1992). Effects of proofreading on spelling: How reading misspelled and correctly spelled words affects spelling accuracy. *Journal of Reading Behavior, 24*, 413–432.

Bradley, L., & Bryant, P. (1985). *Rhyme and reason in reading and spelling.* Ann Arbor: University of Michigan Press.

Brown, A. S. (1988). Encountering misspellings and spelling performance: Why wrong isn't right. *Journal of Educational Psychology, 80*, 488–494.

Brown, K. J., Sinatra, G. M., & Wagstaff, J. M. (1996). Exploring the potential of analogy instruction to support children's spelling development. *Elementary School Journal, 97*, 81–99.

Bruck, M., & Waters, G. (1990). Effects of reading skill on component spelling skills. *Applied Psycholinguistics, 11*, 425–437.

Bryant, P. E., & Bradley, L. (1980). Why children sometimes write words which they do not read. In U. Frith (Ed.), *Cognitive processes in spelling* (pp. 355–370). London: Academic.

Burns, J. M., & Richgels, D. J. (1989). An investigation of task requirements associated with the invented spellings of 4-year-olds with above average intelligence. *Journal of Reading Behavior, 21*, 1–14.

Byrne, B. (1992). Studies in the acquisition procedure for reading: Rationale, hypotheses, and data. In P. B. Gough, L. C. Ehri, & R. Treiman (Eds.), *Reading acquisition* (pp. 1–34). Hillsdale, NJ: Lawrence Erlbaum Associates.

Cassar, M., & Treiman, R. (in press). The beginnings of orthographic knowledge: Children's understanding of simple letter patterns. *Journal of Educational Psychology.*

Castle, J. M., Riach, J., & Nicholson, T. (1994). Getting off to a better start in reading and spelling: The effects of phonemic awareness instruction within a whole language program. *Journal of Educational Psychology, 86*, 350–359.

Cataldo, S., & Ellis, N. (1988). Interactions in the development of spelling, reading and phonological skills. *Journal of Research in Reading, 11*, 86–109.

Chomsky, C. (1979). Approaching reading through invented spelling. In L. B. Resnick & P. A. Weaver (Eds.), *Theory and practice of early reading* (Vol. 2, pp. 43–65). Hillsdale, NJ: Lawrence Erlbaum Associates.

Clarke, L. K. (1988). Invented versus traditional spelling in first graders' writings: Effects on learning to spell and read. *Research in the Teaching of English, 22*, 281–309.

Critchley, M. (1975). Specific developmental dyslexia. In E. H. Lenneberg & E. Lenneberg (Eds.), *Foundations of language development: A multidisciplinary approach* (Vol. 2, pp. 361–366). New York: Academic.

Cronnell, B., & Humes, A. (1980). Elementary spelling: What's really taught. *Elementary School Journal, 81*, 59–64.

Cunningham, A. E., & Stanovich, K. E. (1990). Early spelling acquisition: Writing beats the computer. *Journal of Educational Psychology, 82*, 159–162.

Ehri, L. C. (1986). Sources of difficulty in learning to spell and read. In M. L. Wolraich & D. Routh (Eds.), *Advances in developmental and behavioral pediatrics* (Vol. 7, pp. 121–195). Greenwich, CT: JAI.

Ehri, L. C. (1992). Reconceptualizing the development of sight word reading and its relationship to recoding. In P. B. Gough, L. C. Ehri, & R. Treiman (Eds.), *Reading acquisition* (pp. 107–143). Hillsdale, NJ: Lawrence Erlbaum Associates.

Ehri, L. C., Gibbs, A. L., & Underwood, T. L. (1988). Influence of errors on learning the spellings of English words. *Contemporary Educational Psychology, 13*, 236–253.

Ehri, L. C., & Roberts, K. T. (1979). Do beginners learn printed words better in contexts or in isolation? *Child Development, 50,* 675–685.

Ehri, L. C., & Wilce, L. S. (1980a). Do beginners learn to read function words better in sentences or in lists? *Reading Research Quarterly, 15,* 451–476.

Ehri, L. C., & Wilce, L. S. (1980b). The influence of orthography on readers' conceptualization of the phonemic structure of words. *Applied Psycholinguistics, 1,* 371–385.

Ehri, L. C., & Wilce, L. S. (1986). The influence of spellings on speech: Are alveolar flaps /d/ or /t/? In D. B. Yaden & S. Templeton (Eds.), *Metalinguistic awareness and beginning literacy* (pp. 101–114). Portsmouth, NH: Heinemann.

Ehri, L. C., & Wilce, L. S. (1987). Does learning to spell help beginners learn to read words? *Reading Research Quarterly, 22,* 47–65.

Frith, U. (1980). Unexpected spelling problems. In U. Frith (Ed.), *Cognitive processes in spelling* (pp. 495–515). New York: Academic.

Frith, U. (1985). Beneath the surface of developmental dyslexia. In K. E. Patterson, J. C. Marshall, & M. Coltheart (Eds.), *Surface dyslexia: Neuropsychological and cognitive studies of phonological reading* (pp. 301–330). Hove, England: Lawrence Erlbaum Associates.

Gentry, J. R. (1982). An analysis of developmental spelling in GNYS AT WRK. *The Reading Teacher, 36,* 192–200.

Goswami, U., & Bryant, P. E. (1990). *Phonological skills and learning to read.* Hove, England: Lawrence Erlbaum Associates.

Gough, P. B., Juel, C., & Griffith, P. L. (1992). Reading, spelling, and the orthographic cipher. In P. B. Gough, L. Ehri, & R. Treiman (Eds.), *Reading acquisition* (pp. 35–48). Hillsdale, NJ: Lawrence Erlbaum Associates.

Hatcher, P. J., Hulme, C., & Ellis, A. W. (1994). Ameliorating early reading failure by integrating the teaching of reading and phonological skills: The phonological linkage hypothesis. *Child Development, 65,* 41–57.

Henderson, E. (1985). *Teaching spelling.* Boston: Houghton-Mifflin.

Huxford, L., Terrell, C., & Bradley, L. (1991). The relationship between the phonological strategies employed in reading and spelling. *Journal of Research in Reading, 14,* 99–105.

Jacoby, L. L., & Hollingshead, A. (1990). Reading student essays may be hazardous to your spelling: Effects of reading incorrectly and correctly spelled words. *Canadian Journal of Psychology, 44,* 345–358.

Lie, A. (1991). Effects of a training program for stimulating skills in word analysis in first-grade children. *Reading Research Quarterly, 26,* 234–250.

Lundberg, I., Frost, J., & Petersen, O.-P. (1988). Effects of an extensive program for stimulating phonological awareness in preschool children. *Reading Research Quarterly, 23,* 263–284.

Mann, V. (1993). Phoneme awareness and future reading ability. *Journal of Learning Disabilities, 26,* 259–269.

Mann, V. A., Tobin, P., & Wilson, R. (1987). Measuring phonological awareness through the invented spellings of kindergarten children. *Merrill-Palmer Quarterly, 33,* 354–391.

Mason, G., McDaniel, H., & Callaway, B. (1974). Relating reading and spelling: A comparison of methods. *Elementary School Journal, 74,* 381–386.

Moats, L. C. (1994). The missing foundation in teacher education: Knowledge of the structure of spoken and written language. *Annals of Dyslexia, 44,* 81–102.

Moats, L. C. (1995). *Spelling: Development, disabilities, and instruction.* Baltimore: York.

Mommers, M. J. C. (1987). An investigation into the relationship between word recognition, reading comprehension and spelling skills in the first two years of primary school. *Journal of Reading Research, 10,* 122–143.

Montessori, M. (1964). *The Montessori method.* New York: Schocken.

Morris, D., & Perney, J. (1984). Developmental spelling as a predictor of first-grade reading achievement. *The Elementary School Journal, 84,* 441–457.

Perfetti, C.A. (1992). The representation problem in reading acquisition. In P. B. Gough, L. C. Ehri, & R. Treiman (Eds.), *Reading acquisition* (pp. 145–174). Hillsdale, NJ: Lawrence Erlbaum Associates.

Piaget, J. (1972). Some aspects of operations. In M. Piers (Ed.), *Play and development* (pp. 15–27). New York: Norton.

Read, C. (1975). Children's categorization of speech sounds in English. *NCTE Research Report No. 17*. Urbana, IL: National Council of Teachers of English.

Read, C. (1986). *Children's creative spelling*. London: Routledge & Kegan Paul.

Scarborough, H. S. (1995, March). *The fate of phonemic awareness beyond the elementary school years*. Paper presented at the Society for Research in Child Development, Indianapolis, IN.

Seymour, P. H. K., & Elder, L. (1986). Beginning reading without phonology. *Cognitive Neuropsychology, 3*, 1–36.

Shanahan, T. (1984). Nature of the reading–writing connection: An exploratory multivariate analysis. *Journal of Educational Psychology, 76*, 466–477.

Stahl, S. A., & Murray, B. A. (1994). Defining phonological awareness and its relationship to early reading. *Journal of Educational Psychology, 86*, 221–234.

Stuart, M., & Coltheart, M. (1988). Does reading develop in a sequence of stages? *Cognition, 30*, 139–181.

Templeton, S. (1991). Teaching and learning the English spelling system: Reconceptualizing method and purpose. *Elementary School Journal, 92*, 185–201.

Tornéus, M. (1984). Phonological awareness and reading: A chicken-and-egg problem? *Journal of Educational Psychology, 76*, 1346–1358.

Treiman, R. (1985a). Phonemic awareness and spelling: Children's judgments do not always agree with adults'. *Journal of Experimental Child Psychology, 39*, 182–201.

Treiman, R. (1985b). Spelling of stop consonants after /s/ by children and adults. *Applied Psycholinguistics, 6*, 261–282.

Treiman, R. (1991). Children's spelling errors on syllable-initial consonant clusters. *Journal of Educational Psychology, 83*, 346–360.

Treiman, R. (1993). *Beginning to spell: A study of first-grade children*. New York: Oxford University Press.

Treiman, R. (1994). Use of consonant letter names in beginning spelling. *Developmental Psychology, 30*, 567–580.

Treiman, R., Berch, D., Tincoff, R., & Weatherston, S. (1993). Phonology and spelling: The case of syllabic consonants. *Journal of Experimental Child Psychology, 56*, 267–290.

Treiman, R., Cassar, M., & Zukowski, A. (1994). What types of linguistic information do children use in spelling? The case of flaps. *Child Development, 65*, 1310–1329.

Uhry, J. K., & Shepherd, M. J. (1993). Segmentation/spelling instruction as part of a first-grade reading program: Effects on several measures of reading. *Reading Research Quarterly, 28*, 219–233.

van Bon, W. H. J., & Duighuisen, H. C. M. (1995). Sometimes spelling is easier than phonemic segmentation. *Scandinavian Journal of Psychology, 46*, 82–94.

Varnhagen, C. K., McCallum, M., Burstow, M., Pawlik, L., & Poon, B. (1997). Is children's spelling naturally stage-like? *Reading and Writing: An Interdisciplinary Journal, 9*, 451–481.

Woloshyn, V., & Pressley, M. (1995). Spelling. In M. Pressley & V. Woloshyn (Eds.), *Cognitive strategy instruction that really improves children's academic performance* (2nd. ed., pp. 116–152). Cambridge, MA: Brookline.

13

▼▼▼▼▼▼▼

Phonics and Phonemes: Learning to Decode and Spell in a Literature-Based Program

Robert Calfee
Stanford University

This chapter is written in a context of turmoil within California and elsewhere, as concerned parents and legislators demand a shift from literature-based early literacy programs to "old-fashioned" phonics and spelling. Low test scores (real or purported) are one cause for California's concerns, but similar efforts are welling up in other states. The conflict reflects deep underlying issues, some political, others personal, about the goals of education.

This conflict is probably as divisive in early literacy as anywhere in the curriculum: phonics versus literature, skill versus understanding, passive practice versus eager engagement. In one view, early schooling should inculcate basic skills by teacher-led direct instruction. Virtually all phonics programs incorporate this method (Adams, 1990—note that the citations in this chapter are minimal, mostly as leads to the relevant archival literature; for additional background, see Calfee & Drum, 1986; Calfee & Henry, 1996). From another perspective, the aim is for students to become strategic and purposeful, capable of teamwork as well as individual excellence. Whole language reflects this philosophy, as have predecessors (e.g., Ashton-Warner, 1963; McIntyre & Pressley, 1996; Weaver, 1990). One additional contrast merits comment: the belief that young students differ substantially in their innate capacity to acquire literacy versus the belief (and commitment) that all children are capable of achieving high levels of literacy, regardless of their background and experience.

This chapter describes a framework that incorporates the most promising features of the contrasting positions, not by simple "addition," but by a redesign that goes beyond existing policies and practices. One strategy for achieving balance is to spend part of each reading lesson on standard phonics, and then switch to literary appreciation. This approach to eclecticism, which typifies many classrooms, lacks coherence and is of uncertain effectiveness. Another strategy is a gradual shift over the grades from basics to "the real stuff"—phonics in first grade, comprehension skills by third grade. Both strategies can be found in classrooms and in the basal series that remain the foundation for reading instruction in U.S. schools. If balance means eclecticism, then we have tried it for several decades, and it apparently does not work for many students.

To concretize the current dilemma, imagine a primary (K–2) team of teachers who ask a consultant how they can sustain the advantages of a literature-based program while ensuring that their students acquire skills needed for independent reading and writing. Their literature-based approach motivates students, but a substantial number of students are eager to read but unable to decode unfamiliar words, willing to write but unable to spell words well enough to read them a week later. The teachers worry about two specific phonics issues. First, many students show little interest in learning to decode and spell; they prefer books that they "already know how to read." Second, many students acquire phonics objectives slowly, retention and transfer are limited, and the activities are monotonous. The teachers have adopted a supplemental decoding program. Now they are discussing whether to increase instruction time in phonics, or perhaps assign more students to intensive remediation.

For the past several years I have been "tinkering" with an alternative to these currently available practices; Word Work is a decoding-spelling strand incorporating the policies and practices found in literature-based classrooms (Calfee & Patrick, 1995). The program features include the creation of a "literate community" consistent with whole language philosophy, but with a greater emphasis on explicit strategies for literature analysis, and with a complementary emphasis on teaching students explicit strategies for analysis of English spelling–sound relations.

Word Work differs from typical phonics programs in several ways. First, instruction incorporates principles of social–cognitive learning; instruction is student centered more than teacher directed. Students encounter "real" spelling tests as they revise a work for public display, but they can ask others for help in polishing the work. Second, spelling–sound relations are taught as a meaningfully organized system rather than a list of rote objectives. The program incorporates the *metaphonic* principle: Students are expected to give the correct pronunciation or spelling, but also to explain how they reached it. Third, decoding and spelling are integrated, emphasizing immediate application in purposeful reading and writing. Unlike a step-by-step model by which students first learn to read, Word Work students progress in parallel across all domains of reading and writing. Finally, although teachers high-light spelling–sound patterns in reading selections and writing assignments, neither reading nor writing is limited by the decoding-spelling curriculum. Students may be working on short-vowel patterns, but this does not confine them to "The fat cat sat on the flat mat."

This chapter describes the Word Work program and presents three case studies. The results are that virtually all students acquired the decoding-spelling skills and understanding needed for independent reading and writing in a literature-based program. The program does challenge classroom teachers, because it requires going beyond both free-form literature-based activities and lockstep phonics prescriptions.

THE PHONICS DEBATE: WHAT TO TEACH
AND HOW TO TEACH IT

This volume is set against the continuing debate about reading and writing instruction during the first 3 years of schooling. Here are some observations about what we already know and have yet to discover, based on research and practice (Adams, 1990; Chall, 1983; Chall, Jacobs, & Baldwin, 1990):

Explicit phonics: A traditional phonics curriculum improves early reading as measured by standardized achievement tests, compared with programs that do not include explicit decoding-spelling. Unfortunately, 15% to 35% of phonics-taught students still reach third grade unable to handle grade-level reading and writing tasks. Most research relies on multiple-choice tests; few large-scale evaluations have assessed reading fluency, spelling and writing performance, interest, or motivation.

Phonemic awareness: Students' ability to identify and manipulate speech sounds on entry to school is a strong predictor of success in acquiring literacy, and instructional programs that incorporate phonemic awareness help students, especially those at risk for learning to read. Unfortunately, the construct of phonemic awareness remains fuzzy, with multitudinous definitions and programs of uncertain effectiveness.

Comprehension and composition: Skill and knowledge in handling texts are not an automatic consequence of learning to decode and spell. Immersion in genuine literature and informational books, opportunities to reread familiar stories, and purposeful writing all increase interest in reading, enhance general text knowledge, and expand word knowledge.

Missing from this list is any answer to the question of what to teach. It is assumed throughout the debate that phonics is clearly defined. The job is simply to teach letter-sound relations. Letters are easy to see, and phonemic awareness helps students learn about sounds. What's the problem?

In fact, as the following section shows, the English letter-sound system is a rather remarkable invention, and understanding this system is crucial for the construction of a comprehensible curriculum. The conceptual framework for Word Work builds on the historical and morphophonemic structure of English orthography (Balmuth, 1982; Venezky, 1970), which leads in turn to a definition of phonemic awareness and an explanation for its importance in acquiring phonics. Both the incidental mini-lessons of whole language and the overly specific objectives of the phonics curriculum obscure this structure, confusing students and teachers.

English: A Truly Alphabetic Language

English is a polyglot—many languages. Anglo-Saxon is the foundation, with overlays of French from the 11th-century Norman invasion, Latin and Greek from the English Renaissance, and contributions from around the world reflecting the military and economic dominance of the British (and later) the Americans. Anglo-Saxon, the basis for 95% of the most frequent words, is a collage of languages from the Baltic regions. With origins in German and Swedish, Anglo-Saxon took on a character of its own as successive waves of invaders swept over England, beginning in 200 AD with the Angles and Saxons, continuing with the Vikings and Jutes. Oral traditions dominated during this time. Languages melded and merged, creating an amalgam shaped around a small lexicon of "four-letter" words, with compounds serving for complex constructs. The language was phonetically rich, with multiple dialects.

Catholic missionaries created a written form of Anglo-Saxon-ish using the Roman alphabet. Twenty-four letters were a poor match to 40-plus phonemes, with vowels a particular challenge. In 1066, the Normans complicated matters by adding some 50,000 new words to the Anglo-Saxon base. The English gutturalized the French pronunciation, but print remained fixed, adding a second spelling system to the emerging written language. Romance words were used for more formal discourse—*clam* for plain language, *mollusk* for fancy. Around third grade, today's students begin to encounter these fancy words. This chapter focuses on the Anglo-Saxon orthography that children confront in the primary grades; Romance words will require their own tale.

English orthography is fundamentally alphabetic. Letters represent sounds, although not by simple linear translation. Graphemes, the sound-bearing elements, can be letter combinations like *sh* or *ps*. In a word like *lampshade*, linear reading might yield /lamps-ha-de/—close, but no cigar. Accomplished readers first divide the word into its morphemes or word parts. They can then divide each morpheme into graphemic units; *m* and *p* are two different units, whereas *sh* is a single unit. Consonants are relatively simple, but vowels are a mess. Anglo-Saxon relies heavily on markers to signal vowel contrasts. In the present example, the final *e* acts not as a sound in its own right (although at one time it did), but indicates the "long" pronunciation of the preceding *a*.

Simple "rules" will not work, and educators despair at complexity. There is a simple solution. For the young student, learning to decode and spell depends on sorting words into three categories. The first set, *handy words*, comprises the high-frequency words (the Dolch list) essential for all reading and writing. Many are function words like *the, a, is, was, of,* and *on,* which provide the semantic "glue" for making sentences. They often depart from regular letter-sound patterns. The second set, *topical words*, serves for particular tasks, such as writing about the fall holidays—Halloween, Thanksgiving, and the winter solstice (Christmas, Hanukkah, Kwanza)—which requires a rich array of words, many long and complex, reflecting the many languages and cultures in our nation. In the third set, words are *regular*, in the sense that they follow predictable patterns. They are not especially frequent, nor are they related to any particular topic. Handling these words requires that students be able to "attack" the enormous array of words within their spoken language (although perhaps unknown in print). The foundation for this third set is the consonant-vowel-consonant (CVC) "sandwich," the centerpiece of the Word Work curriculum.

The CVC unit is a user-friendly label for the vocalic center unit that linguists have identified as a fundamental unit in English orthography. In many languages, the contrast between vowels and consonants is not essential for understanding orthographic patterns. Spanish, for instance, relies on unitized consonant-vowel combinations—*ma-me-mi-mo-mu*—much like the syllabaries in languages like Japanese. What distinguishes English is the huge number of CVC combinations, more than 50,000, that arise from its rich array of consonants, consonant digraphs, and consonant blends, combined with the multitude of vowel patterns (Fig. 13.1). These basic building blocks appear as individual words (*tab, fit*), and within syllabic patterns (*rabbit*) and morphological combinations (*hotshot*). The student who has learned to process these patterns as unitized chunks can decode and spell an enormous variety of novel words in print.

Two challenges confront the developing reader in mastering the chunking task. The first is to acquire the concept of the CVC unit. The second is to master vowel correspondences. The Word Work curriculum focuses on these two primary elements.

The CVC Building Block

English is "truly alphabetic." What does this claim mean, and why is it important? The alphabetic principle describes an array of spelling systems in which graphemes represent phonemes. Sometimes the correspondence is

DECODING
Letter-Sound Correspondences

CONSONANTS		
Single Letter	Blends	Digraphs
Consistent and simple correspondences easily learned	Combinations of single letter sounds <u>st</u> a <u>nd</u> <u>pr</u> o <u>ng</u>	Relatively few combinations-- each consistent <u>ch</u> atter <u>sh</u> are <u>th</u> eir <u>th</u> ing <u>wh</u> ere

VOWELS		
Single Letter		
Long vs Short	r and l Affected	Digraphs

mate   mat
Pete   pat
pining   pinning
biter   bitter
nodes   nods
cubed   cubbed
	par pare pal pall
	her here ___
	sir ___ ___
	for ___ ___
		One sound:
		ai/ay maid may
		  ee meet
		oi/oy foil toy
		au/aw taut law
		Two sounds:
		ea breath breathe
		oa boat broad
		oo cook food
		ou/ow
		  round four
		  cow snow

FIG. 13.1. Consonant-vowel matrix for Anglo-Saxon letter-sound correspondences.

fairly simple and consistent; each grapheme represents a single phoneme. The connection is seldom perfect, of course, because variations in oral speech appear in every language. In English, for example, "What you just said" often comes out as "Wha-chue-ju-sed." In contrast, one can speak understandable Spanish by reading consonant-vowel combinations.

English, although fundamentally alphabetical, has numerous surface-level complexities and inconsistencies. Some educators, partly because of these irregularities, and partly from laboratory research on whole-word recognition by skilled readers, conclude that the best way to teach English print is through extensive practice with the word as the unit of analysis: "Just read!" Such "Chinese" readers can be found, but their skill level is typically lower than that of so-called "Phoenician" readers, who have mastered letter-sound relations. Experienced readers can process individual letter-sound units in a word, and rely on this technique when confronted with novel or complex words, sometimes for decoding but especially for spelling.

Phonics programs generally build on some form of syllabary. One strategy is to teach phonogram patterns, consonant + vowel/consonant combinations, in which an initial consonant is added to the phonogram base (*r-at*, *f-at*, *m-at*). Studies show that these onset + rime patterns are more easily acquired than the alternative consonant/vowel + consonant combinations (*ra-n*, *ra-t*, *ra-d*), at least for English.

Neither whole-word nor phonogram-analogy methods require students to operate at the level of individual phoneme–grapheme relations, except perhaps for initial consonants. Curiously, although consonants exist in greater numbers and are phonologically more complex than are vowels, several decades of research show that vowels are most problematic in early decoding and spelling.

The argument for treating English as "truly alphabetic" rests on the large number of CVC building blocks that appear not only as words but as patterns. Learning these patterns is important if students are to gain independent access to literature. Flipping through my worn copy of Frederick's fables (Lionni, 1994), I encounter words like *abandon, reproachful, periwinkle,* and *scatters*. These words are all built of CVC "chunks"; understanding these units can open the door for the young reader to a marvelous collection of stories, even to writing *periwinkle* if she wishes.

Mastering the concept of the CVC "sandwich" is fundamental if the early reader is to handle novel words in reading and writing. Acquiring this concept means understanding the functional difference between consonants (the primary information-bearing units) and vowels (the "glue" that binds the consonants).

Phonemic Awareness as Articulation

Phoneme awareness is important because of the enormous number of CVC combinations in English, mentioned earlier. The gist of the present argument is that (a) full understanding of the alphabetic principle is critical for efficient decoding and spelling of CVC patterns, (b) explicit knowledge of phonemic elements is necessary for students to have something to link to graphemes, and (c) the articulatory dimensions of the consonant system provide the basis for teaching students about phonemes.

Like the alphabetic principle, the concept of phonemic awareness has been defined in various ways (Share, 1995). The most common definition in U.S. schools is "listen for the sounds in a word." This is actually a tough job! It takes considerable insight to know for what to listen. The kindergartner asked to mark all the words that "begin like *bat*" may chose *ball* for the wrong reason and mark *spot* for the right reason. Elkonin's (1963) early work emphasized the capacity to identify the number of phonemes in a spoken word: *fox* has four elements, as does *shucks*. A few programs, most notably Lindamood's Auditory Discrimination in Depth, teach articulation patterns. At the most basic level, the student is taught to lay out a string of colored blocks to mark the number and patterning of elements; *fox* can be written as red-yellow-blue-green, and *shucks* as orange-purple-blue-green.

A crucial element in Word Work is the development of explicit under-standing of the concept of a "sound," to which the key is not listening ability but speech perception. It is not enough to distinguish syllables and rhymes, although these are useful indicators and it helps students to know these concepts. Instead, the critical feature for English orthography is the phoneme, the set of subtle and complex distinctions that mark the contrasts among *bat*, *pat*, and *bad*. The motor theory of speech perception (Brady & Shank-weiler, 1991) suggests that articulation (how phonemes are produced) is the key to perception (how phonemes are heard).

Word Work goes directly to the phoneme–grapheme level. Students are taught individual letter-sound relations for the consonants through the ar-ticulatory principle, using the dimensions of manner, place, and voicing. For example, the phoneme typically represented by *f* is produced by placing the upper teeth on the lower lip and "hissing." The phoneme represented by *v* is made the same way, but the vocal cords are activated slightly before the sound is released. The second step in the decoding-spelling process occurs when students learn to make CVC "sandwiches," in which they "glue" two consonants together with a vowel. The quote marks are intentional; vivid language around familiar terms helps students (and teachers) understand abstract constructs.

Articulatory features come into play in two ways when learning to decode and spell. First is the idea that an English grapheme directs the reader how to produce a sound. In Word Work, this concept is introduced through seven primary consonant phonemes—*p, t, c/k, f, s, m, n*—that are taught in parallel to emphasize the dimensions of manner and place. The first three are stop consonants, the next two are fricatives, and the last two are nasals. Intro-ducing this collection as an organized matrix (Fig. 13.2) supports conceptual insight rather than the rote learning that occurs when correspondences are taught in isolation.

Second, articulation is used to guide production of complete CVC units and to monitor the accuracy of the production. In reading *fat*, for instance, students do not say /fuh-a-tuh/, but /f-a-t/. The teacher models the process of thinking in advance about what the mouth is going to do during the production, and then directs students to check what actually happens as the word is being said. Pronunciation is "stretched out" by elongating the vowel, allowing time for students to focus on each phonological unit.

Spelling CVC units reverses this process. In thinking about how to spell /pan/, for instance, students pronounce the word once or twice, stretching out the vowel and focusing on the consonant articulation. They can see the PTK matrix for visual clues about the relation between articulatory features and the corresponding letters. Spelling is a verbal task during Word Work lessons: "How do you spell /sam/?" "S-A-M." "Check it out! Say /sam/ again and feel what your mouth does."

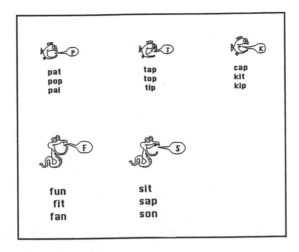

FIG. 13.2. Sample matrix for students displaying articulatory dimensions of place and manner for seven initial consonants in Word Work "Making Sounds."

Reliance on articulation and "stretching" has a direct bearing on the temporal dimension of decoding and spelling. Children identified as "reading disabled" are often described as having "auditory processing" difficulties. They have problems tracking the order of events in a sequence. In fact, analyzing the sequence of sounds in a word is an auditory challenge for everyone. Within a matter of half a second, as a brief part of a much longer and far more complicated sequence, the listener must translate *blend* into "voiced-front-stop + middle-labial-semi-vowel + middle-vowel + middle-nasal + voiced-middle-stop." Normal communication does not require this level of detail, but the reader/writer, confronting *blend* in the midst of a more extended text, faces exactly this challenge—how to convert the graphemes into a reproducible sequence. On the flip side, the student who wants to write about his or her "blended family" must convert the word into a phonemic sequence to which graphemes can be attached in the proper order.

In normal speech, we give little attention to the temporal dimension—we just "talk." Instructing students about the articulatory dimensions of speech gives them control over the temporal dimension. They can stretch out the elements of a word so that each element takes a distinctive shape, while preserving the "whole." This conceptualization of phonemic awareness is distinctive in several ways from most existing alternatives. First, it has little in common with the strategy of teaching that *cat* is /kuh-a-tuh/. Although this portrayal may serve some purposes, it is linguistically bizarre, and ineffective as an instructional technique. On the other hand, the student who reads *cat* and can then describe the shift from one phonemic element to the next possesses strategies of considerable power for decoding and spelling unfamiliar words. Second, the focus is on production more than perception, on how a sound is constructed rather than on "listening more carefully." Third, it emphasizes the structure of the phonemic system rather than specific objectives. The large number of phonemes and phoneme combinations in the English language is a tempting target for behavioral analysis—sufficient objectives to keep a class busy for the better part of the school year, but unfortunately leaving little time for "real" reading and writing.

Word Work helps students grasp the basic dimensions of the phoneme system—quickly—to support productive and independent engagement with print. Research suggests that the interplay between phonemic awareness and acquisition of the concept of letter-sound correspondences is synergistic (cf. Stahl & Murray, chap. 3, this volume; also Bentin & Leshem, 1993). For the child approaching the acquisition of written English, learning rhymes and studying the ABCs is undoubtedly a good thing, but it does not guarantee the type or level of phonemic awareness needed to grasp the alphabetic principle at the level of complex letter-sound correspondences. Explicit instruction on phonemic awareness, however construed, is most effective when directly coupled with the learning of letter-sound relations, and the sooner the better.

Word Work treats consonants and vowels as different phonemic categories: consonants are taught by guiding students to understand their articulatory structure; vowels are taught to be the "glue" that connects consonants; and CVCs serve as "lego pieces" to form more complex words, either by conjoining these basic building blocks into polysyllabic constructions (*porridge, potage*), or by combining base morphemes into compounds (*potpie, potter*).

A MODEL OF CURRICULUM DESIGN FOR EARLY LITERACY

This section of the chapter describes the development of an early literacy program built around the preceding principles, a program that begins with a "story strand" grounded in children's literature, but that also includes a separate and explicit "word strand" for decoding and spelling skills. The complete program, Project READ Plus (Calfee & Patrick, 1995), takes shape not as a collection of prepackaged materials, but as a professional development activity that provides teachers with concepts, structures, and strategies that allow them to make informed decisions about what to teach and how to teach it in order to promote *critical literacy*—the capacity to use language to think and communicate.

All facets of the program are designed to support professional development in the following ways. First, the strands build on a common set of undergirding *principles* about learning, language, and literacy, a conceptual framework that provides teachers a foundation for justifying instructional decisions. Teachers often rely on implicit theories about students; READ Plus offers explicit and practical theories and methods.

Second, the strands are *separable*. Separability must be disciplined; the key is to find the right way to carve a complex task into a small number of distinctive chunks. By focusing on specific chunks, students can grasp the structure that undergirds a domain, and acquire the technical vocabulary for the entire domain. It is also important to link the parts to the whole. In virtually every human endeavor, expertise is not a matter of "part," "whole," "part-to-whole," or "whole-to-part," but instead comprises informed decisions about when and how to employ these strategies.

Third, all strands are inherently *developmental*. The same basic structures and strategies apply across all grades, with content and depth dependent on students' developmental level and interests. Many states and districts assign different stories to each grade. *Charlotte's Web* can be appropriate for any grade level. Kindergartners will appreciate this story in one way, whereas fourth graders see in it a deeper truth about how antagonists can become intimates.

Fourth, every strand emphasizes *organization*, *productivity*, and *transferable knowledge and skills*. These criteria contrast sharply with the microdecomposition typical of objectives-based programs, in which teachers and students are confronted with hundreds of piecemeal outcomes, every objective is allotted time regardless of the pay-off, and learning often disappears after it is tested. In READ Plus, the emphasis is on a small number of high-level outcomes justified by the criteria of coherence (they complement one another), breadth of application, and metacognitive potential—outcomes that span kindergarten through adulthood.

The Phonics "Part"

The program described here, Word Work, is an integrated decoding-spelling program designed for students from kindergarten through second grade. The program combines strengths of whole language and basic skills approaches, but has advantages over both. It is based on the *metaphonic* principle: learning to decode and spell by understanding letter-sound relations rather than by rote practice. The curriculum emphasizes conceptual understanding; instruction is active, social, and reflective, including both direct instruction and small-group problem solving. Part of each day is spent studying letter-sound patterns, based not on a text but instead on a collection of word patterns. Practice and assessment are then grounded in text-based reading and writing.

The Word Work curriculum covers the major Anglo-Saxon spelling patterns: consonants, consonant blends and digraphs, short and long vowels, vowel digraphs, and complex words. It is laid out in an explicit sequence: phoneme awareness and single consonants, short vowels, and long vowels. The program is designed as a component of READ Plus, but can stand alone. It complements most basals and supplementary phonics packages. It is difficult to adapt to strictly linear scope-and-sequence methods. Although compatible with literature-based methods, Word Work uses word collections rather than stories designed around restricted spelling patterns.

The Curriculum Chart. The left-hand panel of Fig. 13.3 displays the primary strand of Word Work as a classroom chart. The idea of the chart is to provide students with the big picture. The right-hand panel provides additional detail about the seven major elements.

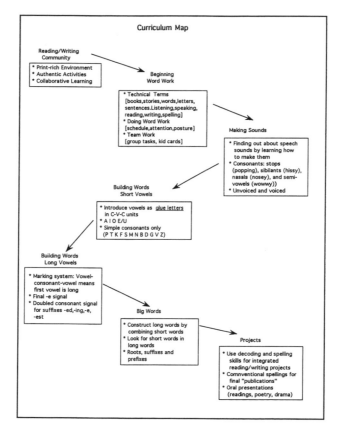

FIG. 13.3. Curriculum charts for Word Work: classroom and teacher versions.

The first and last elements in the chart, Reading/Writing Community and Projects, are curricular "bookends" that anchor the phonics curriculum within a purposeful context for early literacy development. These end points establish and confirm the goals and values of reading and writing at the beginning and end of the school year. The strategy foregoes skills instruction at the outset of the school year, waiting until students' interest has been captured. Likewise, the end of the school year is given over to thematic projects, when skills developed earlier in the year are applied to large-scale student-centered activities.

The second element, Beginning Word Work, accomplishes three outcomes. First, students learn that a special time will be set aside most days to "work with words," to learn to read and spell new words. Second, they are introduced to a vocabulary for talking about reading, writing, and language. Many students, even in the late primary grades, are unclear about ideas that skilled readers (including teachers) take for granted: sentences, stories, words, and so on. If students are to assume responsibility for their own learning, they must know how the language-print system works, and they need a vocabulary to talk about the system. Third, students learn how to work in small groups—dyads and triplets—to solve problems collaboratively. Very young children are seldom adept at cooperative learning; they are egocentric and unskilled at genuine collaboration.

The third element, Making Sounds, introduces the concept of phonemic awareness. Seven basic consonants are presented in this segment as sounds that can be produced or articulated in specific ways. This segment, although brief (a single 2-week lesson block), provides the essential link between letters and sounds during the rest of the curriculum.

The fourth element, Making Words/Short Vowels, introduces students to the construction of consonant-vowel-consonant sequences—words. Short vowels or "glue letters" come first for two reasons. First, the spelling pattern for short vowels is simpler than for long vowels. Second, students learn to distinguish between letter names and letter sounds ("The letter *a* makes the sound /a/"), with the vowel "names" coming later. The short vowels are introduced in order *a, i, o, e/u*, 2-week lesson blocks for each segment. The order reflects pragmatics; *a* is the first and often first learned letter of the alphabet, whereas *i* and *o* are "nice" letters, straight and round! *E* is problematic for various reasons, and so is combined with *u* for the final lesson block.

The fifth element, Making Words/Long Vowels, presents the Anglo-Saxon vowel-marking system for long pronunciations. This element also introduces the major suffixes: *-ed, -s, -ing, -er*, and *-est*. The sixth element, Big Words, presents the concept that long words are combinations of short words. In Anglo-Saxon, compounding is the basic morphological device for creating complex words, setting the stage for the root-affix patterns in the Romance layer of English.

These elements may resemble the objectives in other phonics programs. The difference is that Word Work elements are "big outcomes," covering broad domains, whereas objectives tend to be smaller and more specific. In Making Words/Short Vowel *a*, for instance, the outcome is skill in decoding all CVC patterns in which short *a* is the vocalic center unit. A conservative estimate of the productivity of this principle suggests that students gain access to more than 2,000 CVC building blocks during this 2-week lesson unit. Focusing on larger goals means that learning is more efficient, more transferable, and more comprehensible.

Word Work is a cumulative curriculum. When moving from one element to the next, previous learning is connected to new concepts. After teaching short *a*, for instance, short *i* is introduced as a second glue letter along with short *a*, doubling the number of words in students' repertoire.

The curriculum spirals from kindergarten through second grade. The same objectives are covered in each grade, at different rates and with different emphases, depending on students' developmental levels and individual differences among students and classes.

There are major and minor elements in the curriculum. Major elements include those highly productive patterns essential for fluent reading and readable spellers. Minor elements are specialized patterns added along the way depending on teacher judgment. Critics of any systematic effort to teach letter-sound correspondences often point out irregularities in English orthography. The secondary strand of Word Work includes these minor elements, which students must eventually master, but which do not warrant large time investments. The minor elements occur frequently in printed material, ensuring that students in a print-rich environment have numerous occasions to "read" these patterns (e.g., *-ight*). What about conventional spellings? Parents who readily purchase "Brite Nite Lites" at the local hardware store may be unhappy when their children show them papers with such "invented" or "temporary" spellings, even though the children's work shows extraordinary imagination and coherence. The goal of Word Work is that students quickly reach the point where they can write with facility and ease, and where their work is readable. The secondary strand then responds to parents' and teachers' concerns that students "get it right."

Instructional Design

Both skills-based and whole language programs intermingle skills development with comprehension, and separate decoding and spelling. Word Work lessons reverse this strategy, commingling decoding and spelling as critical elements in reading and writing. The basic instructional strategy begins each instructional segment with a focused lesson that takes a thin "slice of time," early in the morning when everyone is fresh, 3 or 4 days a week, dedicated to the study of "words." Time allocation depends on the activity, but generally amounts to 12 to 35 minutes. Some lessons entail direct instruction of small groups; three groups for 10 minutes each takes 30 to 35 minutes, the upper limit. Whole-class or small-group activities take about 15 to 20 minutes. The idea is to focus on letter-sound correspondences for brief amounts of time, leaving most of the school day for text-level reading and writing.

Word Work sessions are organized into Lesson Blocks, 2-week segments allocated to a specific curriculum element. A block typically begins with teacher-led small-group instruction on a particular curriculum concept (e.g., short *a* words), and ends with teacher-led whole-class assessment. Between these "bookends," the block allows a variety of options, including whole-class, small-group, and individual activities, and some teacher-led reinforcement and review lessons, but most lessons are student centered, the teacher's role being to monitor and facilitate student work. Two weeks is a reasonable amount of time to cover an element, and the sustained emphasis over an extended time supports in-depth learning and application. An important feature of the Lesson Block design is the review at the beginning of the second week. Young children are distracted by weekends (even more by holidays), and the Lesson Block design bridges these interruptions to support cumulative learning.

Small-group problem-solving activities are a distinctive feature of Word Work. The aim is to lead students to become "junior cryptographers." As noted earlier, the metaphonics principle assumes that students benefit from understanding English orthography as a system, and from "thinking" about the alphabetic principle and letter-sound relations. These accomplishments require reflective learning, and thus Vygotskian principles come into play. This strategy calls for students to interact with one another, a tough task for 5- and 6-year-olds. To support these activities, GroupTask cards support students in solving a problem and completing a task. The program also includes Kid Kards as options for classroom practice and take-home assignments. The aim is a balance between individual and group activities, between teacher-directed and student-centered tasks. Students can learn much from one another in group settings when these are genuinely collaborative. They also need to learn how to be responsible for individual work and take-home activities provide a way to link parents to school learning.

GroupTask activities are guided by several principles. First, the tasks are designed to pose "real" problems with open-ended possibilities. The point is not only to find the correct answer, but to justify the work. Task difficulty appears to be a critical factor. Once students have the idea of the basic CVC unit, building short words no longer poses a challenge. At this point, the teacher can assign words like *sassafras* or *discombobulate*.

A second principle is "not whether but when." In primary classrooms with multiple activities, Word Work is sometimes included as a "center."

What if a student never chooses this center? The practical advice is that every student should cycle through every center during each week. If a student has not selected this option by Thursday morning, then he or she no longer has a choice.

A third principle is the importance of not teaching during GroupTask exercises. The teacher should spend this time monitoring and facilitating student interactions and activities, and assessing students' skill and knowledge. Later in the school year, when the teacher has identified individuals who need additional help, GroupTask activities may allow an opportunity for specific instruction. In general, however, this is a time to observe and evaluate.

PRELIMINARY RESULTS

So much for theory and program design—is the concept effective? Word Work is still under development, but pilot evaluations have been conducted in three school sites as part of the developmental activities. Findings from these studies are sketched in this section.

Fruitvale Elementary

South of Stanford University, Fruitvale School serves a varied student population. Some students are from middle-class families fleeing the pressures of the San Francisco Bay Area and Silicon Valley; within reasonable driving distance of the big city, parents can raise their children in a rural setting complete with ponies and horses. Other children are refugees of a different sort, leaving poverty for affordable housing and a more protected situation. And there are still farm-worker families in the Salinas Valley. Fruitvale provided two primary reading programs: Spanish-bilingual and literature-based English. The Chapter I reading specialist was the contact person for Word Work; she had been involved in the early development of READ Plus, and was familiar with social–cognitive strategies for literacy instruction.

Fruitvale implemented literature-based reading in response to the 1987 California Language Arts framework (California Department of Education, 1987). Changing demographics and declining test scores led to concern about the reading program, and the reading specialist approached me in the fall of 1993 to discuss ways to strengthen the program. Discussions with the primary-grade teachers led to implementation of Word Work in January 1994 in several English classrooms: two first-grade classrooms, a first–second combination, and two second-grade classes. During the school year, project staff visited classrooms, consulting with teachers, observing program implementation, collecting samples of student reading and writing, and interviewing teachers and focus groups. Participating teachers were all familiar with literature-based methods. Some were more involved in Word Work than others, judging from classroom observation, and level of participation is noted in the evaluation design.

We collected several indicators of student achievement, including standardized test summaries (CAT-5). Word Work is not primarily aimed toward improved standardized test scores, but students with better decoding and spelling skills should do better on such instruments. The District's Reading Fluency test was administered in the fall, winter, and spring. The measure is the number of words read per minute by each student from one or more passages varying in the number of words and readability level. Each passage is around 180 words in length. Because Word Work is designed to enhance decoding accuracy, reading speed is not necessarily the most appropriate measure, but if the program is effective, then students should become both faster and more accurate. They should also become more competent spellers, and thus we collected writing samples from those classrooms where teachers were willing to provide student work.

The Fruitvale evaluation focused on three questions:

- To what degree did average performance for students in the Word Work curriculum exceed that of students in the regular literature-based curriculum?
- To what degree did Word Work improve the reading performance of students whose achievement was low at the beginning of the school year?
- What was the effect of Word Work on students' spelling and writing performance?

Evidence on the first question came from the standardized tests (Table 13.1). First- and second-grade performance of Fruitvale students was at or above the district average, although the school was the "poor" school in the region. First-grade performance was noticeably higher than average, and exceeded the performance of other schools by 10 to 20 normal curve equiva-

TABLE 13.1
Standardized Language Arts Test Scores (CAT-5 Normal Curve
Equivalents) for Fruitvale Students, Compared With District Averages

	First Grade			Second Grade		
	Vocabulary	Comprehension	Total	Vocabulary	Comprehension	Total
Fruitvale	51	48	51	38	39	38
District	40	39	40	36	37	36

lents. Because decoding skills are important in the early stages of reading acquisition, this pattern suggests a significant impact of Word Work during this critical period.

Additional comparisons come from analysis of within-school effects at Fruitvale on the reading fluency tests. Average effects can obscure fine-grained effects. Stanovich (1986) documented the "Matthew effect"; in any new program, more able students benefit the most. We assessed the Matthew effect by a scatterplot analysis of reading fluency gains for students at different entry levels. Figure 13.4 shows the results. The graphs display the winter–spring profile for each first-grade class. The heavy diagonal line is the constant-performance reference level; if a student read at the same rate during winter and spring testing, he or she would fall near this line. Any point above the line marks a student who gained in reading fluency from winter to spring. In both classes, most students read 40 words or fewer during the winter assessment; imagine a "fence" extending upward from the baseline at this point, and you can see that most students are left of the boundary. During the spring testing, students in the two classes differed greatly. Take the district average of 40 words per minute as a reference point, and imagine another fence that stretches horizontally at the 40-word level. Most students in the moderate-implementation class are below this fence, whereas most (80%) in the high-implementation class are above the fence. Moreover, the greatest gains in the high-implementation class were by students with low winter scores. Only three students "stayed in the cellar" in this class. The one student who performed substantially above average during the winter testing profited as well, scoring at the third-grade level by the end of first grade.

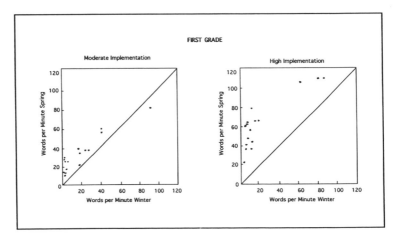

FIG. 13.4. Scatterplots of reading fluency performance in Fruitvale first-grade classrooms.

Phonics programs typically focus on oral reading fluency. A strong argument can be made for the importance of spelling as an indicator of students' knowledge about patterns in the English spelling–sound system. Whole language advocates have argued that readers can rely on context to make sense of print. They are probably right; readers can sometimes guess the general meaning of a passage based on minimal cues. Writers face a more demanding task. Invented spelling, the effort of young students to mimic print, is an important stage in the development of literacy. But if students cannot read their compositions a week or two later, then the function of print has failed.

Student writing samples were limited in quantity and scope, but the data in Fig. 13.5 nonetheless convey an important message. The samples are from the high-implementation first-grade classroom. At Thanksgiving, students struggled to express themselves. By April and May, students composed texts of remarkable creativity and fidelity. The papers are lengthy, interesting, and readable. The literature-based environment encouraged students to write; Word Work provided the spelling skills to support this effort. Students could

---

I AM THANKFUL FOR. . .

my mom And Dad
    my frens
        a cat who plays

my famil wos loif my [my family who
    loves me]
    happy for my dog and a cat
    for chri [Christmas]

the birds in the ski
    my mao cat
        mY dog

My family who loves me
    the birds in the tree
        My dogs that love me

The free Animals in the cuntry
    My nice famule
        My Mom and Dad and step
        Dad thet Love Me

October 1993

MICHAEL'S JOURNAL

One day the clown people couldn't
stat the circus.
A little boy said, "yes, you can."
His dad said,

"I hava monkey." "you do?"
"yes!" "now, you don't!"
"yes, I do!" The monkey
came on the stage.

The show stated, and the kids
and the Dads and the Moms were
there.

I wish that I had a monkey
The monkey did some trixs.
The kids stated claping.

I would play with thaem and
make a bed for him and fed him
an let him woch korttos.

1st Grade - May 1994

ON THANKSGIVING

I had frads over land ate cranberry sauce.

I wae to a pode and I ate trke.

I weh to my grama and I eight turkeye.

I rod biks and turkeye.

I had pugi ply and ate turkey.

I plad with mi csin and I had a good tim.

November 1993

ELENA'S JOURNAL

One day the circus train came
to town.
I lived in the town that they came to.

They had lions & tigers & bears.

Oh, my! Today they are setting up

They are setting up the tents and
the actors & clowns are practicing.

The people came to see it.

The Jugglers are reddy.

Every butty is reddy.

The circus people worked very hard
for this circus, so you could see it.

1st grade - May 1994

FIG. 13.5.   Fall and spring writing samples from the Fruitvale high-implementation classroom. Spring samples are from high- and low-achieving students.

draw on "topical webs" for content words (*clown*), and "word lists" for commonplace spellings (*when*). They were on their own to "attack" other spellings (*reddy* and *butty* for *ready* and *body*). The teacher did allow editorial teams to advise one another about spelling and grammar. Although these papers employ both phonological and conventional spellings, they are of unusual quality for first graders.

Hickory Grove Elementary

In response to the 1987 California Language Arts Framework, Hickory Grove teachers implemented a literature-based program. Hickory Grove serves an upward-oriented middle-class neighborhood in the East Bay region of San Francisco. Most families are successful by dint of hard work. They want the best for their children, and they ask much of the schools. Although teachers concur with these aspirations, there are understandable tensions between developmental growth and surefire results, between basic skills and social–cognitive growth.

Teachers were generally pleased with student achievement, but some parents had expressed concern about phonics and spelling. The district curriculum coordinator learned about Word Work at a November conference, and in January 1995, first-grade teachers at Hickory Grove decided to explore the program. Their input played a vital role in refining sequence, materials, and activities. When should vowel digraphs be introduced? How much emphasis on conventional spellings? How to sustain student interest?

Throughout the school year, Word Work staff provided ongoing support through workshops and conferences with the Hickory Grove teachers. Two assessments were also conducted in December–January and May–June. The first assessment consisted of writing samples from all first graders, 154 students in six classrooms. Four classes were straight firsts, and two were K–1 combinations. Matched pre–post scores were available for 140 students. Missing scores reflect mobility; students who left or entered mid-year did not differ discernibly from the final sample.

Students wrote to two prompts: "A special person" in the winter, and "My summer vacation" in the spring. Each sample was scored by two staff members on the three dimensions: spelling, length, and coherence. Teachers and staff developed the scales collaboratively during the fall of the school year. Both teachers and, to some degree, students knew the criteria. Students understood that these papers were "special," but that they would not be graded on them. Writing was commonplace in the classrooms, and these papers were written under normal conditions. Students had as much time as they wished, and could call on the teacher for assistance. The papers were first drafts.

Forty-six students were also administered the Interactive Reading Assessment System (IRAS; Calfee & Calfee, 1981) in December–January and May–June. IRAS is an individualized multicomponent performance test covering decoding, spelling, vocabulary definition, oral reading, and passage comprehension (narrative and expository), along with metacognitive questions about each component. The data of most relevance here are spelling (15 synthetic words ranging from simple CVCs like *dut* to complex words like *thrinkerlant*), meta-spelling ("How do you know how to spell _____?", a 6-point scale from no response [1] to a well-formed explanation [6]), and sentence reading (ranging from 1.0 to 4.0 in readability). Each teacher identified six students spanning a range of achievement (upper, middle, lower), one boy and one girl at each level.

Writing data are shown in Table 13.2. The main questions in this evaluation center around student progress in the three dimensions. Hickory Grove children enter first grade ahead of the game; the district does not administer standardized tests in the early grades, but about a 1.5 grade-level equivalent. In the 6 months from December–January to May–June, the students moved almost 1.5 units on the 8-point spelling scale, a large and statistically significant shift. Figure 13.6 presents a scatterplot of the pre–post scores. A substantial number of students scored at Levels 2 and 3 on the spelling scale in winter, but virtually all performed at Level 4 or higher in spring. The students were also writing longer (almost a full page) and more coherent (centered around a single topic) essays. For first-grade teachers at Hickory Grove, the most significant outcomes of the writing program were students' enthusiasm about writing, and the capacity to compose interesting, imaginative, and readable papers.

Table 13.3 presents the IRAS data. On spelling, students in December–January could handle simple synthetic words like *dut*, *mape*, and *leb*. In May–June, they spelled complex patterns like *fening*, *sidded*, and *broint*, more typical of second grade. In sentence reading, the 4.5 average means that students were able, on average, to read materials normed for the second half

TABLE 13.2
Pre–Post Ratings [Mean, (SD)] of First-Grade Writing Samples,
Hickory Grove Elementary School, December–January and May–June 1996

	Spelling (1–8)	Coherence (1–6)	Length (1–6)
Pretest			
December–January	3.49 (1.08)	2.30 (1.04)	2.36 (1.32)
Posttest			
May–June	4.96 (1.19)	3.32 (1.00)	3.64 (1.24)
Difference	1.46 (1.01)	1.01 (1.15)	1.28 (1.16)
t-value	17.13 ($p < .001$)	10.39 ($p < .001$)	12.95 ($p < .001$)

Note. $N = 140$.

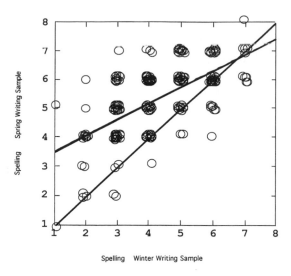

FIG. 13.6. Scatterplot showing spelling scores for winter and spring writing samples, Hickory Grove Elementary School. Upper line is best-fit regression; lower line is no-growth indicator. Data have been jittered to show relative density at each point. $N = 140$.

of second grade. In the 6 months, students had gained more than a full year on this scale.

Word Work emphasizes the metaphonic principle; understanding is as important as performance. First graders improved on the meta-spelling scale, but only slightly. One challenge is that very young students have trouble explaining anything. They are genuine novices, and tend to stay at a surface level when asked "Why?"

Hickory Grove first graders had a successful year. They entered ahead of the game, and finished with a solid mastery of decoding-spelling skills coupled with an enthusiasm for reading and writing. The children were as enthusiastic

TABLE 13.3
Pre–Post Scores [Mean (SD)] of First-Grade Performance on
Interactive Reading Assessment System (IRAS) in Spelling, Meta-Spelling,
and Sentence Reading Subtests, Hickory Grove Elementary School,
December–January and May–June 1996

	Spelling (1–15)	*Meta-Spell (1–6)*	*Sentence (1–8)*
Pretest			
December–January	2.00 (1.75)	1.90 (1.53)	2.53 (2.75)
Posttest			
May–June	4.75 (3.13)	2.35 (0.80)	4.55 (2.55)
Difference	2.75 (1.67)	0.45 (1.01)	2.02 (0.96)
t-value	6.96 ($p < .001$)	1.34 ($p < .05$)	6.64 ($p < .001$)

Note. $N = 140$.

about skill learning as story reading and journal writing. Word Work time was alive with spirited activity, and flowed easily into the other parts of the school day.

Summer in Omaha

The third evaluation addresses the Matthew effect—how to help students in the lowest achievement levels. In spring 1996, the Reading Department of the Omaha Public Schools decided to investigate the potential of Word Work to assist kindergarten "graduates" judged at risk for first grade. Parents of 42 Chapter I students volunteered their children for a 6-week summer school.

First-grade entry is critical. Students who know their letter names, who possess phonemic awareness, who can read simple words and sentences have a clear and lasting advantage over their peers. Helping children who lack these skills to "catch up" is difficult. The purpose of this exploratory effort was to investigate the effectiveness of a concentrated literacy program that combined an explicit and separate decoding-spelling curriculum with comprehension and composition skills in a literature-based environment.

Four teachers conducted the summer program. They had limited familiarity with the program, but received ongoing support and supervision from the district reading coordinator. Class sizes were small, 7 to 12 students. Students spent most of the 3-hour school day reading (a variety of works) and writing ("letter" book, "story" book, and "animal" book). Each day included a Word Work segment, typically around 20 minutes, decoding-spelling concepts directly applicable to the "book work" that occupied the rest of the school day. This summary report presents two sets of data: a teacher checklist assessing letters and letter-sound relations, and a tile test (a performance assessment of letters, words, and sentences).

The district checklist showed that the students could recognize most letters when they entered the program (m = 20/26), but improved over the 6-week experience (m = 23/26). The five-letter tile test of letter names showed the same pattern, and was highly correlated with the teachers' assessments of the complete alphabet. Most children had evidently learned their ABCs in kindergarten, and further refined their knowledge during the summer program. Teaching the ABCs does no harm, but does not guarantee literacy.

More significant for first-grade entry is awareness of letter-sound correspondences, the capacity to read simple words, and oral reading fluency. Students are more likely to succeed in first-grade reading if they can already read. Table 13.4 presents the findings for these outcomes. At the beginning of summer school, these postkindergarten graduates knew fewer than half of the letter-sound correspondences, could read only one or two of five simple words, and were completely stymied when confronted with a short sentence. Six weeks later, the majority knew 20 or more of these relations, and only

TABLE 13.4
Test Scores [Mean and (SD)] for Teacher Ratings of Students' Letter-
Sound Knowledge and Performance on Tile Tests of Word Reading and
Sentence Reading, Omaha Postkindergarten Summer Reading Program

	Letter-Sound (0–26)	Read Words (0–5)	Read Sentences (0–5)
June test	11.2 (5.86)	1.48 (1.55)	0.55 (1.09)
July test	20.2 (3.63)	4.00 (1.34)	2.88 (1.94)
Difference	9.0 (2.67)	2.52 (1.07)	2.33 (1.16)
t-value	15.0 ($p < .001$)	9.91 ($p < .001$)	8.05 ($p < .001$)
September test	16.4 (5.82)	3.62 (1.35)	2.59 (1.94)

Note. $N = 42$ for June and July tests; $N = 29$ for September tests.

one student knew fewer than half of the letter-sound correspondences. Figure 13.7 shows that progress was especially notable for those students with the lowest entry scores. Students also improved dramatically in word and sentence reading during this brief experience. More detailed analyses showed that boys and girls benefited equally, and that gains were present in all four classes. Finally, when the students were reassessed at the beginning of first grade, 6 weeks after the program ended, students had sustained most of the gains.

Observations and teacher interviews suggest that these dramatic improvements were achieved in a motivating, playful environment. The students were not force fed a diet of worksheets; instead, phonics was an active, hands-on activity, interesting in its own right, but also valuable because it allowed students to become adept at independent reading and writing. These findings point to the potential value of focused summer school experiences for at-risk students (Cooper, Nye, Charlton, Lindsay, & Greathouse, 1996).

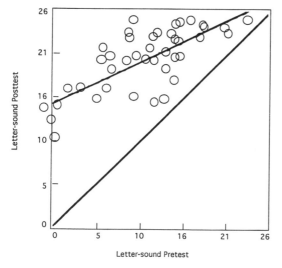

FIG. 13.7. Scatterplot showing letter-sound pre–post data for Omaha summer school postkindergarten project. Teacher assessments of number of letter-sounds identified by each student at beginning and end of six-week summer school. Range from 0–26, $N = 42$.

POLICY IMPLICATIONS: WHAT TO DO?

The "great debate" has raged for decades, and today's situation suggests that the extremes are far more popular than the middle ground. More troubling, the terms of the debate seem little affected by either research findings or practical experience. For instance, the recent California Reading Advisory (California Department of Education, 1996) "encourages" kindergarten teachers to work on phonemic awareness, and then places the task of "teaching reading" on the shoulders of first-grade teachers—a task to be completed by mid-year. Research shows that phonemic awareness is most effectively taught when combined with print awareness. My experience in the "down and dirty" of reading instruction suggests that, although the primary years are a critical time, all children are more likely to become fully competent if the entire primary team works toward this end.

This chapter has meant to convey a few central themes. First and foremost, all American students are capable of attaining high levels of critical literacy, even given today's societal challenges: Continuing declines in family demographics, inadequate social services, and regular trashing of schools and teachers. If a child attends school with some regularity (and most do), we can promote both competence and enthusiasm for reading and writing.

This chapter has focused on print literacy. For students to learn decode and spell, a central requirement is a coherent, developmental curriculum grounded in the features of English orthography, and connected with purposeful activities. English spelling is a sensible and comprehensible match to the spoken language, but both students and teachers need clarity about the system. Today's alternatives (learn on the fly or memorize a thousand objectives) don't work.

A third theme centers around appropriate assessment, which taps into understanding as well as recognition, relying not on "cold turkey" oral reading but on "reading with meaning" passages that merit reading, and downplaying rote spelling tests in favor of accurate and fluent spelling in meaningful contexts.

The final theme emphasizes the teacher's professional role in adapting curriculum and instruction to the needs of diverse students. The professional is knowledgeable about linguistics, child development, and sociocultural variations in language usage. For primary teachers, language and literacy are the most critical instructional domain, and teachers must resist pressures to spread themselves thinly across a broad spectrum foisted on them by policymakers.

The case studies sketched in this chapter show what is possible when first graders are immersed in a decoding-spelling curriculum based on orthographic principles, when instruction employs social–cognitive strategies, and when decoding-spelling is a distinctive curriculum strand directly coupled with purposeful reading and writing. They show how curriculum and instruction can provide the "engine" that produces genuinely powerful learning for all students.

REFERENCES

Adams, M. J. (1990). *Beginning to read: Thinking and learning about print.* Cambridge, MA: MIT Press.

Ashton-Warner, S. (1963). *Teacher.* New York: Simon & Schuster.

Balmuth, M. (1982). *The roots of phonics.* New York: McGraw-Hill.

Bentin, S., & Leshem, H. (1993). On the interaction between phonological awareness and reading acquisition: It's a two-way street. *Annals of Dyslexia, 43,* 125–148.

Brady, S. A., & Shankweiler, D. P. (Eds.). (1991). *Phonological processes in literacy: A tribute to Isabelle Y. Liberman.* Hillsdale, NJ: Lawrence Erlbaum Associates.

Calfee, R. C., & Calfee, K. H. (1981). *Interactive reading assessment system (IRAS)* (rev.). Unpublished manuscript, Stanford University.

Calfee, R. C., & Drum, P. A. (1986). Research on teaching reading. In M. C. Wittrock (Ed.), *Handbook of research on teaching* (3rd ed., pp. 804–849). New York: Macmillan.

Calfee, R. C., & Henry, M. (1996). Strategy and skill in early reading acquisition. In J. Shimron (Ed.), *Literacy and education: Essays in memory of Dina Feitelson* (pp. 97–117). Cresskill, NJ: Hampton.

Calfee, R. C., & Patrick, C. P. (1995). *Teach our children well.* Stanford, CA: The Portable Stanford Book Series, Stanford Alumni Association.

California Department of Education. (1987). *Language arts curriculum framework.* Sacramento, CA: Author.

California Department of Education. (1996). *Teaching reading: A balanced, comprehensive approach to teaching reading.* Sacramento, CA: Author.

Chall, J. S. (1983). *Stages of reading development.* New York: McGraw-Hill.

Chall, J. S., Jacobs, V. A., & Baldwin, L. E. (1990). *The reading crisis: Why poor children fall behind.* Cambridge MA: Harvard University Press.

Cooper, H., Nye, B., Charlton, K., Lindsay, J., & Greathouse, S. (1996). The effects of summer vacation on achievement test scores: A narrative and meta-analytic review. *Review of Educational Research, 66,* 227–268.

Elkonin, D. B. (1963).The psychology of mastering the elements of reading. In B. Simon & J. Simon (Eds.), *Educational psychology in the U.S.S.R.* (pp. 165–179). London: Routledge & Kegan Paul.

Lionni, L. (1994). *Leo Lionni favorites: Six classic stories.* New York: Knopf.

McIntyre, E., & Pressley, M. (1996). *Balanced whole language.* Portsmouth, NH: Heinemann.

Share, D. L. (1995). Phonological recoding and self-teaching: *Sine qua non* of reading acquisition. *Cognition, 55,* 151–218.

Stanovich, K. E. (1986). Matthew effects in reading: Some consequences of individual differences in the acquisition of reading. *Reading Research Quarterly, 21,* 360–406.

Venezky, R. L. (1970). *The structure of English orthography.* The Hague, Netherlands: Mouton.

Weaver, C. (1990). *Understanding whole language: From principles to practice.* Portsmouth, NH: Heinemann.

Motivating Contexts for Young Children's Literacy Development: Implications for Word Recognition

Diane H. Tracey
Kean University

Lesley Mandel Morrow
Rutgers University

The focus of this volume is on word recognition in beginning literacy. The volume provides a comprehensive view and critical analysis of how processes such as phonemic awareness and grapheme–phoneme correspondence knowledge set the stage for early reading success. The book also deals with links between theory and how that translates into practice, specifically related to word recognition.

Our chapter is about motivating contexts for young children's literacy development. Our work has dealt with social and physical contexts that motivate reading and writing. In these contexts, children have the opportunity to practice with print, and our investigations have demonstrated increased achievement in literacy development. The tests we used for measuring achievement were mostly those dealing with comprehension of text. We were also interested in children's sustained engagement in reading and writing and their voluntary motivation to choose to read and write. The study of these social and physical contexts have implications for preparing appropriate settings for the instruction of word recognition skills. When children are voluntarily motivated to read and write, it is apparent that they are practicing with print, and thus enhancing their knowledge about print.

With this in mind, we have structured our chapter in the following way. First, we discuss what theory and research has to say about motivating contexts for learning. Second, we summarize studies we have carried out that include such characteristics and specifically deal with reading and writing. Third, we report on a survey investigating practices in early childhood classrooms where word recognition skills are taught, and analyze the findings to determine if these strategies use elements that have been found to motivate children.

WHAT DO WE KNOW ABOUT MOTIVATING CONTEXTS FOR LEARNING?

According to Wittrock (1986), motivation is the process of initiating, sustaining, and directing one's own activity. Maehr (1976) defined it as returning to and continuing to work on a task and, like Wittrock, suggested that true motivation includes sustained engagement. If we transfer this general definition of motivation to describe readers and writers, we would say that motivated readers and writers are individuals who choose to read and write on a regular basis for long periods of time, for a specific purpose, and in several contexts. Gambrell, Codling, and Palmer (1996) elaborated on the concept of motivation as it is related to reading. They stated, "Motivation is defined as goal-directed behavior that is mediated by social, cognitive, and affective factors. Motivation to read, then, is more than effortful activity or time spent on the task (Corno & Mandinach, 1983), and is reflected in how children think about themselves as readers and how they think about reading tasks and activities" (p. 2). As we read through the literature concerning motivating elements and contexts, we realized that there isn't just one way to motivate, and that different children will be motivated by one or more combinations of factors, including settings, experiences, and conditions. Next we describe the work of several writers who have contributed to our general understanding of motivational contexts and learning.

Csikszentimihalyi (1978) suggested that challenge is an important aspect of motivation. An activity will be motivating if it is challenging but not beyond the skill of the learner. Learners must see a purpose for the challenges set before them, the goals must be clear, and learning experiences must result in enjoyment and perceived success (Csikszentimihalyi, 1978).

Erickson (1995) found that when children were given responsibility for their learning they were more likely to be motivated to work toward a goal than were children who were in situations controlled by the teacher. These controlled situations are characterized by an overemphasis on rules, procedures, and time restraints for completing projects (Oldfather, 1993). Students need some degree of autonomy and an open-ended atmosphere in which they can raise questions and search for answers. The factors within open-ended tasks that relate to motivation are opportunities for challenge, student control, personal interest, and engaging in social collaboration with peers to accomplish goals (Turner, 1995).

Oldfather (1993) and Turner (1995) suggested that the social constructivist theory contains elements that provide learning settings that tend to be motivating. Social constructivists view learning as an active process in which knowledge is constructed by individuals, based on their personal experiences and prior knowledge. In this view, learning is a social process by which learners construct knowledge together, from, and with each other (McCombs, 1991).

In classrooms that incorporate the constructivist theory into practice, learning is student centered around topics of interest to children. Students are encouraged to take risks, express ideas, and have choices as to what they will learn and how they will go about achieving their goals. In addition to the characteristics already listed, children are involved in the responsibility of directing many of their learning experiences, and have input into the evaluation of their performance. Students must perceive success in order to be motivated to continue working on a task. This success comes with the selection of activities that are challenging but can be achieved, and with the support of the teacher to help guide experiences (Bandura, 1989; Ford, 1992). Elements of social constructivism are apparent in children's interactions with each other and literacy materials during unstructured literacy center time. These experiences have been found to be positively related to both children's motivation to read and reading achievement levels (Morrow, 1997).

Access to materials (i.e., having easy access to a wide variety of books and literacy-related activities) and the authenticity of tasks (i.e., tasks that are closely tied to meaningful activities) are two elements that promote motivation (Morrow, 1990). Kindergartners have been found to engage in reading and writing activities in a purposeful and sustained manner when they have access to reading and writing materials through literacy-enriched centers with authentic themes designed in their classrooms. Examples of authentic tasks include activities such as writing letters that will actually be sent, writing recipes that will actually be used, and writing in journals for personal reflection. Examples of authentic themes include study of areas of interest to students across the curriculum, such as studying underwater life or dinosaurs from multiple content areas such as science, social studies, math, art, and the language arts.

Finally, Skinner and Belmont (1993) revealed that teachers who have clear goals promote motivation, but, in addition, teachers must supply support in the form of scaffolding and positive reinforcement for information they want children to learn.

Table 14.1 summarizes the theoretical elements described in this section that have been found to motivate learning.

RESEARCH TREATMENTS THAT MOTIVATE STUDENTS TO READ AND WRITE

In this section we present a summary of pertinent studies, to take a closer look at the characteristics found that motivate children to read and write.

TABLE 14.1
Theoretical Elements That Have Been Found to Motivate Learning

1. Activities that provide for choices of materials and experiences for learning.
2. Activities that challenge, but can be accomplished.
3. Activities that give the learner responsibility and some control over the learning process, such as self-direction, selection, and pacing of learning activities and materials.
4. Activities that involve social collaboration with peers or adults.
5. Activities that are facilitated by teachers who model, guide, and scaffold information to be learned.
6. Activities that are meaningful and functional by using authentic materials and settings.
7. Activities with conceptual orientations that add interest to what is being learned (content area topics).
8. Activities that offer time for practicing skills learned in settings that are independent of the teacher.
9. Activities and materials that are easily accessible.
10. Activities that offer the child a feeling of success.

A correlational study in 30 nursery school classrooms and 37 kindergartens found positive relationships between children's voluntary use of literature during free choice times (i.e., times during the day when students were allowed to choose their own activities within which to participate), and the physical design of literacy centers in classrooms (Morrow, 1982). Based on the results of this investigation, an intervention study was carried out with kindergartens. There were 12 kindergarten classrooms, with an average class size of 20. The rooms were randomly assigned to either one control condition or to one of three experimental conditions: the design of literacy centers only, the implementation of a literature program only, and both design and program implementation of a literature. There were three classrooms in each condition. The purpose was to see if children could be motivated to select the literacy center for reading and writing during a center time, as opposed to other centers in the classroom, such as, art, dramatic play, and manipulative learning games (Morrow & Weinstein, 1982).

With the information from the original correlational study (Morrow, 1982), treatment rooms were designed with literacy centers that were accessible, with varied genres of children's literature available for use, and choices of activities to engage in reading and writing. For example, children could choose from literacy-related props such as felt board and story character activities, headsets with taped stories, and puppets. Furthermore, the literacy center area was designed to be attractive—with elements of softness such as rugs, pillows, stuffed animals, and rocking chairs—to make them as enjoyable as possible.

Children had the opportunity to select from a wide variety of materials, activities, and peers with whom they could work. Through demonstrations, teachers modeled activities for students before the students used them. The materials represented a wide variety of experiences for different ability levels and interests; therefore, there were challenges for all, but success could be achieved. After teachers modeled the use of materials, children selected activities. Because they were to complete the task selected, they had clear goals and responsibilities set before them. The results of the study indicated that in all treatment rooms more children chose to use the literacy centers during free-choice periods than did children in the control rooms where the centers included only a shelf of books. Thus, it was now apparent that using factors found to motivate learning in other settings could produce the same results in settings for reading and writing.

As a result of the success of these investigations, another similar study was carried out (Morrow & Weinstein, 1986). The purpose of this study was to determine whether children's voluntary use of library centers and their attitudes toward reading could be positively affected by involvement in a literature program emphasizing the enjoyment of books. Six second-grade classes were assigned to either a control group or one of two experimental groups: a group in a school-based program or a group in a school- and home-based program. The treatment for this study was the same as the one previously described in the kindergarten investigation.

Questionnaires and observations were used to assess students' attitudes and behaviors before, during, and after involvement in the program. The results indicated that voluntary use of the library center during free-choice time in school significantly increased in both experimental groups. Moreover, this effect continued after the intervention had ended. Girls engaged in library center activities significantly more than did boys, and were more responsive to the intervention. However, achievement level was unrelated to library center use or to responsiveness. The intervention had no effect on students' attitudes toward reading, nor on reading habits at home. Because the results of a parent questionnaire suggested that parents did not fully implement the home-based program, increases in use of the library center in both experimental groups were attributed to the school-based interventions.

As a result of these studies, we continued this line of work to determine if the increased motivation on the part of the children to read and write in the treatment rooms enhanced reading achievement (Morrow, 1992). We were interested to find out if student's engagement enhanced their literacy achievement. This study was carried out in nine second-grade classes ($N = 166$) that were assigned to either one control group or one of two experimental groups: one in a school-based program only, and one in a school- and home-based program. Standardized and informal written and oral tests of comprehension were used to determine growth in literacy. Use of literature was measured by child surveys concerning after-school activities and records of books read in school and checked out to read at home. Interviews with teachers and children determined attitudes toward the reading. Children were engaged in similar treatments as described earlier to motivate reading and writing, including: the design of literacy centers in classrooms; teacher-guided literature activities in which the teacher led the students through specific teacher directed lessons; and periods for free-choice, independent reading and writing.

The results of this study again indicated that children in the experimental groups performed significantly better than did those in the control group, on all literacy measures except for the standardized test, in which no differences were found. Also, no differences were found in the performance of the children in the home- and school-based program versus the school-based program alone. These findings suggest that when children had the opportunity to self-select tasks, had many choices for engaging in reading and writing, and had time to practice literacy activities, they met with success. The children in this study experienced both intrinsic and extrinsic rewards. They found pleasure through their engagement in reading and writing, and their scores on literacy achievement tests increased.

In the study just described, children did not improve on the standardized tests administered by the school district. Therefore, another investigation, similar to the one just presented, was initiated (Morrow, Pressley, & Smith, 1995). The treatment was expanded to include content integration with literacy instruction. The content area on which we focused was science. We added this component to determine if we could enhance achievement more, because it has been found that concept orientation (in this case, the content area) enhances motivation (Guthrie et al., 1996). The study took place in six third-grade classes ($N = 128$) that were assigned to either one control or two experimental groups (a literature/science program and a literature-only program). The literature-only program was similar to the second-grade study just discussed (Morrow, 1992). The treatment in the literature/science group was the same as in the literature-only treatment group, but was also included in the literacy centers: children's literature that focused on science topics studied by third graders in the schools, and modeled writing of narratives with science themes. The addition of concept-oriented materials presented topics that were of interest to the children, and also provided science material in a motivating context different from the usual textbook presentation.

The results from this study demonstrated that children in the literature/science group did significantly better on the literacy measures such as story retellings, rewritings, written original stories, and probed comprehension tests—and the standardized test of reading and language—than did those in the literature-only group. Furthermore, the literature-only group did better than the control group on all literacy measures except for the standardized measure. There were no differences between the groups on number of science facts used in science stories written. In the test of science concepts, the literature/science group did significantly better than did both the literature-only group and the control group. From observations of children's activities during periods of independent reading and writing, we found that children in the experimental rooms voluntarily selected science books to read and about which write. This added practice that did not occur in the control rooms, plus the modeling of children's literature with science topics, were elements that helped to increase performance. The addition of a conceptual orientation (by including the science component) that provided additional interest and choices as well as practice in literacy experiences for the children, increased motivation to engage in activities.

Another study sought to determine if the voluntary literacy behaviors of preschool children could be increased in type and quantity through design changes, by including reading and writing materials in thematic play centers (Morrow, 1990). Thirteen preschool classes were distributed into one control group and three different experimental groups: one in which thematic play with literacy materials was guided by teachers; one in which thematic play with literacy materials was not guided by teachers; and one in which books, pencils, and papers were supplied in unthemed dramatic play areas with teacher guidance.

The treatment rooms with themes involved settings that were authentic and meaningful for children, with concept orientation such as a veterinarian's office when the class was studying about animals and a post office when they studied about the community. In a veterinarian's office setting, for example, there were an appointment book, a telephone, appointment cards for patients, and forms for doctors to write prescriptions and reports on patients. In the doctor's waiting room, there were magazines and books for reading. The type and quantity of literacy behaviors in each of the three experimental settings were determined by direct observation prior to intervention, during intervention, and after a delayed period of time. Literacy behaviors increased significantly in all the experimental groups over the control group. Thematic play with teacher guidance yielded greatest gains; the provision of books, pencils, and paper with teacher guidance yielded the next greatest gains; thematic play without teacher guidance yielded the third greatest gains. The effect of the treatments continued after a delayed period of time (Morrow, 1990).

Combined, the studies presented found many elements that seem to motivate children: children had choices in both activities and peers with whom to work, the social settings were carefully designed for learning, the teachers engaged in guidance and modeling, and the challenges culminated in success experiences. Additionally, students were given time for working independent of the teacher, had access to a wide range of literacy materials, and engaged in activities that were conceptually oriented and therefore were embedded in meaningful and functional contexts. Thus, these elements, which have been found to contribute to motivational contexts for literacy learning, need to be considered in relation to teaching word recognition skills.

HOW TEACHERS ARE TEACHING WORD
RECOGNITION SKILLS

From the studies presented in this chapter it is apparent that when certain characteristics exist in a classroom, students can be motivated to read and write and increase literacy achievement. We can assume that these children's enhanced scores on reading comprehension and writing have had a positive impact on word recognition skills. Relatedly, increased exposure or experience with print has been shown to increase word recognition performance (Stanovich, 1992). Therefore, we can conclude that these motivating contexts have helped with developing children's knowledge about print.

The contexts we have described do motivate children to read and write. However—as the other chapters in this book stress—direct, explicit experiences in learning to read words accurately and fluently are also needed. An integration of our principles of motivation and explicit instruction in word recognition would appear to offer an optimal setting for beginning literacy. Thus, in our next study we investigated whether motivating elements were being incorporated by classroom teachers into lessons specifically designed to teach phonics and phonemic awareness, and, if so, what did these lessons look like? Here, we conducted an observational survey of classroom practices to observe and describe types of strategies used in teaching phonics and phonemic awareness in early childhood classrooms (Morrow & Tracey, 1997). This research provided us with an opportunity to determine if strategies used by teachers to teach phonics and phonemic awareness incorporate elements that have been found to motivate children's interest in learning.

A Description of the Project

Sixty-five graduate and undergraduate students enrolled in a teacher education program were trained to observe and record incidents of instruction in phonemic awareness and phonics instruction in early childhood classrooms. For this study, *phonemic awareness* was defined as any occurrence that drew children's attention to the sounds within words. Phonics lessons were defined as instruction focusing on the association of speech sounds with printed symbols (Burns, Roe, & Ross, 1992). Student observers recorded, in detail, all incidents of phonemic awareness and phonics instruction, including dialogue that occurred during their classroom visits.

The observations took place in 76 classrooms. Of these, 29 were preschool classrooms, 20 were kindergarten, 13 were first grade, and 14 were second grade. The classrooms were visited during a 4-month period. Each room was observed every third week for the entire school day. There were 6 visits per room, for a total of 456. The classrooms were located in districts of varied socioeconomic levels, and mixed racial and ethnic backgrounds. Some classrooms were located in urban, low socioeconomic status (SES), and racially diverse communities, whereas others were situated in more middle-class, homogeneous, suburban areas. Although the classroom teachers were informed that the student observers would be taking notes about classroom practices, they did not know the focus of the note taking. Thus, it was hoped that the activities observed were as natural as possible. At the conclusion of the data collection period, the teachers were interviewed regarding how they taught phonics and phonemic awareness and the importance they placed on their development in literacy instruction. Their comments were then compared with the recorded observations of their practices.

After all observations were completed, they were read and categorized. The categories that emerged are defined as follows.

Explicit Instruction. This is the systematic, sequential presentation of phonemic awareness and phonics skills using isolated, direct instruction strategies with lessons that were largely controlled by the teacher. Explicit instruction, as it was most often used in these classrooms, used worksheets that tested knowledge in phonics and phonemic awareness. The following description of a phonics lesson that Mrs. Molsen carried out with her first-grade class represents what we are calling *explicit instruction*:

Mrs. M.:   Please take out your phonics book and turn to page 63. This page shows pictures which begin with the *ch* sound and some pictures which do not. Remember *ch* is called a *digraph* because it is made up of two letters that make a new sound that is different from the usual sound of each letter. Print the letters *ch* next to every picture that begins with a *ch*. If a picture does not begin with *ch* put an *x* over the picture.

Authentic Instruction. This includes learning integrated within meaningful or functional contexts. Incidents of authentic instruction are usually unplanned and happen spontaneously when the teacher or a child points out a phonic element. When this occurs, the teacher takes the opportunity to guide and scaffold for students. Authentic phonics instruction often occurs in activities such as the morning message, language experience charts, and storybook reading when the teacher or child notices phonic elements within a text and discusses them as they arise. There is no inclusion of explicit systematic instruction.

In the following episode, Mrs. Jones helped her class compose a thank-you letter to the class mother. It demonstrates how this teacher took advantage of a spontaneous situation to create an authentic learning experience in phonics.

Mrs. J.:   Mrs. Sherry took us to that wonderful concert, and I think we should write her a thank-you note. Remember to start your note with "Dear Mrs. Sherry."

Tricia: What letter does her name *Sherry* start with?

Mrs. J.:   Can anyone help Tricia?

Tim: It starts with *sh*. The *sh* together says *Sherry*.

Mrs. J.:   Very good Tim. *Sh* makes the sound that we hear in *show* or
           shine. Can you think of other words that have the sound like
           Sherry? (Tricia raises her hand.)

Tricia: Well, there's *show* and *shine, shower, share,* and *Shelly's* name.

Mrs. J.:   That was great, Tricia. (Mrs. Jones wrote the words on a
           chart and continued with the original activity in which the
           children were writing thank-you notes.)

Balanced Approach.   This is the term we are using for phonics instruction
in which both explicit instruction and authentic experiences are used together.
The teacher seems to have a plan for phonics instruction by providing
meaningful settings for learning with explicit strategies as well. The following
description of Mrs. Singer and her kindergarten class illustrates what we
called a balanced approach.

Mrs. Singer's class was learning about animals. She planned to focus on
the consonant *p* during the unit, because the letter appeared frequently in
texts and discussions about animals. She read the book *The Pet Show* (Keats,
1972), and children noticed the letter *p* in the book title as well as in *Peter
Rabbit* (Potter, 1903), and *Petunia* (Duvoisin, 1950). On this particular day
Mrs. Singer read *Katy No-Pockets* (Payne, 1972), which is about a kangaroo
in need of a pocket. After the story, she put on an apron full of pockets. In
each pocket were little animal figures. Each of the animal's names began
with the letter *p*, such as a *pig, puppy, peacock*, and a *panda bear*. Children
were given a chance to take the figures out of Mrs. Singer's pockets and
name them. She wrote these words on a chart entitled *Animal Names Beginning with "P."* Mrs. Singer gave out worksheets showing pictures of the
animals that had been in her pockets, which children identified by writing
the letter *p* in a space provided. She asked the children to look around the
room for things beginning with the letter *p* to list on their worksheets, and
place in the pockets of her apron. During literacy center time, Mrs. Singer
encouraged children to continue to look for words beginning with the sound
of *p*, to collect in their "Very Own Book of Sounds," and to share what they
found with their friends.

Grade-Level Differences

A total of 722 observations of phonics instruction were recorded from the
76 classrooms. We grouped the first- and second-grade observations together
because we had fewer rooms at those levels.

The results of the survey reveal that 72% of the phonics lessons observed in preschool were categorized as authentic, compared to 33% in kindergarten and 21% in first and second grades. In the explicit instruction category, 19% of the preschool observations were considered explicit, compared to 56% of the incidents in kindergarten and 67% in first and second grades. A balanced approach was observed in 9% of the preschool observations, in 11% of the kindergartens, and in 12% of the first and second grades. Neither phonemic awareness nor phonics instruction was reported in 72 of the observations, which represented 10% of the total incidents recorded.

An examination of the phonics instruction observed across grade levels found that preschool teachers engaged their children in authentic experiences in their phonics instruction (which included motivating elements we have identified) more often than did teachers at other grade levels. Children were more involved through verbal interaction and hands-on projects at this level than they were in the other grades. Teachers at the preschool level appeared to be concerned with making the learning fun, and many lessons were done in a way that directly related to the children's lives. Also, in preschool many of the references to phonemic relationships appeared more spontaneous than planned. In contrast, the observations of kindergartens revealed mostly explicit instruction or a skills-based approach. Literacy lessons were teacher directed, with a set of discrete skills that were taught sequentially.

In first and second grades, 67% of the phonics lessons were categorized as explicit. The following excerpt from a transcript illustrates a typical first or second grade phonics lesson.

Ms. Green had written the following words on a chart:

Word Families
ame: name, game, fame, same
ide: ride, side, hide, slide

She told the children that these were word families, because the ends of the words had the same letters. They read the two family letter combinations—*ame* and *ide*—out loud, as well as the words that followed. Ms. Green distributed worksheets and said, "Cut and paste the words that end in *ame* on the left side of your page and those that end in *ide* on the right. Place different letters at the beginning of the word families to form new words."

A small percentage of teachers at all levels used a balanced approach to phonics and phonemic awareness instruction, meaning that their lessons used a combination and integration of both explicit and authentic instruction. (See Pressley, Wharton-McDonald, & Mistretta, chap. 15, this volume, for a further description of balanced instruction.) The following example illustrates the use of a balanced approach in a second grade.

Ms. Davis had been teaching word families to her class. She began this lesson by reading *Goodnight Moon* (Brown, 1947) and told the children to listen for all the word families they heard. At the conclusion of the story, she explicitly reviewed the concept of word families with her students. She then had the students recall families of words from the story and recorded them on the chalkboard. The children were given a worksheet that provided practice in building words from different combinations of word families. After Ms. Davis was assured that the children understood the concept, she gave them an opportunity to apply what they had learned in a meaningful context. In this case, Ms. Davis gave pairs of students a sheet with the story *Goodnight Moon* typed on it. The students' job was to write their own version of the story using the original as a model. Ms. Davis helped them brainstorm word families to use in place of the ones they heard in the story. The students then chose the word families they wanted to use. Megan and Stacey's story illustrates what they learned from Ms. Davis's lesson:

Our Word Family Story Based on Good Night Moon

In the small blue room, there was a small blue broom
And a tiny red nest, and a tiny pink vest
There were three big rockets, sitting in pockets
And one big cat, sitting on a mat
And there were three gray mice, skating on some ice
Goodnight room, goodnight broom
Goodnight nest, goodnight vest
Goodnight rockets, good night pockets
Good night cat, sitting on a mat
And Goodnight mice, skating on some ice

CONCLUSIONS, IMPLICATIONS, AND FUTURE DIRECTIONS

The most commonly used strategy we observed for teaching phonics was explicit instruction. As observed, these lessons typically had fewer of the motivating characteristics previously identified, such as: fewer opportunities for choices of activities, fewer opportunities for self-direction and self-pacing, fewer opportunities for social collaboration, fewer opportunities involving authentic context, and fewer opportunities involving concept orientation. In contrast, the observed authentic and balanced lessons had more of the characteristics listed as motivating (e.g., they were embedded in meaningful contexts, and children had the opportunity for some self-direction and social interaction). However, neither of these instructional approaches were used as frequently as explicit instruction, except at preschool level.

The findings of the observational survey regarding the ways in which phonics is taught in early childhood classrooms (Morrow & Tracey, 1997), combined with the existing knowledge base about motivational contexts for young children's literacy development (Morrow, 1982, 1990, 1992; Morrow, Pressley, & Smith, 1995; Morrow & Weinstein, 1982, 1986; Turner, 1995) suggest that current practices in teaching phonemic awareness and phonics relationships may be improved with the inclusion of more elements known to promote young children's motivation in literacy learning. Using Table 14.1 as a guide, some of the elements that would be easiest to integrate into phonemic awareness and phonics instruction would be providing students choices of materials and experiences for learning; giving students more responsibility and control over their learning, such as self-direction and self-pacing; and using more social collaboration during lessons.

The incorporation of the elements described previously into the classroom requires adept classroom management skills by the teacher, because alternatives to whole-class instruction are necessary for use of each of the elements. The importance of teachers' strong classroom management skills in relation to children's early literacy instruction has been documented by Pressley, Wharton-McDonald, and Mistretta (chap. 15, this volume), and is apparent in this situation. Teachers must be able to monitor and manage multiple groups of children in the classroom—including individuals, pairs, small groups, and heterogeneous and homogeneous groups—for these motivational elements to be successfully implemented.

In addition to strong classroom management skills, the classroom teacher seeking to make phonemic awareness and phonics instruction more motivational should be encouraged to create a literacy center in the classroom. The literacy center is an area of the classroom, most often a carpeted corner, that contains a large variety of materials and activities designed to promote literacy growth. These may include (but are not limited to): a well-organized and large collection of children's reading materials; and a wide range of literacy-related props and activities, such as puppets, flannel boards, tape recorders, role movies, and chalk stories (see Morrow, 1996, for a full description of how literacy centers are created and managed). Additionally, writing materials may be included in the literacy center. Writing materials can include a variety of paper and writing implements, computers, printers, typewriters, magnetic letters, and so on. Other options for the literacy center are board and card games related to literacy learning, and stuffed animals, pillows, rocking chairs, and beanbag chairs to make the center warm and inviting.

By its nature, use of a literacy center in the classroom incorporates many motivational features. Among others, these include: opportunities for choice, self-direction, self-pacing, social collaboration, and practice independent of the teacher; materials that are accessible; and activities that are meaningful, functional, and that often offer experience with conceptual orientations.

Thus far, we have discussed aspects of classroom management and the establishment of a literacy center as factors that can contribute to increased motivation for phonemic awareness and phonics instruction. However, it is also apparent that high-quality modeling, guiding, and scaffolding by the teacher are important to student motivation (Skinner & Belmont, 1993). Combined with the elements of creating activities that are appropriately challenging, and therefore lead to success experiences for students (Csikszentimihalyi, 1978), these elements suggest that teachers must do more than just create learning environments for their students; they must also be connected, responsive, and in tune to their students' academic needs. These factors compose the direct instruction, or explicit aspect of instruction, and are as important to motivational teaching as are the classroom management and classroom design aspects.

Pressley and others (Pressley & Woloshyn, 1995) described the importance of high-quality explicit instruction and the steps necessary to achieve high-quality explicit instruction. Briefly, they include: (a) telling students what you are going to teach them, and why it is important for them to learn it; (b) modeling the desired skill; (c) providing guided practice to the students in the use of the desired skill, with a gradual release of responsibility; (d) providing guided practice with materials that increase in difficulty until mastery at grade level is achieved; (e) developing self-monitoring in students as they learn the skill, so that they are aware of their ability (or inability) to use the skill effectively; (f) teaching students to abandon an ineffective strategy for an effective strategy, if necessary; and (g) convincing students that the effort they expend to deploy skills will be directly related to their achievement. Underlying these steps is the belief that in high-quality explicit or direct instruction, skills are taught in great depth and with great care.

How is it, then, that in many of the chapters in this volume (see, e.g., Pressley, Wharton-McDonald, & Mistretta, chap. 15; Gaskins, chap. 9), explicit instruction was associated with high achievement, whereas in our own investigation (Morrow & Tracey, 1997) explicit instruction was associated with a low incidence of motivational elements? We believe that the answer to this question lies in the quality of the explicit instruction provided. In Pressley et al.'s work, as in Gaskins', explicit instruction was provided by outstanding and exceptionally well trained teachers. In contrast, the explicit instruction we observed was explicit instruction *as it is most often taught in primary grades.* Unfortunately, most teachers whom we observed taught phonics and phonemic awareness using traditional explicit instruction, which lacked motivational components, rather than the sophisticated explicit instruction referred to by Pressley and Woloshyn, 1995 (Pressley, 1990; Pressley, Wharton-McDonald, & Mistretta, chap. 15, this volume) and Gaskins (chap. 9, this volume), which would be more motivational.

What, then, should phonemic awareness and phonics instruction look like if they are going to be motivational for children? First, they must be viewed as being embedded in the context of the classroom environment, one that is run by a caring, responsive, and capable teacher, rather than being viewed as aspects of early reading acquisition that occurs in a vacuum. Within this environment, the teacher should posses strong classroom management skills, strong classroom design skills, and strong explicit instruction skills. A glimpse into a hypothetically ideal classroom might have one group of the children cognitively and socially engaged in free-choice literacy center activities with peers, one group reading or writing quietly about authentic tasks at their desks, and one group involved in a high-quality explicit instructional experience with their teacher. Clearly, the children learning about phonemic awareness and phonics relationships in these contexts would be more motivated than would students learning about phonemic awareness and phonics relationships through traditional explicit instruction.

Current research indicates that a strong foundation in letter-sound relationships is essential for children's success with reading and writing development (See Ehri, chap. 1; Goswami, chap. 2; Treiman, chap. 12, this volume). We have not, however, yet determined the relative impact of explicit, authentic, and balanced instruction on children's reading achievement. Studies to determine which strategies are the best are necessary for future research (see Pressley, Wharton-McDonald, & Mistretta, chap. 15, this volume). Although this is a meaningful research direction and intervention studies in this area are needed, it may be many years before we know the importance of these distinctions for children's learning. In the meantime, we suggest that educators make a conscious effort to examine and reflect on the strategies they use for teaching phonics, in order to select the best type of experiences for the children they teach. When examining these experiences, we urge educators to reflect on the 10 elements presented in Table 14.1, which represent motivating aspects of learning. We believe that increased self-reflection on these elements of the learning process, as well as on the topic of phonemic awareness and phonics in general, will ultimately lead to improved instruction for children.

REFERENCES

Bandura, A. (1989). *Social foundations of thought and action: A social cognitive theory.* Englewood Cliffs, NJ: Prentice-Hall.

Brown, M. W. (1947). *Goodnight moon.* New York: Harper.

Burns, P. C., Roe, B. D., & Ross, E. P. (1992). *Teaching reading in today's elementary schools.* Boston: Houghton-Mifflin.

Corno, L., & Mandinach, E. (1983). The role of cognitive engagement in classroom learning and motivation. *Educational Psychologist, 18,* 88–100.

Csikszentimihalyi, M. (1978). Intrinsic rewards and emergent motivation. In M. Lepper & D. Green (Eds.), *The hidden cost of reward: New perspectives on the psychology of human motivation* (pp. 205–216). Hillsdale, NJ: Lawrence Erlbaum Associates.

Duvoisin, R. (1950). *Petunia.* New York: Knopf.

Erickson, H. L. (1995). *Stirring the head, heart, and soul.* Thousand Oaks, CA: Corwin.

Ford, M. E. (1992). *Motivating human.* Newbury Park, CA: Sage.

Gambrell, L. B., Codling, R. M. & Palmer, B. M. (1996, Winter). *Elementary students' motivation to read* (National Reading Research Center Reading Research Report No. 52). College Park, MD: University of Georgia and University of Maryland, National Reading Research Center.

Guthrie, J. T., Van Meter, P., McCann, A. D., Wigfield, A., Bennett, L., Poundstone, C. C., Rice, M. E., Faibisch, F. M., Hunt, B., & Mitchell, A. M. (1996, Spring). *Growth of literacy engagement: Changes in motivation and strategies during concept-oriented reading instruction* (National Reading Research Center Reading Research Report No. 53). College Park, MD: University of Georgia and University of Maryland, National Reading Research Center.

Keats, E. J. (1972). *The pet show.* New York: Macmillan.

Maehr, M. L. (1976). Continuing motivation: An analysis of a seldom considered educational outcome. *Review of Educational Research, 46,* 443–462.

McCombs, B. L. (1991). Unraveling motivation: New perspectives from research and practice. *The Journal of Experimental Education, 60,* 3–88.

Morrow, L. M. (1982). Relationships between literature programs, library corner designs, and children's use of literature. *Journal of Educational Research, 75,* 339–344.

Morrow, L. M. (1990). Preparing the classroom environment to promote literacy during play. *Early Childhood Research Quarterly, 5,* 537–554.

Morrow, L. M. (1992). The impact of a literature-based program on literacy achievement, use of literature, and attitudes of children from minority backgrounds. *Reading Research Quarterly, 27,* 250–275.

Morrow, L. M. (1997). *Literacy development in the early years: Helping children read and write* (3rd ed.). Boston: Allyn & Bacon.

Morrow, L. M., Pressley, M., & Smith, J. K. (1995). *The effects of a literature-based program integrated into literacy and science instruction on achievement, use, and attitudes toward literacy and science* (Research Report #37). College Park, MD: University of Maryland and Georgia, National Reading Research Center.

Morrow, L. M., & Tracey, D. H. (1997). Strategies used for phonics instruction in early childhood classrooms. *The Reading Teacher, 50*(8), 2–9.

Morrow, L. M., & Weinstein, C. S. (1982). Increasing children's use of literature through program and physical design changes. *Elementary School Journal, 83,* 131–137.

Morrow, L. M., & Weinstein, C. S. (1986). Encouraging voluntary reading: The impact of a literature program on children's use of library centers. *Reading Research Quarterly, 21,* 330–337.

Oldfather, P. (1993). What students say about motivating experiences in a whole language classroom. *The Reading Teacher, 46,* 672–681.

Payne, E. (1972). *Katy no-pockets.* Boston: Houghton-Mifflin.

Potter, B. (1903). *Peter rabbit.* New York: Scholastic.

Pressley, M., & Woloshyn, V. (1995). *Cognitive strategy instruction that really improves children's academic performance* (2nd ed.). Cambridge, MA: Brookline.

Skinner, E., & Belmont, M. (1993). Motivation in the classroom: Reciprocal effect of teacher behavior and student engagement across the school year. *Journal of Educational Psychology, 85,* 571–581.

Stanovich, K. E. (1992). Speculations on the causes and consequences of individual differences in early reading acquisition. In P. B. Gough, L. C. Ehri, & R. Treiman (Eds.), *Reading acquisition* (pp. 307–342). Hillsdale, NJ: Lawrence Erlbaum Associates.

Turner, J. C. (1995). The influence of classroom contexts on young children's motivation for literacy. *Reading Research Quarterly, 30,* 410–441.

Wittrock, M. C. (1986). Students' thought processes. In M.C. Wittrock (Ed.), *Handbook of research on teaching* (pp. 297–314). New York: Macmillan.

15

▼▼▼▼▼▼▼

Effective Beginning Literacy Instruction: Dialectical, Scaffolded, and Contextualized

Michael Pressley
Ruth Wharton-McDonald
Jennifer Mistretta
University at Albany, State University of New York

Our most fundamental assumptions are that there are some very good elementary-level literacy teachers, and much about effective literacy elementary literacy education can be learned by studying their teaching. Such a perspective contrasts with alternative approaches to the understanding and development of pedagogy, the most popular of which have been philosophical analyses (Noddings, 1995). Contemporary language arts, in particular, has been dominated by alternative philosophies of education and development (Goldhaber, in preparation; Pepper, 1942).

Thus, at one end of the spectrum, whole language educators make strong assumptions about the inevitability of the development of literacy if children are immersed in reading and writing (see Weaver, 1994). Their metaphor is the naturally developing child. In Pepper's (1942) term, whole language theorists are organismic in their thinking. At the other extreme are those who embrace the metaphor of the child as a machine, such as a computer. From this mechanistic perspective, what children become is determined largely by the quantity of input. Direct teaching and practice of skills strengthens associative connections in the machine, with the machine's functioning improved by repeated experiences. In general, skills-based decoding instruction and direct teaching of reading strategies of various sorts have been conceived in such mechanistic terms (Adams, 1990).

In contrast, we do not believe that effective instruction is most likely to come about from dedication either to organismic or mechanistic philosophy. Rather, our view is that insights about how to teach effectively should come from careful study of effective teaching, with such analyses, as much as possible, free of philosophical biases. Our approach is not aphilosophical, however; rather, excellent teaching seems consistent with theories and metaphors not considered by the advocates of either whole language or direct instruction, with the latter part of this chapter dedicated to these alternative conceptions

Several years ago, when the program of research discussed in this chapter was first conceived, there was a search of the literature for analyses of expert literacy instruction. The studies of effective elementary classrooms that we found tended to focus on issues of management and pedagogy without regard to the content being covered (e.g., the various process–product analyses; Rosenshine, 1979). Closer to the mark were testimonials about the practice and power of particular approaches to reading instruction. Those writing the testimonials, however, were selected not because they were particularly effective teachers, but because of their commitment to a type of instruction, most frequently whole language (e.g., Ohanian, 1994; Shannon, 1994; Weaver, 1994; see the bibliography in Smith, 1994, for many examples). Systematic study of teachers who were known to be effective in promoting the reading and writing of their students seemed not to exist. The research summarized in this chapter was intended, in part, to begin to fill this somewhat surprising gap in the literature, to analyze elementary literacy teaching selected for its excellence.

THE NATURE OF OUTSTANDING GRADE 1 TEACHING

What is described in this section is a grounded theory of outstanding Grade 1 teaching (Strauss & Corbin, 1990). The researcher who is attempting to develop a grounded theory spends a great deal of time observing behaviors in a setting of interest and interviewing informants. He or she goes through the data systematically as it comes in, looking for meaningful clusters and patterns—behaviors that seem to go together logically. (That is, data collection and analyses are interwoven enterprises.) This stage of analysis results in a number of categories, each of which is supported by observational and/or interview evidence. With every new round of data collection, there is opportunity to look for support or nonsupport of categories—to compare tentative conclusions based on early data with conclusions suggested by new data. Eventually, there is a stable set of categories, which are then defined precisely and organized in relation to one another. Data collection continues until no new categories, defining features of categories, or relationships between categories are being identified.

In 1994–1995, Wharton-McDonald, Pressley, and Mistretta observed the teaching of nine Grade 1 teachers in the Albany, New York, area. Their purpose in doing so was to construct a grounded theory of outstanding Grade 1 literacy instruction. The first challenge in the research was to find a group of outstanding teachers, as well as a group of teachers whose practices and beliefs could be compared with those of the outstanding teachers. Wharton-McDonald, Pressley, and Mistretta (1996) asked language arts supervisors to nominate teachers whom they considered to be outstanding in promoting the literacy of their students; the supervisors were also asked to identify teachers who were more typical of the Grade 1 teachers in their district. The supervisors made a case for each teacher's participation, which was based on observations of teaching, indications of literacy achievement (e.g., reading test achievement, written products), and parental feedback. Four school districts participated, with three of the districts serving predominantly lower-middle-class families and the fourth serving an upper-middle-class population.

More About the Teachers and Their Impact on Students

Of course, we desired as much information as possible about the effectiveness of the teachers in this study. Hence, one goal of the study was to understand both the practices that promoted literacy and the literacy-related outcomes themselves. Thus, as the researchers conducted their observations, they were particularly attentive to possible indications of achievement. In the end, three types of information were viewed as telling about the effectiveness of teaching. First, engagement as defined by an informal measurement: Every 10 to 15 minutes, the observer would look around the classroom and calculate percentage of students attentively engaged in academic activities. The classrooms varied with respect to this dimension, with some characterized by consistently high engagement, even when the teacher was not present or attending to the class. Others were more variable in engagement.

Second, reading level was defined by the difficulty levels of books that students were reading at the end of the year. Various indications of reading level were accepted, from basal level being read in class to the estimations of reading level published on the back covers of many trade books. There was wide variation between the classes by the end of the year, from ones in which most students seemed to be working regularly with texts that were at or above grade level to others in which many students were regularly reading books intended for low or middle Grade 1 reading.

Third, writing was appraised by examining the stories and essays that children wrote. In some classrooms, typical compositions were several pages long, reflecting knowledge of a variety of writing conventions, good spelling, and appropriate punctuation. The writing in these classrooms often reflected real coherence in expression, with a single topic developed over the pages of writing. At the other extreme were classrooms in which writing typically was less than a page long—usually two to three sentences. In these classrooms, topical development and mechanics typically were much less impressive (e.g., "I luv my mommy. I luv daddy. I luv my dog to").

By the conclusion of the study, the researchers were in agreement that there were really three clusters of teachers in the study. Three teachers conducted classrooms where student engagement was typically high, reading levels were at or above grade level, and writing was relatively coherent and sophisticated. Three classrooms were at the other extreme, with much more variable and often low engagement, and more modest indications of reading and writing achievement. Three classrooms were in the middle. Notably, outstanding teaching and high student achievement was not predicted from socioeconomic level of the school, because the most affluent district provided one teacher in the middle group and one in the lower group. Two of the three teachers in the highest achievement group came from the district serving the most economically disadvantaged of the districts in our study. In general, the supervisors' original ratings were supported. In three of the four districts, the outstanding teachers were placed in higher categories than were the more typical teachers. The one exception was the most disadvantaged district, which supplied two outstanding teachers. The nominated typical teacher from this school could only be viewed as typical in the context of an outstanding primary literacy program, which this school district had.

Developing Models of Each Teacher's Teaching

Each teacher's classroom was observed at least 10 times, with two of the observers typically visiting 4 or 5 times apiece, and the third observer visiting 1 or 2 times. The observations took place from December 1994 to June 1995. Although the observations varied from 45 to 120 minutes in length, they were typically between 60 and 90 minutes long. One goal of the observations was to develop a grounded theory of instruction in each class. To this end, observers developed extensive field notes. These were analyzed following each visit, with subsequent visits informed by tentative conclusions emerging from the data and questions suggested by analyses of the data from previous visits. The two observers who conducted most of the observations were continuously in contact with one another, sharing emerging conclusions and relating issues to one another that needed to be resolved in order to understand each teacher's teaching. By the end of the observations, all three observers were satisfied from the data on hand with the conclusions about teaching drawn for each teacher.

The observational data were supplemented with data from two formal interviews with the teachers. The first, which occurred several months into the study, was semi-structured to permit teachers to express their philosophy and to allow the researcher conducting the interview to seek clarification from the teacher about some of the instructional practices seen up until that point. The data from this interview then were used to refine the theory that was emerging; these interview data also informed subsequent observations. The second interview occurred in May or June and was intended as a member check on the observations made (Lincoln & Guba, 1985), including an opportunity for each teacher to comment on the model that the researchers were developing of his or her teaching. Thus, the emerging model of a teacher's language arts instruction was shared with the teacher at this point. In doing so, the researcher avoided presenting valuations to the teacher, which was important given that some teaching behaviors were construed negatively by the researchers. Thus, when probing one teacher about her tendency to criticize students publicly and by name when they were inattentive, the researcher offered the conclusion to the teacher that she provided public, negative feedback to students when they were off task. In general, teachers agreed with the descriptions of their teaching and with the researcher models of their teaching presented to them. Revisions of the models as a result of the interviews typically involved adding or deleting a particular practice to/from a list of "frequently observed activities." In only one instance did a teacher disagree with a comment describing his or her classroom.

Summarizing Across the Nine Models of Teaching

The nine individual models of teaching that were developed became the data for construction of a higher-order grounded theory, one specifying the commonalities in teaching across the nine teachers as well as the aspects of teaching that distinguished the three outstanding teachers from the others. Basically, the researchers compared and contrasted the categories of teaching across the nine teachers until they were satisfied that they had identified the commonalities across classrooms and the features distinguishing the excellent teachers from the others.

The following conclusions held with respect to at least seven of the nine classrooms: The classroom was a positive place, with the teachers consistently letting their students know that they cared about them. There was little competition. There were classroom routines, so that much of the time students just knew what they were supposed to be doing. A variety of teaching configurations occurred across the day, with it not unusual for a day to include some whole- and some small-group instruction, as well as both cooperative learning and independent work.

Elements of whole language philosophy and pedagogy included, for example, the extensive use of trade books, the teacher modeling a love of reading as he or she read to students, and the use of process writing. Still, skills instruction occurred as well, including some direct instruction of decoding, punctuation, capitalization, and spelling. Worksheets were a common occurrence in support of the development of such skills. Finally, all of the

teachers recognized the importance of parental participation in children's
literacy development. Table 15.1 details some of the characteristics observed.

As we expected, there also were discernible differences between the classrooms in ways that linked to student achievement. The best teachers in the
sample were masterful classroom managers. They were so good, in fact, that
classroom management was hardly noticable! In these classrooms, students
were busy and appeared happy, with virtually no misbehavior observed. The

TABLE 15.1

Instructional Characteristics Observed in at Least Seven of the Nine Grade 1
Classrooms in the Wharton-McDonald, Pressley, and Mistretta (1996) Study

Skills and authentic literacy activities:
   Some direct instruction of decoding strategies or rules.
   Instruction and practice of decoding skills in the context of authentic literature.
   Trade books available for student reading.
   Time for independent reading.
   Teachers modeling a love of reading.
Writing instruction:
   Daily writing activities.
   Students writing primarily connected text.
   Writing process includes rough draft with revisions.
   Writing process includes teacher conferences.
   Writing topics chosen primarily by the teacher.
   Instruction in basic rules of punctuation and capitalization.
Spelling programs.
Use of some worksheets.
Classroom arrangement:
   Desks arranged in small groups.
   Rug area with easel for group instruction.
   Small table for groups and teacher conferences.
   Information posted around the room on commercial and teacher-made posters.
Instructional grouping:
   Both whole-group and small-group teaching configurations.
   At least some cooperative learning activities.
   Students read or wrote in pairs.
   Some independent seatwork (most often expressive writing activities).
Reinforcement:
   Students received lots of positive attention throughout the day.
   Some verbal negative feedback used to address student misbehavior or inattention.
Classroom atmosphere and teacher dedication:
   Teachers dedicated to helping students grow and achieve.
   Classroom atmosphere consistently conveyed caring for students.
   Classroom atmosphere noncompetitive.
   Students appeared to be comfortable with classroom activities.
   Instructional planning evident.
Parent participation:
   Recognition of the importance of parental participation and modeling in children's
   literacy development.
   Reported variation in parent participation from year to year—regardless of teacher practices.

worst that happened in these classrooms was off-taskedness, which typically ended quickly, with the teacher moving in to get the student back on task in a quiet, quick, and positive way. One of the three top teachers had a classroom chart, which included for each student a green card (everything okay), a yellow card (a warning), and a red card (unacceptable) for each student. Yes, occasionally a student had to flip from the green to the yellow card, but we never saw a red card. Moreover, a yellow card was always an isolated yellow card. This compared to other classrooms in the study that used a similar card system, with many more yellow and red cards typically seen on those charts.

The top three teachers in the Wharton-McDonald et al. (1996) study were also skillful managers of the human resources available to them. Thus, resource teachers who "pushed in" to these classrooms were always busy providing instruction and assistance to students. In contrast, resource teachers often were underused by the more typical teachers—for example, spending a great deal of time on the periphery of the classroom with nothing to do as the classroom teacher conducted a whole-group lesson.

One reason why the students were so engaged in the best classrooms was that there was a high density of instruction. Mornings in the best classrooms seemed jam-packed compared to more relaxed paces in the other classrooms. Moreover, the mornings in the best classrooms were crammed with activities that connected with one another. Reading materials were connected to writing topics, and literacy instruction was tied to content instruction. For example, one of the outstanding teachers integrated her lessons on nutrition, a required part of the Grade 1 science curriculum for the district, with readings such as *Cloudy With a Chance of Meatballs*, which motivated writing of balanced menus in the style of the children's book. In contrast, down the hall, in a classroom in the bottom third of the sample, the same nutrition curriculum was covered with food posters and drills, with the closest linkage to literacy being the inclusion of a song that included the names of many different foods. Some of the distinguishing characteristics of the best teachers in the study are presented in Table 15.2.

In contrast to the best classrooms, more typical classrooms had large portions of time that were not as literacy demanding. For example, in one

TABLE 15.2
Distinguishing Characteristics of the Best Teachers in the
Wharton-McDonald, Pressley, and Mistretta (1996) Study

- Masterful classroom management.
- High density of instruction and activity.
- Reading, writing, and other instruction well integrated.
- Good balancing of whole language and explicit skills instruction.
- High expectations that students would learn.
- Extensive use of scaffolding.
- Consistent encouragement of self-regulation.

of the more typical classrooms in the Wharton-McDonald et al. (1996) study, there was a great deal of copying, something almost never observed in the classrooms of the three best teachers. In another, much of the literacy instruction was devoted to communications activities that occurred in a sharing circle, with most of the discussion during this sharing not related to what the children were reading or to other academic content.

The atmosphere in the three best classrooms was qualitatively different as well. Although eight of the nine classrooms were pleasant places in which to be, the classrooms with outstanding teachers were places filled with the message that students can learn, that they can and will be good readers and writers. Every student was stroked for his or her achievements, and the positive feedback was sincere. We recall discussions with each of the three best teachers in which they beamed at the progress being made by weak students. These teachers were determined that students in their classes would develop as readers and writers. In contrast, there was more acceptance of failure in other classrooms in the study, for example, more willingness to believe that lack of progress simply reflected that the students were not yet ready to read and write.

We had several typical classrooms in the study in which the teachers were determined to be as consistent as possible with whole language, including the downplaying of skills instruction. These classrooms just did not "cook" like the three best classrooms, with boredom often very easy to detect, and end-of-the-year achievement in reading and writing not as apparent. We also had two classrooms in which skills were paramount. These classrooms did not cook either, with boredom easy to spot, and reading and writing achievement in these classrooms not even close to the end-of-the-year performances we observed in the best classrooms.

One of the reasons that the students in the best classrooms were busy, happy, and learning was that they received help as they needed it. The three best teachers in the Wharton-McDonald et al. (1996) sample were exceptionally active in scaffolding students' learning (Wood, Bruner, & Ross, 1976), providing hints and prompts when students faltered. These three teachers were terrific at spotting someone having difficulties, moving in, and quickly providing hints, suggestions, or other supports that permitted the student to make progress. Much of the reason that balancing of skills and larger literacy tasks worked in the best classrooms was that students received assistance as they attempted to read more difficult texts and as they drafted and revised what they wrote. The assistance often involved prompting students to use the skills they were learning; for example, prompting them to sound out words they wanted to read or write.

The help that was given to children in the best classrooms did not make the children dependent on the teachers, however. Quite the contrary—the best classrooms were notable because of the self-regulation of the students in them. Much of the time the students in these classrooms worked independently or with other children, without the immediate attention to the teacher. One of the strengths of the best teachers was that they developed students who could do much of what was required of them without adult assistance. That was one of the reasons the engagement ratings were so high. The children were productive, regardless of whether the teacher saliently monitored them.

The final characteristic to emerge from the analysis of the three really outstanding teachers was their awareness of purpose. Not only were they skillful and engaging models, facilitators, and managers, but the best teachers were highly aware of both their practices and the purposes that drove those practices. When asked to describe the intended purpose of a particular activity (such as the teacher reading aloud), the outstanding teachers as a group were clear and articulate about their intentions. There was nothing haphazard about literacy instruction in these classes. This was in contrast to some of the other teachers who justified some frequently observed activities as useful for developing good habits or giving the children something to do while the teacher worked with small groups.

The observers were struck that despite the commonalities among classrooms, every classroom in this study had its own personality, including the three headed by the best teachers. Selecting only one classroom to describe in more detail, thus, is somewhat deceptive. Space constraints prohibit us from describing more than one, however. By considering in greater detail the teaching of one of the three outstanding teachers, we think that the complexity of an outstanding Grade 1 class will be clear. For detailed description of the teaching of another one of the outstanding teachers in this study, see Pressley et al. (1996).

ANDY'S TEACHING

One of the three outstanding teachers was a middle-aged male named Andy. Andy's classroom was an extremely attractive world. Andy never criticized students. The following type of remark was typical when things got a little out of hand: "I hear productive talk, but how about a little softer." When other adults entered the classroom, nothing stopped. Indeed, student engagement was invariably high in Andy's class, with students attentive during their whole-group and small-group lessons and working hard when on their own. Moreover, student time mostly was spent on actual reading and writing, for example, with very little time devoted to illustrating stories the students had written.

Why were Andy's students so self-regulated? Andy strongly encouraged self-regulation, regularly praising students for making decisions and taking responsibility. There were lots of comments like: "Some of you already had the words in alphabetical order before I told you to do so. Good." Each group of desks had a bin of easy-reading books, with students making their own choices about which ones to read. On their own, students selected books from the "Reading Is Fundamental" project that were related to ongoing themes in the class. Andy taught his students to read "inside your heads." He encouraged students to monitor whether what they were reading was making sense, and to reread when it did not. Before writing, Andy urged students to attend to mechanics themselves, although mechanics, in fact, were checked by the teacher as part of his monitoring of writing. The classroom included a writing checking chart so that students could check their own writing and begin revision rather than wait for the teacher. Students practiced a variety of simple thinking skills, such as comparing and contrasting and summarizing. These skills occurred in the context of other activities. For example, students were encouraged to plan, an important critical thinking skill, as part of their end-of-basal projects. The students in Andy's class were self-regulated because Andy consistently encouraged them to self-regulate. There also was a lot of cooperation in this classroom, with kids checking each other's work and helping one another work through difficult materials.

Tasks given to students were always within reach of them, with Andy providing extensive scaffolding for students when they experienced difficulties, often providing hints appropriate to the problems of particular students. For example, when one group of students was having difficulty differentiating the habitats of ducks and chickens, Andy pondered aloud to himself, "I wonder if it might have something to do with dealing with water." When a student had difficulties with spelling a word during writing, Andy prompted the student to think about the sounds in the word. There were lots of comments like: "Shawn, is that the way we used those letters when we did the other words? Think about it." Shawn went on to spell *rule* correctly.

Consistent with whole language philosophy, excellent literature was extremely important in Andy's class. There were many discussions of what had been read. Student writing typically involved responses to high-quality stories and trade books. Anything but consistent with whole language, however, Andy's class included systematic coverage of a basal.

That Andy was not married to whole language philosophy comes through in many other ways, however. In this classroom, skills instruction intelligently complemented the reading of literature and student writing. There was extensive phonics instruction, both in formal lessons and online as part of mini-lessons. Simple phonics rules were taught (e.g., "bossy *e*"). This occurred in the context of spelling instruction, for example, with lists of words that exemplified particular phonics principles. During the reading of a story, there was often a discussion of words with particular characteristics (e.g., a word with a "short *o*" sound). During small-group lessons, there often were word analysis activities, for example, finding the little words in big words. Workbook pages complemented instruction, sometimes, when Andy believed the students could benefit from such work.

Andy consciously stimulated students to think as they did skill activities, however, often requiring explanations from them. There were lots of exchanges like this one during a whole-group alphabetizing activity:

Andy: Why did you put *whale* before *woman*?

Tommy: Both start with a *w* but I used the second letter. "H" comes before "o", so whale before woman.

Andy: That's right. . . . Your group has been learning how to alphabetize using the second letter . . . This one is tricky because one letter in it can have 2 different sounds.

Eddy: Huge (pronounced correctly).

Andy: Why is it tricky?

Eddy: Because *g* can have hard *g* or soft *g* sound.

Andy: That's right. Sometimes *g* can say [makes hard *g* sound] and sometimes [makes soft *g* sound]. So that's why this word needs a little extra practice.

There also is explicit attention to vocabulary development in Andy's classroom. There were many sight words posted around the room and sight word drills.

There were strong ties across the curriculum, for example, with the gardening theme in the spring being represented in reading, writing, and a class science activity—as well as in students' self-selected reading from sources such as the "Reading Is Fundamental" books. Andy fostered a strong home–school connection as well, with homework (e.g., spelling) that he carefully monitored.

REFLECTING ON ANDY'S TEACHING RELATIVE TO REPORTS FROM EXCELLENT PRIMARY-LEVEL TEACHERS THROUGHOUT THE NATION

Another study was conducted in conjunction with the Wharton-McDonald et al. (1996) project just described. Pressley, Rankin, and Yokoi (1996) asked reading supervisors around the United States to identify their very best kindergarten, Grade 1, and Grade 2 teachers. All nominated teachers received a letter indicating that they were were among a select sample of teachers who had been identified as effective primary reading teachers by their supervisors. The letter included a short questionnaire requesting three lists of 10 practices the teacher believed were "essential in her or his literacy instruction." Each teacher generated one list for good readers, one for average readers, and one for weaker readers. The questionnaire emphasized that the teacher's lists should include only practices that actually occurred in his or her classroom. The response rate to this request was more than 83%: 113 of the 135 nominated teachers responded.

The 300+ practices the teachers cited in response to the short questionnaire were categorized. All 300+ practices were probed on a second questionnaire assessing reading and writing instruction. Each item on this questionnaire was one that a teacher could answer objectively (e.g., the frequency of the teacher's use of an instructional practice on a seven-point Likert scale, from never to several times daily). This questionnaire was sent to all of the teachers who returned the initial questionnaire. A total of 86 questionnaires were returned (76% response rate).

What did these outstanding primary-level teachers report that they do? Some of the highlights included the following:

• The teachers reported creating literate environments (e.g., in-class libraries; listening, reading, & writing centers).

• Reading of outstanding children's literature is central in the curriculum, with lots of reading throughout the day.

• There is a lot of writing.

• Literacy instruction is integrated with the rest of the curriculum and extension experiences.

• Many skills are taught, including those prerequisite to reading (e.g., auditory and visual discrimination, attending and listening skills), concepts of print, letters and their sounds, the alphabetic principle, decoding strategies and phonics, vocabulary and sight vocabulary, spelling, text elements (e.g., cause-and-effect relations, theme/main idea, character analysis, etc.), comprehension strategies (e.g., prediction, visualization), and critical thinking skills (brainstorming, categorization, and recalling details). These skills are taught and practiced both in the context of reading and writing and in isolation.

• They use a variety of teaching approaches, including modeling of literacy skills and strategies, and positive attitudes toward literacy. There is lot of practice of reading and writing as whole tasks, but also of unmastered skills, including of phonics, letter recognition, and spelling. Some of the skills practice takes place in the context of reading and writing, but some is isolated, including by workbooks and worksheets. Mini-lessons based on student need were reported as common.

• There is great concern for individual achievement and productive participation of all students in the class. Children learn at their own pace, with more intense instruction provided for those children who need it. The same elements of reading and writing instruction are emphasized for good versus weak readers.

• Teachers attempt to motivate literacy by reducing risks for attempting literate activities, providing positive feedback, setting an exciting mood, and encouraging students to believe they can be readers and writers.

Notably, the three strongest Grade 1 teachers in the Wharton-McDonald et al. (1996) study did almost everything on the Pressley, Rankin, and Yokoi (1996) list! When the outcomes in the two studies are combined, there is a strong case for the conclusion that outstanding primary-level literacy classrooms are intense experiences, filled with high-quality reading and writing as well as skills instruction. In short, both Pressley, Rankin, and Yokoi (1996) and Wharton-McDonald et al. (1996) supported the perspective that outstanding literacy teachers are balanced in their instruction, immersing their students in reading and writing experiences but also teaching skills (McIntyre & Pressley, 1996).

PHILOSOPHIES OF AND METAPHORS FOR LITERACY DEVELOPMENT THAT MAKE SENSE IN LIGHT OF EFFECTIVE PRIMARY-LEVEL LITERACY INSTRUCTION

When the data from the two studies discussed in this chapter are considered, it is clear that neither the nativist nor the mechanistic conception of literacy development is adequate. An alternative possibility is dialecticism—that developmental processes inherently involve contradiction and conflict (Riegel, 1972, 1976). For example, the prime mechanism for cognitive development according to Piaget is equilibration, which involves both assimilation and accommodation—contradictory mechanisms.

According to the dialectical perspective, both the child and the environment are very active in development. This perspective also recognizes that development occurs simultaneously at different levels; for example, with the changing nature of wholes sometimes affecting the functioning of parts, and changing parts sometimes affecting the functioning of the whole. Thus, from this perspective, it seems sensible that the reading and writing of whole texts could promote the development of the lower-order skills involved in reading and writing; it also seems sensible that improvements in lower-order skills promote the development of reading and writing of whole texts.

At a minimum, reading and writing whole texts provides contextualized practice of skills the child is acquiring. It probably does more than that, however. The experiences of reading and writing whole texts make clear why skills development is important, in part energizing skills development. For example, reading of real text can make obvious the need for decoding skills, as it simultaneously makes obvious the value of practicing sight words. Decontextualized practice of skills and learning of sight words, in turn, makes reading of wholes even easier and permits access to new wholes. That is, skills practice and sight word learning can do much to maintain motivation for reading and writing. Reading of real text is not a grabber for the child who lacks decoding skills! Attempting even more challenging texts is also unlikely for that same child.

We regularly watched Andy and his students live the dialectical experience of reading and writing of wholes that motivated learning of parts, with ever-more challenging texts read and better texts written as new skills were developed. Classrooms are meant for dialectical contradictions, for wholes and parts to interpenetrate, and as they do, for both whole functioning and part functioning to improve, continually feeding off one another. Quantitative changes in skills translate into qualitative changes in whole functioning; qualitative changes in whole functioning, in turn, translate into quantitative changes in part functioning.

Literacy Instruction as Scaffolded Experience

Vygotsky's notion of teaching in the child's zone of proximal development plays out in excellent Grade 1 literacy classrooms. According to this perspective, learning occurs when children are working on tasks that are just a bit beyond them, a bit challenging. The role of the teacher is to give students tasks that are within their reach, at least with some teacher support. Then, the teacher provides just enough support to permit the child to continue to make progress (Hogan & Pressley, 1997).

Scaffolded skills instruction is very constructivistic. Teaching within the zone of proximal development is student sensitive—stimulating students to experiment with skills—with adaptations of skills continually occurring as students apply them to new tasks (Harris & Pressley, 1991; Pressley, Harris, & Marks, 1992; for other versions of the perspective that what is taught by the teacher is a beginning point for student construction of knowledge, see Elbers, 1991; Iran-Nejad, 1990; Wittrock, 1992).

None of the three excellent teachers whom Wharton-McDonald et al. (1996) observed expected their students to understand skills based only on teacher explanations and modeling. Rather, they expected the students to acquire skills slowly, with a great deal of scaffolding required as students attempted to apply the skills during reading and writing. They scaffolded well, with scaffolding being the prime bridge between whole and parts. Because the focal tasks in the excellent classrooms were reading of whole texts and student composition of new texts, scaffolding took place in the context of these holistic activities. The scaffolding was often at the skill level; for example, punctuation, spelling, or sentence construction. Sometimes story construction would be facilitated by orienting students to the parts of the story, such as the characters and their development, the setting, the problems the characters experienced, and the resolutions of the problems. Such scaffolding of parts permitted the child to make progress in reading whole texts and writing whole stories.

Literacy Acquisition as Contextualized Experience

Social context matters in development, a position summarized by contextualist philosophies of development (e.g., Bronfenbrenner, 1979, 1989), with development determined by a variety of contextual variables in interaction. The largest contextual variable determining the course of the Grade 1 year is the child's teacher. The child's life is very, very different as a function of the person who teaches him or her in Grade 1. For example, if one of Andy's students had had one of the more typical teachers in the Wharton-McDonald et al. (1996) sample, his or her experience of Grade 1 would have been very different . . . and so likely would have been his or her literacy achievements. The teacher affects the child's environment in many ways, including through print and writing experiences, which in turn affect the developing child.

Excellent teachers are culturally determined, however. They translate the ideas they have encountered in coursework, professional journals, and workshops, with these inputs affected and informed in part by curriculum theory and research. The ideas of whole language and mechanistic theorists only come to pedagogical life through the translations of classroom teachers. The excellent teacher balances contextual forces. Thus, none of our three excellent teachers were married exclusively to any one curriculum product, although they were aware of and used fluidly a variety of publishers' materials available in the modern educational context. Although each of the three outstanding teachers in the Wharton-McDonald et al. (1996) sample was aware of standardized tests demands and the standards their students would face in the higher grades, with these affecting their teaching somewhat, none of these concerns dominated their teaching.

The most salient contextual variable for excellent teachers is their students. The outstanding teachers we studied knew where their students were every day, and were always intervening to ensure that each student made progress. The students never fell victims to some overarching educational philosophy, never were less important than the philsophy. The excellent teachers' commitments were much more to the kids in their classrooms than to being whole language teachers or basal teachers or anything else than being the best Grade 1 teacher they could be.

CONCLUDING COMMENT

Excellent primary-level instruction in reading and writing is extremely complex, largely because it is the result of a number of contextual forces. The teacher is an important contextual variable, the provider of what can seem like contradictory experiences, such as a whole language curriculum that involves a great deal of explicit teaching of skills. This contradiction works well in excellent classrooms, because the teacher scaffolds the child's application of skills as part of real reading and real writing.

The organismic and mechanistic perspectives do not go far enough. Thinking about primary-level literacy acquisition as involving dialectical contradictions, scaffolding, and many contextual influences is more realistic. We came to the envisionment of skilled primary-level literacy teaching as dialectical, scaffolded, and contextualized from spending time watching and interviewing excellent teachers, the individuals best in the position to inform a model of excellent primary-level teaching. By being so grounded in our approach to the development of instructional theory, we believe that the theory that has emerged is more complete, more sensible, and more credible than alternatives that were developed somewhat removed from actual teaching (i.e., they were a university-based curriculum theorist's conception of the teaching–learning process).

ACKNOWLEDGMENTS

The support from the National Reading Research Center for the writing of this chapter and conducting the research on which it is based was complemented by support from University at Albany, SUNY, including a Presidential Fellowship for Wharton-McDonald. The authors are especially grateful to the nine Albany-area Grade 1 teachers who welcomed them into their classrooms during 1994–1995.

REFERENCES

Adams, M. J. (1990). *Beginning to read.* Cambridge, MA: Harvard University Press.

Bronfenbrenner, U. (1979). *The ecology of human development.* Cambridge, MA: Harvard University Press.

Bronfenbrenner, U. (1989). Ecological systems theory. In R. Vasta (Ed.), *Annals of child development* (Vol. 6, pp. 187–251). Greenwich, CT: JAI.

Elbers, E. (1991). The development of competence and its social context. *Educational Psychology Review, 3,* 73–94.

Goldhaber, D. (in preparation). *Why we are: Theoretical perspectives on human development.*

Harris, K. R., & Pressley, M. (1991). The nature of cognitive strategy instruction: Interactive strategy construction. *Exceptional Children, 57,* 392–404.

Hogan, K., & Pressley, M. (Eds.). (1997). *Scaffolded instruction: Advances in teaching and learning*. Cambridge, MA: Brookline.

Iran-Nejad, A. (1990). Active and dynamic self-regulation of learning processes. *Review of Educational Research, 60*, 573–602.

Lincoln, Y. S., & Guba, E. G. (1985). *Naturalistic inquiry*. Newbury Park, CA: Sage.

McIntyre, E., & Pressley, M. (1996). *Balanced instruction: Strategies and skills in whole language*. Norwood, MA: Christopher-Gordon.

Noddings, N. (1995). *Philosophy of education*. Boulder, CO: Westview.

Ohanian, S. (1994). Call me teacher & who the hell are you. In C. B. Smith (Ed.), *Whole language: The debate* (pp. 1–15, 58–61). Bloomington, IN: ERIC Clearinghouse on Reading, English, and Communication.

Pepper, S. (1942). *World hypotheses*. Berkeley: University of California Press.

Pressley, M., Harris, K. R., & Marks, M. B. (1992). But good strategy instructors are constructivists!! *Educational Psychology Review, 4*, 1–32.

Pressley, M., Rankin, J., & Yokoi, L. (1996). A survey of instructional practices of primary teachers nominated as effective in promoting literacy. *Elementary School Journal, 96*, 363–384.

Pressley, M., Wharton-McDonald, R., Rankin, J., Mistretta, J., Yokoi, L., & Ettenberger, S. (1996). The nature of outstanding primary-grades literacy instruction. In E. McIntyre & M. Pressley (Eds.), *Balanced instruction: Strategies and skills in whole language* (pp. 251–276). Norwood MA: Christopher-Gordon.

Riegel, K. (1972). Influence of economic and political ideologies on the development of developmental psychology. *Psychological Bulletin, 78*, 129–141.

Riegel, K. (1976). The dialectics of human development. *American Psychologist, 31*, 689–700.

Rosenshine, B. V. (1979). Content, time, and direct instruction. In P. L. Peterson & H. J. Walberg (Eds.), *Research on teaching: Concepts, findings, and implications* (pp. 28–56). Berkeley CA: McCutchan.

Shannon, P. (1994). The answer is "Yes" & People who live in glass houses. . . . In C. B. Smith (Ed.), *Whole language: The debate* (pp. 48–51, 81–99). Bloomington, IN: ERIC Clearinghouse on Reading, English, and Communication.

Smith, C. B. (Moderator). (1994). *Whole language: The debate*. Bloomington, IN: ERIC Clearinghouse on Reading, English, and Communication.

Strauss, A., & Corbin, J. (1990). *Basics of qualitative research: Grounded theory procedures and techniques*. Newbury Park, CA: Sage.

Weaver, C. (1994). *Understanding whole language: From principles to practice* (2nd ed.). Portsmouth, NH: Heinemann.

Wharton-McDonald, R., Pressley, M., & Mistretta, J. (1996). *Outstanding literacy instruction in first grade: Teacher practices and student achievement*. College Park, MD: National Reading Research Center.

Wittrock, M. C. (1992). Generative learning processes of the brain. *Educational Psychologist, 27*, 531–542.

Wood, S. S., Bruner, J. S., & Ross, G. (1976). The role of tutoring in problem solving. *Journal of Child Psychology and Psychiatry, 17*, 89–100.

Author Index

Q

Quinlan, P., 134, *137*

R

Rack, J. P., 20, *39*, 142, 149, *159*, 161, *186*, 190, 207, 208, 246, *260*
Ramsay, D. S., 95, 97, *119*
Randazza. L. A., 94, 101, 103, 107, 111, 112, *116, 119*
Rankin, J., 365, 367, 369, *373*
Rapala, M. M., 162, *185*
Rashotte, C. A., 80, 82, *87*, 162, 165, 166, 167, 168, 174, 175, 178, 176, *187, 188*, 205, 208, 245, *262*, 275, *287*
Ratcliff, R., 130, 131, *137*
Raven, J. C., *260*
Rayner, K., 10, *40*
Raz, I. T., 265, 273, 276, 278, *286*
Rea, C. P., 132, 135, *137*
Read, C., 16, 26, *40*, 82, *87*, 150, *159*, 292, 298, *313*
Reed, M. A., 112, *118*
Reese, L., 266, 272, 282, *285*
Reitsma, P., 8, 12, 27, *40*
Reznick, J. S., 99, *118*
Rhine, W. R., 135, *136*
Riach, J., 303, 304, *311*
Rice, M. E., 346, *356*
Richgels, D. J., 298, *311*
Richman, B., 44, *60*
Richmond-Welty, E. D., 43, 44, 54, *62*, 123, 124, 125, 126, 127, 128, 129, *138*
Riegel, K., 369, *373*
Ring, J., 181, 183, *186*, 201, *208*
Robbins, C., 10, 22, *37*, 49, 55, 56, *60*
Roberts, K. T., 294, *312*
Robertson, C., 179, *186*
Roe, B. D., 348, *355*
Roper/Schneider, D., 19, *38*
Rosenshine, B. V., 358, *373*
Rosinski, R., 9, *38, 40*
Rosner, J., 66, 67, *87*
Ross, E. P., 348, *355*
Ross, G., 364, *373*
Rourke, B. P., 180, *185*
Routh, D. K., 46, *60*, 66, *85*
Rozin, P., 78, *87*, 90, 91, *116, 118*
Rudel, R. G., 162, 164, 165, *185, 187*
Rudorf, E., 26, *38*
Rumelhart, D. E., 6, *40*, 132, *137*
Russell, G., 150, *159*
Ruyter, L., 150, *159*
Ryan, E. B., 142, 144, 149, 154, *160*
Ryan, S. M., 162, 167, *185*

S

Salter, W., 179, *186*
Saltmarsh, J., 13, 32, *37*, 143, *158*
Samuels, J., 9, *39*
Satlow, E., 214, *232*
Sattler, J. M., 169, *187*
Savin, H. B., 67, *87*
Sawyer, D. J., 179, *187*
Scanlon, D. M., 46, *62*, 239, *262*
Scarborough, H. S., 149, 150, *159*, 169, *187*, 279, 280, *286*, 301, *313*
Scher, D., 264, 266, 269, 272, 273, 275, 280, 282, *284, 286*
Schmidt, R. A., 135, *137*
Schneider, W., 46, *61, 62, 63*
Schommer, M., 10, *37*, 215, *232*
Schooler, L. J., 123, *136*
Schuder, T., 214, *232*
Schwartz, R. G., *118*
Scott, J. A., 278, 282, *284*
Seergobin, K., 134, *136*
Segui, J., 98, *115*
Seidenberg, M. S., 107, *118*, 122, 123, 124, 126, 127, 128, 129, 132, 133, 134, *136, 137, 138*, 142, 144, 145, 146, 147, *159, 160*
Seifert, M., 146, *158*
Semrud-Clikeman, M., 191, *207*
Senechal, M., 266, *286*
Serpell, R., 264, 266, 269, 272, 273, 275, 280, 281, 282, *284, 286. 287*
Seymour, P. H. K., 144, *159*, 298, *313*
Shafrir, U., 142, *159*
Shanahan, T., 293, *313*
Shankweiler, D. P., 15, *39*, 45, 46, *60, 61*, 65, 66, *86, 87*, 90, 91, 112, *114, 117*, 145, 146, 147, 149, *158, 159*, 161, 162, 164, 174, 178, 180, *185, 186*, 196, *207*, 239, *260*, 322, *340*
Shannon, P., 358, *373*
Share, D. L., 15, *40*, 77, 78, *86, 87*, 91, *118*, 161, 165, *187*, 202, *208*, 237, 239, 240, 246, *260, 261* 258, *260, 261*, 321, *340*
Shaywitz, B. A., 162, 173, 174, 178, 180, *185. 187*
Shaywitz, S. E., 162, 173, 174, 178, 180, *185, 187*
Shea, P., 149, *158*
Shepherd, J., 31, *40*
Shepherd, M. J., 296, 297, *313*
Shillock, R. C., 92, *114*
Shockley, B., 282, *284*
Shucard, D. W., 95, 97, *119*
Shucard, J., 95, 97, *119*
Shvachkin, N. K., 97, *119*

Subject Index

A

AB-BC paradigm, *see* Catastrophic interference
Access to materials, motivation for learning, 343, 344, 345
Accuracy
    consistency ratio of orthographic segment, 126
    site word learning, 23
Achievement, best teaching practices by outstanding teachers, 368–369
Acoustic information, spoken word recognition, 104
ADD, *see* Auditory Discrimination in Depth program
Adolescence, prediction of proclivity toward reading, 255–257
Affixes, decoding, 7, 8
    Age of acquisition (AOA), later word representations, 101
    mispronunciation in spoken word recognition, 105–106
Alliteration skills
    exposure relation to phonological awareness and early reading, 278
    word recognition development, 273–274
Alphabet
    English orthography history, 318–319
    home experiences relation to development of word recognition, 266, 269
    knowledge
        beginning reading, 34, 275–276
        learning at home, 84
        phonological awareness, 79–81
        disabled readers ability, 32
        reading and spelling correlation, 28, 296

site word learning, 12–24, *see also* Site word learning
strategy
    use in spelling before use in reading, 298–300
    Word Work program, 319, 324
Alphabet books, phonological awareness and reading, 80–81, *see also* Picture books
Analogy, word recognition development
    acquiring spoken versus written language, 41–42
    analogies in other orthographies, 51–52
    integrating orthographic analogies in the classroom, 57–58
    interactive theories of reading development, 53–54
    levels of phonological awareness, 44–46
        learning to read other orthographies, 46–47
    orthographic analogies
        classroom practice, 54–56
        rime units in English, 47–49
    phonological awareness and reading, 46
    rime awareness and rime analogies in English, 50–51
    spelling system of English, 43–44
Analogy strategy
    decoding, 78
    learning to read, 10, 34
    site word learning, 22
Analytic language skills
    dyslexic versus normal readers, 190–191
    training and reading ability, 176–177
AOA, *see* Age of acquisition
Arabic, phonological deficits in dyslexia, 150, 151, 152
ART, *see* Author recognition test

385

training and phonological awareness relation to reading, 80, 82, 176
Letter-sound knowledge
    at-risk and delayed readers, 213
    instruction in primary grades, 304
        phonological processing relation to beginning reading, 275
    learning to read, 34
    phonetic cue reading, 77
    synergism with phonemic awareness, 324
    training and benefits of spelling, 296, 297
    Word Work program, 322, 327
        Omaha Public Schools, 337, 338
    site word learning, 14–15, 16–17, 20, *see also* Mnemonics
Letter-string choice (LSC) test, orthographic versus phonological processing and variance in word recognition
    first grade, 241, 242, 243
    first through third grade, 246, 247, 248, 249
Letters
    knowledge
        exposure and beginning word recognition, 278
        learning to read, 33
    patterns
        decoding and learning to read, 7
        development and site word learning, 17, 22–23
        pronunciation confusion and phonological deficits in Arabic dyslexics, 152
        symbol matching in strategy training study, 197
Lexical diffusion, word representation, 98, 100
Lexical knowledge, learning to read, 7, 34
Lexical memory, site word learning, 19, *see also* Memory
Lexical representation, *see* Word representation
Lexical restructuring model (LRM)
    developmental origins of phonemic segments, 90–96, *see also* Phonemic segments, developmental origins
    links with phonemic awareness and reading ability, 108–113
    word representations, *see also* Word representations
        early, 96–100
        later, 100–108
Library centers
    motivation for learning, 345
    home experiences and word recognition, 265, 267
Lindamood Auditory Conceptualization (LAC) test, strategy training study, 200, 201
Lindamood Auditory Discrimination in Depth, teaching articulation patterns, 321
Linearity, English spelling system, 291

Linguistic awareness, *see* Phonological awareness
Linguistic complexity, phonological awareness skills relationships, 68–69, 72
LISREL analysis, alphabet knowledge and phonological awareness, 80
Literacy
    acquisition
        children's spelling, 300
        contextualized experience, 371
    assessment through print exposure, 237–239
    home activities and development of word recognition, 264–266, 267, 268
    lifetime and early start in reading, 256
    -related props and motivation for learning, 353
    scaffolding, 370–371
    switch to phonics and phonemes, 315–316
Literacy centers, motivation for learning, 344–346, 353, 355
Literacy instruction, beginning
    best teaching practices by outstanding teachers, 368
    model of teacher experiences, 365–367
    nature of outstanding first grade teaching, 358–365
    philosophies for literacy development, 369–372
    teacher model versus report of excellent national primary-level teachers, 367–369
Literacy program
    at-risk and delayed readers
        being word detectives and keeping a language log, 221–222
        book discussion, 227
        building a word wall, 215
        completing a compare/contrast worksheet, 218
        completing a rhyming word sort, 217–218
        fully analyzing words, 218–219
        generating and reading rhyming words, 216
        independent reading and response, 227
        literature, 230–231
        looking through words, 224
        parent-read-aloud book report, 226
        participating in Echo reading, 223–224
        playing ready-set-show, 216–217
        playing what's in my head, 218
        process writing, 230
        reading group, 227–230
        reading predictable rhymes, 220–221
        reading to a partner, 224–225
        reading tongue twisters, 217
        self-assessing word knowledge, 222